English for Academic Purposes
A guide and resource book for teachers

CAMBRIDGE LANGUAGE TEACHING LIBRARY

A series covering central issues in language teaching and learning, by authors who have expert knowledge in their field.

In this series:

English for Academic Purposes

A guide and resource book for teachers

R. R. Jordan

CAMBRIDGE
UNIVERSITY PRESS

PUBLISHED BY THE PRESS SYNDICATE OF THE UNIVERSITY OF CAMBRIDGE
The Pitt Building, Trumpington Street, Cambridge CB2 1RP, United Kingdom

CAMBRIDGE UNIVERSITY PRESS
The Edinburgh Building, Cambridge CB2 2RU, United Kingdom
40 West 20th Street, New York, NY 10011–4211, USA
10 Stamford Road, Oakleigh, Melbourne 3166, Australia

First published 1997

Printed in the United Kingdom by Bell and Bain Ltd, Glasgow

Typeset in Adobe Garamond 8/10pt

A catalogue record for this book is available from the British Library

Library of Congress Cataloguing in Publication data applied for

ISBN 0 521 55423 3 hardback
ISBN 0 521 55618 X paperback

CE

Contents

Contents

Contents

Contents

List of figures

List of abbreviations

ARELS	The Association of Recognised English Language Services
BALEAP	The British Association of Lecturers in English for Academic Purposes
CALL	Computer Assisted Language Learning
COBUILD	COLLINS Birmingham University International Language Database
DDL	Data-driven Learning
EAP	English for Academic Purposes
EFL	English as a Foreign Language
EGAP	English for General Academic Purposes
ELT	English Language Teaching
EOP	English for Occupational Purposes
EPP	English for Professional Purposes
ESAP	English for Specific Academic Purposes
ESL	English as a Second Language
ESP	English for Specific Purposes
EST	English for Science and Technology
EVP	English for Vocational Purposes
IELTS	International English Language Testing System
LSP	Languages for Specific Purposes
L1	first language/mother tongue
L2	second language/medium of communication
NCELTR	National Centre for English Language Teaching and Research (Australia)
NNS	non-native speaker (of English)
NS	native speaker (of English)
OHP	overhead projector
PSA	present-situation analysis
RELC	Regional Language Centre (Singapore)
TEFL	Teaching English as a Foreign Language
TENOR	Teaching English for No Obvious Reason
TOEFL	Test of English as a Foreign Language
TSA	target-situation analysis
UETESOL	University Entrance Test in English for Speakers of Other Languages

Acknowledgements

To BALEAP members, past and present, with affection

In a book of this nature there are many people to thank, the doing of which gives me great pleasure. First and foremost, I thank my former colleagues at Manchester University, Ken James and June O'Brien, for providing study leave cover for me during the first half of 1992. This made possible the groundwork for the book. In addition, I thank June most warmly for her willingness to share ideas and materials, and for allowing some examples of teaching materials to be reproduced: in particular, the study skills workshop, correcting code, report conversion, and part of the syllabus in Appendix 1.1. I thank Ken for the original idea for *Figure 16*: socio-cultural components. I also thank the ELT Unit at Manchester University for the loan of books, and some materials – parts of which have been reproduced.

I am most grateful to BALEAP members for kindly taking part in the original Questionnaire Survey in 1991/92 and for giving permission for the information to be used. For specimens of timetables and questionnaires, and additional information, I am grateful to the following: Penny Adams, Alan Barr, Mike Beaken, Meriel Bloor, George Blue, Doreen du Boulay, Peter Brown, Joanna Channell, Michael Chiles, Don Dunmore, Clare Furneaux, Martin Hewings, Margaret Khidhayir, Jo McDonough, Anne Marshall-Lee, Hilary Nesi, Graham Perry, Rod Revell, Pauline Robinson, Celia Shalom, Susan Thompson, Alan Tonkyn, Graham Trengrove, John Trzeciak, Joan Turner, Cyril Weir.

In addition, I am very grateful to the following for their advice and help: Jo McDonough – BALEAP Research Register; Richard West – needs analysis and testing; Gary Motteram – CALL and video; Hilary Nesi – CALL; Caroline Moore – The British Council. Pat Hurst, Education Librarian at Manchester University, deserves a special thank you for her willingness to find references for me, and for her excellent memory of the location of items.

I wish to thank the following for kindly providing me with information about the EAP situation in courses, universities, or countries, they know well: John Morley – Australia; Anncha Lindeberg, Mirjaliisa Charles, Elizabeth Heap-Talvela, Deborah Mason – Finland; William Dodd – Ireland; Donald Sim – Israel; Dorothy Humphreys – Nepal; Samina Amin Qadir – Pakistan; John Swales – USA.

Four anonymous readers' reports were most helpful for their detailed comments and useful suggestions. I also thank my editors at Cambridge: initially, Elizabeth Serocold; later, and particularly, Alison Sharpe, for her strong support and constructive advice; Helena Gomm, for her thoroughness throughout; and Jane Clifford, for her liaison, and consultation at all stages.

I am grateful to the following publishers for kindly providing books that enabled me to widen the scope of my research and to bring it up-to-date: Heidi Mulvey and Peter Donovan – Cambridge University Press; Yvonne de Henseler – Heinemann ELT; Angela Royal – Charles Letts; Liz Huntley, Kathryn Derbyshire and Karen Groves – Longman ELT; Susan Holden – Macmillan/Phoenix ELT; Gary Hall - Open University Press; Sarah Ashton – Oxford University Press; Brian Holmes and Mirjana Ilic – Prentice Hall International/now Phoenix ELT; Theo Schröder – Phoenix ELT.

I warmly thank Richard Jordan and Hamayoun Choudry for kindly undertaking the detailed task of typing the first draft of the Bibliography. Last, but very far from least, I thank my wife, Jane, for sharing me with EAP for so long!

Together with my publishers I should like to thank the following for permission to reproduce copyright material: Pat Howe, Ken James, Bill Jones, Jo McDonough, Ron Mackay, Alan Matthews, Fred Nixson, June O'Brien, Teresa O'Brien, Gillian Walsh and Richard West.

My apologies if I have inadvertently omitted anyone to whom acknowledgement is due.

Bob Jordan

Addison Wesley Longman for the extract on p. 6 from *Longman Dictionary of Language Teaching and Applied Linguistics* by J. C. Richards, J. Platt and H. Platt; the extract on p. 111 from *Communication in the Classroom: Applications and methods for a communicative approach* by K. Johnson and K. Morrow; the extracts on p. 154 by J. Channell and on p. 159 by R. Carter and M. McCarthy in R. Carter, C. N. Candlin and M. McCarthy (Eds) *Vocabulary and Language Teaching*; the extracts on pp. 172 and 174 from *Process Writing* by R. White and V. Arndt; the extract on pp. 187–188 from *Listening in Language Learning* by M. Rost and C. N. Candlin; the entry for the word 'ambiguous' on p. 209 from *Longman Dictionary of Contemporary English*, 1987; the extracts on pp. 313 and 329 from *Panorama* by R. Williams; the extract on p. 326 from *Count Me In: Understanding numbers in English* by S. Elsworth, reprinted by permission of Addison Wesley Longman Ltd; the table on p. 96 (top) from *Study Abroad: A Manual for Asian Students* by B. Ballard and L. Clanchy, 1984,

Acknowledgements

reprinted by permission of Longman Malaysia Sdn Bhd; the extract on p. 244 from *How to Write Essays* by B. Ballard and L. Clanchy, reprinted by permission of Addison Wesley Longman Australia; Little Brown for the extract on p. 13 from *Learn How to Study* by D. Rowntree; Cambridge University Press for the extract on p. 24 from 'Needs analysis in language teaching' by R. West, *Language Teaching* 27(1); the extract on p. 51 from *Teaching Faster Reading: A Manual* by E. Fry; the exercises on p. 119 from *Study Tasks in English* by M. Waters and A. Waters; the extract on p. 159 from *Developing Reading Skills* by F. Grellet; the extract on p. 191 from 'Training lecturers for international audiences' by T. Lynch in J. Flowerdew (Ed.) *Academic Listening: Research Perspectives*; the diagram on p. 201 and the extracts on pp. 317 and 319–320 from *Study Skills in English* by M. J. Wallace; the entries for the word 'ambiguous' on p. 210 from *English Pronouncing Dictionary* by D. Jones, 15th edition, P. Roach and J. Hartman (Eds) and *Cambridge International Dictionary of English*, 1995; the extract on pp. 211–212 from *How To Choose an English Dictionary*, 1995; the extracts on pp. 230, 232 and 233 from *Genre Analysis* by J. Swales; the extracts on pp. 243 and 333 from *Study Writing* by L. Hamp-Lyons and B. Heasley; the extracts on pp. 253 and 259 from *English for Specific Purposes: A learning-centred approach* by T. Hutchinson and A. Waters; the extract on p. 300 from *Study Reading* by E. Glendinning and B. Holmström; the extract on pp. 312–313 from *Study Listening* by T. Lynch; the extract on pp. 318–319 from *Study Speaking* by T. Lynch and K. Anderson; Phoenix ELT for the extract on p. 36 from 'Socialisation into the academic community: linguistic and stylistic expectations of a Ph. D. thesis as revealed by supervisor comments' by T. Dudley-Evans and the tables on p. 54 from 'Language learning within academic constraints' by G. M. Blue, both in P. Adams, B. Heaton and P. Howarth (Eds) *Socio-Cultural Issues in English for Academic Purposes. Developments in ELT*; the extract on p. 59 from *ESP today: A Practitioner's Guide* by P. C. Robinson; the chart on p. 68 from 'Project writing: the marriage of process and product' by M. Bloor and M. J. St John, in P. C. Robinson (Ed.) *Academic writing : process and product. ELT Documents 129*; the extract on p. 110 from 'Making materials work in the ESP classroom' by T. Hutchinson, in D. Chamberlain and R. J. Baumgardner (Eds) *ESP in the classroom: practice and evaluation. ELT Documents 128*; the extract on p. 134 from 'A consumer's guide to ELT dictionaries' by R. West, the questionnaire on pp. 135–136 from 'Which materials?: a consumer's and designer's guide' by M. P. Breen and C. N. Candlin, and the extract on p. 137 from 'Not so obvious' by J. Dougill, all in L. E. Sheldon (Ed.) *ELT textbooks and materials: problems in evaluation and development. ELT Documents 126*; the extracts on pp. 169–170 and 308–309 from *Writing* by R. White and D. Mc Govern; the extract on p. 175 from 'Don't correct reformulate!' by J. Allwright, in P. C. Robinson (Ed.) *Academic writing: process and product. ELT Documents 129*; the extracts on pp. 198 and 199 from 'Do you mind if I come in here? – a comparison of EAP seminar/ discussion materials and the characteristics of real academic interaction' by T. Lynch and K. Anderson, and the extract on p. 199 from 'Talking heads and shifting bottoms: the ethnography of academic' seminars by C. Furneaux, C. Locke, P. Robinson and A. Tonkyn, both in P. Adams, B. Heaton and P. Howarth (Eds) *Socio-Cultural Issues in English for Academic Purposes. Developments in ELT*; the extract on p. 213 from 'English as a Foreign Library' by C. Primrose, in G. M. Blue (Ed.) *Language, Learning and Success: Studying through English. Developments in ELT*; the extract on p. 221 from 'The product before: task-related influences on the writer' by L. Hamp-Lyons, the extract on pp. 221–222 from 'Teaching examination answer writing: process, product and placebo?' by T. Lynch, and the extract on p. 224 from 'A consideration of the meaning of 'discuss' in examination questions' by T. Dudley-Evans, all in P. C. Robinson (Ed.) *Academic writing: process and product. ELT Documents 129*; the extract on p. 251 from 'Planning a pre-sessional course in English for Academic Legal Purposes' by P. M. Howe, and the extract on pp. 285–286 from 'Letting the students choose: a placement procedure for a pre-sessional course' by M. Ward Goodbody, both in G. M. Blue (Ed.) *Language, Learning and Success: Studying through English. Developments in ELT*; the extract on p. 301 from *Reading* by D. Mc Govern, M. Matthews and S. E. Mackay; the extract on pp. 323–324 from *Campus English* by D. Forman, F. Donoghue, S. Abbey, B. Crudden and I. Kidd; the extract on p. 324 from 'Peer evaluation in practice' by T. Lynch, in A. Brookes and P. Grundy (Eds) *Individualisation and autonomy in language learning. ELT Documents 131*; The Bell School of Language for the extract on p. 44 from *Non-native Speakers of English at Cambridge University* by G. Geoghegan, 1983; Elsevier Science Ltd for the extract on p. 49 from 'The role of writing in graduate engineering education : A survey of faculty beliefs and practices' by S. Jenkins, M. K. Jordan and P. O. Weiland, *English for Specific Purposes* 12(1), © 1993; the extract on pp. 168–169 from 'Science research students' composing processes' by P. Shaw, *English for Specific Purposes* 10(3), © 1991; the extracts on p. 217 and 331 from 'Teaching bibliographic documentation skills' by T. Lynch and I. McGrath, *English for Specific Purposes* 12(3), © 1993; the extract on p. 235 from 'The graduate seminar: another research process genre' by B. Weissberg, *English for Specific Purposes* 12(1), © 1993; the extract on pp. 240–241 from 'Hedges and textual communicative function in medical English written discourse' by F. Salager-Meyer, *English for Specific Purposes* 13(2), © 1994; the extract on pp. 283–284 from *Approaches to Self-assessment in Foreign Language Learning* by M. Oskarsson, © 1980. Reprinted with kind permission from Elsevier Science Ltd, The Boulevard, Langford Lane, Kiddlington, OX5 1GB, UK; TESOL Inc. for the extract on p. 96 (bottom) from 'On the notion of culture in L2 lectures' by J. Flowerdew and L. Miller, *TESOL Quarterly* 29(2), © 1995; the extract on p. 132 from 'Survey of materials for teaching advanced listening and note-taking' by L. Hamp-Lyons, *TESOL Quarterly* 17(1), © 1983; the extract on p. 153 from 'Teaching academic vocabulary to foreign graduate students' by A. V. Martin, *TESOL Quarterly* 10 (1), © 1976; the extract on pp. 180–181 from 'Listening comprehension: Approach, design, procedure' by J. C. Richards, *TESOL Quarterly* 17(2), © 1983 by Teachers of English to

Acknowledgements

Speakers of Other Languages, Inc. Used with permission; The Hong Kong Polytechnic University for the quote on p. 100 from *The Hong Kong Poly University Students Handbook*; Oxford University Press for the extract on pp. 117–118 from 'Study skills and study competence: getting the priorities right' by M. and A. Waters, *ELT Journal* 46(3), © 1992; the extract on p. 131 from 'Evaluating ELT textbooks and materials' by L. E. Sheldon, *ELT Journal* 42(4), © 1988; the table on p. 133 from 'Survey review: textbooks for teaching writing at the upper levels' by L. Hamp-Lyons and B. Heasley, *ELT Journal* 38(3), © 1984; the extracts on pp. 155 and 156 from 'Applying semantic theory to vocabulary teaching' by J. Channell, *ELT Journal* 35(2), © 1981; the extract on pp. 156–157 from 'Vocabulary learning: the use of grids' by P. D. Harvey, *ELT Journal* 37(3), © 1983; the extract on pp. 184–185 from 'The effect of discourse markers on the comprehension of lectures' by C. Chaudron and J. C. Richards, *Applied Linguistics* 7(2), © 1986; the extracts on pp. 142 and 330 from *A Study Skills Handbook* by M. Smith and G. Smith, © 1990; the entries for the word 'ambiguous' on pp. 209 and 210 from *Oxford Advanced Learner's Dictionary of Current English*, 4th edition 1989, *The Concise Dictionary of Current English*, 8th edition 1990 and *the Oxford Thesaurus (an A–Z Dictionary of Synonyms)*, 1991 by Permission of Oxford University Press; Heinemann Educational for the extract on p. 150 from *Teaching Vocabulary* by M. J. Wallace, reprinted by permission of Heinemann Educational, a division of Reed Educational and Professional Publishing Ltd; Heinle & Heinle Publishers for the chart on p. 152 and the extract on p. 162 from *Teaching and Learning Vocabulary* by I. S. P. Nation, © 1990; C. J. Kennedy for the extract on p. 160 from 'From printout to handout: grammar and vocabulary teaching in the context of data-driven learning' by T. Johns, *English Language Research Journal* 4:27–45; HarperCollins Publishers for the entry for the word 'ambiguous' on p. 210 from the *Collins COBUILD English Dictionary*, © HarperCollins Publishers, 1995; the extract on pp. 284–285 from *Study Skills for Higher Education* by J. Floyd, © HarperCollins Publishers Limited; The University of Birmingham for the extract on p. 231 from *Genre analysis and ESP* by T. Dudley-Evans, *English Language Research Journal*, Vol. 1, 1987; Open University Press for the extract on p. 299 from *Teaching Students to Learn* by Graham Gibbs, 1981; The Michigan University Press for the extract on p. 306 from *Academic Writing Skills for Graduate Students* by J. M. Swales and C. B. Feak, © 1994; Macmillan Education for the extracts on pp. 315, 321 and 332 from *Learning to Study in English* by B. Heaton and D. Dunmore; Deborah Mason for the extract on p. 325 from 'Project work with students of household sciences', *ESP SIG Newsletter*, January 1995; Blackwell Publishers for the extract on pp. 354–355 from *Materials and Methods in ELT* by J. McDonough and C. Shaw, 1993.

Introduction

Background

This book is the culmination of twenty-one years' experience of teaching EAP at the University of Manchester and overseas. It has been written with the realisation that, although there are a number of practice books in EAP for students, no book currently exists for teachers that surveys the whole field of EAP. It is normally covered in small sections in ESP books. This, then, gives a comprehensive overview of the whole subject for teachers, and has arisen out of my 1989 state-of-the-art article on English for Academic Purposes for the journal *Language Teaching* (Jordan 1989).

In recent years, there has been a world-wide increase in demand for EAP or study skills courses, varying in length from two weeks to one year or more. EAP is needed not only for educational studies in countries where English is the mother tongue, but also in an increasing number of other countries for use in the higher education sector.

Readership

Because of the increase in demand for EAP, there has been a commensurate increase in demand for qualified and experienced teachers of EAP. This book is intended for experienced EFL teachers, native speakers or non-native speakers, perhaps with some experience of EAP/ESP/study skills. They may be attending a teacher-training or higher degree/diploma course, where EAP is a main or subsidiary component, perhaps combined with ELT, ESP or Applied Linguistics. It is also intended for experienced EFL teachers who may not be attending a course but who would like information about EAP or who would like to place their knowledge of EAP in a wider context. They may be working in relative isolation, and would like to be able to compare their approach with alternatives, or to compare material they are using with other books, or to write their own EAP (EGAP/ESAP) material. This book contains a number of examples of published material and exercises, as well as research reports, thus enabling comparisons to be made. It also provides information about, and examples of, research in EAP.

Purpose and approach

The purpose of the book is to provide a reasonably straightforward, step-by-step account of the coverage of EAP, noting its scope, approaches, developments, issues and research findings, in addition to methods and materials. The book is intended to be informative and user-friendly, and to serve as a resource and reference book, for teachers working on their own as well as those attending a course. Although the book is designed to be read through chapter by chapter, it may also be dipped into as needed. This applies particularly to the Appendices.

The approach that I have taken is not dogmatic: it considers different viewpoints and ways and methods of teaching EAP, but leaves you to think, discuss and form your own opinions. These will be based on your personal experience combined with the conclusions that you draw from your reading and discussion of aspects of this book. While reading about different approaches and trends, it is important to bear in mind that the ultimate objective is to assist students to learn as efficiently as possible.

In the belief that one can always learn from other disciplines and approaches, I have included, in Chapter 1, some references to study skills books available for the English mother-tongue situation. These books are often overlooked in EAP settings. Some of them may be of direct help, especially for use with more advanced students; others may serve the purpose of giving ideas for developing different approaches or materials. Study skills do not exist only for non-native speakers of English. There is increasing evidence that mother-tongue students at university level need to be catered for, as the notice below from an English university in the 1990s indicates.

STUDY SKILLS FOR UNDERGRADUATES

The University is once again organising a series of free study skills seminars for undergraduate students.

Topics for this term are: 27 January – Taking and Making Good Notes; 3 February – Understanding and Analysing Questions; 10 February – Generating Ideas and Creating Essay Plans; 17 February – Planning Essays; 24 February – The Elements of a Successful Essay; 3 March – Quotations, References and Bibliographies; 10 March – Report and Project Writing for the Sciences; and 17 March – Introductions, Conclusions and Paragraphs.

Organisation

The book is divided into three parts. **Part I** serves as an introduction to EAP and study skills, explaining scope and background and putting various aspects and components into context. It also provides illustrative data on a number of the main areas.

Part II looks in depth at English for General Academic Purposes. It examines the different study skills, noting research findings that are relevant and giving examples of different approaches. It also gives some examples from practice books that are commonly used.

Part III focuses on English for Specific Academic Purposes. After looking at the various features and analyses concerned with academic discourse, it concentrates on areas of subject-specific language that are relevant to EAP teachers, including the production of teaching materials. It ends with a look at examples of ongoing research.

References

There are a large number of references to books, journals and research reports: full details are given in the References. They range from brief references to quotations, examples and specimens of material. In some cases, the quotations are lengthy: this is to enable you to obtain a flavour of the originals, with their individual styles and emphases. There are several reasons for including such a large selection of references:

a) To show a variety of approaches and ways of doing something. As there is often a tendency to teach in isolation, only knowing your own course/classes, there is an advantage in seeing alternatives. You will be exposed to different views on problems or areas for concern, and also see what is happening elsewhere. Perhaps some will be relevant to your needs.

b) To serve as a stimulus or starting point for your own ideas for teaching, developing materials or further research. In addition, to enable you to pursue matters further if you need more details or in-depth information.

c) To provide an overview or survey of approaches to various aspects of EAP, especially from the viewpoint of researchers and practitioners through their research articles and reports. Many of the journals are difficult or impossible to obtain unless you have access to a large ELT or academic library. This access is provided vicariously through the quotations and summaries included in the book. Similarly, some of the books referred to are out of print and may be difficult to find: extracts from some of them are included for purposes of exemplification, especially in Part II.

Introspect and discuss

Each chapter ends with a section entitled **Introspect and discuss**. This consists of a number of questions and discussion topics or activities. The purpose of these questions is to raise your awareness of issues as well as to give you an opportunity to compare your own experience with that of other people. If you are attending a course, many of the questions and activities may be prepared and discussed with a partner. Certainly, there would be benefit from a discussion and comparison within the group. A main purpose is to stimulate thought about aspects of your reading or your teaching: this can be done whether you are attending a course or reading the book on your own. Essentially, it is to help you to stand back, reflect, and to view matters in a more objective and critical way.

Not all the questions or activities are appropriate for all readers; nor would you want to do all of them. The intention is to provide a range and a choice: you will need to be selective and to choose those activities that are relevant to your needs and interests. You can also add other questions of your own. Many of the activities that are proposed can be done in pairs or small groups. If you are on a course, you and your tutor can decide which activities should be discussed or compared, and how.

You should note that the questions are arranged in chronological order, following the same sequence of the issues as they are raised in each chapter. In short, the aims of the section are to encourge you to think, discuss, compare and evaluate.

BALEAP survey

In the winter of 1991/92, I sent a questionnaire to members of the British Association of Lecturers in English for Academic Purposes (BALEAP), of which I am a founder-member (see Appendix 3 for an account of BALEAP and the Survey). The replies to the questionnaire were used to form the basis of parts of Chapter 4, regarding EAP course design, and in Part II, some of the books commonly used by EAP professionals. The Survey provided data for the first time on what actually happens on EAP courses.

Lastly . . .

In Part III, some detailed examples are given from one discipline – economics. This is my particular area of interest and it, therefore, allows me to speak from experience. However, the principles involved can apply to other subjects: economics should thus be seen as an exemplar.

Part I English for Academic Purposes and study skills

1 EAP and study skills: definitions and scope

1.1 What is English for Academic Purposes (EAP)?

A provisional, rather general, working definition of EAP, which we shall enlarge upon shortly, is that 'EAP is concerned with those communication skills in English which are required for study purposes in formal education systems' (ETIC 1975).

1.1.1 Background

The first recorded use of the term 'English for Academic Purposes' appears to be in 1974 (Johns, T. F. 1981); by 1975 it was in more general use. The published proceedings of the joint SELMOUS-BAAL Seminar at Birmingham University in 1975 on 'The English Language Problems of Overseas Students in Higher Education in the UK' were entitled *'English for Academic Purposes'* (Cowie and Heaton 1977). *'English for Academic Study'* was used by the British Council (ETIC 1975) as the title of its collection of papers, mostly on English for Science and Technology. One of the papers was 'Developing Study Skills in English' (Candlin *et al.* 1975).

Study skills were coming increasingly to the fore in the 1970s in practice material for students of English. An early book in the USA was *Study Skills for Students of English* by R. C. Yorkey (1970). In the UK, J. B. Heaton wrote *Studying in English: A practical approach to study skills in English as a second language* (1975). In 1979, the first title in the Collins Study Skills in English series appeared (James *et al.* 1979).

In Britain, increased professionalism in the teaching of EAP at university level was indicated by the re-naming in 1989 of an older-established group to the British Association of Lecturers in English for Academic Purposes (BALEAP). (See Appendix 3.)

1

1.1.2 Range of settings

EAP takes place in a variety of settings and circumstances. These range from an entirely English-speaking context (e.g. UK, Ireland, USA, Canada, Australia, New Zealand, etc.) to the students' own countries. These countries may have English as a Foreign Language (EFL), e.g. Germany, Finland; or as an official/second language (ESL) or medium of instruction in schools and/or colleges, e.g. anglophone African countries, India. The students may need EAP for higher education studies in their own country, e.g. for reading academic texts; or for higher education in L1 countries, e.g. all skills may be needed. They may also use EAP on pre-departure courses in their own countries before studying abroad. See Chapter 4, the section on 'International EAP courses' for examples of the variety of settings.

The teachers may be native speakers of English (NS) or non-native speakers (NNS). The courses may be pre-sessional, i.e. held before an academic course begins, and usually full-time, or in-sessional, i.e. held during an academic term or semester, and usually part-time. These latter courses are usually attended by students at the same time as they are studying their mainstream subjects. In addition, the courses may be 'short', e.g. 4–12 weeks, or 'long', e.g. 6–12 months, or longer. Courses may include formal teaching programmes, self-access situations, distance-learning materials or CALL (computer-assisted language learning).

EAP courses in UK universities are normally run by Language Centres, English Language (Teaching) Centres or Units, or departments with various other broadly similar names. If they are not free-standing, the majority are located in Departments of English, Linguistics, (Modern) Languages or Education. The pattern in other countries will vary but tends to be rather similar.

The settings and situations, like other aspects of education, are subject to change. To take an example in the UK, in 1992, 36 new universities were created from the previously-named polytechnics. In common with the older-established universities, they actively sought to increase their intake of overseas students in order to improve their financial position. Together with the expansion of the European student-exchange programmes, ERASMUS and TEMPUS, the increased numbers of non-native speakers of English entailed a growing need for EAP at tertiary level in the UK.

In different sections of this book, reference will be made to the various settings referred to above. The international nature of EAP and ESP (English for Specific Purposes) is emphasised in a wide-ranging survey article by Johns and Dudley-Evans (1991).

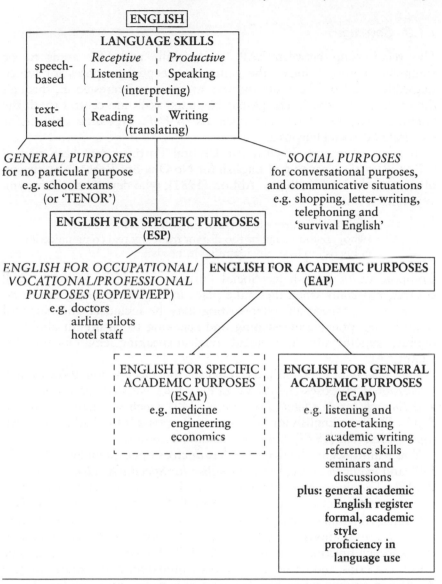

Note: In the USA a more usual model for the categories of ESP is as
follows (Johns 1991). (This is similar to ETIC 1975.)

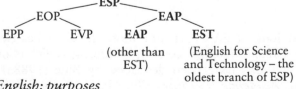

Figure 1   English: purposes

1.1.3 Coverage

The relationship between EAP, study skills and ESP needs to be examined. Figure 1 shows the generally accepted purposes for which English is needed. The route that we are mainly interested in, through the diagram, is boxed. The global language skills are central to all the language purposes. Our path takes us to *ESP*, bypassing English for General and Social Purposes.

In some situations, English for General Purposes has been named 'TENOR' – 'the Teaching of English for No Obvious Reason', no reason obvious to the learner, that is. Abbott (1981), who devised this acronym, explained it thus:

> Most of the world's learners of English are schoolchildren ...
> [who] are too young or too distant from any real communication
> in English to have any identifiable 'needs'.

Components of English for Social Purposes are often added to EAP courses, especially when they take place in English-speaking countries. For example, aspects of letter-writing may be included, and 'survival English', i.e. practice in listening and speaking to ensure an ability to operate functionally in a local English-speaking environment (see Chapter 4).

ESP has two main strands: English for Occupational/Vocational/Professional Purposes (EOP/EVP/EPP), which we shall only touch on, and *English for Academic Purposes (EAP)*, which we shall consider in depth. The term English for Educational Purposes (EEP) had earlier been used by Strevens (1977), but this is seldom used now.

You will notice in the diagram that *doctors* appears under EOP/EVP/EPP, and *medicine* is listed under *English for Specific Academic Purposes* (ESAP). This is to highlight the essential difference between the two strands of ESP. For example, under EVP/EPP, material has been devised for trainee doctors to give them practice in doctor–patient interaction in casualty consultations (a very restricted situation): the material is based on 23 speech functions (Candlin *et al.* 1977). For students studying to be doctors, a book and cassettes have been prepared, under ESAP, to give practice in reading textbooks, listening to lectures and so on (e.g. James 1989).

1.1.4 EAP

We can now look at EAP in a little more detail. It has two divisions: it 'may be either *common core* or *subject-specific*' (Coffey 1984). These two divisions have been described by Blue (1988a) as *English for General Academic Purposes* (EGAP) and *English for Specific*

Academic Purposes (ESAP). A large proportion of the common core element is more usually known as 'study skills', and that is the label that will be used for those elements in this book. Some examples of study skills are given in the diagram, e.g. listening and note-taking. Study skills will be looked at in detail in this chapter as well as in Part II.

Subject-specific English is the language needed for a particular academic subject, e.g. economics, together with its disciplinary culture. It includes the language structure, vocabulary, the particular skills needed for the subject, and the appropriate academic conventions. This will also be examined in detail later.

In the past, some authors regarded EAP and study skills as being synonymous (Robinson 1980, 1991). However, the majority view, more recently, is that study skills is the key component in EAP – 'it is difficult ... to conceive of an EAP course which is not centred on study skills in English' (Phillips and Shettlesworth 1978) – but that EAP includes something in addition to this (see Jordan 1989 for a full discussion; this also includes an extensive bibliography on all aspects of EAP). These additional features can be summarised as *a general academic English register*, incorporating *a formal, academic style*, with *proficiency in the language use*. These features will also be looked at later.

1.1.5 Students and study skills

Many students, whose mother tongue is not English, already possess study skills to an advanced level in their own language. They may simply need help to transfer their skills into English and, possibly, to adjust them to a different academic environment. However, they may need help with the other elements of EAP, e.g. style. Equally, there will be many students who do *not* already practise study skills efficiently in their own language or in their own country, or who do not possess all the study skills needed for effective study through the medium of English.

The students' needs may differ according to the learning environment. For example, students from educational systems very different from those in the UK, Australia or North America may need considerable help with various study skills and the academic conventions attached to them if they go to study in those countries. There may be substantial differences, for instance, between the structure and conventions attached to an academic discussion in Indonesia, Nepal or China, and a seminar for postgraduates in a British university. An added complexity is the different cultural conventions involved in academic argument. It is clear that an assessment of students' needs is crucial. These aspects will be discussed in subsequent chapters.

The first requirement of students will be the development of study skills to an appropriate level for the subject(s) to be studied, in conjunction with the development of language proficiency. Once students are over the basic hurdle of study skills and language adequacy, they then have to 'learn the academic code'. This will involve a number of elements, depending on the level of education being pursued, i.e. undergraduate, post-graduate, research and so on. It may include adapting to a new academic system, within a different cultural environment, which has its own conventions. It may also involve observing the nature of the relationships between academic staff and students, and among students themselves. In turn, these relationships involve attitudes and expectations, some of which are expressed through language.

These, then, are the settings for EAP. In what follows, the various components and aspects of EAP will be considered in some detail: we shall look at examples of published material, data from surveys and research findings. Many of the issues raised above will be looked at in the light of evidence and experience.

1.2 What are study skills?

A dictionary explanation of study skills encapsulates the essence:

> abilities, techniques, and strategies which are used when reading, writing or listening for study purposes. For example, study skills needed by university students studying from English-language textbooks include: adjusting reading speeds according to the type of material being read, using the dictionary, guessing word meanings from context, interpreting graphs, diagrams and symbols, note-taking and summarizing.

> (Richards, Platt and Platt 1992)

A reasonably comprehensive list of study skills in the study situations in which they are likely to be needed is set out in Figure 2. Some authors regard such an all-inclusive list as the 'broad' interpretation of study skills. A 'narrow' view is that the term 'study skills' is reserved for the more mechanical aspects of study, e.g. reference skills, the use of the library, the layout of dissertations and theses, the use of footnotes, bibliography, etc. (Robinson 1991). As Robinson (1991) says, 'all these skills need to be taught to the native speaker of English as well as the non-native'. This aspect will be considered shortly.

Earlier in this chapter, Figure 1 showed language skills separate from, but basic to, study skills. Figure 3 (adapted from Jordan 1977a) shows the integrated relationship of the skills. The receptive skills are seen as necessary inputs to the productive skills, with each receptive skill having its place with each productive skill, depending on the appropriate study situation or activity. Note-taking is seen as an adjunct to listening or reading (i.e. receptive skills), but also as a lead-in to, or link with, the productive skills of speaking or writing, e.g. listening to a lecture, taking notes, and then making use of the notes to make comments in a seminar or in writing an essay.

STUDY SKILLS

STUDY SITUATION/ACTIVITY	STUDY SKILLS NEEDED
1 *lectures/talks*	1 listening and understanding
	2 note-taking
	3 asking questions for: repetition, clarification and information
2 *seminars/tutorials/ discussions/ supervisions*	1 listening and note-taking
	2 asking questions – as above
	3 answering questions; explaining
	4 agreeing and disagreeing; stating points of view; giving reasons; interrupting
	5 speaking with(out) notes: giving a paper/oral presentations, initiating comments, responding; verbalising data
3 *practicals/ laboratory work/field work*	1 understanding instructions: written and spoken, formal and informal
	2 asking questions; requesting help
	3 recording results
4 *private study/reading* (journals and books)	1 reading efficiently: comprehension and speed
	2 scanning and skimming; evaluating
	3 understanding and analysing data (graphs, diagrams, etc.)
	4 note-making; arranging notes in hierarchy of importance
	5 summarising and paraphrasing
5 *reference material/ library use*	research and reference skills viz.:
	1 using the contents/index pages
	2 using a dictionary efficiently
	3 understanding classification systems
	4 using a library catalogue (subject and author) on cards, microfiche and computer
	5 finding information quickly (general reference works and bibliographies)
	6 collating information
6 *essays/reports/projects/ case studies/dissertations/ theses/research papers/articles*	1 planning, writing drafts, revising
	2 summarising, paraphrasing and synthesising
	3 continuous writing in an academic style, organised appropriately
	4 using quotations, footnotes, bibliography
	5 finding and analysing evidence; using data appropriately
7 *research* (linked with 3–6 above)	*in addition to 3–6 above*:
	1 conducting interviews

7

| | 2 designing questionnaires |
| | 3 undertaking surveys |

8 *examinations*:

a) *written*
  1 preparing for exams (techniques)
  2 revision
  3 understanding questions/instructions
  4 writing quickly: pressure of time

b) *oral*
  1 answering questions: explicitly, precisely
  2 explaining, describing, justifying

Skills generally applicable:

1 organising study time efficiently, i.e. time management
2 logical thinking: constructing arguments – use of cohesive markers and connectives; recognising weaknesses and bias in arguments; balance; critical analysis
3 accuracy
4 memory: recall; mnemonics
5 using computers/word processors

N.B. The term *reference skills* is sometimes confused with the generic term *study skills*.

Figure 2   Study skills and situations

1.3   The native speaker and study skills

At a basic level, it may be noted that study skills are not something acquired instinctively. To take an example, silent reading, which is often taken for granted, is not automatically acquired but learned. In this section we shall look briefly at the situation with regard to native English-speaking students in the UK. There is a body of evidence from a number of research findings which demonstrates the need for study skills instruction or courses of various kinds. The proposition is that if many English mother-tongue students need help with study skills, then it is equally likely that many non-native speakers will also need help if they have to study in English.

One small instance of research was a survey carried out by the Students' Union of Manchester University (1979) among students in the Faculty of Science. There were a number of findings, among them that 'the university should provide information and courses designed for students to acquire study skills'. Beard and Hartley (1984) surveyed different aspects of higher education in Britain with evidence from a number of sources. One of their conclusions was that 'students need to develop effective study skills if they are to become effective independent learners'.

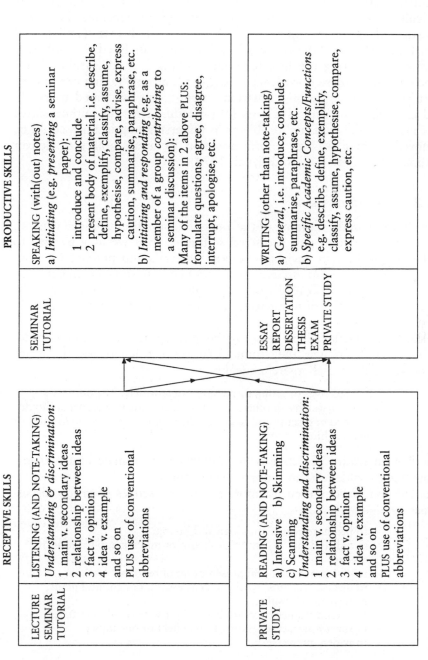

The following content appears within the figure:

STUDY SKILLS

RECEPTIVE SKILLS

LECTURE
SEMINAR
TUTORIAL

LISTENING (AND NOTE-TAKING)
Understanding & discrimination:
1 main v. secondary ideas
2 relationship between ideas
3 fact v. opinion
4 idea v. example
and so on
PLUS use of conventional
abbreviations

PRIVATE
STUDY

READING (AND NOTE-TAKING)
a) Intensive   b) Skimming
c) Scanning
Understanding and discrimination:
1 main v. secondary ideas
2 relationship between ideas
3 fact v. opinion
4 idea v. example
and so on
PLUS use of conventional
abbreviations

PRODUCTIVE SKILLS

SEMINAR
TUTORIAL

SPEAKING (with(out) notes)
a) *Initiating* (e.g. *presenting* a seminar
   paper):
   1 introduce and conclude
   2 present body of material, i.e. describe,
     define, exemplify, classify, assume,
     hypothesise, compare, advise, express
     caution, summarise, paraphrase, etc.
b) *Initiating and responding* (e.g. as a
   member of a group *contributing* to
   a seminar discussion):
   Many of the items in 2 above PLUS:
   formulate questions, agree, disagree,
   interrupt, apologise, etc.

ESSAY
REPORT
DISSERTATION
THESIS
EXAM
PRIVATE STUDY

WRITING (other than note-taking)
a) *General*, i.e. introduce, conclude,
   summarise, paraphrase, etc.
b) *Specific Academic Concepts/Functions*
   e.g. describe, define, exemplify,
   classify, assume, hypothesise, compare,
   express caution, etc.

Figure 3   Study skills: receptive and productive skills

1.3.1 Lectures and note-taking

The lecture system is a common feature of higher education. Understanding lectures, with the concomitant skill of note-taking, presents difficulties for many students. This method of teaching has been investigated in some depth by Bligh (1971/72), Brown (1978), and Beard and Hartley (1984). Beard and Hartley analysed a number of studies investigating the link between note-taking and learning. They concluded that 'there is evidence to suggest that note-taking can aid the learning process in certain situations, note-taking is related to recall, and reviewing one's notes is a useful procedure'. All the authors agree that many of the students' problems in understanding lectures could be removed if there was an improvement in lecturers' ability to deliver lectures (see Chapter 12, and Lynch 1994).

1.3.2 Group discussions

If we have an understanding of the aims of group discussions in general, and of the problems and proffered solutions, then we may be able to make use of these in devising courses, materials and practice for non-native speakers. Group discussions are looked at in some detail below as this is an area of considerable difficulty for many students. (The expressed difficulties of non-native speakers in seminars are looked at in Chapters 3 and 13.)

Beard and Hartley (1984) employ the term 'group discussion' in order to avoid confusion, as they found that some teachers use the terms 'seminar' and 'tutorial' interchangeably:

> The objectives of group discussion range widely. The objective which outweighs all others in importance ... is that students should be helped to discuss and to clarify difficulties arising from lectures or other teaching sessions.

Another important objective is 'to obtain more intimate and personal contact with students than is possible in lectures'.

Beard and Hartley then list more specific objectives of group discussions:

- to promote critical and logical thinking;
- to aid students in solving problems or making applications of theory;
- to give practice in oral presentation of reports;
- to discuss students' work, such as essays, designs and plans, experimental results;
- to extend studies to topics beyond those covered in lectures;
- to survey literature relating to one field or one topic;
- to widen interests;

- to change attitudes;
- to provide feedback to staff on (1) students' progress and attitudes, and (2) the effectiveness of their teaching.

Perhaps the biggest problem noted in group discussions is that students do not participate. Various reasons have been suggested for this, which can be summarised under the following headings:

- shyness
- lack of self-confidence
- unwillingness to begin
- lack of knowledge of the subject
- unsuitable topic for discussion
- over-large room and/or group
- inhibiting seating arrangement of students and tutor
- monopolisation of time by persistent talkers (including the tutor).

Beard and Hartley go on to look at different research findings aimed at helping students to talk in groups. Hawkins *et al.* (1981) found that most discussion was between people sitting opposite each other; people sitting next to each other spoke less. In addition, it was noted that students will not talk to those they cannot see.

Beard and Hartley also reported on the findings of Bligh *et al.* (1975) who considered that the teacher should, as far as possible, withdraw from a central, dominant position. They also proposed that teachers should:

- not correct students' first contributions to a discussion;
- not state an opinion too firmly as it may inhibit students;
- not answer questions that other students could answer.

EAP tutors could doubtless utilise some of the further findings of Beattie (1982), reported by Beard and Hartley:

- the tutor spoke much of the time and was involved in a disproportionate number of exchanges;
- a student was far less likely to be followed in discussion by another student than by the tutor (the talk was mainly channelled through the tutor);
- the tutor tended to follow on students' contributions with minimum delay, so leaving little opportunity for the other students to organise their thoughts;
- the tutor commonly interrupted the students by cutting in when they were nearing a possible completion point.

Some possible roles for tutors and students are listed in Beard and Hartley (based on Schmuck and Schmuck 1971). These can be helpful to a tutor in providing a purpose to group discussions and enabling students to maximise benefit from them:

11

Some possible roles for teachers and students in group discussions

Initiating	Starting things off, suggesting new ideas or new ways of looking at what you're discussing.
Seeking information	Asking for relevant facts or authoritative information on a subject.
Giving information	Supplying relevant facts or relating personal experiences.
Giving opinions	Stating an opinion about something the class is considering: perhaps challenging consensus or complacency.
Clarifying	Restating something that someone has said. Translating a poorly worded statement into a clear one.
Elaborating	Building on previous comments, giving examples.
Controlling	Making sure that everyone who wants to gets a chance to speak.
Encouraging	Being receptive and responsive to comments.
Setting standards	Supplying and asking for criteria to judge the different ideas that are discussed.
Harmonizing	Reducing tension: getting pupils to explore their differences.
Relieving tension	Diagnosing what causes frustration during discussions and trying various remedies.
Coordinating	Extracting the key ideas from what's been said and integrating them: helping the group to use and to build on each other's ideas.
Orientating	Defining where you think the class is in their discussion and where you think they have to go.
Testing	Checking with your class as to where they feel the discussion should be going.
Consensus testing	Checking with the group to see how much agreement has been reached: protecting the divergence of views.
Summarizing	Reviewing what's been said, pulling together ideas and comments.

1.3.3 *Academic writing*

Academic writing occupies a large proportion of students' study time. For a variety of reasons it causes difficulties. Beard and Hartley assess different authorities and strategies and, unsurprisingly, conclude that planning an essay is essential. The requirements that they comment on are: the need to select relevant material, present a reasoned argument, evaluate evidence and draw appropriate conclusions. Comment is made on the particular difficulty of writing both the introduction and the conclusion. They stress the need for redrafting, rewriting and competent presentation. In this connection, Rowntree (1970/76) provides a useful checklist for students' use when rewriting essays. He first advises them to put the essay aside for a few days so that they can re-read it more critically:

A check-list

Here are some useful questions to ask yourself about it:
1. Does the essay answer the question or deal with the topic that was set?
2. Does it cover all the main aspects and in sufficient depth?
3. Is the content accurate and relevant?
4. Is the material logically arranged?
5. Is each main point well supported by examples and argument?
6. Is there a clear distinction between your ideas and those you have brought in from other authors?
7. Do you acknowledge all sources and references?
8. Is the length of the essay right for its purpose?
9. Is it written plainly and simply, without clumsy or obscure phrasing? (A good test is to *read it aloud*.)
10. Is the grammar, punctuation and spelling acceptable, and is it neatly and legibly written?

Writing genres are also examined briefly by Beard and Hartley, in particular the scientific article. After giving an overview of the different parts of the paper (typically: title, abstract, introduction, materials and method, results, discussion, conclusions, literature cited and acknow-ledgements), they provide helpful comments on redrafting and editing text. They also examine the three main types of writers' blocks: physical, procedural and psychological.

1.3.4 A student-centred approach

Having seen that there is often a need for assistance in developing study skills, we can now turn to look at what has been recommended. In a refreshing approach, Gibbs (1977) raised the question of 'teaching study skills' when observing that 'conventional attempts to teach students how to study – in the sense of *telling* them how to study – have tended to cause a multitude of problems for students'. They produced a 'gap between knowing and doing' with advice which 'sometimes involves a very threatening attack on existing ways of doing things'. Gibbs had observed that students often reacted negatively to being *told*, for example, how to take notes from lectures. They felt comfortable with their own methods and techniques, even if they were inefficient, and felt insecure if told to change them. Gibbs advocated 'self-discovered learning' by means of 'structured groups' of students discussing how and why they did something. The basic purpose is to increase students' awareness and their self-confidence.

Gibbs developed his student-centred approach (1981) by posing questions or setting exercises related to learning, which are tackled in a structured group. First, the students start with their own experience and ideas, and then widen these by comparing and contrasting with others in the group. The approach:

> requires students to work alone, then in pairs, then in small groups of four or six, and finally in a plenary session involving the whole group and chaired by the tutor.

Gibbs' comments are based on experience with students for whom English is the mother tongue. He was concerned about 'telling/advising' as opposed to 'doing/practising'. In this sense, courses in EAP/study skills for non-native speakers have a better record as they invariably contain practice, often in the form of problem-solving exercises, tasks or projects. In addition, they usually aim to increase students' awareness of alternative ways of studying, and to give information, apart from improving their language ability. Nevertheless, there are still lessons that can be learned from Gibbs' approach, especially with regard to awareness-raising, developing self-confidence, and the use of the structured group format for discussions (for examples of this, see the 'pyramid discussion' in Chapter 13).

At the beginning, we referred to the fact that some non-native speakers may already possess an ability to use study skills in their own language. It will be apparent, therefore, that it is essential to discover their needs. Methods of needs analysis will be examined in Chapter 2, after we have looked at study skills material for mother-tongue speakers.

1.4 Study skills books for native speakers of English

1.4.1 Overview

There is a vast array of literature of all kinds aimed at helping pupils and students, whose mother tongue is English, with aspects of study skills. The levels range from primary school to college or university, and from class-based practice material to individual self-help, self-study books. For many years books have existed for all kinds of learners, including those who left school without qualifications and who wish to return to study after a considerable gap. Some also cater for those studying on their own and following correspondence/distance-learning courses.

The purpose of this section is to survey some of the types of material published for native English speakers; it is seldom referred to in books for NNS. Some of the books are eminently suitable for the more advanced NNS. In other cases, some of the advice, ideas, methods or practice are appropriate. In yet further cases, some of the activities and tasks can be adapted for use. Certainly, there is overlap between study skills for NS and NNS. The latter can undoubtedly learn something from books or ideas for the former. One small booklet, *Effective Learning Skills*, ILEA (1981), summarises the attitude: 'The most useful form of learning for life is learning how to learn'. In fact, *Learning How To Learn* (by R. M. Smith) is the title of one of the useful Open University publications.

In study skills books for NS, language difficulty as such is naturally not normally a serious consideration; the focus is on the skills themselves. Frequently, these include getting started, organising your time, where to find information, using libraries, reading skills, making notes, memory, writing essays and exam revision. Advice and self-questioning play a large part. Practice is sometimes given through activities and discussion. Sometimes examples are shown, but not always an explanation of 'how to do it'. Bearing this in mind, you might find some of the material or activities useful, especially if suitable adaptations are made.

It is necessary to bear in mind that the books are academically and culturally bound to the L1 country (UK, USA, Australia, etc.). This may be an advantage if students are attending courses in these countries, otherwise it may not. Another aspect to bear in mind is the level of sophistication of the book, i.e. the age group of the intended readership.

A number of the books refer to planning and organising study, using time, methods of study, timetables and other features associated with the structure of studying. These aspects are sometimes ignored in NNS study skills courses, often on the assumption that undergraduates or postgraduates have nothing to learn in this regard. Clearly it depends on individual students and their educational background: their needs should be carefully checked.

Publications aimed at British undergraduates, and mature students taking Open University courses, also contain sections useful to students going to study in the UK. In this respect, study skills books published by the Open University and the National Extension College, Cambridge, are particularly relevant. An excellent all-round book for students is *Going to University* by J. McIlroy and B. Jones. It discusses the whole system of higher education in Britain in a practical way. It gives information on the structure of a university, the hierarchy and titles of staff and the system of qualifications. It then proceeds to give examples of good practice in a variety of study skills.

Some of the books are geared to the needs of advanced students, for example, writing dissertations and theses, doing research and studying for a PhD. These will be particularly useful for reference by teachers who do not themselves have such higher qualifications but who may have students studying at that level.

From time to time, quality newspapers carry articles aimed at helping students. *The Guardian* newspaper is one such paper that, over the years, has maintained a high profile with regard to education and students. Appropriate articles can be a useful source of up-to-date information and often provide fruitful topics for comparison and discussion.

1.4.2 Advice and strategies

PRODUCING A GOOD ESSAY

Advice is given in the form of criteria made memorable by the acronym ASPRESCO (from *Going to University* by McIlroy and Jones):

> Answer (the question)
> Structure (clear)
> Presentation (tidy)
> Reading (wide range)
> Evidence (used to support arguments)
> Style (appropriate)
> Clear thinking
> Originality (or play safe!)

This is followed by 'The ten-point plan for writing good essays':

1. Understand the title
2. Generation of ideas
3. Preliminary essay plan
4. Assembly of resources
5. Reading
6. Note-making
7. Detailed essay plan
8. First draft
9. Second draft
10. Final reading

EFFECTIVE READING

Several books refer to the well-tried and widely-used system of reading textbooks, known as 'SQ3R', developed by F. P. Robinson in 1946 in *Effective Study*. (This method is included in other early books: *How to Study* by H. Maddox, and *Learn How to Study* by D. Rowntree.) The method has been adapted for NNS (e.g. Yorkey 1970/82; Heaton 1975; Floyd 1984). It ensures a high degree of understanding and remembrance.

SQ3R has five stages which are as follows:

Survey: Glance rapidly through the whole material before reading any part of it, in order to discover the purpose and organisation of the book.

Question: Formulate appropriate questions to ask yourself for each section/chapter: this will give a purpose to the reading.

Read: Read carefully and thoroughly, if necessary turning back some pages to ensure understanding. The reading purpose is to find answers to the questions (e.g. the main idea of a section). Read through first and then make notes at the end of each section.

Recall: At the end of each section, try to remember the content. Read the questions again and try to provide answers. Check and amend notes.

Revise: Check the accuracy of your recall by a quick survey,
(or Review:) and try to answer the questions. Re-read as necessary. Double-check notes.

FASTER READING

Various books exist on methods to increase reading speed. Clearly, a student is at a disadvantage if faced with a long reading list if he or she can only read slowly. 'Slowly' is, of course, subjective, and will vary from reader to reader, and will depend on the text-type. It is easier to read a light novel quickly with understanding than a densely-packed textbook.

Reading speed courses usually discuss the causes of slow reading. These invariably include reference to eye movements (i.e. mechanical) and brain function (i.e. comprehension). Factors considered are: eye and recognition span; reading word-by-word instead of in word groups/ thought units; eye regressions along the line; excessive finger-pointing; slowness in word recognition; poor vocabulary range; vocalising (i.e. mouthing words); sub-vocalisation (i.e. saying the words silently to oneself); and inability to predict language.

Methods to improve reading efficiency usually involve exercises and practice in increasing vocabulary range, anticipation of language, improved comprehension, awareness of eye movements, variable reading speed and timed reading passages.

It is essential for students to be able to skim and to scan texts. Skimming involves the quick reading of a text – not every word – in order to understand the gist or main points of a passage, i.e. the overall meaning. Scanning involves quickly looking through a text, or surveying it, in order to find specific information. When skimming and scanning, a student should be looking at the heavy information words (or 'content

17

words', i.e. nouns and verbs) rather than the grammatical or structural words (e.g. articles, prepositions).

Reading speed is normally measured in words per minute (wpm). Over the years various measures and estimates have been made of slow, average and fast reading speeds for serious reading material. Less than 200 wpm is considered slow, about 250 wpm average, and above 300–400 wpm fast (Tabachnick 1969; De Leeuw and De Leeuw 1965). In 1972 I conducted an experiment with my wife and myself (both native English-speakers). Averaging both our speeds we found that reading aloud we read at 194 wpm, reading to ourselves but mouthing words audibly we read at 293 wpm and reading silently we read at 385 wpm.

NOTE-TAKING

Allied to reading, listening, understanding and remembering, is note-taking. It is a necessary skill for later reference or revision purposes. Traditionally, note-taking is linear, i.e. one point follows another down a page. Aspects of this may be the use of layout, capital letters, headings, systems of numbering, indentation, underlining, abbreviation symbols, etc. One tendency of linear note-taking is that it is apt to become unnecessarily lengthy, whereas only a maximum of 10 per cent of the original is normally needed for recall purposes.

An alternative system of note-taking has been promoted by Buzan (1982) under the label of 'mind maps'. The note-taking starts from the topic listed in the centre of the page and then expands outwards in different directions making use of key words and images linked to each other. Buzan also calls these *patterned notes*; they are essentially visual.

Variations on 'mind maps' have been produced: they are known as branching notes or diagrams, and may look like a spider's web. Many people consider that branching notes are more memorable than linear notes because of their visual impact. They may be especially useful for note-taking during lectures as they allow notes to be developed in a flexible way as the lecture proceeds, and allow the relationships between ideas to be noted more clearly. (Examples of some of the note-taking systems will be shown in Chapter 12.)

1.5 Introspect and discuss

1. Do you accept the definition of EAP given near the beginning of the chapter? Is there anything you would wish to modify? Why? Are there any changes that you would propose to *Figure 1*?
2. What place does EAP have in your country? What types of EAP courses are there?

3. *Figure 2* gives a fairly comprehensive list of study skills and the situations in which they might be used. Are there any other study skills that you would want to add to the list?
4. Which of the study skills have caused *you* the most difficulty in the past? Do you know why?
5. From your experience, what are the main reasons why students have difficulty in participating in group discussions?
6. From your observations, which are the biggest mistakes that teachers make when conducting group discussions?
7. A checklist of questions was drawn up by Rowntree for students to ask themselves after they have written the first draft of an essay. Compose a list of suitable questions for *teachers* to ask themselves after they have conducted a group discussion.
8. An example is given of a student-centred approach by Gibbs. If possible, emulate his approach by discussing your experiences of learning foreign languages: which methods worked best for you, and why?
9. Whatever your mother tongue, did you use any books in your own language to help you develop study skills at secondary or tertiary level? Can you remember in which area(s) you found them most helpful?
10. If you were to write an article aimed at helping undergraduates to organise their studies, which aspects would you emphasise?
11. Try to devise a suitable acronym containing advice for students about to start their studies in another country.
12. Faster reading is discussed and examples are given of reading speeds. If you do not know your average reading speed, in words per minute, find out what it is (perhaps with the help of a partner).
13. Try different techniques to see which helps your reading speed and understanding to improve most. Compare restrictions of eye movements, with reading in word groups, with removal of any sub-vocalisation, with prediction of language/content.

2 Needs analysis

In broad terms, needs analysis can be described as:

> the process of determining the needs for which a learner or group of
> learners requires a language and arranging the needs according to
> priorities ... [it] makes use of both subjective and objective
> information.
>
> (Richards *et al.* 1992)

The various dimensions involved in analysing needs can be seen in the
following imaginary, but plausible, case study.

2.1 An imaginary case study (1)

Gopal, a young man from Nepal, wants to go to a university in the UK
to study for an MA in Economics. His sponsor, the Ministry of Finance,
wants Gopal to study Development Economics, thinking that this might
be more advantageous to the needs of a developing country. Gopal's
opinion is not asked; he is told that a financial award is only available
for Development Economics. Naturally he agrees, and is delighted to
have the opportunity of studying abroad: he has not been outside Nepal
before. He hopes that he will go to University 1 where his friend went
and was happy.

Gopal is asked to take a British Council English Test (IELTS test from
UCLES) in their office in the capital, Kathmandu. He does so, feeling
fairly confident of the outcome as he has been studying and using
English for some years. Rather to his surprise, he is told that he needs a
pre-sessional English course for eight weeks before his academic course
begins. He feels somewhat apprehensive as he thought that his English
was adequate for the course. Certainly his English was better than that
of many of his friends. However, he appreciates that his earlier arrival
will give him a chance to settle in, adjust, become acclimatised and so
on. He feels a little disappointed when he then hears that he is to go to
University 2 and not University 1. Nevertheless, he looks forward to
studying there and appreciates that the extra English course will be paid
for, and will also be held at University 2. It will give him time to
orientate.

The brightness of the prospect becomes a little tarnished when Gopal is told, late in the day, that University 2 will only accept him for the Master's course if he first takes the one-year Diploma course. He would need to do well in the exams at the end in order to be accepted for the MA course, which would then be a further year's study. Gopal's government reluctantly agrees to his release for two years, and the British Council agrees to find funds for the extra year. But does Gopal agree?

Gopal knows from his friends' experiences that if he does not agree to the change, then it is goodbye to a scholarship for some years. The decision is made difficult by the fact that his young wife and two-year-old child will miss him terribly, and he will miss them. Two years is a totally different proposition from one year's absence.

Gopal's household, like most in Nepal, consists of an extended or joint family, in other words, his parents and brothers and their families, as well as his wife and child. They are a close-knit group. As with most major concerns, the whole family discusses Gopal's problem. It is reluctantly decided that for the sake of his career, they will agree to two years' study abroad. Perhaps Gopal will be able to make arrangements for his wife and child to follow later; but he knows this will be expensive.

Gopal's friend, Mohan, advises him, from his own experience, not to try to take his wife and child with him at the beginning. He tells him that if he does so, he will spend the first few weeks sorting out accommodation and everyday living difficulties, and will only speak Nepali at home. As a result, he will not obtain maximum benefit from the English course. Mohan also warns him that he will hardly understand anyone when he first arrives, and that he will find the food and climate difficult to adjust to. By taking his wife and child with him at the beginning, Gopal would be making a difficult task more complex. However, Gopal wants to discuss this with his wife to see how she feels. He anticipates that he will be homesick, perhaps lonely, and will probably suffer from culture shock, and the presence of his family would help to alleviate this.

2.1.1 Whose needs?

It can be deduced from the realistic illustration above that there are several points of view to be considered in the process of examining needs:

- the Ministry of Finance and Government of Nepal;
- the British Council, in Nepal and the UK;
- staff of the Diploma Course in Development Economics at University 2, and the course director of the Pre-sessional English course;
- Gopal and his family.

21

In other words, the sponsor, the subject specialists, the language course designer and teachers, and the student.

The needs to be taken into account, apart from the subject matter of Development Economics and the requirements of the department, might appear to be mainly language and study skills. However, from Gopal's point of view, there are a number of other considerations, e.g. orientation in an alien academic environment and adaptation to different study modes and expectations; adjustment to a foreign culture with its social language, customs and conventions and so on (see Chapter 6). A broad approach is taken by Dubin and Olshtain (1986) who refer to 'societal needs' ('ways in which the members of the community use or need to use the LWC' – 'language of wider communication' or world language).

2.2 Analysis

Needs analysis should be the starting point for devising syllabuses, courses, materials and the kind of teaching and learning that takes place. This has been recognised for some time (e.g. Higgins 1966; Richterich in Trim *et al.* 1973/80; Strevens 1977; Coffey 1984).

Under the umbrella of needs analysis, other approaches have been incorporated. These include: target-situation analysis, present-situation analysis, deficiency analysis, strategy analysis, means analysis, language audit and constraints. In addition, other terms have been proposed for 'needs'. These include: necessities, demands, wants, likes, lacks, deficiencies, goals, aims, purposes and objectives. They will be commented on shortly. For a full discussion of all aspects of needs analysis, together with an exhaustive bibliography, see the excellent article by West (1994). (See also Robinson 1991; Mackay and Palmer 1981.) Cunningsworth (1983) gives a brief overview of needs analysis throughout the 1970s.

Implicit in needs analysis is the requirement for fact-finding or the collection of data. The data, for example, about the students, the subject to be studied, etc. can come from a variety of sources and can be collected by various methods. The starting point is to pose some fundamental questions (Richterich 1983) which can help us to see the appropriate type of analysis and the data needed. After noting the questions, and the type of responses they will elicit, we shall look at the different approaches to analyses before examining the different methods of collecting data.

2.3 Questions

1. *Why* is the analysis being undertaken? (to determine the type of syllabus and content, materials, teaching/learning; for placement on

an appropriate course; to inform EAP teachers through articles in journals ...)

2. *Whose* needs are to be analysed? (the student's; the sponsor's – institution or country; the specialist department ...)
3. *Who* performs the analysis? *Who* decides what the language needs are? (sponsor; teacher; student; researcher/consultant ...)
4. *What* is to be analysed? (target situation; present situation; deficiencies; strategies; means; constraints; necessities; lacks; wants ...)
5. *How* is the analysis to be conducted? (tests; questionnaires; interviews; documentation ...)
6. *When* is the analysis to be undertaken? (before the EAP course/tuition; at the start of the course; during the course; at the end of the course ...)
7. *Where* is the EAP course to be held? (in the target country, e.g. UK; in the student's own country; in a third country ...)

At this stage it will be helpful to look at a summary of the steps involved in conducting a needs analysis, before we look at the different approaches.

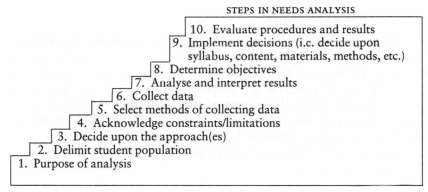

STEPS IN NEEDS ANALYSIS

10. Evaluate procedures and results
9. Implement decisions (i.e. decide upon syllabus, content, materials, methods, etc.)
8. Determine objectives
7. Analyse and interpret results
6. Collect data
5. Select methods of collecting data
4. Acknowledge constraints/limitations
3. Decide upon the approach(es)
2. Delimit student population
1. Purpose of analysis

Figure 4   Steps in needs analysis

2.4   Approaches to needs analysis

2.4.1   *Target-situation analysis*

A landmark in the development of needs analysis, and probably the best-known framework for *target-situation analysis* (TSA), is the rigorous model devised by Munby (1978). Munby's approach focuses on the students' needs at the end of a language course, and target-level performance. Munby is concerned with communicative syllabus design, and his procedures are very detailed. The core of his model is the

'Communication Needs Processor' (CNP) in which account is taken of 'the variables that affect communication needs by organising them as parameters in a dynamic relationship to each other'. After operating Munby's model, the end product is a profile of the students' language needs. The needs profile is then converted into a 'communicative competence specification', from which a sequenced syllabus can be drawn up. The routes through the model to arrive at the syllabus go either via a 'language skills selector' or via a 'meaning processor' and 'linguistic encoder'. A useful and straightforward summary, with exemplification, is contained in Hawkey (1980).

'Munby's attempt to be systematic and comprehensive inevitably made his instrument inflexible, complex and time-consuming' (West 1994). As a result, all subsequent systems of needs analysis have aimed at simplicity. In addition, Munby's:

> model collects data *about* the learner rather than *from* the learner ... As a reaction, more recent needs analysis procedures have been developed which deliberately adopt a very different starting point, reasserting the value of the judgement of the teacher or involving the learner from the start.
>
> (West 1994)

Two other criticisms have been levelled at Munby's model: that practical constraints should be considered at the start of the needs analysis procedure (Munby considered them after the procedure had been worked through); and that the language items chosen for practice in ESP/EAP should reflect those used in the real world (Munby's classifications of language were derived from social English). Nevertheless, in spite of the criticisms, Munby's approach and model have been very influential: either developments have stemmed from his work, or as a result of reactions to it.

2.4.2 Present-situation analysis

A different approach is provided by Richterich and Chancerel (1977/80) who propose a *present-situation analysis* (PSA). The PSA ascertains the students' state of language development at the beginning of the language course. The sources of information are: the students themselves, the teaching establishment and the 'user institution', e.g. place of work, sponsoring body, etc. The methods of collection of data are surveys, questionnaires and interviews. Information is sought on levels of ability, resources and views on language teaching/learning. Essentially, the learner is at the centre of the system, which includes the surrounding society and culture.

There have been developments in needs analysis which have stemmed from the two approaches described above. In many ways, they are refinements to the two starting positions of present situation and future/ target situation. In practice, course designers are likely to want information concerning both TSA and PSA. Consequently, the resulting analysis will be a combination of the two approaches. Further developments in needs analysis are now considered.

2.4.3 Learning-centred approaches

Hutchinson and Waters (1987) advocate a *learning-centred approach*. They draw a distinction between learn*er*-centred and learn*ing*-centred. *Learner-centred* infers that 'learning is totally determined by the learner' (and thus probably does not truly exist); whereas *learning-centred* involves learning as a 'process of negotiation between individuals and society' (which includes teaching, syllabus, methods, materials, etc.). Hutchinson and Waters compare 'target needs' (what the learner needs to do in the target situation) with 'learning needs' (what the learner needs to do in order to learn). It should be borne in mind that Hutchinson and Waters refer specifically to *language* needs and not other aspects.

Hutchinson and Waters consider the kind of information that it is necessary for the course designer to obtain from an analysis of *target needs*. They pose several questions, each one sub-divided into more detailed questions:

- Why is the language needed?
- How will the language be used?
- What will the content areas be?
- Who will the learner use the language with?
- Where will the language be used?
- When will the language be used?

Similarly, Hutchinson and Waters pose questions to analyse *learning needs*:

- Why are the learners taking the course?
- How do the learners learn?
- What resources are available?
- Who are the learners?
- Where will the ESP (or EAP) course take place?
- When will the ESP (or EAP) course take place? (*my brackets*)

Hutchinson and Waters sub-divide target needs into 'necessities', 'lacks' and 'wants'. By 'necessities' (also called 'objective needs') they mean what the learner has to know in order to function effectively in the target situation (this would involve obtaining information about the situations in which the language will be used, e.g. lectures, seminars, etc., and the

25

discourse components and linguistic features commonly used in them, e.g. functions, structures, vocabulary, etc.). This is frequently known as TSA (see Chambers 1980). Many language courses are short and cannot fulfil all the requirements of the objectives of TSA. The objectives of such courses are better regarded as short- or medium-term goals or aims. 'Lacks' represent the gap between the target proficiency and what the learner knows already. Generally, the necessities that the learner lacks can form the basis of the language syllabus: this is often referred to as *deficiency analysis*. Both 'necessities' and 'lacks' can be regarded as being objective.

The third sub-division is the 'wants' or subjective needs of the learner. 'Bearing in mind the importance of learner motivation in the learning process, learner perceived wants cannot be ignored' (Hutchinson and Waters 1987). This point had been noted by Bowers (1980):

> If we accept ... that a student will learn best what he *wants* to learn, *less* well what he only *needs* to learn, less well still what he neither wants *nor* needs to learn, it is clearly important to leave room in a learning programme for the learner's own wishes regarding both goals and processes.

Learners may feel they have certain 'wants' which may conflict with the views of sponsors, course designers, etc. For example, a language course may focus on reading and writing because that will be the core of the subject-course the students will be attending. The students, however, may feel they want to develop their spoken English more, as this is their weakest skill. They want to function actively in the English language environment around them. There is no easy answer to this, but it is important that these views are taken into consideration. This aspect is considered in the context of the *negotiated syllabus* in Chapter 4.

McDonough (1984) had earlier drawn attention to these differences and their importance:

> It must be the experience of many teachers that their target specification seems to break down with a group of learners who *want* to learn a variety of English or a particular skill that was not originally envisaged in their programme, *demand* that their programme be set up in a particular way because they have certain *expectations* of the whole teaching-learning process that they bring with them, and *estimate* their own strengths and weaknesses according to certain criteria.

McDonough is concerned with the learner's perceptions and attitudes, and the need, somehow, to take account of these with the goal-oriented needs analysis: the ability to be flexible and to adapt a course programme.

Learners' involvement in the needs analysis process can have benefits

(Nunan 1988b). In particular, learners obtain a clearer idea of what can be achieved, how it can be done, and the time-scale involved.

2.4.4 Strategy analysis

In the 1980s the focus of needs analysis turned more towards the methodology employed to implement language programmes (Nunan 1988b). This involved not only methods of teaching, but also methods of learning. In other words, observing the preferred learning styles and strategies of students.

Allwright (1982) was a pioneer in this area: his starting point was the students' perceptions of their needs in their own terms. In this respect, Allwright makes a distinction between *needs* (the skills which a student sees as being relevant to him/herself), *wants* (those needs on which the student puts a high priority in the available, limited time), and *lacks* (the difference between the student's present competence and the desired competence). These terms match those later adopted by Hutchinson and Waters (see above). Allwright's concerns were to help students to identify skill areas and their preferred strategies of achieving the skills (see Dickinson 1987 for a discussion). Related areas in a strategy analysis are preferences in group size, correction procedures and methods of assessment.

Problems have arisen where students utilise learning strategies or styles that are perceived by teachers to be inappropriate or inefficient, e.g. rote learning, and a passive, teacher-dependent approach to language learning. In such cases, it becomes important for teachers on EAP courses to raise awareness of: cultural differences (where they exist), academic cultural conventions, differences in learning strategies and methods of teaching. Consequently, learner training and the development of learner autonomy become important. All of this will assist in preventing the frustration of expectations where students are studying in a different environment.

2.4.5 Means analysis

An important strand in the development of needs analysis is the attempt to adapt language courses to local situations; in other words, to accommodate what are frequently seen to be 'constraints', e.g. cultural attitudes, resources, materials, equipment, methods. This approach has been called *means analysis* (Holliday and Cooke 1982), and involves a study of the local situation, i.e. the teachers, teaching methods, students, facilities, etc. to see how a language course may be implemented. This is the reverse order of the usual approach.

The importance of this approach is that it starts from a positive premise, in other words, what might be achieved with certain, given factors. It allows sensitivity to situations in any country and discourages the imposition of alien models (of teaching, methodology, learning, etc.). Holliday (1994a and b) develops this further into what he terms 'a learning-centred approach', which acknowledges the social context of education, and gives more latitude to teachers. It can be termed 'an environmentally-sensitive teaching approach'. The purpose is to prevent alienation caused by imported teaching methods that may be culturally inappropriate. As an example, group work and teacher monitoring is only one method in a communicative approach – not the only one. It can be inappropriate in a large class, of perhaps 300 students.

Holliday compares large- and small-class cultures, and discusses appropriate methodology. He notes that communicative activities:

> can take more forms than simply practising oral communication in pairs and groups. They can involve text analysis, for example, when students communicate, not so much with each other as with a text, to solve a language problem about how the text works.
>
> (Holliday 1994a)

2.4.6 Language audits

Language audits will not be of great concern to most EAP teachers. They are large-scale exercises in defining language needs carried out for companies, regions or countries. They provide data and may propose training or educational policies to be implemented over a period of time: for example, a language audit might be conducted into the use of English as a medium of instruction in higher education in a country (see West 1994).

2.4.7 Diagrammatic summary

An attempt is made in Figure 5 to summarise the various approaches and terms used in needs analysis.

2.4.8 Methods of collecting data

So far we have looked at needs analysis in general. For an EAP needs analysis we would need to know which *subject* was going to be studied, and at what level, and the *language* necessary for this. We would also need to see which of the *study situations* and the related *study skills* (listed in Chapter 1) were relevant for the students. Then we would need to assess the students' current abilities in English and study skills in order to determine the gap, and thus their needs. (See Chapter 18 for an

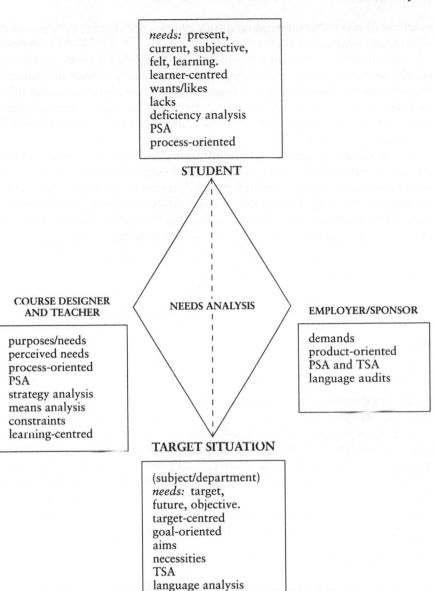

Note: Some terms can be assigned to more than one 'pole' in the diagram.

Figure 5   Needs analysis: summary

example of economics, including a framework/checklist for the provision of remedial practice in syntax and lexis.)

If the students were going to study in an English L1 country, then it would be useful to find out if they had previous experience of studying through the medium of English. It would also be useful to discover their awareness or otherwise of different cultural and academic conventions. In this connection, information about their educational background is relevant.

The methods for gathering data about the learners are summarised in the 14 sections below. The methods used employ various techniques: documentation, tests, questionnaires, forms/checklists, interviews, record-keeping and observation. The methods are given in an approximate chronological order. However, it should be noted that information may be obtained by different methods almost simultaneously.

1 ADVANCE DOCUMENTATION

Advance documentation can be requested for information about educational background, previously attended courses (especially if through the medium of English), references as to abilities and any other relevant aspects.

2 LANGUAGE TEST AT HOME

A *language test* can be conducted in the students' *home country* before they are accepted by a university, etc. overseas, or before they join a course. Such a test should indicate their strengths and weaknesses and indicate the length and type of language course needed (e.g. a three-month pre-sessional English course, EAP) before starting their main subject course. An example of such a test is the *IELTS* test by UCLES (Cambridge). The test can be taken in more than 100 countries in approved centres, most of which are British Council offices which supervise the administering of the test locally (see Appendix 4).

3 LANGUAGE TEST ON ENTRY

A *language test* can be conducted *on entry* to the target institution. This entry test could provide diagnostic information and indicate the students' language learning priorities for short courses or part-time classes. Many institutions have developed their own entry or proficiency tests and sometimes use these to construct a profile of learning difficulties and needs. Such tests may take a variety of forms, ranging from multiple-choice questions on grammar and vocabulary to dictations, note-taking tasks, reading comprehension, speech production checks, and diverse writing assignments – paraphrasing, summarising, analysing data, describing, open-ended questions, essays, etc. (See Chapter 5 for more information on tests.)

4 SELF-ASSESSMENT

Students can be asked to *assess themselves*. There are various ways of doing this: most involve the use of questionnaires, forms or checklists (see Oskarsson 1980; Dickinson 1987). A straightforward way is for the students to complete a form indicating their ability at, for example, the language skills of listening, speaking, reading and writing, perhaps on a rating scale ranging from very good to poor, or numbered (1–5 or 1–10), which has to be ticked or circled, etc. They could also be asked if they can carry out certain tasks in English, indicated by yes/no or graded. Additionally, they could be asked to list language/skills areas in which they need practice. This information could also be gathered at an interview, perhaps in conjunction with a test.

EXAMPLES OF SELF-ASSESSMENT PROCEDURES

Specimens of the examples referred to below are given in Appendix 1.1.

a) The first example ('Speaking') is from Oskarsson (1980), regarded as the standard work on self-assessment. Descriptive rating scales (from 0–5) are used for the skills of listening, speaking, reading and writing, which are listed separately in a self-assessment form. Students are asked to put a cross in the boxes corresponding to their level in each skill.

b) The next example is also from Oskarsson (1980) and is for self-assessment in spoken language at the 'threshold level'. This is the term used by the Council of Europe to indicate the minimum level of language proficiency which is needed to achieve functional ability in a foreign language. This example covers asking and answering questions, giving information, description and explanation. The instructions and descriptions are to be translated into the student's mother tongue. The students have to indicate (Yes/No) their ability to perform certain tasks in English. (The first 10 tasks only are shown, out of a total of 30.)

c) The third example is from Floyd (1984). It is concerned not only with language: it requires students to assess their current abilities (26 are listed – only the first 12 are shown) in the performance of a wide range of study skills for higher education. Students indicate their present level of ability by circling the appropriate number. The form is used as part of a continual assessment process: it is repeated towards the end of the course and improvements are noted.

d) The final example is from Ward Goodbody (1993). It shows a self-assessment placement questionnaire used at the beginning of an EAP course. The nine-band descriptive rating scale shown is comparable with the IELTS and English-Speaking Union's scale and levels (see Appendix 4). The questionnaire makes use of open-ended questions, and contains different areas of focus. It asks the students to think about their language level, learning strategies, learning priorities and their views on classroom management.

Ward Goodbody (1993) describes the benefits of using the self-assessment questionnaire in conjunction with a test. Teachers' assessments were also made during interviews with the students when the questionnaires were discussed. The students were from a wide range of countries and were both undergraduate and postgraduate. Ward Goodbody reported a high degree of correlation between the students' and teachers' assessments, and of satisfaction with the procedure. It should be noted, however, that detailed comparisons were only made with listening and speaking:

> Students seemed much happier with their groups and there were no complaints. Indeed, all the teachers remarked on the excellent group dynamics in their classes.

Ward Goodbody regarded the questionnaire as 'a useful part of a sensitising process where students take responsibility for their learning'. She noted that the questionnaire helped the students to focus on the content and aims of the course.

The advantages of involving students in self-assessment, and raising their self-awareness of language skills and abilities, are not in doubt. However, in a different approach, Jordan (1977b) asked students to describe their four language skills by a rating scale ranging from very good to poor. No descriptions were supplied with the labels. Students, therefore, had to determine their own yardstick for the terms.

Jordan compared the students' self-assessment ratings with their scores in a proficiency test at the beginning of EAP courses. Of the students whose scores were below 40 per cent (i.e. sufficiently low to warrant full-time English tuition for several months), 50 per cent had described their *written* English as either *very good* (6 per cent) or *good* (44 per cent); 41 per cent had described it as *weak*, and only 9 per cent as *poor* – probably the most apt description. There appeared to be a tendency for students at the lower end of the scale to overestimate their language ability, while some at the top underestimated theirs. However, they appeared to assess their listening and speaking more realistically. In this respect, the findings more closely resembled those of Ward Goodbody.

Blue (1988b) also used a descriptive rating scale for self-assessment of the four language skills at the beginning of a pre-sessional EAP course. He noted that 'many learners are unaccustomed to thinking of language in terms of the different skills involved'. Blue found that some cultures tended towards overestimation, while others tended towards underestimation.

The findings so far are unclear, except that:

> the teacher still has a very important role to play in advising students in the area of needs analysis ... and guiding them towards more accurate self-assessment.
>
> (Blue 1988b)

Clearly, more research is needed in this area; until then, self-assessment as the *only* criterion for placement on a course should be treated with caution.

5 OBSERVATION AND MONITORING

Students' difficulties can be *observed* in English classes and in written homework assignments. This is particularly suitable for perceiving speaking and listening difficulties, and for noting students who lack self-confidence and who may need extra help. Similarly, *monitoring* in a language laboratory can help in identifying specific oral/aural difficulties. If records are maintained of major and repeated difficulties/errors, a useful bank of information can be accumulated to help in determining appropriate advice and practice, and as a basis for materials development.

6 CLASS PROGRESS TESTS

Information can also be obtained from informal *class progress tests*, which are a feature of many courses of more than four weeks' duration. Although these tests are often designed to motivate students, they also provide additional feedback on learning difficulties. If a systematic collection is made of repeated errors and areas of difficulty in writing, diagnostic use can be made for correction, i.e. *error analysis* (see Chapter 19). Written homework can be used in the same way.

7 SURVEYS

Surveys of students' language and skills use and difficulties can be undertaken by means of *questionnaires* given directly to the learners. If this is done on a sufficiently large scale, an overall picture will emerge of students' perceived needs. In addition, it will be possible to build up a *profile* of a typical student attending the EAP course (listing background, language, study characteristics together with typical uses of English and the difficulties experienced). This can be useful in discussions with subject departments, administration, and in briefing new staff for EAP courses.

In Appendix 1.1 an example is shown of a questionnaire given to postgraduates studying in Britain to ascertain their use of spoken English and any problems arising (Jordan and Mackay 1973). It shows the breakdown of the skills of listening and speaking into their use in different situations, thus helping to raise students' self-awareness of their language use and possible areas of difficulty. Part of the outcome of the resulting survey is looked at in the next chapter. Questionnaires can also be given to various other groups, e.g. sponsors, teachers, representative users in the target situation, staff in the subject departments.

8 STRUCTURED INTERVIEW

The *structured interview* is discussed by Mackay (1978) (an example is shown in Appendix 1.1). It consists of prepared questions to which the answers are noted or recorded, allowing follow-up of points arising. Mackay strongly favoured this method of gathering information, and highlighted its advantages:

'Firstly, since the gatherer is asking the questions, none of them will be left unanswered as frequently happens in questionnaires. Secondly, the gatherer can clarify any misunderstanding which may crop up in the interpretation of the questions. Thirdly, and perhaps most advantageously, the gatherer can follow up any avenue of interest which arises during the question and answer session but which had not been foreseen during the designing of the structured interview'. Mackay and Bosquet (1981) discuss this further, in the context of curriculum development.

Even a straightforward *interview* (without the aid of a detailed questionnaire) can reveal a considerable amount about a student's listening and speaking difficulties together with other information about skills, attitudes, expectations, etc. However, the usefulness of the interview is improved if areas for questioning are pre-planned.

9 LEARNER DIARIES

Learner diaries (or journals) can be used as a way of gaining insights into students' learning experiences, as they are based upon introspection. They can be used to supplement, in a qualitative way, the often quantitative information supplied by end-of-course questionnaires. The conventional questionnaire indicates to the course director the extent to which the students were or were not satisfied with the course and its components; learner diaries can inform the tutors of the items that students enjoyed, found difficult, did not understand, etc., sometimes with reasons given.

O'Brien (1989) analysed 15 student diaries which were maintained for four weeks during an eight-week Pre-session English course at Manchester University (written up three times a week). The study was non-directive, the only guidance being 'Record whatever comes into your mind when you think back to your time in the classroom.' Four categories were found to reflect the focus of the diaries: course input, tutor performance, learner performance and external factors affecting study (home-related anxiety, food and accommodation and personal variables). Taking the first category, course input, the diary entries revealed a clear set of criteria to be in operation in the selection of items for inclusion: information content, apparent usefulness, interest/enjoyment value and personal involvement. In conclusion, O'Brien found that the diary entries, as evaluation feedback, could provide a basis for the tutors and students to work towards a 'negotiated syllabus' within the framework of a tightly structured course (see Chapter 4 regarding a negotiated syllabus).

Parkinson and Howell-Richardson have also noted that 'diaries can be a rich source of information about learners' (1990). Their investigation in 1986–87 was of the diaries of 51 overseas students, filled in each day over a period of 7–10 days while attending general English courses at the Institute for Applied Language Studies, Edinburgh University. The diaries consisted of headings for the students to react to: 'in-class activities', 'out-of-class activities', 'my problems', and 'what I have learned'. They then provided a grid so that students could estimate the amount of time engaged in linguistically relevant activities outside the classroom. One main conclusion reached was that the data 'showed a high correlation between rate of improvement and the amount of time which students spent outside class in social interaction with native speakers of English.'

10 CASE-STUDIES

The *case-study* approach can be utilised as a way of obtaining in-depth information and insights; in other words, putting some meat onto the bones of generalisations. Case studies can be very time-consuming but, like the analysis of learners' diaries, they can be very illuminating. One such EAP case study was made by James (1984a) of a Brazilian student writing a thesis on his research in the sociology of medicine. James divided the written mistakes into three categories: (1) those which frequently led to a breakdown in meaning; (2) those which frequently led to a blurring of the meaning; and (3) those which distracted the reader from the meaning conveyed.

In the most serious category, a breakdown in meaning, James found that there were four main reasons for the breakdown: over-long or over-complex sentences; faulty referencing; lexical difficulties; and weaknesses in the signposting of connections and relationships. A blurring of the meaning was caused by: inefficient ordering, inappropriate weighting and functional incoherence. James' conclusion has widespread relevance:

> students need help with what they find most difficult. What they find most difficult can only be discovered by observing them at work on the job.

Dudley-Evans (1988b) built upon James' findings by looking at four students' drafts of the 'discussion of results' section of their theses in plant biology. Photocopies of first and final drafts were compared, with supervisors' comments noted. Dudley-Evans reported that the great majority of changes made by supervisors were in the interpretation of the results presented, and in the structure of the argument presented. He concluded that the language tutor may be in a position to explain the 'move structure' of sections of a thesis more effectively than the subject supervisor (who may be less conscious of the patterns). Dudley-Evans suggests that the following moves are found in the discussion section of plant biology dissertations:

> (1) Background information (2) Statement of result (3) (Un)expected outcome (4) Reference to previous research (comparison) (5) Explanation of unsatisfactory (or surprising) result (6) Deduction (7) Hypothesis (8) Reference to previous research (support) (9) Recommendation (10) Justification.

In a further case study, of a PhD thesis (by a British student – an 'apprentice writer'), Dudley-Evans (1991) examined and categorised the supervisors' comments. There were three broad headings and each was subdivided:

> A. Organisation: 1 layout 2 punctuation 3 genre conventions
> B. Content: 1 factual errors 2 expansion and clarification of content
> C. Language: 1 spelling mistakes 2 grammar 3 tense choice
> 4 cohesion 5 sentence order 6 lexical choice (which included not only technical terms but also formality and style) 7 strength of claim.

> The most striking aspect of the analysis of the (supervisors') comments is the similarity of the problems that the student encountered to those that an overseas PhD student with a good command of English encounters ... the main adjustments the student had to make were the adoption of a more formal and clearer style, and the inclusion of discussion of all relevant points

11 FINAL TESTS

The *final test* at the end of a course provides information on learning difficulties (apart from other aspects, e.g. teaching difficulties, inappropriate material) not only for the course director but also, if used constructively, for the student. If the students are informed of areas of difficulty or weakness, they can make use of this as the basis for self-improvement.

12 EVALUATION/FEEDBACK

In addition to an end-of-course test, there is usually final *evaluation* or *feedback*, often in the form of *questionnaires*, to both students and staff. In conjunction, or separately, there may also be a round-up *discussion* between students and their tutor(s) at which the main features of the course that were liked and disliked can emerge. Suggestions can also be made for improvements for the next course.

13 FOLLOW-UP INVESTIGATIONS

Follow-up investigations can be carried out some time after a course has finished, both with the students and the receiving subject-specialist department. With students, this often takes the form of a questionnaire, designed to ascertain, in the light of their subsequent experience, which parts of the course they found most and least useful.

With staff in the receiving departments, a questionnaire may also be used, or a letter, or an interview. There may be several purposes to such departmental follow-up but one of them should be to see what their perceptions are of student performance, and the continued difficulties of the students. EAP course staff and subject tutors can see if their perceptions of student needs and difficulties match, and in which areas course content or emphasis need to be changed.

14 PREVIOUS RESEARCH

The final method for gathering information about the needs and deficiencies of learners is by examining *previous research*. This, of course, will have involved using the methods of data collection already described above, but it may save some time if the research is relevant to the students or type of course under consideration.

The research can take a number of routes, for example:

1. analysing the language used in different modes and registers, noting the frequency of occurrence of items and using this as a basis for investigation;
2. analysing the situations in which students experience difficulty, and testing some of the features and skills employed in the situations.
3. A number of other routes are also possible, e.g. investigating particular groups of learners, perhaps from a particular language background or studying a particular subject.

Over the years, a considerable body of research has been built up, some published and appearing in journals and books, some unpublished and residing in university libraries. Some examples of early research are given below (from Jordan 1977b); later research can often be traced through articles in journals and reports of conference proceedings.

1. The lecture is a teaching mode which presents considerable difficulty for most students, at least for the first few months. Wijasuriya (1971) investigated 46 hours of taped lectures in order to classify and count the occurrences of discourse-markers and inter-sentence connectives. Both types of cohesive elements are important for understanding an argument, recognising a change of direction in an argument and anticipating a line of argument.
2. Holes (1972) investigated the difficulties of the lecture situation for overseas students on a one-year postgraduate course. Of particular difficulty was found to be the use of colloquial language and of register-switching by lecturers.
3. The listening situations causing the greatest difficulty for first-year postgraduate students of science studies were identified by Morrison (1974). These situations comprised not only seminars and tutorials, in which questions and discussion are necessary and expected, but also informal lectures, in which there may be some questions and discussion. Features of spoken discourse causing persistent difficulty in seminars, tutorials and lectures were then identified. These features consisted of the referential system (logical connectors, reference and predictability), lexis (especially idiom and nominalised groups) and some aspects of phonology (speed of delivery, accent and pronunciation).

The different methods of collecting data for needs analyses are summarised in Figure 6.

2.5 Summary

There is a danger that with so many approaches, methods of data collection and variables, you may feel overwhelmed. You might even begin to feel like the 'needs analysis juggler' shown in Figure 7! What is important, however, is to remember that there is no single approach to needs analysis, and that circumstances are different and change.

In practice, most needs analysis choices will be determined by time, money and resources. What is essential, however, is that there is planning in advance. After deciding what is strictly relevant and necessary, sufficient time must be allowed for carrying out the step-by-step procedures listed in Figure 4. This can be helped by deciding in

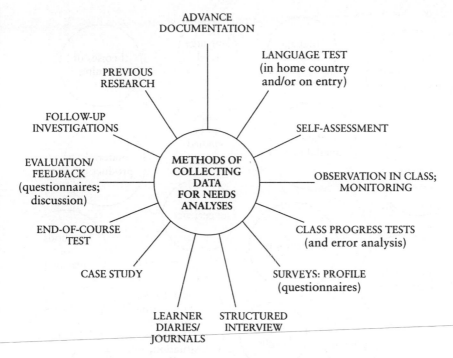

Figure 6   Methods of collecting data for needs analyses

advance the answers to the list of questions posed (Why? Whose? Who? What? How? When? Where?).

When the answers are in place, the syllabus can be designed. Early consideration will be given to determining if the EAP course will be for undergraduates (who may need practice in all language skills and study skills) or postgraduates (who may need to focus on certain skills only, and whose needs may depend on whether or not they are doing research). The main type of writing practice can be outlined: essays, reports, dissertations, etc. Depending on the number of students studying the same subject, decisions can be made about the organisation of subject-specific language learning (e.g. whole class, groups, individuals, self-access; projects, homework, oral/written reports, etc.).

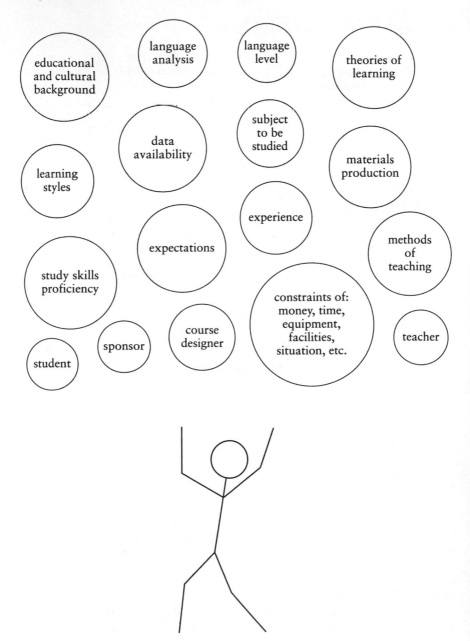

Figure 7   The needs analysis juggler

2.6 An imaginary case study (2)

To conclude this chapter we can take an overview of various aspects of needs analysis, as applied to the Nepalese student, Gopal. You will recall that he is attending an eight-week pre-sessional EAP course in Britain prior to starting a one-year postgraduate diploma course in Economic Development. We know that his one-year course will consist of lectures, seminars/tutorials, giving papers/making presentations, essays and examinations; it will be essential to read large numbers of journals and books.

In broad terms, Gopal has the same language difficulties as many overseas postgraduates studying in British universities. He scored 6.0 on the IELTS test. He has difficulty in:

a) understanding fluently spoken English, especially when the language is informal and colloquial;
b) understanding the variety of English native-speaker accents;
c) using the polite conventions of the language;
d) communicating functionally, especially in asking questions for appropriate purposes;
e) taking an active part in discussions and seminars;
f) reading quickly or understanding the complexities of academic prose;
g) understanding lectures, and taking notes, especially when they are delivered informally in a seemingly unstructured way;
h) writing formal, academic English; writing concisely; writing quickly (in exams).

Gopal's cultural and other difficulties will be looked at in Chapter 6.

2.7 Introspect and discuss

1. Have you ever been involved in any kind of needs analysis for EAP? What was your starting point? How did you proceed? What difficulties did you have?
2. A number of fundamental questions are posed as part of the planning for need analysis. In addition, Figure 4 contains the steps involved in undertaking a needs analysis. Can you think of any further questions to add, or steps to undertake?
3. Attention is drawn to the desirability of taking into account the learner's 'wants' when designing a course and materials. How might this be achieved in practice?
4. Fourteen methods are described for gathering data for needs analyses. Which methods do you consider are the most important from the practical point of view of a course director and teacher?

41

5. Three examples are shown of parts of self-assessment procedures from Oskarsson and Floyd (see Appendix 1.1). Look at them critically; which do you think is best and why? Could you improve on them in any way?
6. An example is given of a self-assessment questionnaire for students commencing a pre-sessional EAP course (Ward Goodbody 1993 in Appendix 1.1). Devise a short questionnaire for EAP teachers about to teach on an EAP course: find out their abilities, self-confidence, preparedness, difficulties, etc.
7. As a preparation for a structured interview, draw up a list of questions to ask a partner about his/her difficulties in teaching EAP.
8. The uses of learner diaries are discussed. Can you see any practical difficulties involved in this kind of undertaking?
9. Follow-up investigations with subject-specialist departments are mentioned. Devise a list of suitable questions to ask staff in such a department in order to obtain their views on the usefulness of the EAP courses that you organise. Their students attend your EAP courses before going on to study in their department.
10. Figure 7 shows the needs analysis juggler. Are there any other items that might need to be juggled with?

3 Surveys: students' difficulties

The previous chapter referred to the use of questionnaires in surveys of students' language and study skills difficulties. In this chapter we shall be looking at some of these surveys and other investigations, and the information that they provide about difficulties and needs. In some cases, the surveys focus on one or two language or study skills, in others, they encompass a wide range. Most of the investigations looked at are in the UK and the USA, as more has been reported from these countries, but a few others are also included. The students who are reported on are from most parts of the world. The research findings provide a necessary background for later issues, particularly those involving syllabus and course design, and the use of appropriate materials. They also give ideas for the type of investigations that can be conducted, and possible areas for further research.

3.1 Surveys: a note of caution

A number of surveys are reported below; they seem, at times, to show different results or different emphases. Care needs to be taken in interpreting the results to ensure that you are comparing like with like. Clearly, students in different countries may have different difficulties and needs, just as students studying different subjects may.

The requirements of different subjects and courses of study may vary. For example, if the examination at the end of a course is of the objective, multiple-choice type, and only involves ticking boxes, then practice in examination *writing* will not be needed. Instead, there will be a greater need for reading comprehension, the comprehension of instructions and questions, and the precise use of language. If a course is heavily lecture-based, listening comprehension and note-taking may cause greater difficulty and, therefore, will need more practice.

You need to check if the surveys have involved staff or students, or both. This has several implications: perhaps it is the *staff* assessment of the *needs* of the *subject*; or of the *staff* observation of the students' *difficulties*; or of the *staff* assessment of the students' *needs*. Alternatively, it may be of the *students'* assessment of the *skills needed* by the *subject*, compared with *their views* of their own *difficulties* and,

43

therefore, *needs*; and so on. Another way to view this is the distinction between 'necessities' and 'lacks' in Hutchinson and Waters' terms (1987; and see Chapter 2). 'Necessities' are the requirements of the target situation, while 'lacks' are the difficulties experienced by the students (the gap between the target proficiency and what is known already).

It should also be remembered that students in some EFL situations may have some native English-speaking lecturers. For these students, listening comprehension in English may pose the biggest problem, whereas in other situations, reading ability in English may be the greatest difficulty and need. An extra dimension to be considered is that on English courses containing mixed students – mixed for nationality, subject, age, etc. – the mixture may vary from year to year, with a commensurate change in questionnaire results. Thus direct comparisons between years may not be easy. For example, it is almost certain that a survey of a course containing 70 per cent European undergraduates would show different results (difficulties/needs) from one containing 70 per cent Asian postgraduates.

3.2 Overview

In 1980, fairly large-scale research was conducted at Cambridge University (Geoghegan 1983) into the language difficulties of overseas students, both undergraduates and postgraduates, during their first term. It will be seen from the summary table below that spoken language (in seminars and 'oral expression' combined), writing and taking notes in lectures created the biggest problems.

Rank order of difficulty: all students	*percentage declaring area 'most difficult'*
1. Participating in seminars	28%
2. Written work	23%
3. Oral expression	14%
4. Taking lecture notes	11%
5. Understanding lectures	9%
6. Reading at adequate speed	4%

(based on Geoghegan 1983)

This research, in a sense, summarises other surveys that have been conducted before or since, at least in the context of non-native speaking (NNS) students studying at universities in the UK. Invariably, it is the same three broad areas of study skills that appear as the major causes of difficulty for students, i.e. listening and speaking in seminars, academic writing, and listening, with understanding, and note-taking in lectures.

We shall now look at research findings that have focused on some of the details of these three broad areas.

3.3 Spoken English and seminars

A survey of the spoken English problems of overseas postgraduates at the Universities of Manchester and Newcastle-upon-Tyne (Jordan and Mackay 1973) was mentioned in the last chapter (the questionnaire is in Appendix 1.1). It showed that on arrival in the UK, *understanding spoken English* was the biggest difficulty for 70 per cent of the postgraduates taking part in the survey. Six months later it had fallen to second place (39 per cent). Expressing themselves in *speech* (involving fluency and self-expression) was the second biggest problem for 48 per cent of students on arrival. After six months it had become the biggest problem, for 42 per cent.

The most persistent problem for the students was the inability to express themselves adequately in the spoken language. One factor was that, for various reasons, the students spent little time in actually speaking English in a typical day, i.e. there seemed to be little opportunity to practise. Fifty-six per cent of the students said that they had not met as many native speakers (NS) of English as they would have liked.

The above findings were largely borne out by Blue (1991) who conducted a questionnaire survey of overseas and EEC students at Southampton University, 1988–1989. Jordan's and Blue's surveys found that a large proportion of the students spent one hour or less per day speaking English to NS and, sadly, that a sizeable proportion had made no British friends. By the middle of the academic year, both surveys found that speaking in seminars was the area of greatest difficulty.

The overall pattern of both these surveys corresponds closely with that found at Cambridge University, reported above.

In an American survey, Johns, A. M. (1981) noted that listening was ranked first as a requirement for success in university by more than 50 per cent of the staff. A large-scale investigation was conducted at Yarmouk University, Jordan (Zughoul and Hussein 1985). Students and faculty members completed questionnaires. Both students and staff agreed that 'the most needed skill for success at the university level is listening comprehension'. These are examples of target-situation analysis. The following is an example of present-situation analysis. In another survey, at five universities in the USA, overseas students were asked to list skills in order of difficulty: speaking was first (35 per cent), closely followed by listening (32 per cent) (Christison and Krahnke 1986).

SEMINARS

Participation in seminars or academic discussions has been noted as an area of major difficulty: basically, students do not participate. The reason that they do not take part has been referred to, generally, in Chapter 1; more specific reasons are as follows. Johns and Johns (1977) devised a questionnaire in order to investigate difficulties caused by different teaching modes. The following difficulties in discussions were specified:

(i) comprehension of spoken English ('they speak too fast'; 'they mumble'; 'vocabulary is idiomatic');

(ii) the pressing need to formulate a contribution quickly ('I can't think what to say');

(iii) shyness about the value of a contribution ('I might say something wrong');

(iv) inability to formulate an idea in English ('I don't know how to say it in English');

(v) awareness that a given function may be realised in various ways ('I don't know the best way to say it');

(vi) frustration about being unable to enter the discussion ('some students speak too much').

Investigations into the reality of seminars – the form that they take and the language functions and skills involved – are looked at in Chapter 13.

3.4 Academic writing

Written work has been referred to as being one of the major causes of concern for students. One study (Jordan 1981) looked at the writing difficulties of overseas postgraduates attending writing classes at university in the UK. On a six-point scale, ranging from 'no difficulties' to 'a lot of difficulties', they were asked to comment on their own writing problems. In the higher ranges of difficulties ('a number' to 'a lot'), the order of headings selected by students (%) was as follows (1 below). It will be noted that vocabulary, style and spelling loom large, closely followed by grammar.

1. students

vocabulary	62%
style	53%
spelling	41%
grammar	38%
punctuation	18%
handwriting	12%

A similar questionnaire was given to academic staff teaching the students, asking what caused *them* the most difficulties when reading the writing of overseas students (2 below).

2. staff

style	92%
grammar	77%
vocabulary	70%
handwriting	31%
punctuation	23%
spelling	23%

Style, grammar and vocabulary appear to cause the staff a higher level of difficulty than the students: the predominance of academic style, in particular, should be noted. Spelling bothers staff less than it does the students but, understandably, handwriting poses more problems for staff than students!

Below are listed some of the specific difficulties referred to by the students (where 10 per cent or more listed the same problem). Comments by staff varied. Some made the point that where the students had a very different first script (e.g. Arabic and Thai), often they had mechanical difficulty in writing and, especially, writing quickly. Lack of brevity was commented on: some students seemed to have difficulty in writing concisely.

Vocabulary	Using a word correctly	21%
	Own lack of vocabulary	15%
	Confusion caused by similar sounding/ looking words	12%
Style	Writing in a formal style (Some mentioned the differences between formal and informal styles and the difficulties of separating them.)	12%
Spelling	Trying to write what is heard (guessing, leading to mistakes)	15%
	Confusion of similar sounding words	15%
Grammar	Verbs: tense formation and use; active/ passive use	26%
	'Agreement' of verb and subject (e.g. stem + s ... 'it seems')	10%
Punctuation	Not aware of it (Just under 10% said they only used a full stop.)	12%
Handwriting	Writing quickly	35%

Weir (1988c) conducted a much more detailed and wide-ranging survey among staff and students into the writing difficulties of overseas students. He concluded that:

> subject tutors are more concerned with content than with mechanical accuracy features ... it is the relevance and adequacy of the subject content, the clarity of the message and the arrangement and development of written work which clearly stands out as the most important criteria in subject tutors' assessments of written work.

In this connection it should be noted that subject tutors are often linguistically unaware, and cannot always distinguish a poorly conceived idea from an idea that is expressed through inadequate English. In other words, subject tutors may assume that something has been poorly understood when, in fact, it has been understood but badly expressed.

A different aspect of writing difficulties was explored by Bloor and Bloor (1991) who analysed the writing of overseas students at Warwick University and their retrospective views of their expectations about writing in English. The Bloors' investigation provides a link with the problems of learning styles and culturally different norms which will be explored in Chapter 6. They found that 50 per cent had expected to be assessed on the basis of objective-type examinations and not on the basis of written term assignments. These false expectations stem from the fact that many students may believe that universities have universal academic conventions.

The Bloors also noted the problems that can be caused by unintentional plagiarism through lack of awareness of the need to acknowledge all sources in the writing of essays or research reports (plagiarism is discussed in Chapter 6). They also observed that:

> there are clearly identifiable cultural differences in the degrees of directness and concession permitted (or encouraged) in academic writing in different languages.

They give examples of some students being unaware of the need to use hedged propositions. They had been taught to write directly and to avoid modification in essay writing in their own language. In these cases, some of the students' difficulties can be solved by direct instruction and explanation – which has to be given by the EAP teachers.

Further research into overseas students' academic writing was conducted by Richards and Skelton (1991) at Aston University. In a small-scale investigation they looked at:

> the willingness with which British and overseas postgraduate students are critical in their written coursework, and at the manner of that criticism.

They concluded that 'overseas students evaluate less, and evaluate less critically'.

Jenkins, Jordan and Weiland (1993) conducted a survey of the role of writing in graduate engineering programmes in six engineering faculties in American universities which had a large number of NNS students. One part of the questionnaire to faculty staff asked the respondents whether they evaluated the writing of NS and NNS graduate students by the same standards. Thirty-six per cent said that they used different standards; 'several wrote comments such as "I try to, but it's impossible"'. The table below shows the major features which received more lenient evaluation standards in the American engineering research.

Writing Standards Evaluated Differently for Non-Native Speakers of English as Percentages of Total Faculty Sample

Writing skills feature evaluated differently	%
9. Presenting ideas in organized way	7
10. Logical connections	13
11. Stating problem clearly	7
15. Overall writing ability	21
16. Quality of content	5
17. Grammar/sentence structure	25
18. Appropriate vocabulary	24
19. Punctuation and spelling	22
20. Ability to self-correct own work	13
21. Avoiding plagiarism	7
26. Importance of writing for department	11

It seems the input of time by advisers/supervisors on helping students with their MSc theses was considerable. They estimated that more than 25 per cent of the writing was done by the staff themselves.

Another American survey – into the writing needs and difficulties of first-year doctoral students (both NS and NNS) was conducted at Stanford University in 1987 (Casanave and Hubbard 1992). The survey was based on questionnaires from faculty staff in humanities, social sciences and science and technology departments. Casanave and Hubbard questioned the timing of appropriate writing classes for doctoral students. They noted that at the beginning of doctoral pro-grammes, students are more concerned about the course content than their English. They felt that academic writing courses would be more fruitful if they were timed more closely to when the students were required to do their content writing. By this time, students would also be 'more familiar with the writing style of the major journals of their field'.

3.5   Lectures and note-taking

In a survey of overseas students in higher education in Britain, Campbell (1973) reported that:

> about 85 per cent of the students interviewed complained of the difficulties faced in their studies, whether it be 'language' or 'difficulty in taking lecture notes' ... Practically all students admitted that at first there was a problem comprehending lectures because of the lecturers' accents.

One of Campbell's main conclusions was that lectures should be taped and the main points listed on duplicated lists. Both should then be made available to students.

It is of interest to note that in an investigation into note-taking among students (66 NS and 63 NNS) at the University of Arizona, the conclusion was reached that:

> the effective L1 and L2 note-takers were those who compacted large amounts of spoken discourse into propositional-type information units; transcribed content words using abbreviations, symbols and a limited number of structure words ... Terseness of note-taking ... rather than mere quantity seems to be an essential ingredient of effective L1/L2 note-taking.
>
> (Dunkel 1988)

Dunkel's conclusion for teaching was that students should be provided with 'skeleton notes' containing the major points of information in the lecture. They would then be able to concentrate on understanding the content of lectures.

3.6   Reading

Although the research at Cambridge University (Geoghegan 1983) showed reading to be a relatively minor problem for students compared with the other three main areas, nevertheless, we shall look at it briefly as the greatest *need* of students is the ability to read textbooks. This 'need' was expressed by 90 per cent of students surveyed by Ostler (1980) in an American university. In a similar type of university survey among faculty members in Saudi Arabia, Hohl (1982) found that reading was ranked first by 48 per cent as a requirement for success in university. It is likely that in most EFL university situations, reading academic texts will be the biggest requirement for students. The two surveys do not indicate if students had difficulties with reading.

3.6.1 Reading speed

In any self-assessment or questionnaire-based survey, students almost always cite reading as the skill causing them least difficulty. This is probably correct, at least in relation to the other skills. However, this does not mean that students have no problems at all with reading. The most usual difficulty is that indicated in Geoghegan's analysis at Cambridge (1983), i.e. an inability to read at adequate speed (also borne out by other surveys viz. Jordan and Mackay 1973 and Blue 1991).

One early study in the USA (Plaister 1968) reported on a reading course for foreign students which contained timed reading exercises:

> Most of our students are word-by-word readers and, as a
> consequence, read at very low rates – 125 to perhaps 150 words
> per minute.

It was noted in Chapter 1, in looking at the reading speeds of native-speakers of English, that less than 200 wpm is regarded as slow. Certainly my experience of teaching overseas postgraduates is that the maximum reading speed for many is 150–160 wpm.

Probably the first exponent of reading speed techniques, and the writer of a course in faster reading for use overseas, was Fry (1963a and b). He distinguished three kinds of reading speeds and then compared the performance of a poor reader and a good reader. This is tabulated below (Fry 1963a). He based his reading speeds on those acquired by students before and after attending his courses; he regarded 250 wpm as an attainable minimum.

Speed		Poor reader	Good reader
Slow	*Study reading speed* is used when material is difficult and/or high comprehension is desired.	90–125 w.p.m. 80–90 % comp.	200–300 w.p.m. 80–90 % comp.
Average	*Average reading speed* is used for everyday reading of magazines, newspapers and easier text-books.	150–180 w.p.m. 70 % comp.	250–500 w.p.m. 70 % comp.
Fast	*Skimming* is used when the highest rate is desired. Comprehension is intentionally lower.	Cannot skim	800 + w.p.m. 50 % comp.

THE THREE SPEEDS OF READING

Fry's reading course (1963b) is based upon thirty timed reading passages, followed by multiple-choice comprehension questions. Such courses often bring gains in reading speed and comprehension rate immediately after completion, but longer term benefits are less clear (Beard and Hartley 1984).

3.7 Experience and expectations

From all the surveys referred to in this chapter, it will be seen that there is clear evidence of the need for some kind of help with study skills and language practice. What form that help should take will be looked at in the following chapters. However, at this stage, a question needs to be posed that was referred to in Chapter 1. Do students already have experience of using study skills in their own language, and simply need to transfer these skills to their studies in English? Or do they need to practise the study skills themselves because they are inexperienced in using them? The answer, as may be expected, is mixed.

In order to discover students' experience in using study skills, a questionnaire was devised and given to postgraduates attending a pre-sessional EAP course at Manchester University in the summer of 1988 (Jordan 1993). Most of the students were from Asia and Europe, with a smaller proportion from the Middle East; the subject areas were largely in the humanities and social sciences. The questionnaire was in two parts: the first part endeavoured to ascertain students' experience of study skills in their own country, and the second part attempted to elicit their expectations of studying their own subject after the EAP course had finished. The questionnaire results are included in Appendix 1.1.

The main findings from the questionnaire were that many students receive no instruction in study skills in their own country, including the use of a library. This aspect alone becomes important when students are from countries where libraries are closed-access, i.e. they fill in a request form and the book is brought to them. If they are then faced with open-access libraries (where they find books themselves), they may need considerable help at first.

Other findings were that students normally play an active part in question and discussion situations, and that they often receive close guidance in academic writing. It will be readily seen that if this experience is combined with the students' expectations of studying in Britain (e.g. expectations of help from subject tutors), and set alongside the realities of academic study as known in universities in Britain, a number of mismatches or discrepancies or frustrations may emerge. All of this must give food for thought to EAP course designers and tutors.

Furneaux *et al.* (1991) conducted a survey at Reading University which also involved the experience and expectation axes for overseas students. The questionnaire focused on views of the nature of seminars and perceptions of participant roles and participation. The questionnaire was given to both NNS postgraduates and NS lecturers. Furneaux *et al.* found that there was broad agreement between both groups about the nature and purpose of seminars, though the lecturers gave greater weight to presenting a paper, 'and little weight to listening and taking notes, whilst the reverse is true for the students' (other details are given in Chapter 12).

One lesson to be learned from some of the findings above is for subject tutors especially. They need to be informed of the expectations of overseas students:

> so that the tutors may be more aware of possible causes of disappointment, frustration and incomprehension. In some cases, the tutors may be able to help, e.g. by an explanation of *their* expectations of students' work, and by showing a model piece of writing (preferably by a British student).

(Jordan 1993)

Other investigations highlight the likely mismatch between students' expectations and those of the staff. Sherman (1992) looked in particular at the problems caused by a mismatch between expectations of staff and students over university students' academic writing. Further evidence is provided by Channell (1990), Thorp (1991) and Bloor and Bloor (1991).

3.8 Introspect and discuss

1. A note of caution about comparing surveys was sounded at the beginning of the chapter. A number of reasons were given to explain why results may vary. Can you think of any other variables that might cause results to differ?
2. It was stated near the beginning that 'it is almost certain that a survey of a course containing 70 per cent European undergraduates would show different results (difficulties/needs) from one containing 70 per cent Asian postgraduates'. What major differences would you expect? Why?
3. The three broad areas of study skills causing most difficulties for students are: seminars, academic writing and note-taking in lectures. Does this match your experience? Which of these would you like to pursue in depth? Why?
4. A survey of overseas and EEC students attending pre-sessional EAP courses and in-sessional classes was conducted at Southampton University in 1988–89 (Blue 1991). One part of the questionnaire

was concerned with factors that had helped or hindered the students' language improvement. The factors are listed below in rank order. Do these factors and their order match your experience? Which factors do you consider to be the most important? Could you add any factors to either group?

Table 8.18: Factors that have helped language improvement

1. Talking to native speakers informally
2. Listening to the radio, watching TV, etc.
3. Attending lectures, seminars, etc. in department
4. Attending in-sessional English classes
5. Individual language learning
6. Talking to other non-native speakers
7. Their own positive attitudes
8. Sympathetic staff in university department

Table 8.19: Factors that have hindered language improvement

1. Too much work for the main course of study
2. Not making friends with native speakers
3. Sickness

5. a) In the section on academic writing, tables are given of student and staff responses to a questionnaire on writing difficulties (Jordan 1981). Do any of the results surprise you? In view of the differences displayed between staff and students, which aspects of writing should receive emphasis in an EAP course?

 b) Ask your colleagues (or students) to rank in order the six aspects of writing shown according to their own difficulties with writing, with the item causing most difficulty first. How do the results compare with the two tables shown?

6. Information is given about three kinds of reading speeds (Fry 1963a). Do you know your own reading speed, or that of your students? It can be found by counting the number of words in a text and then noting accurately, in minutes and seconds, the time it takes to read it. By dividing the number of words by the reading time, the result is given in words per minute, e.g. a text of 650 words read in $2\frac{1}{2}$ minutes = 260 wpm. It is probably best to take the average of three timed readings to obtain a more reliable reading speed. (You may already have found this out from the task at the end of Chapter 1.)

7. Below is a summary list of many of the areas of difficulty for non-native speakers of English to emerge from the various surveys.

 a) Which three areas would you emphasise on a short, intensive EAP course (4–8 weeks)? Why? Compare your choices with a colleague and discuss any differences you may have.

Note: This activity is similar to that described as 'pyramid discussions' (see Chapter 13).

b) Would you omit any of these areas from a short course? Which ones, and why?

1 seminar/discussion strategies
2 academic writing: essays, reports, etc.
3 lecture comprehension and note-taking
4 reading at adequate speed
5 spoken language: self-expression and fluency
6 social interaction with native-speakers
7 writing quickly
8 sentence structure and grammatical exercises
9 development of appropriate vocabulary
10 subject-specific writing
11 punctuation and spelling
12 reading comprehension
13 library skills
14 developing self-confidence
15 listening to different English accents
16 writing in a formal, academic style
17 developing critical approaches

8. Construct a brief questionnaire (list the precise questions to be asked) to find out the *views* of your colleagues on the *value* of questionnaires in discovering students' language difficulties for purposes of syllabus and course design, and materials production.

4 EAP syllabus and course design

So far we have looked at some of the necessary background to drawing up a syllabus – needs analysis and indications of students' difficulties. Now it is appropriate to look at the syllabus itself. Basically, a *syllabus* is a specification of what is to be included in a language course. Designing a syllabus involves examining needs analyses and establishing goals. It then entails the selection, grading and sequencing of the language and other content, and the division of the content into units of manageable material.

The *methodology* employed in implementing the syllabus will include materials selection and development, and will involve a selection of the learning tasks, activities and exercise types, and how they are to be presented, in a particular environment, for teaching and learning; it will conclude with assessment and evaluation. In other words, in a simplified sense, the syllabus is concerned with 'what' and the methodology with 'how'. Together they cover the planning, implementation and evaluation of a language course. Excellent descriptions and discussions of syllabus design are included in Robinson (1991), Nunan (1988a; 1988b), Hutchinson and Waters (1987), McDonough (1984), Johnson (1982), Mackay and Palmer (1981), Dubin and Olshtain (1986), Coffey (1984), Candlin *et al.* (1975; 1978), McDonough and Shaw (1993), White (1988b), Breen (1987).

Once the syllabus has been drawn up, the *course* can be designed, and then realised by means of *timetables*, and finally evaluated by utilising various kinds of *feedback* (see Chapter 5). All of this will be discussed after the syllabus has been examined in greater detail. The actual implementation, involving methods (of teaching and learning) and materials, will be examined separately in Chapter 7. The following figure summarises the stages and considerations involved in designing EAP courses.

We shall now discuss an EAP syllabus, after which we shall look briefly at other types of syllabus insofar as they are relevant to EAP syllabuses. Following this, we shall examine EAP course design, and possible differences between short and long EAP courses. Then we shall consider EAP course components and timetabling, after which we shall look at some EAP courses that take place in a variety of countries. Finally, we shall discuss aspects of feedback and evaluation of courses.

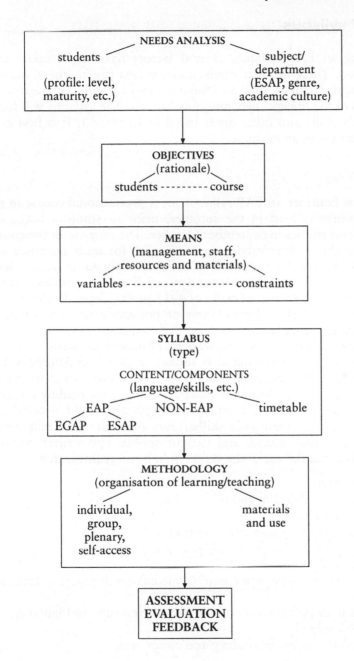

Figure 8   EAP course design: summary

4.1 EAP syllabus

In designing an EAP syllabus, several factors have to be taken into consideration. These include: *needs, aims, means* (the teachers, materials, equipment, facilities, time and finance), and *variables* or *constraints* (limitations of the 'means' become 'constraints'). The syllabus will focus on the study skills and other areas listed in Chapter 1; it is best considered by means of an example.

4.1.1 Example

We will now consider an EAP syllabus for a pre-sessional course in the UK. The course is held in the summer, prior to students beginning university-level studies in September/October. The purpose of the course is to develop the students' ability to use English for study purposes in a range of skills. It is fairly typical of syllabuses aimed at tertiary-level students from a variety of countries and mixed disciplines coming to study in the UK. The courses are normally of 4–12 weeks, depending on needs, and may be aimed at undergraduates or postgraduates. The elements included will be adapted to suit the length of course and the language level of the students, together with their particular future study needs.

The example we are looking at is shown, in detail, in Appendix 1.1; the outline only will be looked at here. The syllabus was originally devised in the 1970s to focus on separate study skills: reading comprehension, academic writing, listening comprehension and note-taking, academic speech and reference skills. Over time, the sub-components were developed and refined, and various spoken and written projects were added so that the use of the skills could be more integrated.

Core components:
1. Reading comprehension and note-taking
2. Academic writing
3. Listening comprehension and note-taking
4. Academic speech (oral presentation and seminar practice)
5. Reference/research skills
6. Grammar/vocabulary workshop (remedial/developmental language practice)
7. Life in Britain (information on life and institutions, and language for 'survival' English)
8. Self-access (language laboratory and computers)

Short-term target activities:
a) for components 1, 2 and 5:
    i)   Library project (familiarisation)
    ii) Study project (literature-based, extended writing)

b) for components 3 and 4:
   i)   Plenary lectures/group seminars (guest lecturers: replicate depart-
        mental situation)
   ii) Tutor seminars (short talks + questions/discussion)
   iii) Student seminars (oral presentations + questions/comments)
   iv) Interview/questionnaire project (pair work surveys by question-
        naire + oral reports)

Evaluation/assessment:
i)   Tutorials (individualised feedback on progress and discussion of
     problems)
ii) Evaluation (questionnaire at the end)
iii) Assessment (self-; peer- and tutor-assessment; at end, a written test;
     after the course, a report is sent to the department and sponsor)

Many features of this syllabus example are still current. However, there have been developments and changes during the 1990s, especially moving away from teaching discrete skills. The reading and writing components are more closely integrated, with a largely text-based focus to the writing. With the input now based more upon texts, a greater emphasis has been placed upon genre analysis, summarising, para- phrasing and the integration of source text, with appropriate references. This is particularly useful for postgraduates who will be involved in research.

More stress has been put on student-led seminars in their own subject areas (ESAP). Conciseness and relevance are encouraged in the short talks, which are preceded by a one-minute oral abstract. Greater emphasis has also been placed on learner-training for self-access use of a resource centre, and for promoting autonomous learning.

If we examine the outline and details of this particular EAP syllabus (Appendix 1.1), we may discern that it is comprised of a combination of several different types of syllabus or approach. We may readily identify components that are language skills, study skills, functions, projects, topics and situations. We may also surmise that there are language forms/structures, and tasks involved. This mixture of approaches is quite usual and desirable (McDonough 1986). In addition:

> we should treat all approaches as being simultaneously available
> and try to find what is most suitable for a particular situation.
>
> (Robinson 1991)

As Robinson points out:

> one reason for the continuing life of the language form and function
> syllabuses is that they are familiar to teachers. In a situation where
> teachers lack confidence and need a lot of support, such well-tried
> ... approaches may be the best to adopt.

4.2 Types of syllabus

At this stage, it is useful to look briefly at a number of different types of syllabus that have been used over the last few decades (see Yalden 1987). Parts of these will often overlap with, or be incorporated within, an EAP syllabus, as we have seen in our example. Hutchinson and Waters (1987) give numerous examples from course books based on most of the types of syllabus listed below. We shall not discuss the pros and cons of the various approaches but give references to follow up for further details and discussion (see Robinson (1991) for a schema incorporating the different approaches).

The various types of syllabus can be subsumed under three broad headings, which indicate their overall kind of approach:

a) **Content** or **Product** (focusing on the end result)
b) **Skills**
c) **Method** or **Process** (focusing on the means to an end)

4.2.1 Type a: Content/Product

1 GRAMMATICAL/STRUCTURAL/LANGUAGE FORM

This is one of the oldest and exists in a variety of forms (e.g. Hornby 1954, 1959). In essence, a grammatical syllabus focuses on aspects of grammar, e.g. verb tenses, sentence patterns, articles, nouns, etc. and then grades them for teaching, supposedly from the simple to the complex, and according to frequency and usefulness. It usually entails a cumulative step-by-step approach. If implemented with an emphasis on the spoken language, it is often referred to as an *oral-structural method*. Grammatical structures and structural words were used as the basis for some well-known course books in the 1960s and 1970s (e.g. Herbert 1965; Ewer and Latorre 1969; Swales 1971).

2 NOTIONAL-FUNCTIONAL

This lists conceptual meanings (*notions*: e.g. time, space, quantity) expressed through language (logical relationships, etc.), and the communicative purposes (*functions*) for which we use language (e.g. greetings, requests, apologies, description, comparisons, cause and effect, etc.). The origins of a functional syllabus can be traced back to Hornby (1954). However, the names most readily recalled in connection with such syllabuses and their methodology are Wilkins (1976), Munby (1978) and Johnson (1982); for an excellent practical overview see Littlewood (1981). Because this approach stresses communication, the processes of communication are often utilised in the teaching/learning, e.g. problem-solving, obtaining information, interacting with people. This syllabus is often called 'the communicative approach'.

3 SITUATIONAL

This lists the situations or contexts in which the language will be used, and analyses the language needed for those situations. For example, in an EAP course in an English-speaking country, the situations in which students might find themselves, can be utilised, e.g. registration with the institution and the police; opening a bank account; finding accommodation; visiting the doctor or dentist, etc.; and various academic settings.

4 TOPIC

A topic-based syllabus may have a similar approach to that based on situations. Topics are selected from the students' specialist studies and the language analysed: appropriate syntax and lexis are then practised. Examples from economics (ESAP) might include: economic growth, economic development, industrialisation, international trade, inflation, etc. As with situations, the sequence of topics may have several alternatives.

5 CONTENT-BASED

Although all the above types of syllabus are based on content of one form or another, 'content-based' has come to mean, in recent years, the particular requirements of specific academic disciplines, e.g. economics, engineering, etc. In other words, such a syllabus or approach focuses on teaching students the language, skills and academic conventions associated with their particular subject and its content (subject-matter). Genre analysis (see Chapter 16) helps to determine which skills/conventions can be generalised, if at all, across disciplines (Johns 1988a). For an example of an integrated EAP/subject content course, based on sociology, see Gaffield-Vile (1996).

4.2.2 *Type b: Skills*

6 SKILLS

Sometimes this involves a syllabus being based on one or more of the four traditional *language skills*. In such a skills-based syllabus, the constituents of the skills are often highlighted – the *sub-skills* or *micro-skills*. For example, reading (which may be described as a *macro-skill*) may be sub-divided into a number of micro-skills, e.g. skimming, scanning, reading for information, ideas, opinions, etc. Where some of the micro-skills involve more than one language skill, e.g. summarising – for both writing and speaking, there may be courses in *learning skills*, with the stress on effective strategies. *Cognitive skills* are closely allied to language and learning skills, and their development is a necessary part of specialist disciplines, thus, in turn, affecting ESAP, e.g. planning and organising information.

If study purposes are added to language skills, then a *study skills* syllabus may be developed. For example, if the style of formal writing is combined with an appropriate structure and academic conventions, various types of academic writing will ensue, e.g. essays, reports, dissertations, etc. In turn, these will often specify or practise appropriate language (thus combining syllabuses). *Communication skills* is a term used for an approach that focuses on the means of effectively conveying information, ideas, opinions, etc., e.g. in a talk, the style of presentation and use of aids, etc. will be stressed. Robinson (1991) has suggested that:

> skill-based syllabuses are something of a half-way house between content or product syllabuses on the one side and method or process syllabuses on the other.

4.2.3 Type c: Method/Process

The two following types of syllabus focus on some kind of task to be performed. After target tasks are analysed, pedagogic tasks can be listed and selected after negotiation between student and teacher. The purpose of the tasks is to develop the methods or processes involved with learning activities. (For a full discussion see Long and Crookes 1992.)

7 PROCESS

The focus is the learner and learning processes and preferences. A process syllabus considers the questions:

> who does what with whom, on what subject-matter, with what resources, when, how, and for what learning purpose(s)?
>
> (Breen 1984)

The negotiation process is part of the syllabus: among sets of options, the final selection is made by students. An example of a task might be agreeing on a definition of a problem, organising data, followed by discussion.

8 PROCEDURAL/TASK-BASED

The basis is a problem or task, with teaching/learning aimed at cognition and process. The task needs to be intellectually challenging in order to maintain students' interest. The aim is to complete the task and to focus on meaning. Pedagogic tasks often involve opinion-gap, reasoning-gap, and information-transfer activities. Using maps to plan itineraries, etc. would be an example of an appropriate task. The procedural syllabus is associated with the work of Prabhu (1987) in India. Task-based language learning is described in detail, with its implementation at King Abdulaziz University, Jeddah, Saudi Arabia, in Wilson (1986). Skehan (1996) usefully discusses some of the problems associated with a task-based approach, for example, the potential focus away from form towards lexis. He draws attention to the need for some kind of principled task sequencing.

9 LEARNING-CENTRED/NEGOTIATED

These focus on the learner, with the learner responsible for making a number of decisions (Nunan 1988b). Although the primary focus is on processes/methods, a choice of approaches is possible: a tailor-made syllabus for an individual; adapting a syllabus in the light of perceived needs; providing a range of alternatives or options of content and methods; self-access (Dickinson 1987; Sheerin 1991); self-determined, self-directed. Blue (1988b) gives an example of an initial questionnaire for self-directed learning. After listing language skills and their micro-skills, for each one it poses the question: How necessary is it? What is your present level? Priority? Time available?

In particular, a learning-centred approach:

> will be concerned with the development of and sensitisation of
> learners to their role as learners ... A focus on the development of
> learner autonomy and independent learning skills will be
> particularly important in systems which can offer the learner only
> short-term courses.
>
> (Nunan 1988b)

An interesting discussion and perspective on negotiated syllabus is contained in Clarke (1991) and Bloor and Bloor (1988). Bloor and Bloor, from their own experience in designing courses based on negotiation, see three major areas that can be negotiated for self-access learning: various aspects of language use (skills, genres, etc.); target levels of competence; preferred study modes.

4.3 Conclusion

Broadly speaking, the approaches adopted in an EAP syllabus are likely to be a combination of other syllabus types – a 'multi-syllabus' (conceptualised in Figure 9). The combination may be designed laterally or in hierarchical layers. The types of syllabus included may depend on the country in which the EAP course is being organised. It may reflect the approach to teaching English that is current in the country or in its education system. Consequently, throughout the world, there will be a variety of EAP syllabuses in existence at any one time.

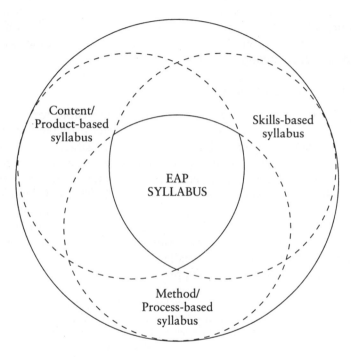

Figure 9   The basis of an EAP syllabus

4.4   EAP course design

4.4.1   Constraints or variables

The main components of the syllabus having been agreed upon, and the objectives outlined for each section, the next task is to design the course around the syllabus. In practice, this will be restricted by several factors, the main ones being:

1. *tutors*: number available and their experience and capabilities
2. *students*: number and nationalities to be catered for; their language level

3. *other staff*: administrative, secretarial, technical, social, welfare
4. *time*: length of the course: full-time or part-time (frequency); weeks, days, hours
5. *space*: number of rooms, room size (furnishings – fixed or movable); location and proximity
6. *facilities/equipment*: library, resource centre, language laboratory, cassette recorders, TV and video, computers, overhead projectors, photocopier, books, journals, stationery and other materials
7. *accommodation*: hostels or other arrangements for students; proximity (transport, if necessary)
8. *finance*: budget – size, fixed or variable; method and speed of payment
9. *other influences*:
   – past experience
   – motivation of students: their attitudes and expectations
   – need for variety
   – a belief in learning by doing
   – awareness of non-EAP needs
   – need to be commercially viable
   – 'common sense'

A usual approach is to prepare for a course based upon the previous course, amended in the light of feedback, and then modified again according to perceived needs and constraints. As Robinson (1991) comments:

> ESP course design is the product of a dynamic interaction between a number of elements: the results of the needs analysis, the course designers' approach to syllabus and methodology, and existing materials (if any). All of these are modified by the contextual constraints.

Some course directors may feel that they are performing a balancing act between academic and other factors (see Figure 10), and between various constraints. However, as usual, one of the secrets to success is planning sufficiently far ahead. Later, compromise and flexibility may well be needed.

As some of the larger EAP courses get more and more complex, and the course director is more of a manager, the efficient use of time becomes more important. White *et al.* (1991) discuss the issues involved in time management, identifying priorities and drawing up action plans. They also look at a timetable planning sequence which involves an analysis of: the courses and their components; session length; teacher hours; teachers' responsibilities, areas of expertise and preferences; vacations; room availability; and cost.

On a course there is often insufficient time to cover all that is desired.

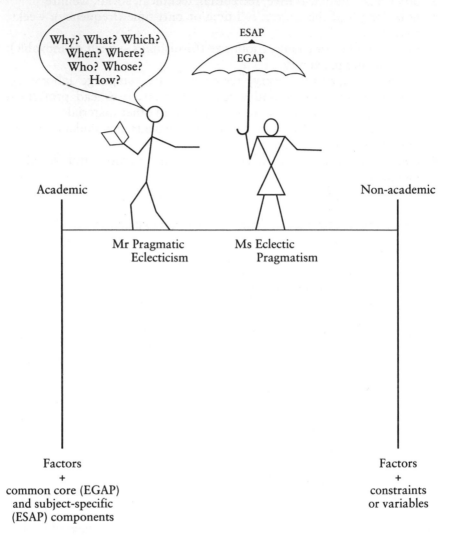

Figure 10   *The course design balancing act*

Consequently, it is usually preferable to concentrate on those areas causing the most difficulty or that will be most needed for the students' specialist studies. Thus appropriate needs analyses are essential.

An example of flexibility, pragmatism, or compromise, might be as follows. The course directors would like to give more responsibility to all the tutors to negotiate parts of the syllabus regarding spoken language with their students. They realise that some of their staff are not sufficiently experienced to cope with the demands that this may make upon them. Consequently, they provide course books and teachers' notes for these staff and brief them on other parts of the syllabus. Each group of students is timetabled to meet the experienced members of staff who will then specialise in negotiating with them the spoken language aspects. Depending on the outcome of the negotiations, either the experienced staff will take all the spoken language sessions, or they will organise appropriate ones for the less experienced staff.

In another example, the course directors have been unable to engage the services of a guest lecturer in one of the disciplines that several of their students will be studying later. The directors wanted an authentic voice for the subject. As an alternative, they have made available some audio-cassettes and a video of some introductory lectures on the subject. They have also prepared some appropriate worksheets to go with the cassettes. They place all the material in a resource centre for the students to use on a self-access basis.

4.5   An alternative course design: projects

An alternative to designing a course in which study skills and other components are practised either separately or integrated with varied subject matter, is to focus on a project or research exercise. Provided that the project is in some way related to the students' interests or future subjects of study, it will serve as a realistic vehicle for fully integrated study skills and language practice. If carefully chosen, the project or research task can become all-engrossing and provide a motivation of its own.

One particular advantage of project work is that it can overcome a difficulty that might exist with teaching study skills to some students. Blue (1993) has commented that some postgraduates think they are being patronised by being taught study skills. They think their existing skills should be adequate for their studies. With project work, particular problems – language or skills – can be dealt with as they arise.

Bloor and St John (1988) distinguish three types of project. The first is a *Group project*, in which 'a piece of real research is undertaken by the whole group, with each individual student taking one aspect for detailed study'. The second is a *Mini-research project* where 'individual students engage in social studies type research involving, for example, question-naires, survey techniques and interviews'. The third type is a *Literature-based project* which is 'based on selective reading on a topic of interest' and is 'suitable for individual work where the object is to encourage students to read selectively in their subject field with a specific purpose in mind'. Bloor and St John comment that this type of project is the most common and the easiest to administer. Their chart, reproduced below, summarises the processes involved in project work, which leads to a combination of process and product. (See Chapter 11 for a discussion of 'process v. product in academic writing'.)

Project writing: Stages, activities and skills for literature-based projects

Stages	Activities	Skills
Teacher's introduction	Specifying the task	Discussion
Planning	Finding relevant literature	Library reference skills
	Selecting interesting texts	Speed reading/skimming/ scanning
	Making a proposed reading list	Basic bibliography preparation
	Establishing topic	Writing: headings/note form
	Outlining proposals	
Consultation and revision	Presenting written proposals to group/supervisor	Consultancy skills/discussion
Preparation (Tutor consultation)	Reading on the topic	Intensive reading
	Summarising literature	Note-making/paraphrasing
	Organising ideas	'Realisation of schemata'
	Taking a position	
Drafting (Tutor consultation)	Writing the body of the text	Advanced writing skills
	Checking message	Use of dictionaries/reference
	Revising and rewording	books/notes
	Re-ordering	
Writing-up (Tutor consultation)	Writing introduction, conclusion	Advanced summarising
	contents, index, bibliography	Research skills
	Layout	Proof reading
	Checking for accuracy	
Presentation	Binding, titles, acknowledgements	Seminar skills
	Oral presentation to group	

The research task approach, in providing a framework for practising study skills, is recommended by Budd (1989), who describes, in some detail, the ups and downs of a four-week pre-sessional study skills course. He concludes that the research project 'replicated real-life processes in an unforeseen, but nevertheless very productive way'.

For teachers inexperienced in organising project work, a good intro-duction is provided by Fried-Booth (1986). She discusses it in a very practical way, stressing the organisational aspects. She also includes a number of real case studies. The resources necessary for project work are discussed in some detail by North (1990), who outlines a system for providing a 'mini-library'.

Even if a project does not provide the vehicle for the whole course, nevertheless, there is a strong case for allocating at least 10 per cent of course time (perhaps more) to projects. Some examples of projects within the EAP syllabus were referred to earlier in the chapter (and see Appendix 1.1). It will be noted that they focused on projects for individuals and pairs. Whole-group projects, as outlined by Bloor and St John (1988), are quite possible within the context of a course. If the group is heterogeneous (regarding nationalities and disciplines), so much the better. An interesting project, with a real informational purpose and a useful outcome for the students, would be to investigate existing welfare provisions for overseas students in the educational institution, and to recommend extensions of the provision if gaps are found.

4.6 Pre-sessional EAP courses

Many British universities and colleges have developed pre-sessional EAP courses for their overseas students to attend before starting their specialist studies. These courses are normally of 4, 8 or 12 weeks' length and are full-time in the summer: they usually provide 20–25 hours of tuition a week. We shall call these 'short courses'.

An obvious feature of short courses is pressure of time, which entails a careful prioritising of needs, focusing on the essentials. Strevens' (1977) list of criteria still applies, i.e. only include what is required by the learner's purposes viz. restriction, selection, themes and topics, communicative needs. Although short EAP courses usually try to cover nearly all aspects of EAP, they normally emphasise the components that are of immediate concern to the students. These might be, for example, listening and understanding and taking notes; familiarisation with the library and its resources, so that a student can function independently in this respect; the academic conventions associated with academic writing, etc.

If the course is geared to the needs of students from one particular department or discipline, it might focus entirely on that subject area, i.e. ESAP. Thus all the practice can evolve round the specific needs of the subject and of the students' lacks in that area. For example, if discussion of the subject causes difficulty, the course might focus on helping students to make short presentations (3 minutes, extending to 15 minutes), to listen carefully to such presentations, to make notes, to ask questions at the end and to express opinions.

An example of the main components of the syllabus in a short EGAP course is shown in Figure 11. This is an average of many such short courses mounted by British universities and shows the percentage of course time allocated to each component. This will be discussed shortly, in the context of EAP course components.

Academic writing	25%
Listening & note-taking	15%
Academic speech	15%
Reading comprehension	15%
Reference skills	5%
Individual project	10%
Various components	15%
	100%

Figure 11   Example of a short EGAP course

4.7 In-sessional, part-time courses

A distinction needs to be made between full-time and part-time courses. In the UK, a fee is normally charged for the full-time short courses described above; the courses are usually self-financing. As well as the short, full-time courses in the summer, many UK universities run part-time EAP classes during term-time as a service to their overseas students. These classes are often free (or covered by the departmental fee), and are attended by students who have already registered for their subject-specialist course. The classes usually specialise in, for example, essay writing, developing confidence in speaking in a discussion group, taking notes while listening to subject-specific lectures, etc. Such classes are often held in lunch breaks or at other times when students are free from their departmental timetable commitments.

Typically, the part-time classes focus on one area of need, frequently in blocks of two hours a week, e.g. academic writing, seminar practice. An advantage of the classes is that they can be geared to the students' immediate and known needs. Links can be established with the specialist departments and information/feedback given in both directions. A disadvantage can exist in the case of students who are at a lower language level. They often need a full-time EAP course, but for various reasons do not or cannot attend, e.g. because of lack of time or money. In their case, the progress can be very slow and they may tend to stop attending classes. They often say that they need to spend all their time on the specialist subject as they have so much reading and writing to do. In this case, a vicious circle can develop in which there is no progress in any direction.

4.8 Long EAP courses

A number of UK universities organise one-year, full-time EAP courses. These are typically divided into three ten-week terms. In some cases, they are certificated by the universities with an examination at the end, and the courses are validated by external examiners.

We shall look at the main differences between long EAP courses and short ones, noting any issues that arise. It may be that some of the concerns of these long courses will also be experienced by long EAP courses held in other parts of the world. We shall be looking at these later in the chapter.

4.8.1 Content balance

There are various approaches to the question of balance between EAP/ study skills and general English. One big determining factor is the language level of the students at the beginning of the course: the lower the level, the more general English that is needed. For example, lower-level students may have about 80 per cent general English and 20 per cent EAP, while intermediate (+) students may have 30 per cent general English and 70 per cent EAP.

An approach favoured by several centres is for the balance to shift throughout the course; thus:

Term 1: one-third EAP, two-thirds general
Term 2: two-thirds EAP, one-third general
Term 3: nearly all EAP.

Linked with this is the notion of phasing in, or building up, in a quantitative and qualitative way. For example, starting with basic study skills and encouraging very short oral presentations, to finally giving a short talk at the end. Similarly, progressing from basic infrastructural skills (e.g. library use and information retrieval) to writing very short accounts, to writing short essays, to finally writing a long project.

An alternative approach is to concentrate on EAP tasks and to provide general English as a response to any needs arising. This may be organised on an individual basis or a group basis, depending on the type of need and its general applicability.

4.8.2 Motivation

Most long, full-time courses have some problems with sustaining interest and motivation over a long period. This is one reason why courses are often divided into blocks of time (e.g. a month or a term) with short-term aims or goals for each block: these sometimes take the form of a project or group assignment. One way to sustain interest that has been tried is gradually to reduce the number of staff contact hours, with more time given to self-access and independent study. Staff can be on hand to give help or advice, as needed. In some cases, motivation is provided by the purpose of the course: students might be working towards specific IELTS test scores. They, thus, have a clear aim in view.

4.8.3 Smaller numbers

In the UK at least, the number of students attending the long courses is smaller than the number attending the short courses. This brings its own advantages and disadvantages.

We will look at some of the disadvantages first. Because the numbers are smaller, the language levels and range of abilities within one group may be wider (in order to make the course viable in terms of finance). This may make the work of the teacher more difficult. There may also be a wide range of subject specialisms. In addition, there may be a concentration of speakers of the same language, if some countries have made a block booking for a particular purpose or reason. This may upset the balance with respect to other mother tongues, and entail some reorganisation of groups or activities.

On the other hand, there are some distinct advantages to having smaller numbers. Because there is more time to develop the different components in the syllabus, the pace can be slower with more time devoted to individualised help. A closer rapport can be built up between teacher and students, with all its advantages.

4.8.4 Time of year

As the course is running throughout the academic year, there are some advantages because of this. For example, the students can join in main-stream university activities and make more contact with other students. This may not be possible during short courses in the summer.

Perhaps more importantly, from the point of view of course content, it is easier to obtain information and informal help from specialist depart-ments, e.g. regarding books, journals, topics, advice, etc. This may enable the course, or components within it, to have a greater content focus. Easier contact with departments can result in a greater exchange of information; for example, the EAP course director can advise the department(s) how certain students are coping and the kind of progress they are making.

4.8.5 Evaluation

The methods of course evaluation and feedback are broadly the same as on short EAP courses: these are looked at in some detail in the next chapter. However, because the course is long, there is very often more time and opportunity for *formative* evaluation to take place. In other words, feedback is provided by the students and staff at various stages during the course which enables the ensuing parts of the course to be modified. As with short courses, there is *summative* evaluation at the end.

4.9 EAP course components

The following information is based on the BALEAP Survey carried out in 1991/92 (referred to in the Introduction and Appendix 3). In the nature of a survey, the data that are revealed are retrospective. Consequently, you are now reading an historical account. However, I believe that the main course outline and EAP components are still relevant and of use to prospective course directors. In addition, no other such analysis of EAP courses has been undertaken before: the resulting data allow some comparisons to be made (see Jordan 1996a). Clearly, not all EAP courses will or should adopt the pattern of components and time allocation indicated below: this will vary according to the exact purpose of the course and the precise needs of the students. However, the information given here shows what was current practice among EAP professionals and will provide some guidelines or, at least, a starting point.

The data about course components that follow are divided into EAP and non-EAP components. Subsequent chapters will be looking at the content and type of materials used within these different components.

Figure 12 gives the overall picure of pre-sessional EAP courses in the survey. Not all the courses contained all the components listed (see Jordan 1996a for full details). The components shown here are in descending order of frequency on EAP courses. For example, academic writing appeared in 100 per cent of the courses, while self-access/individualised learning appeared in 12 per cent. Among the non-EAP components, 'grammar' occurred in 47 per cent of the courses, while 'media' appeared in 12 per cent. All the courses surveyed had 50 per cent or more of the time allotted to EAP components; 81 per cent had 70 per cent or more time for EAP, while 30 per cent of the courses had 100 per cent of the time for EAP.

The proportion of time spent on the various components presumably reflects the importance of that component to the students and their future needs. The components indicate that there are several syllabuses, combined or in layers viz. content, skills, project. Subject-specific aspects and academic writing feature as the most important, but integrated study skills and individual study project (which is also integrated) are also very important. English for Social Purposes is as important as several of the study skills areas presumably because the courses took place in Britain and the students needed to be able to function in the wider environment. This element would not be expected in many of the courses in EFL/ESL countries.

If a similar survey were to be conducted today, I might expect a greater emphasis on integrated areas and skills, and more time devoted to self-access or individualised learning.

	Course components	Average % time spent on components
A	EAP COMPONENTS	
1	Academic writing	25%
2	Listening and note-taking	15%
3	Academic speech (oral presentations and seminar strategies)	14%
4	Reading comprehension and strategies	16%
5	Library/reference/research skills	9%
6	Integrated study skills	16%
7	Individual study project	18%
8	Note-making (from reading)	18%
9	Subject-specific topics/language	30%
10	Guest lectures/plenaries	7%
11	Individual tutorials	–
12	Self-access/individualised learning	10%
B	NON-EAP COMPONENTS	
1	Grammar	12%
2	English for Social Purposes	16%
3	Computer literacy	8%
4	Vocabulary development	11%
5	Pronunciation/language laboratory	–
6	Media: newspapers/TV/video	–

Notes:
1. As always, one needs to be careful in interpreting statistics or in trying to claim too much for them.
2. Only components mentioned by 10 per cent or more of BALEAP members are included.
3. The 'average % time' column totals more than 100 per cent because it is an average of all the courses, and not all courses include all the components.

Figure 12   Overall picture of EAP courses (based on Jordan 1996a)

4.10   Content of EAP components

An area of concern in devising or selecting appropriate practice material for EAP components is the suitability of the content of the talks to be listened to, for instance, or the passages to be read. If there is a group of homogeneous economists, it should be possible to select an apt text on economics. Most groups in the UK, however, are of mixed disciplines. What kind of content, therefore, is the most appropriate? The short answer is, it varies. This can be seen from Figure 13, based on the survey. All EAP courses, to a greater or lesser degree, contain a mixture of content. The survey showed that 91 per cent of courses contain three or more types of content, with an average of four to five types.

	Content	1st choice for:
1	General study skills	31%
2	International issues*	27%
3	Subject-specific	27%
4	British life and institutions (or British studies)	4%
5	Educational issues	2%
6	Others: mixed (see examples below)	9%

(* Books that are useful, on account of their international themes, are Brieger and Jackson 1989; Potter 1991)
Examples of other content
a) Language as an object of study
b) Host culture/cross-cultural aspects/inter-personal relations
c) Current affairs
d) General matters of academic interest

Figure 13   Content of EAP practice materials

Clearly, the vast majority of courses will have a combination of the first three content areas listed above. Some aspects of the content are looked at in the whole of Part II as well as in other chapters.

4.11 Non-EAP components

The purpose of including non-EAP components in an EAP course is threefold:

1. to serve as a necessary adjunct to the main study skills:
   - *grammar* is often incorporated with academic writing (and is considered together with it in Chapter 11);
   - *vocabulary development* is often combined with reading comprehension (but is looked at separately in Chapter 10);
   - *pronunciation* may be combined with aspects of academic speech (and is looked at briefly in Chapter 13) or regarded as an individual matter to be pursued in a *language laboratory* (see Appendix 2);
2. to fulfil a perceived present or future need:

- *social/survival English* in an English-speaking country (see below);
- familiarisation with *TV news and newspapers*: to keep abreast of current affairs (see Grundy (1993a) for ways to utilise newspapers);
- hands-on experience with *computers*: useful later in producing essays and dissertations in subject departments;
3. to provide useful variety:
   - *video* material;
   - *mini-projects* (Fried-Booth (1986) has several suggestions that can be used or adapted).

4.11.1 Social/survival English

In Figure 1 on page 3, English for Social Purposes is shown as a separate entity from EAP. In the purist sense, this is accurate, particularly if you look at EAP in EFL countries where English is only being used for the subjects being studied. However, when the EAP courses are held in English-speaking countries it is highly desirable to include some practice in the spoken language needed for everyday living, often referred to as 'survival English'.

A principled approach to survival English has been made by Nation and Crabbe (1991) who investigated the needs of students, and analysed language guide books for visitors. They devised a syllabus and divided the language items into eight categories; adapted for students (as opposed to business travellers), they are:

1. greetings and being polite
2. shopping – numbers, money, weights, size and measure
3. reading signs
4. getting to places
5. finding accommodation
6. ordering food – names of dishes and drinks, and cooking terms
7. talking about yourself
8. controlling and learning language

Typically, such syllabuses include dialogue practice, based on a situational approach, e.g. opening a bank account, at the post office, registering with the police, etc. It might also include making enquiries over the telephone and understanding the responses.

Another aspect of social English to consider is that reported by Nunan (1991) in the context of NNS in Australia. The advanced learners nominated conversation with NS and practising English outside the classroom as the two aspects that most helped them to learn English. The more practice you have in using a language, the more comfortable you become with it, and the less inhibited you feel about using it in other contexts. In addition, students learn a lot from each other, and the more they are able to exchange information and ideas and opinions, the better they will understand the content of their course.

4.12   Timetabling: priorities, balance and structure

One possible approach to course design, and subsequently timetabling, is as follows. The main components are decided upon in the light of the needs analyses. They are, perhaps, presented in the order in which students have the most difficulty, combined with some grading of tasks and prioritising of skills use. A balance and variety can be achieved in a number of ways; some of them are discussed below.

The course director, in taking into consideration all aspects of the course, will decide what should be included in the *introductory day*. A decision will need to be taken on whether or not to have an initial test to use as a basis for dividing students into groups. This may depend on the philosophy of the course (that such tests are unnecessary, that self-assessment is sufficient, that other factors are more important, etc.). It may also depend on the amount of prior information available on the students, e.g. if they have IELTS test scores and profiles, if they are from a similar background, if they are all going to study the same subject, etc. Often the introductory day will include a tour of the campus and facilities to help with orientation. It will also include some kind of explanation of the course content and philosophy, organisation, and the books and other materials to be used.

After deciding on the first day, decisions will then be made about the first week, the morning sessions compared with the afternoons, the first block or half compared with other blocks or the second half, etc. One method of helping to see an overview of the whole course is to draw up a plan of the course structure, divided into weeks and morning and afternoon sessions. It is then easier to see if there is an appropriate balance and variety (receptive versus productive skills; intensive versus less intensive study; individual, group or plenary work; phasing components in and out; different tutors for morning and afternoon sessions and/or for specific course components). In addition, the detailed daily timetable could be changed every fortnight or month to prevent staleness creeping in.

An example is given in Figure 14 of a possible course structure. Note that it does not indicate the frequency or amount of time devoted to the components. The fact that the components are listed individually does not necessarily imply that they must all be timetabled separately. As students have difficulty with listening and understanding on arrival, listening comprehension and note-taking has been timetabled for the mornings, but changed to the afternoons half-way and then phased out.

STRUCTURE OF AN EIGHT-WEEK EAP COURSE

MAIN COMPONENTS	1	2	3	4	5	6	7	8	am or pm
Tests	X			X				X	am
Listening comprehension and note-taking	X	X	X	X					am
				X	X	X			pm
Academic writing	X	X	X	X	X	X	X	X	am
									pm
Spoken language (seminars)									am
		X	X	X	X	X	X	X	pm
Reading comprehension									am
	X	X	X	X	X	X	X	X	pm
Library and reference skills									am
	X	X							pm
Individual project		X	X	X	X	X	X	X	am
									pm
ESAP: subject-specific					X	X	X	X	am
									pm
Self-access									am
			X	X	X	X	X	X	pm
Social English	X	X	X	X	X	X	X		am/pm
Guest lectures and seminars					X	X	X	X	am
									pm
Individual tutorials	X	X	X	X	X	X	X	X	am
									pm

Key: ▨ ◨ = presence of the component

Components not included (that might have been): grammar, use of computers, other projects, life in Britain ...

Figure 14   Example of an eight-week course structure

Academic writing is considered to be one of the essential core components and is practised each week in the mornings. However, the frequency of the sessions may be reduced as more time is devoted to the individual project.

Familiarisation with the library and its facilities is concentrated into the first two weeks, then phased out. Guest lectures are not introduced until the second half of the course, by which time the students will have had more time to adjust to understanding different voices, and to coping with a possibly different academic system. Self-access is introduced after the first two weeks, taking over from library and reference skills. The time devoted to it could be gradually increased as the course progresses.

4.13   Timetable examples

Two examples are given in Figure 15 of different types of timetables, perhaps reflecting different approaches, or different stages in the same course. *Example A* shows a more conventional timetable divided into sessions which are clearly demarcated. Not unusually, the morning sessions give the impression of more intensive work, while the afternoon seems to have less pressure. This would logically match the students' concentration span and the tiredness factor as the day progresses. *Example B* indicates a less tight structure to the timetable. More choice is indicated, with options and a possibly more flexible approach. There might also be more closely integrated study skills practice.

Many EAP courses give an afternoon free for students (mid-week or end of week). In addition to the items shown in the examples, most courses arrange a social programme: this will include some evening activities, often a one-day coach visit at the weekend, and an end-of-course party. Frequently, social organisers or social assistants are employed for these activities. They provide another useful point of contact for the students.

There are a number of approaches to timetabling that are possible. To some extent they may depend on the experience of the EAP teachers: for example, less experienced teachers may need more guidance, thus the timetable may be more detailed. Students, also, may prefer a timetable that indicates the structure and content of the day or week.

4.14   International EAP courses

In this section we shall look at a range of types of EAP courses mounted in English L1 and EFL/ESL situations, with examples taken from different parts of the world.

4.14.1 English L1 countries

Before looking at examples of EAP courses, it is useful to look at the situation with regard to teachers. In the USA, UK, Australia, etc. it is usual, with a few exceptions, to employ NS as teachers. The teachers are unlikely to speak (all) the students' languages; they will know very little of the students' backgrounds – educational and cultural – at the beginning of the course. However, they will often have access to the

79

English for Academic Purposes and study skills

TIMETABLE EXAMPLES

Example A

	9.30–10.15	10.15–11	B R E A K	11.15–12	12–12.30	L U N C H
Monday am	Listening comprehension and note-taking	Academic writing		Plenary 'Academic writing'	Seminar: in groups	

	1.30–2.15	2.15–3	B R E A K	3.15–4
Monday pm	Reading comprehension	Social English		Self-access

Example B

	9.30–10.15	10.15–11		11.15–12	12–12.30	
Tuesday am	Individual project or Resource centre (self-access)			Grammar workshop or Language laboratory or Private study		

Figure 15   Timetable examples

specialist subject departments that the students will be attending after their EAP course. Consequently, they can be well aware of the target situation needs and its academic culture.

A number of *Australian* universities offer similar tertiary-level language programmes to those described earlier, with similar emphases on the different study skills. A good example is Macquarie University, Sydney, which has pre-entry and pre-sessional study skills and EAP courses for immigrants and overseas students. It houses the National Centre for English Language Teaching and Research (NCELTR) which is involved in wide-ranging research and publications in many areas of EAP. Similarly, Charles Sturt University, Waga Waga, organises four-week intensive study skills courses and ten-week EAP courses.

In the *USA*, many universities organise EAP courses and have a long history of doing so. A good example is the English Language Institute at the University of Michigan, which offers an intensive summer academic language skills programme for NNS. This focuses on classroom and oral presentation skills, lecture comprehension and note-taking skills, academic writing (including dissertation writing), academic reading and vocabulary, and academic speech and pronunciation.

80

In the *Republic of Ireland*, EAP courses at University College, Cork, are organised by the Language Centre, and held in the summer. They cater for two main categories of students: those under European exchange programmes (ERASMUS/LINGUA/TEMPUS), and those from several Asian countries, e.g. Japan, Malaysia, Hong Kong, China, Taiwan. Their four-week (intensive) and ten-week (extensive) courses cover the same areas as courses described earlier. At the end of the course, students take the IELTS exam.

Examples of courses similar to those described above can also be found in other English L1 countries, e.g. *Canada* and *New Zealand*.

4.14.2 EFL/ESL countries

In these countries, there are usually monolingual classes, with the NNS teacher speaking the same language as the students. There may also be some NS teachers as well. The NNS teachers may know a lot about the students' backgrounds regarding language difficulties, education and culture. The teachers may also have access to specialist departments and their requirements if they are in the same institution. However, the teachers may know less or little about the academic environments if the students are aiming to study abroad.

As the education systems, and academic and cultural conventions, are likely to be different from those in the UK, USA, etc., it is likely that there will be differences with aspects of the EAP courses. There may be different approaches regarding methodology, materials, emphases, prioritising, use of the mother tongue, etc.

EFL

Nepal is an example of a country in which the British Council arranges EAP courses as preparation for students going to study in the UK. The courses are geared to the needs of the IELTS exam, and normally students must pass with minimum grades of about 6.0 in order to be accepted by UK universities. Such courses are normally in blocks of 4, 8 or 12 weeks, all the year round. They are cheaper to run than those in the UK, though students often benefit from short 'topping up' courses in the UK afterwards. After teaching basic reference skills (library use, classification systems and dictionary use), the courses concentrate on the following:

- listening comprehension and note-taking (as note-taking in English is new for many students);
- listening and speaking (to help with the IELTS interview; the spoken language is a big area of difficulty – pronunciation, intonation and fluency);

– reading and writing: especially organising information.

There is very high motivation on these courses as the students want to study abroad. The courses perform the function of a stepping stone. They are held in the capital, Kathmandu: it may be the first time that students have been separated from their families but they are secure in their own environment. It is often the first contact that students have had with a Western teacher. NNS may also teach on the courses, with their attendant advantages of knowing the language (Nepali is the lingua franca), education system and likely cultural difficulties. Such courses are very important in confidence building.

Israel is an example of a country in which university EAP courses largely concentrate on academic reading. Students of most subjects need to read widely in English (textbooks and journals); consequently, courses promote skills in comprehension, skimming, scanning and vocabulary development.

Finland provides an interesting contrast to Israel in that the focus of many of the university EAP courses is academic writing. Although the two official languages (Finnish: 93 per cent of the population; Swedish: 6 per cent of the population) are used in higher education, there is an increasing demand from faculties and students to write and publish in English, especially for theses for the MSc and PhD. For example, in Helsinki, the Helsinki School of Economics, the Swedish School of Economics, Helsinki University of Technology and Helsinki University, all organise courses in writing for research purposes. The courses are staffed by both NNS and NS, and are particularly in demand from social scientists, scientists and technologists.

In some cases, writing clinics are arranged, often in the form of seminars, at which 'how to write a research paper' or 'how to structure a thesis' is the main theme, followed by individualised practice. Writing skills and the writing process itself are emphasised; particular attention is given to: the use of metatext, structure, cohesion and style. In addition to these courses, most language centres in Finland organise reading comprehension courses for scientists, for example, and the skills needed in giving oral presentations. One advantage of homogeneous classes (Finnish-speaking) is that language interference difficulties (both at macro- and micro-levels) can be anticipated and their avoidance explained and practised.

ESL

In *Pakistan*, both Urdu and English are official languages. At university level, EAP courses mostly focus on reading specialist texts and the discourse conventions of academic writing, especially for science students. Although the students' perceived need is for spoken English, the academic requirement is mostly writing, which is catered for by part-time classes, mostly staffed by NNS. A particular difficulty for the teachers is the shortage of suitable EAP materials available, and their relatively high cost for students.

In *Hong Kong*, there are also two official languages, Cantonese and English. Most university courses are officially conducted in English, although in practice a mixture of Cantonese and English is often used. The students are all Cantonese-speakers, most of whom have been educated at Chinese-medium schools. Consequently, when students study at university, they frequently need help with English. A good example is Hong Kong Polytechnic University, which runs a wide range of degree courses.

The service English section of the English Department, which is staffed by a balanced mix of NNS and NS, provides a large number of EPP courses on a part-time basis. In addition, they have developed EAP courses which take place during one semester for two hours a week. The course units concentrate on developing reading and writing skills, with some emphasis on making oral presentations and seminar practice. The sessions are organised on the basis of discussions, role-play, and individual and group activities.

4.15 Introspect and discuss

1. Figure 8 summarises, in a flow chart, the various strands involved in EAP course design. Is there any other 'box' that you would wish to add to the diagram? If so, what would you include in it, and where would you place it?
2. An extensive example is given of an EAP syllabus emanating from the 1970s (see Appendix 1.1). If you were designing a syllabus today, would you amend it in any way? If so, how and why? (You may prefer to return to this question after you have finished reading the book.)
3. Examples are given of several projects incorporated in the syllabus. Can you think of any other projects that it would be useful to include?
4. From your experience, can you add any topics to the list given for student discussions?
5. If you were devising an EAP course, which type(s) of syllabus would you choose as the basis for it (content/product, skills, method/ process...)? Why?
6. Bloor and Bloor (1988) suggest three major areas for negotiation in self-access learning. Do you have any views on these?

7. What are the advantages and disadvantages of totally self-access language learning?
8. From your experience, which are the major and which are the minor constraints or variables in designing courses? Have any been omitted from the list given?
9. On a light-hearted note, Figure 10 shows two course directors balancing various aspects of a course. Suggest which kind of book Mr Pragmatic Eclecticism is reading! What kind of response might Ms Eclectic Pragmatism make to all the questions put forward by the other course director?
10. If you have any experience of long EAP courses, does it match the description given here? Are there any significant differences?
11. Figure 12 gives details of a survey of UK EAP courses. Do any of the results surprise you? Which? Why?
12. What advantages and disadvantages can you see in the choices of content for EAP practice material (Figure 13)?
13. Figure 14 gives an example of the structure of an eight-week EAP course. Outline the structure for the content of the *first day* of an intensive EAP course in your country.
14. Two examples (A and B) are given of timetables in Figure 15. Which other approaches to devising a timetable can you suggest?
15. Do you have any experience of teaching on EAP courses in the types of countries exemplified in the section 'International EAP courses'? Were these courses different in any respects from the ones described here? What were the major problems encountered?

5   Evaluation: students and courses

Chapter 2 referred to *tests* as one source of information, among several others, in needs analysis. Chapter 4 mentioned *feedback* during and after EAP courses. Both aspects form part of the process of *evaluation*, which is an intrinsic part of learning and teaching. The purpose of evaluation is 'to collect information systematically in order to indicate the worth or merit of a programme or project ... and to inform decision making' (Weir and Roberts 1994), both from the point of view of development and the end product. Evaluation applies to both students and to courses as a whole, and can make use of *quantitative* methods, e.g. tests, and *qualitative* methods, e.g. observations, interviews, and questionnaires.

First, we shall look at the different test types, bearing in mind that testing is only one component in the evaluation process (Rea-Dickins and Germaine 1992). Then we shall look at evaluation more generally under the umbrella term 'feedback'.

5.1   'Test' and 'examination'

The words 'test' and 'examination' are often used synonymously. Some-times a distinction is made according to the criterion of formality or external/public, where test is 'smaller', local, less formal and often part of an ongoing process of evaluation or feedback. However, this distinc-tion breaks down when well-established, formal public exams are known as 'tests'. Nevertheless, in this chapter, the word 'test' will be used to refer to the various evaluation procedures utilised in EAP courses. 'Examination' will be used when referring to the public exams (even when they are called 'tests'!): these are looked at in Appendix 4.

5.2   Tests: differences

Underlying all the tests that follow is the essential difference between *objective* and *subjective* tests.

Objective tests, or items, have only one or a small number of correct answers, e.g. multiple-choice items. They can be marked by a machine (computer) or with a template overlay or by an experienced person. They can usually be marked quickly and reliably.

Subjective tests, or questions, are usually open-ended (e.g. essays, reports, open comprehension questions, talks) and give greater freedom in the answers. Markers must be experienced teachers who have to use their own judgement. Such tests take time to mark, and there may be discrepancies between markers.

Receptive skills can be tested objectively, but *productive* skills usually require subjective testing. Tests should normally cover a full range of skills and therefore 'most good tests contain both objective and subjective types of items' (Heaton 1990, who clearly illustrates these tests).

Most teachers on EAP courses will be involved with some of the following test types; they may need to construct some themselves. The type of test that they set will depend upon the purpose for which it is needed.

5.3 Tests: types

Most EAP courses contain some kind of testing of students, often for different purposes. There may be an *entrance test* to determine whether or not the students' language level is appropriate for the course (it might be too low or too high). Sometimes the results of internationally recognised exams are used for this purpose, e.g. IELTS or TOEFL (see Appendix 4).

Individual institutions may use their own internal tests which they validate by feedback and follow-up. Such an example is given by James (1980), who surveyed one year's intake of overseas postgraduate students at Manchester University, noted their English test results and correlated them with their academic performance the following year by means of a questionnaire sent to the subject tutors. The test (Chaplen Test: a speeded grammar and vocabulary test, which takes 28 minutes to administer) showed that two out of three students who scored less than 40 per cent proved to have negligible or inadequate English for their academic work. Such information can be used predictively and acts as a warning for low scorers to receive as much help as possible, and for the receiving departments to be informed of their (potential) difficulties.

5.3.1 Placement test

Once students are accepted for a course, there may be a *placement test* to help decide which class/group they are to go in. As the test is concerned with students' present language ability, it will probably be general and/or wide-ranging in order to give an overall assessment of their level. The test may consist of multiple-choice grammar and vocabulary questions, reading comprehension, cloze passages, etc. It may test all the language skills rather than focus on one or two.

In forming groups for teaching, other factors may be taken into consideration, e.g. the balance/mismatch of a student's receptive/productive language skills; the desire to separate speakers of the same language so that they do not dominate a group nor use their own language together in class.

A feature of placement tests is that the results are needed quickly so that groups can be formed without delay. Often students are also interviewed by a tutor so that there can be a check on oral production and fluency; personality aspects can also be noted.

5.3.2 Progress/diagnostic test

Courses may also give tests every four weeks or so: these are often called *progress tests*. Such tests have several functions: they provide information on progress being made and areas of difficulty remaining, i.e. they provide screening, indicating what help is still needed. They also act as a spur or motivation for students by setting short-term goals.

Judgement is needed about the frequency of such tests: if they are given too often, they become an end in themselves, and any pleasure there might be in learning is destroyed. However, if they are held in the spirit of giving information to the student as well as to the teacher, they can be invaluable. Students can be helped to learn the areas of difficulty revealed by the tests – often called *diagnostic tests*. The type of test can often seem like an extension of a lesson or similar to previously used material or unit in a book.

An account of using a diagnostic test for grammar is given by Johns (1994). He describes the popularity of remedial grammar classes at Birmingham University based on areas of grammatical difficulty revealed by the test, which is structurally based and contains 130 items.

5.3.3 Achievement/attainment test

At the end of a course a final test is often conducted to see if students have learned what they should have been taught. In other words, it covers the syllabus or course books and is usually set by the course director for all the classes on the course. The final test on an EAP course may reflect the language needs of the target situation and contain a simulation of study skills in use (e.g. listening to a talk, making notes, writing a report, etc.). The results may be used in a report to a receiving department or a sponsor. More formal achievement tests, i.e. examinations, are set by external bodies.

A true *achievement test* will have constant standards from one course to the next and from year to year. It shows the standard reached by a student in relation to other students at the same stage. Few EAP courses will have such consistency because of the changing nature of courses and students.

5.3.4 Proficiency test

A proficiency test looks forward, assessing the suitability of students for specific courses, from the point of view of their control of the language. Such tests are not based upon particular syllabuses, books or teaching programmes. However, there may be books or courses which aim to help students to pass such exams. Examples of such tests are some of the public examinations, e.g. IELTS. This aims to assess the ability of a student to follow a university course in an English-speaking country.

Blue (1993) reports on research into IELTS test scores correlated with students' academic success in British universities. Students who scored 6.5 in the test had a failure rate of 6 per cent; for those scoring 6.0, the failure rate increased to 19 per cent. Students who scored 5.5 had a 30 per cent chance of failure. Clearly, language proficiency plays an important part in academic success. Other instances supporting this conclusion are given in Robinson (1991).

5.4 Tests: general features

5.4.1 Basic principles

1. Every test should be *reliable*, i.e. it should measure precisely what it is supposed to measure; it should have consistency.
2. Every test should be *valid*, i.e. it should only measure what it is supposed to measure, not something else (e.g. it should not rely on external knowledge, or depend on a student's personality).
   Content validity relates to what is included in a test. This is decided by considering the purposes of the test and then designing the test to reflect the areas to be assessed, in appropriate proportions. For example, a test of an oral presentation would need to include subject content and language as well as delivery, otherwise it would have low content validity.
   Face validity is the degree to which teachers and students think the test measures what it claims to measure. In other words, a subjective judgement of the test: does it seem reasonable, include appropriate content, have a suitable level of difficulty, etc., i.e. do people have faith in it?

3. Every test should be *economical* – of time and cost. In other words, the principle of *practicality* is essential. This is an administrative area which involves setting, marking, equipment, arrangements, etc.

5.4.2 Norm-referenced and criterion-referenced tests

In the literature on testing, mention is frequently made of norm- and criterion-referenced tests. Briefly, a *norm-referenced* test shows how a student's performance compares with that of others who have taken the test at the same time, e.g. in the top, middle or bottom sector. It is often used for selection purposes, but it does not say if a student can perform a particular task. Usually it is general purpose English that is tested.

A *criterion-referenced* test measures a student's performance in relation to clearly-stated criteria. It:

> provides information which is directly interpretable, and can be related to performance in real life.
>
> (Skehan 1988)

In ESP/EAP, such tests are sometimes called *performance-based* tests, as they may contain simulated real-life tasks, e.g. reading several extracts from journals in order to write an essay. These tests are discussed by Allison and Webber (1984); an example is the IELTS test. A useful survey of approaches to, and books/articles on, testing in EAP/ESP, is contained in Robinson (1991).

5.5 Feedback

There are two main types of evaluation that are utilised to obtain information about the course itself. The first is *formative* evaluation which is concerned with the development process and is usually informal. In EAP courses it often takes the form of meetings between students and tutors where views can be exchanged, e.g. weekly tutorials. As a result of this feedback, aspects of the course can be adapted in an ongoing way. A case study of the procedures involved at Reading University is contained in Weir and Roberts (1994).

The second type occurs at the end of a course: it is *summative*. Students will normally be given a questionnaire to complete anonymously: it will usually include questions relating to the content and organisation of the course, and may also ask about social activities and accommodation arrangements. Tutors may also discuss the course with their groups and thus obtain an overall picture of certain aspects. Tutors themselves may also complete a questionnaire and have discussions with the course director, and give their views on the course. A full discussion of evaluation in ELT is contained in Rea-Dickins (1994), who provides a very extensive bibliography.

An example of student evaluation is given in Jordan (1993). He averaged the course feedback on the various EAP components over a five-year period (1986–1990) and found that 'academic writing' and 'personal project' were awarded the two highest grades (on a five-point scale) by 89 per cent and 88 per cent of the students, respectively. Jordan also conducted a follow-up analysis of student attitudes to the pre-session courses after they had been in their subject departments for one term (about three months) following their attendance on the courses. He found that 79 per cent of the students replying to the questionnaire rated the course as being either 'extremely relevant' or 'relevant' to their subsequent studies (the top two grades on a five-point scale).

Post-course evaluation by the receiving departments is also highly relevant. This may take the form of questionnaires, open-ended questions and/or interviews. The prime purpose is to check on the departments' perception of the effectiveness of the course, its strengths and weaknesses, difficulties still facing their students, and if the departments' grading of students matches that of EAP tutors (see Tonkyn *et al.* 1993 for an example and discussion).

Follow-up comparisons of the assessments of students' language proficiency by the EAP teachers and subsequent departmental tutors are often called 'tracer studies'. These studies are invaluable as a check on the appropriateness and effectiveness of the course content and its methodology to the students' future needs. Tonkyn *et al.* (1993) conducted a tracer study at Reading University and found that there was a fairly high degree of agreement between EAP teachers and academic tutors regarding students' English proficiency. However, they did find that academic tutors placed a 'heavy reliance on oral work for diagnosis of language problems'. As a result, Tonkyn *et al.* urged departments to give more written tasks earlier in their courses to verify in a more balanced way the nature of language difficulties. They also found that there was considerable agreement between teachers and tutors on the importance of certain factors for academic success: the main ones listed were diligence, language proficiency, critical intelligence, combined with active participation.

Armed with all this feedback, the course director is in a position to modify certain aspects of the next course. Probably the ideal situation is to be able to devise ahead the syllabus and overall course design, together with the first week's timetable. Then, depending on the needs of the students on the next course, detailed timetabling beyond the first week can be provided after the course has started. In reality, this may not be possible, but some kind of in-built flexibility is normally needed in a course design. For example, most courses will need to order books and materials before the course starts. However, they may have ordered/ accumulated sets of books of different levels or approaches, so that various components of a course may be adapted to the needs of the newly-arrived students.

A pertinent question to ask in the context of evaluation is: has the customer (student/sponsor/department) received value for money (Alderson and Beretta 1992)? This suggests some kind of quality assurance which would need external criteria and independent evaluation. For EAP courses at British universities, there is an accreditation scheme operated by BALEAP (see Appendix 3). Full details are included in Appendix 4.1 of Weir and Roberts (1994) who look at the code of practice and the checklist of documentation involved. The scheme's assessment criteria are listed by O'Brien (1996):

> a. Management and administration
> b. Staffing
> c. Resources and facilities
> d. Course design
> e. Teaching
> f. Assessment
> g. Student welfare
> h. Course evaluation

O'Brien first discusses problems associated with any quality assurance scheme. She divides these into three questions:

> 1. What to assess?
> 2. Accountability, promotion or development?
> 3. External assessment or self-regulation?

She then examines the teething difficulties of the scheme and discusses their implications; these involve:

> – report writing
> – interpretation of assessment criteria
> – management of the visit
> – administration of the scheme.

A different approach to institutional evaluation is outlined by Mackay, Wellesley and Bazergan (1995). They describe a collaborative self-evaluation scheme being developed in a number of language centres in Indonesia. The purpose is to permit language centre staff to assess their practices and activities, and to identify strategies that will guarantee the sustainability of their centres when external project support is no longer available. They make use of a performance indicator framework which represents the language centre by means of a profile of its major characteristics.

Another self-evaluation scheme, based on a team approach trialled at

Southampton University, with an internally designed checklist appropriate for EAP courses, is described by Blue and Grundy (1996).

5.5.1 End-of-course questionnaires

Finally, we can look at some examples of the types of questionnaire that students might be asked to complete at the end of an EAP course. The following are based on specimens from pre-sessional EAP courses at UK universities, but they could be adapted to any situation.

1. The shortest, simplest kind poses a few open-ended questions about certain features of the course, giving students complete scope to say what they like, but with very little guidance. Its ultimate use is probably very limited.
   e.g. What did you think of ...
   - i) The study skills sessions?
   - ii) General language development?
   - iii) The questionnaire project?
     etc.
2. This is also brief: it leaves the choice to the students about what to comment on, but gives guidance in the sense that it seeks views on the best/worst aspects. This will probably provide polarised information. Combined with a more detailed questionnaire, its value would be enhanced.
   e.g. i) What did you enjoy most on the course?
   - ii) What did you enjoy least?
   - iii) What would you like to have changed on the course:
     a) added?
     b) omitted?
   - iv) Do you have any other suggestions?
3. All the main course components can be listed, and opinions sought, on a scale (ranging from three-point to ten-point), as to their value: 'extremely valuable ... of no value'. An example is shown in Appendix 1.1. Students can also be asked to rate and compare items in the categories 'useful/valuable' and 'interesting/enjoyable', and to indicate if more or less time should be spent on the components. If this more detailed questioning is combined with example 2 above, a clearer and more useful picture will probably emerge.
4. Students can be asked to make judgements about their own improvements, in a fairly detailed way, in the different language and study skills. This changes the focus of the questionnaire from the course as such to the students themselves. It has the advantage of increasing self-awareness. However, in order to provide an overall

evaluation of the course, it is probably better given in conjunction with one of the other types above.

e.g. SPEAKING: My speaking has improved in the following areas:
(scale: 5 strongly agree; 4 agree; 3 not sure; 2 disagree;
       1 strongly disagree)
– presenting information
– discussing
– asking questions
– pronunciation (etc.)
– others: please specify

5.6 Introspect and discuss

1. What experience do you have of placement tests? Have you found that one type is preferable to others? Is it necessary to have one at all at the beginning of an EAP course?
2. Do you have any views on the use of progress/diagnostic tests on EAP courses? Which type do you prefer? Why? From your experience, are there any real benefits to the students in taking such tests on short EAP courses (i.e. 4–12 weeks)?
3. How would you design an end-of-course EAP test for students who will go on to study in different specialist departments? What kind of items would you include?
4. From your experience, which kinds of feedback do you think are the most useful for course directors to guide them in modifying current or future courses?
5. Four types of end-of-course questionnaire for evaluation purposes are exemplified. Which type do you prefer? Can you suggest other types?

6 Learning styles and cultural awareness

6.1 An imaginary case study (3)

In Chapter 2 we looked at an imaginary case study of a student from Nepal. We noted that, apart from the subject to be studied and any language difficulties, there were other factors to be considered. These involved differences in academic environment, study modes, expectations and aspects of the whole culture.

To continue our case study a little further, in the UK, Gopal attends an eight-week pre-sessional EAP course prior to starting his studies in Development Economics. One day he attends a lecture on the system of government in Britain: it is given by a guest lecturer from the Department of Government. After the plenary session, the course tutors will be discussing the lecture and its particular difficulties with the students in their classes. Meanwhile, Gopal is feeling confused because of interweaving and conflicting thoughts and observations.

During the lecture, Gopal tries, with difficulty, to write down almost everything the lecturer says and writes on the blackboard. But he notices that some students only write brief notes, while one or two others are writing notes in a kind of diagram. He is rather surprised when one student asks a question. Still others, he notices, are talking together quite a lot. Gopal does not find the lecture easy to follow: the lecturer seems to make jokes, but Gopal cannot understand them. His friend tells him they are jokes about politicians, TV programmes and cricket, but he observes that only the course tutors and a few other students are laughing. In addition to all this, he finds the subject of Constitution, Commons, Lords, Westminster, Crown, councils and committees, rather confusing.

Although this scene is imagined, the difficulties for Gopal are not: they are highlighted by the incidents depicted. To summarise, we have the following considerations:

- *learning styles*: in turn, will lead to *learning strategies* and *learner training*;
- *academic culture*: stems from the educational system and disciplinary culture, with recognised conventions; can result in mismatches of expectations;
- *general culture*: stems from the surrounding society and pervades all aspects of life;

- *British studies*: sometimes referred to by the older name of 'British life and institutions', provide the content of some of the practice material on British EAP courses (listed in Figure 13).

This chapter will look at each of these four aspects in turn.

6.2 Learning styles and strategies

A *learning* (or *cognitive*) *style* is the particular approach by which a student tries to learn. Major influences which condition or shape the way learners think and study are: the educational system, the socio-cultural background and personality variables. *Learning strategies*, on the other hand, are the ways in which learners try to understand and remember new information, e.g. techniques for learning new words in a foreign language.

If students are studying EAP in their own countries, then they will normally retain the learning style they have utilised throughout their school life. Problems need only arise if their teachers expect them to learn or practise in a way different from their normal way. This might occur if the teachers are NS, or if the teachers have been trained to teach EAP in a different way, e.g. while abroad. Clearly this situation needs to be resolved by explanation, and by negotiation, if at all possible.

If, on the other hand, students are studying EAP in an English L1 situation, there might easily be a conflict between their customary learning style and that presumed or expected in the target situation. In this case, explanation, exemplification and practice are needed so that adjustment can be facilitated.

Ballard and Clanchy (1984) draw attention to differences in learning styles and academic cultures, and raise students' awareness of expectations in English-speaking educational systems. They take the view that, with prior knowledge, students can be prepared to adapt to an alien system. They will 'need to change habits of thinking, studying and learning to suit the demands of the foreign education system'. A vital need, Ballard and Clanchy have found, is to develop an analytical and critical approach to learning; and for students to present their 'judgements in a persuasive and reasoned argument'. They succinctly analyse cultural variations in styles of learning: their summary table is shown below.

Areas of difficulty in study activities noted by Ballard and Clanchy are: working independently, relations with supervisors, participating in discussions and extended writing in English (especially a thesis). Ballard (1984) discusses separately an integrated approach to cultural adjustment with regard to a course in academic writing. The main strategies that Ballard and Clanchy recommend students to adopt are: observe, practise and participate, as 'these three strategies provide a sound basis

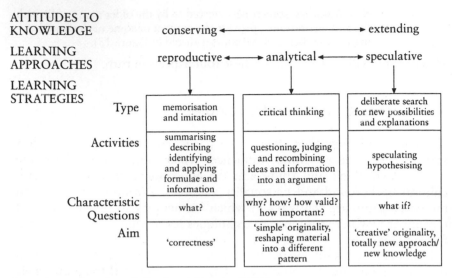

Learning styles – from Ballard and Clanchy (1984)

for successful study in a foreign culture' (see also Ballard and Clanchy 1991).

In an investigation of cross-cultural aspects of lectures delivered by NS to NNS students (Cantonese-speakers), Flowerdew and Miller (1995) noted cultural differences in attitudes to lectures as portrayed by Hong Kong students (see also Chapter 12). They noted that the students' moral education was firmly based on 'those Chinese historical, cultural and traditional philosophical patterns broadly referred to as *Confucianism*'. Flowerdew and Miller summarise those aspects of Confucianism which perhaps most noticeably contrast with Western values in the context of lectures in the following table.

Confucian and Western Values as They Relate to Academic Lectures

Confucian	*Western*
– respect for authority of lecturer	– lecturer valued as a guide and facilitator
– lecturer should not be questioned	– lecturer is open to challenge
– student motivated by family and pressure to excel	– student motivated by desire for individual development
– positive value placed on effacement and silence	– positive value placed on self-expression of ideas
– emphasis on group orientation to learning	– emphasis on individual development and creativity in learning

(From Flowerdew and Miller 1995)

In the situation where ESP courses are run predominantly by NS for NNS students in the students' own country, consideration needs to be given to the traditional cultures and technologies of that society. This aspect is stressed by Barron (1991) in the context of Papua New Guinea. He argues that ESP approaches and materials need to be adapted to include appropriate local cultural elements to enable students to make the necessary transitions.

A useful overview and summary of the various language learning styles is provided by Oxford *et al.* (1992), who put into perspective the different approaches. They also make a number of suggestions for dealing with style in multicultural tertiary ESL/EFL classrooms. Their proposals involve raising an awareness of learning styles in a class and accommodating these by means of different activities, presentations and groupings. Nunan's advice (1991) is similar:

> If your class consists of learners with a range of strategy preferences, then you will need to provide a range of learning options and activities in class.

These can include a mixture of: teacher-led and student-led activities; individual, pair work, small group, and class activities; plenary sessions, and self-access work.

In a related area to learning styles, Widdowson (1981) discusses cognitive style and specific purpose. He concludes that the best that can be done is:

> to design EAP programs by direct reference to the methodologies of subjects concerned (e.g. physical sciences/social sciences) on the grounds that these must of their nature incorporate the cognitive styles associated with their particular areas of inquiry.

This is discussed by Flowerdew (1986) who proposes a process of observation in ESAP classrooms in order to build up a 'profile of the cognitive styles required by the academic discipline in a particular local setting'. This analysis could then be related to 'what is known about the intellectual abilities of the "good language learner"'. The course designer might then be able to combine this information to devise more appropriate courses.

There is a considerable amount of literature on learning styles and strategies. References only will be noted here for any follow-up that might be required. For a discussion of *serialist/holist* and *converger/ diverger* learners, see Widdowson (1981). Willing (1988) categorised learners, in Australia, as: *concrete*, *analytical*, *communicative* and *authority-oriented*. Other research in Europe and the USA divided students' learning styles into four basic perceptual types: *visual*, *auditory*, *kinesthetic* and *tactile* (see also Reid 1987; Wenden and Rubin 1987; Melton, 1990; O'Malley and Chamot 1990).

6.2.1 Learner training

Awareness raising, of self and others, with regard to learning styles and strategies, is a positive development in EAP. In this way, students can see that there is not just one way of learning or achieving something, and that some ways may be more effective than others. In a structured form, this has become learner training. Its big advantage is that it can help students to be more responsible for their own learning, so that when a short EAP course finishes, they can continue the learning process more independently and with more self-confidence. This area is discussed in more detail in the next chapter.

The strategies that can be employed in learner training are discussed and exemplified by Ellis and Sinclair (1989: the teacher's book). They start by helping students to reflect on themselves as language learners and on the language itself and, later, to experiment with different learning strategies. The activities focus on the learning process, they are 'informed' (i.e. the students are informed of the rationale to the activity), and they have a useful outcome (see also Willing 1989).

6.3 Academic culture

Academic culture consists of a shared experience and outlook with regard to the educational system, the subject or discipline, and the conventions associated with it. These conventions may, for example, take the form of the respective roles of student and lecturer/tutor/supervisor, etc. and their customary behaviour; or the conventions attached to academic writing, with its structuring and referencing system. These latter considerations will be looked at in Chapters 14 and 16. If a student enters this culture as an outsider from a different academic culture, there will inevitably be some mismatches of expectations, or misunderstandings, which may occur at two levels. Firstly, the student has to adjust to the organisation, system and ethos of the university: in other words, a process of socialisation. The next step is a more specific kind of acculturation:

> each discipline has its distinctive content, orientation, language and methodology which must be recognised and learned.
>
> (Ballard 1984)

Brumfit (1993) discusses some of the issues relating to disciplinary culture. He gives the example of advanced studies in arts and social sciences where there is often an equality between student and teacher and where 'judgements may be genuinely open'. He compares this with technical subjects where some skills have to be imparted and where there cannot be the same equality of judgement present. This is clearly related to genre analysis appropriate to particular academic groups and disciplines; this will be looked at in Chapter 16.

6.3.1 Some cultural differences

Various studies have looked into the difficulties students experience as a result of academic cultural clashes. Dudley-Evans and Swales (1980) focused on students from the Middle East (Southwest Asia and North Africa) with Arabic as their mother tongue. They recorded differences caused by educational and cultural backgrounds in the matter of revision for examinations. Other studies are included in Greenall and Price (1980): specific cultural profiles that are considered relate to students from Iran, the Middle East, Thailand and the Indian sub-continent.

The mismatching of expectations by students and academic staff is a recurring theme in research reports. It was noted by Bloor and Bloor at Warwick University, regarding writing and examinations (see Chapter 3), and by Jordan (1993) at Manchester University, regarding help from subject tutors. It is also noted by Thorp (1991) who is concerned about a 'negative picture being built up of the students' by staff because of 'culturally different norms of interaction'. She looks at examples from questioning in lectures and essay writing, and concludes that the giving of adequate information and explanations, with appropriate discussion, is a prelude to necessary awareness-raising.

Major differences in expectations between overseas students and British university staff were noted by Furneaux *et al.* (1988) who questioned a group of research students at Reading University. They were asked to rank the personal qualities they thought a research student should have:

> The students gave a low ranking to such qualities as curiosity, the ability to be critical and honesty – all of which the academics considered essential. By contrast, the students placed a high value on being methodical and precise.

Under the intriguing title of 'Teaching spectacles and learning festivals', Coleman (1987) describes classroom behaviour in some Indonesian universities which would strike Western observers as extremely informal. The students have considerable respect for their teachers, but university English classes are regarded as a ritual in which the participants have ritually prescribed roles. The teacher is 'active, respected, ineffective', and the student is 'passive, respectful, inattentive'. In other words, students spend a great deal of the time ignoring the teacher and talking to each other. If this behaviour is transferred to an EAP course or university class in the UK, for example, there could be conflict. Thus explanation is essential. This example, and others, are discussed in Holliday (1994b).

Difficulties can also arise with efforts to introduce individualisation or independent study into EAP courses. Students might be from a culture based on close family groups and small communities, for example Nepal, Hong Kong and other Southeast Asian countries. Such students frequently work together, solving problems as a group, and are accustomed to studying in relatively crowded conditions. They can have severe difficulties if prevented from collaborating with friends; the uninitiated Western teacher might assume they are 'cheating'. Explanation and help is required. More predictable difficulties can loom for students who are from cultures where the sexes are segregated at all levels of study, and where teachers will be of the same sex as the students. They can suffer a form of culture shock when placed in a mixed group or class as in the UK and other Western universities.

6.3.2 Plagiarism

In a number of countries, particularly in Asia, there is considerable respect for the printed word and those in authority. Consequently, it is quite normal for students to quote from authorities/books without feeling the need to acknowledge the source; nor is it necessarily expected. Criticism of published works is unacceptable as it displays disrespect for authority. Consequently, students will often present extracts from books or articles in an uncritical way (Cortazzi 1990).

The problems can be imagined for students coming from an educational background as above to a North American or European university with its different academic conventions: in particular, the need to acknowledge all sources and to avoid any hint of plagiarism. The concept of plagiarism needs to be explained and practice given in making bibliographic references (Hamp-Lyons and Courter 1984; Swales and Feak 1994; see Chapter 14).

A number of institutions are aware of the different attitudes towards plagiarism and the need to acknowledge sources. For example, *The Hong Kong Polytechnic University Student Handbook* for 1995 contains an appendix 'Guidance notes on avoiding plagiarism, on bibliographic referencing and on photocopying of copyright materials'. The university views plagiarism as a serious disciplinary offence. It defines and explains plagiarism by several quotations from dictionaries (basically, 'the representation of another person's work as the candidate's own, without proper acknowledgement of the source'). It then shows how sources are referred to: using direct quotations or paraphrases. Finally, it demonstrates how to cite bibliographic references.

The Sunday Post (Bangkok, Thailand 18/2/96) carried a feature article entitled 'Cheating to Get Master's Degree' in which it investigated methods by which students receive help in writing their theses. It concluded by looking at the lack of understanding of the role of footnotes and quotations in academic papers. A professor commented, 'We should tell students about the importance of original academic work so people who copy others' academic work will be ashamed of themselves.'

6.3.3 Academic conventions (UK)

ACADEMIC HIERARCHY

If care is not taken, confusion can be caused at the outset even by seemingly trivial matters, for example a lack of understanding of the titles of the academic staff. The ones commonly used in British universities are, in descending order: professor, reader, senior lecturer/tutor, lecturer/tutor; plus supervisor, who may be any one of these. Many postgraduate students seem to assume either that academic titles are the same as in their own country (suitably translated), or are the same, for example, in the UK, USA, Canada, Australia, New Zealand, etc. Ballard and Clanchy (1984) sensibly include appendices giving information about degrees and academic titles in Britain, the USA and Canada.

The title 'professor' is one that probably causes the most confusion. In Britain, it is used only for the highest grade of university teacher who 'holds a chair' in a subject; heads of department are usually professors. In many other countries, including the USA and Canada, it is used to mean a university teacher: thus, there may be grades of professor, e.g. full professor, associate professor, assistant professor, etc.

The confusion, and resulting embarrassment, is confirmed by a small-scale survey I undertook in the summer of 1993 among postgraduate students from all over the world who were attending an EAP course at Manchester University. Some of the results were:

- 45 per cent were not confident that they understood the meanings of the different academic titles;
- 50 per cent were not certain which title and name to use when meeting staff.

ACADEMIC BEHAVIOUR

If you consider in detail the routines and behaviour of academic life (combined with its norms and expectations), you will realise that there is a formidable list of conventions that NS take for granted but which may be sources of puzzlement, misunderstanding and confusion for NNS. Such a list can be created for any academic environment and then compared with others. The list given below gives some examples for the UK; it is far from exhaustive.

a) If a student is late for a seminar/tutorial, an apology is normally expected (often with a reason given for the lateness); this infers that punctuality is expected (at all times).

b) If a student is late for a lecture, a quiet entry with the minimum of disturbance is expected (an apology is not usual).

c) While a lecturer or teacher is speaking, students are expected to listen and not talk among themselves (unless asked to do so).

d) Lecturers often speak informally, with digressions and asides, including extraneous cultural references and jokes (this aspect is noted in Flowerdew 1994).

e) Libraries are quiet places for private study; conversation is not expected inside and is not welcome.

f) Staff are normally available/accessible for making appointments to meet, etc.

g) Appointments are normally necessary to discuss research/studies, etc.; staff are not often free at a moment's notice for an impromptu/ ad hoc meeting, especially if it is likely to be lengthy.

h) If a student knows in advance that an appointment cannot be kept, he/she should inform the supervisor/tutor accordingly and make another appointment.

i) If teachers/ lecturers have their office doors slightly ajar, it can mean they are 'in' and possibly available to casual callers; conversely, a closed door can mean 'not in' (but not necessarily). Different cultural conventions and attitudes regarding open/closed doors are discussed by Kramsch (1993). Students should be aware that it is quite in order to knock on a closed door to see if an occupant is available.

j) If a student is making a presentation in a seminar group, it is considered common courtesy to listen in silence (other students should not talk among themselves); it is also polite to try to join in any ensuing discussion or to ask questions. It is also considered impolite to pick up papers noisily, sort through books, pack bags, etc. while another student or the teacher is talking.

k) Essays usually have to be handed in to the teachers/tutors by a set date (and, perhaps, time); it is considered important that they are handed in punctually (this is usually strictly observed for assessed essays).

l) If a student is being interviewed for a course, etc., it is not normally expected nor wanted that the student should proffer original copies of all qualifications/certificates/references/ translations at the beginning of (or during) the interview (unless specifically asked to provide them). If these are wanted, they will normally be checked before or after – and notice will be given.

m) There are polite conventions for addressing staff: these will vary considerably, depending on the attitudes of the institution and individual members of staff. It may be formal – expecting titles, etc. to be used – or informal – expecting first names to be used. What is not acceptable is a mixture of the two, so that a title is used with a first name, e.g. 'Mr Bob' is wrong! Many overseas students have difficulty in using first names appropriately, and often feel embarrassed at doing so.

It will be clear from all the above that there are several implications for EAP teachers. They include:

a) the need to state explicitly, and explain, aims and expectations;
b) the importance of appropriate and adequate information;
c) the usefulness of awareness-raising activities;
d) the need to be aware of one's own cultural norms (both students and teachers);
e) the fruitfulness of discussing comparisons (both similarities and differences) in cultural norms.

6.4 General culture

From the moment that students arrive in the English-speaking community, they find that the cultural norms of that society pervade all aspects of their life and impinge on their studies in a variety of ways. Their first weeks in the country, perhaps attending a pre-sessional EAP course, are spent in acclimatising and adjusting to their new way of life.

In 1988 Underhill (1991) conducted a 'culture shock' survey of 350 foreign students at private language schools in Britain. Their most serious problems, in rank order (1 = the most serious problem) were:

1. food and eating habits
2. English language not good enough on arrival
3. difficulty in making friends
4. British attitude to foreigners
5. official procedures
6. polite language
7. travel by public transport
8. pub and café culture
9. daily schedule
10. life in the host family
11. teaching methods

Students attending EAP courses at British universities often add other problems to those listed above. These include: homesickness, loneliness, separation from family and friends, accommodation problems, colder/ wetter weather, different relationships between people, different customs and attitudes (towards women, children, the elderly, the family unit, religion, etc.).

Although culture shock can have its positive side, for example, excitement caused by the prospect of something new and interesting, its negative aspects are the causes of concern. These may involve feelings of discomfort, sadness, uncertainty, insecurity, anxiety, frustration, fear, hostility, often linked with incomprehension and false expectations, leading to a feeling of 'not belonging' coupled with a sense of loss of what is familiar. A clear and useful appraisal of culture and cultural studies is contained in Lavery (1993).

The problem for many students is that they have no experience or knowledge of the way of life before commencing their EAP course, unless it is obtained from stereotyped portrayals of people in their school textbooks. Some students, however, may be better informed through TV and the media generally.

EAP teachers who are interested in making a comparison of models that have been proposed for the analysis of culture are recommended to read Hughes (1986). Such models 'offer an opportunity for culture study to proceed in a systematic, comparative and comprehensive manner'. Cultural goals can be established and may be divided into four categories (Valette 1986):

> developing a greater awareness of and a broader knowledge about the target culture; acquiring a command of the etiquette of the target culture; understanding differences between the target culture and the students' culture; and understanding the values of the target culture.

One model of cultural analysis (by Nelson Brooks) examined in Hughes (1986), involves the asking of key questions, divided into two categories: those that highlight the individual (or psychological) aspects of culture, and those that are of an institutional kind. Examples of the former deal with needs, motives, desires and purposes, e.g. How do you tell right from wrong? How do you treat a guest? How do you view the opposite sex? What are you superstitious about? Examples of the latter involve ideas, beliefs, customs and forms of organisation, e.g. Under what system of government do you live? What is the money system you use? How do you get from place to place? Hughes also looks at some techniques for teaching cultural awareness.

In fact, it is the raising of cultural awareness that will be the focus of what follows. This seems to be one of the most useful functions that teachers can perform on an EAP course: helping students to come to terms with realities.

6.4.1   Techniques for raising cultural awareness

a) *Newspapers*: these are a good source of cultural information; local papers will give more of a flavour of everyday life in towns. Aspects of culture revealed in newspapers are discussed by Blatchford (1986). Grundy (1993a) contains over 100 activities which make use of newspapers; some of the exercises, if adapted, would be suitable for use with *TV* (e.g. news broadcasts).

b) *Video*: a number of published ELT video tapes are a good visual source of cultural information.

c) *Talks/discussions*: some topics may be suitable for giving information to students in a plenary session, perhaps prior to having a discussion; others may be more suitable for group discussion and comparison. Some examples of possible topics are:
 – culture shock (including psychological, emotional, social and health aspects)
 – taboo subjects/language
 – the use of euphemisms
 – politeness in language and in gestures
 – body language
 – naming systems
 – hospitality customs
 – religious festivals
A useful list of topics and questions is contained in Brooks (1986).

d) *Role play/dramatisations*: these can be used to initiate discussion and introspection, and can be acted out by ethnic groups, e.g. different modes of greeting and reactions to those greetings. Archer (1986) uses 'culture bumps' as the basis for her role plays:

> 'A culture bump occurs when an individual from one culture finds himself or herself in a different, strange or uncomfortable situation when interacting with persons of a different culture ... [it] occurs when an individual has expectations of one behavior and gets something completely different'.

e) *Culture quizzes/tests*: an increased cultural awareness about the target culture can often be stimulated by means of a quiz (perhaps a test, e.g. Valette 1986). Bowers (1992) gives an example of a culture quiz, divided into four parts representing the different sources of culture: *memories* (the substance of group recall, e.g. What were the names of the Beatles?); *metaphors* (shared perceptions, e.g. What does it mean to say that an Englishman's home is his castle?); *maxims* (implicit and explicit guides to behaviour, e.g. Whose rule is this – that the customer is always right?); and *myths* (viz. literary, religious, historical heritage, etc., e.g. Can you identify the pairs? Romeo and ..., Jack and ..., David and ...).

A suitably devised quiz can be an instrument to encourage the exploration of the local environment and thus meet aspects of the local culture in a fairly short time. An added bonus is that pressure is put on the students to communicate with local people. A time limit can be set (e.g. a half-day, a day, a weekend) for pairs of students to find the answers in a *local orientation quiz.* Questions might cover the following areas:
– location of certain public buildings/services/amenities
– opening and closing times
– prices of admission (reductions for students?)
– bus numbers for travel from A to B
– certain telephone numbers
– coach/train timetables
– meaning of some public signs
– shopping: where to buy certain items

6.5 British studies

The increasing interest in British studies (or American, Canadian, Australian studies) is linked with the move towards more content-based (text/project-based) ELT. It involves an inter-disciplinary approach, drawing upon various strands, such as literature, history, social sciences, economics, politics, the arts, etc. Its presentation in EAP courses is sometimes connected with international issues or a contrastive approach, in which there is a mixture of information giving and discussion. Under its older name of 'British life and institutions' it was noted in Chapter 4 as a choice for content on EAP courses. Fanning (1993) has discussed its inclusion in EAP courses as an aid in providing cultural background.
   Examples of topics include the following:

- the system and institutions of: central and local government, political parties, law, education
- the economy, agriculture, industry, banking and finance
- religion
- national holidays and festivals
- the arts
- sport
- daily life: work, eating, leisure
- family life

The British Council has produced an invaluable annotated bibliography, *British Studies,* available from its office in Manchester (Bibliographic Services Section). The British Council in London publishes a free international newsletter, *British Studies Now* (available from the Literature Department). In addition, the Central Office of Information in

London produces useful reference material: *Britain: An Official Hand-book* and *Aspects of Britain* (both sold by HMSO).

6.6 Conclusion

It will be clear from the foregoing that the more that students' awareness can be raised about the academic and general culture surrounding them, the better they will be able to cope with their studies and to join in student life. To this end, EAP courses usually include socio-cultural components. A summary of some of these is included in Figure 16.

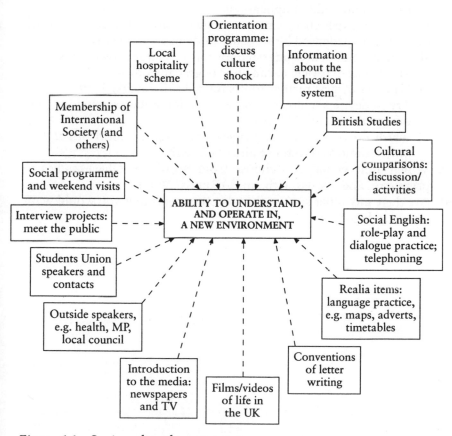

SOCIO-CULTURAL COMPONENTS IN AN EAP COURSE (UK)

Figure 16   Socio-cultural components

6.7 Introspect and discuss

1. What kind of learning style do you think you utilise? Have you always had the same approach?
2. Have you ever taken part in any form of learner training? If so, what form did it take?
3. Which main academic cultural differences (compared with those in the UK, the USA, etc.) have you noted from any country you have lived/worked in?
4. What kinds of plagiarism have you observed while teaching? Has the plagiarism been intentional or unintentional?
5. A list of examples a) – m) is given for academic behaviour and conventions in UK universities. Can you add to the list? How do they differ from those in a country you are familiar with?
6. At the end of the section on academic culture, five implications for EAP teachers of the differences in academic culture are listed. Can you suggest any other implications?
7. From your experience, can you suggest any other culture shock difficulties experienced by students studying in another country?
8. Several techniques are suggested for raising cultural awareness.
   a) From your experience, can you suggest any others?
   b) Can you suggest further topics for talks/discussions?
   c) Try to devise a 'culture quiz' suitable for students going to study on a tertiary-level EAP course.
   d) which areas would you suggest covering in a *local orientation quiz* – additional to those already listed?
9. Which topic would you choose from British (or other) studies to present to, and discuss with, an EAP class? Why?
10. Are there any other socio-cultural components that you would want to add to Figure 16?

7 Methodology and materials

The methodology appropriate to EAP is dependent upon that of ESP in general, of which it is a branch. Thus, the closely linked and inter-weaving strands of functional syllabus, communicative and learning-centred approaches, and authenticity, relevancy and appropriacy in language and materials, are all relevant to EAP. Much has been written about these various facets: a selection of the views with their different emphases will be considered below. We shall then try to draw together the threads into a coherent whole.

A useful summary and critical analysis of language teaching methods generally is provided by Nunan (1991) and Richards and Rodgers (1986). References to materials in this chapter will only be in general. Specific study skills and examples from published books will be looked at in Chapters 9–15.

7.1 Methodological principles

Phillips (1981) proposed that the Language for Special/Specific Purpose (LSP) course must set the student various tasks, and that these tasks 'must reflect the structural characteristics of the learner's special purpose' and must be as integrated as possible and not divided into minute, discrete elements. Within the context of EAP this could mean, for example, a set of lectures or a series of seminars. Acceptance of this approach entails the adoption of four essential principles:

1. *reality control*: 'control of the difficulty of the task demanded of the LSP student is exercised by means of the procedures of simplification appropriate to the field of activity constituting his or her special purpose';
2. *nontriviality*: 'the learning tasks required of the student must be ... perceived by the student as meaningfully generated by his or her special purpose';
3. *authenticity*: 'the language that the student acquires through fol-lowing the LSP course ... must be the language naturally generated by his or her special purpose';
4. *tolerance of error*: 'errors of content and of formal adequacy are to

be judged as unacceptable only to the extent that they entail errors of communicative adequacy'.

7.2 Principles of learning

To Phillips's four methodological principles may be added Hutchinson's (1988) nine fundamental principles of learning, which 'can provide a reasoned basis for the interpretation of ESP language needs into an effective ESP methodology':

1. Learning is development.
2. Learning is a thinking process (i.e. cognitive).
3. Learning is an active process.
4. Learning involves making decisions.
5. Learning a language is not just a matter of linguistic knowledge.
6. Second language learners are already communicatively competent.
7. Learning is an emotional experience (i.e. affective).
8. Learning is not systematic.
9. Learning needs should be considered at every stage of the learning process.

Hutchinson enlarges on each of the nine principles and, for teachers, his seventh principle of learning ('an emotional experience') is of particular interest:

> The good teacher will try to minimise the negative effects of the learner's emotional reactions to learning and will instead try to boost the positive emotions. This might involve:
> – using *pair* and *group* work to minimise the stress of speaking in front of the whole class;
> – structuring tasks so as to enable learners to show what they *do* know rather than what they *do not*;
> – giving learners time to think and work out answers;
> – putting more emphasis on the process of getting the answer rather than the product of the right answer;
> – making interest, fun and variety primary considerations in the design of tasks and activities, not just an added bonus.

Finally, motivation 'indicates the inseparability of the cognitive and affective sides of the learner' as it is initiated by the learner first wanting to think about learning something.

Hutchinson and Waters (1987) list a number of techniques that can be applied to lessons in order to put into practice Hutchinson's nine fundamental principles. They are: gaps, variety, prediction, enjoyment, an integrated methodology, coherence, preparation, involvement, creativity and atmosphere in the classroom.

7.3 Principles of communicative methodology

Morrow (1981) is 'interested in ideas that might help us to see that our students can use the language they learn in order to communicate'. To this end he espouses five principles of communicative methodology:

1. *Know what you are doing.*
   'Every lesson should end with the learner being able to see clearly that he can do something which he could not do at the beginning – and that the 'something' is communicatively useful';
2. *The whole is more than the sum of the parts.*
   '... a crucial feature of a communicative method will be that it operates with stretches of language above the sentence level, and operates with real language in real situations';
3. *The processes are as important as the forms.*
   The aim is to replicate as far as possible the processes of communication. Two of these processes are as follows:
   1 *Information gap*: the purpose of communication in real life is to bridge this gap. The 'concept of information gap seems to be one of the most fundamental in the whole area of communicative teaching';
   2 *Choice*: 'another crucial characteristic of communication is that the participants have choice, both in terms of what they will say and, more particularly, how they will say it ... Deciding on these under the severe time pressure which language use involves is one of the main problems which foreign users of a language face';
4. *To learn it, do it.*
   Although the teacher can help, advise and teach, only the learners can learn: they must, therefore, become involved in the activities and learn by doing;
5. *Mistakes are not always a mistake.*
   With the aim of developing the communicative ability of the students, it may be necessary to be flexible enough to treat different things as 'mistakes' at different stages in the learning process; in other words, not every error should be corrected.

To the process or technique of 'information gap', Hutchinson and Waters (1987) have added other types of 'gap': media, reasoning, memory, jigsaw, opinion and certainty.

7.4 Communicative activities

The emphasis above has been on communication and ways of achieving and practising it. Johnson (1982) adds to this:

fluency in communicative process can only develop with a 'task-orientated teaching' – one which provides 'actual meaning' by focusing on tasks to be mediated through language.

The focus is thus 'on the ability to understand and convey information content'.

Littlewood (1981) discusses the purposes of communicative activities and their contribution to language learning:

1. they provide 'whole-task practice', i.e. the total skill;
2. they improve motivation;
3. they allow natural learning;
4. they can create a context which supports learning.

The activities can be divided into those that use language to share information (e.g. often in small groups and with a 'game' element), and those that process information (e.g. to discuss it or evaluate it; an example is 'jumbled sequence' activities). In addition, the activities are usually learner-directed and often involve pair and small group work.

Johnson (1982) proposes five principles for a communicative exercise typology which are, in essence, based on problem-solving and task-orientation. He illustrates these with several examples:

1. *information transfer* (e.g. reading information to extract data in order to fill in a form);
2. *information gap* (e.g. information is known by only one student in a pair and it can be conveyed by different exercises to the other student);
3. *jigsaw* (an example of co-operative learning in which each member of a small group has a piece of information needed to complete a group task; perhaps the best-known published example of this is *Listening Links* by Geddes and Sturtridge, Heinemann 1979);
4. *task dependency* (the principle by which a second task can only be done if the first task has been successfully completed, e.g. listening to, or reading, something and then using the information to produce something, e.g. a report (oral or written);
5. *correction for content* (the principle argues that 'at some stage the student's language production should be judged on its communicative efficacy in relation to a specific task'; an example of this is the pair work technique 'Describe and Draw', in which one student describes an illustration, diagram, etc. to his/her partner and the partner tries to reproduce the item from the description and questioning; see Chapter 13 for an example).

In discussing ESP exercise typology, Coffey (1984) maintains that the main consideration:

must be that of authenticity. All ESP work is in essence a simulation of a real-life task ... Serendipity is therefore one of the main virtues required [of the ESP writer]: the ability to find an authentic text that will fit pedagogic needs.

Coffey attaches importance also to role-play, self-directed learning, and team-teaching (see below).

7.5 Authenticity

Authenticity of language has been referred to by Phillips and Coffey above. It has also been discussed by a number of other writers to whom you are referred for the detailed arguments that surround the subject (e.g. Wilkins 1976; Morrow 1977; Phillips and Shettlesworth 1978; Widdowson 1979; McDonough 1984; Kennedy and Bolitho 1984; Breen 1985; Hutchinson and Waters 1987; Robinson 1980 and 1991; Kramsch 1993; and Clarke 1989 in particular for a very detailed discussion and bibliography).

McDonough (1984) has listed a number of terms that are used with regard to authenticity – 'genuine', 'authentic', 'real', 'natural', 'scripted', 'contrived', 'semi-authentic', 'semi-scripted', 'simulated', 'simulated-authentic'. Clearly there are 'gradations' or different degrees of authenticity of language. However, the issue is not simply one of authenticity of 'language data', but of purpose or task, and from the writer's/speaker's point of view, and from the reader's/listener's. Possibly one solution is to view authenticity from at least four angles – authenticity of: language input, task, event and learner experience (Maley, in Fried-Booth 1986).

Essentially, there are two points at issue. Firstly, what exactly do we mean by an 'authentic text'? Secondly, should only authentic texts be used in the ESP/EAP classroom? There are no easy answers to these questions: discussion has raged backwards and forwards since the 1970s.

In the most straightforward interpretation, one can say that an authentic text will be that which is normally used in the students' specialist subject area: written by specialists for specialists. It is not written for language teaching purposes. Using an authentic text (or speech recording) in a classroom does pose certain problems and raise certain questions. As the text has been removed from its original context, are you certain that the language learning context is appropriate? Is the topic, purpose and language level appropriate and relevant for the students? Why do you really want to use the text? What do you hope the students will gain from it? Depending on the answers to these questions, it may be preferable to use an adapted text or a specially written one (as long as you can ascertain that it is suitable for the students).

My own feeling is that there is nothing intrinsically wrong with non-authentic texts, especially in the earlier stages of language learning: it depends on the pedagogic purpose in using the texts. However, as soon as students can cope with texts from their own subject area, they should have the opportunity of reading (listening to) them. This presupposes that there is a clearly-defined and appropriate purpose – communicative and pedagogic – combined with a meaningful context, and that information gap and task-dependency principles can be adhered to.

Lee (1995) distinguishes between *text authenticity* and *learner authenticity*, building upon Widdowson's (1979) similar distinction. However, she stresses the need for learners to have positive perceptions about the materials they are using. Lee describes and discusses the positive reactions of students in Hong Kong to their involvement in a variety of tasks based upon newspaper articles, selected according to topics of relevance and interest: role-play activities, report writing, projects and short oral presentations.

Wong, Kwok and Choi (1995) also discuss the use of authentic materials at tertiary level on EAP/ESP courses in Hong Kong. They refer to the use of company reports, journals, magazines, TV programmes and newspaper articles. They illustrate their approach by reference to a newspaper article on vegetarian diets which was used as the basis for a number of discussion and writing activities. Thus 'authentic materials can serve as a bridge between the classroom and the outside world'.

Obtaining examples of authentic spoken language can sometimes be a problem in NNS situations. One way to overcome this, and to provide realistic listening practice for students, is to set up a small radio station on campus. Varieties of NS accents can be recorded (e.g. British, American, Canadian, Australian, etc.), and the programmes and news broadcasts can supplement classroom teaching. A successful experiment in Shanghai is described by Yu (1995).

7.6 Case studies, role-play and simulations

Huckin (1988) stresses authenticity or realism in language teaching and, in addition to problem-solving and team-teaching, cites *case studies* as being an appropriate means of reproducing the 'real world', as they can contain a 'realistic, complex, ill-defined problem that has many possible solutions, none of them ideal' – a suitable activity for group work. Huckin stresses the value of case studies in providing an opportunity for students to form sound arguments and engage in persuasive communication; this entails what he terms *higher-order reasoning*. The real benefit is that:

> the student is placed in a situation where his linguistic needs exceed his linguistic resources. He is thus driven to seek help from the language teacher and, which is perhaps even more important for the development of communicative competence, to develop strategems that allow him to engage in communication despite linguistic shortcomings.

Role-play (i.e. students act the parts of different participants in a situation) is differentiated from *simulations* (in which students are themselves in a problem-solving situation). McDonough (1984) looks at the potential of simulations (see also Sturtridge 1977) and, in the context of EAP, finds the academic seminar or tutorial an obvious stimulus. To this one could add lectures, and use of the academic library. She also looks at the part played by pairs and small groups in the problem-solving methodology and stresses that the need is for the 'negotiated settlement rather than the imposed solution'.

Maley (1981) sounds a note of caution regarding the choice of activity for problem-solving. One important criterion is the proportion of *input* (text, visuals, instructions, apparatus, etc.) to *output* (the learning that takes place) involved in a given activity. The best activity is one that involves a low input and a high output.

Many of the communicative activities referred to involve argumentation between students in pairs or small groups. Sometimes the activities highlight differences of opinion between students; some take on the character of games or competitions and spotlight individual students. If these activities are overplayed, the effect may be to disturb feelings of group unity. As a counterbalance to the 'competitive' activities, Hadfield (1992) has proposed a whole range of activities to help develop a positive group 'atmosphere' in which the group can jell. The variety encompasses activities aimed at forming the group ('breaking the ice; thinking about language'), maintaining the group ('opinion- and value-bridging; confidence-building'), and ending the group experience ('positive feelings; evaluating').

McDonough (1984) notes that:

> within any group of learners, there will be a greater or less differential of:
> – pace of learning;
> – amount of target language already known;
> – subject/professional knowledge;
> – type of subject or profession;
> – status;
> – time available for language learning;

  - motivation and interests;
  - expectations of language learning.
  All these factors ... suggest that some degree of individualisation
  and relevance is necessary.

7.7   Individualisation and autonomy

Several authors have discussed the need for varying degrees of individualised learning and learner autonomy (e.g. Brookes and Grundy
1988; McDonough and Shaw 1993). In a nutshell, the main reason for
advocating learner autonomy is that students on short EAP courses (in
the UK, etc.) need to be able to continue their EAP learning without EAP
teachers after they have moved on to their specialist studies. They will
only be able to do this if they have been helped to do so while on the
EAP course (Kennedy and Bolitho 1984).

The means of developing learner autonomy or independent learning
are discussed in detail by Dickinson (1987). He uses the blanket term
self-instruction to cover a number of situations in which students work
'without the direct control of a teacher'. As Dickinson points out,
unfortunately, the same label may be used by different writers to mean
rather different things. Here we shall only note the main labels that are
used:

  - *individualised instruction* (methods and materials adapted for an
    individual);
  - *self-direction* (the learner makes decisions but does not necessarily
    implement them);
  - *self-access materials and learning* (appropriate materials for self-
    instruction);
  - *autonomy* (the learner is totally responsible for decisions and their
    implementation).

See also Dickinson and Wenden (1995), who edit a special collection of
articles on autonomy, self-direction and self-access in language teaching
and learning.

Linked with the above are *self-access centres, self-assessment,* and
distance learning. All are discussed at length, with extensive bibliographies, by Sheerin (1991) and Hill (1994). Self-access systems are discussed
in Little (1989; 1993). See also Appendix 2.2.

Distance learning, in the context of EAP/ESP, is discussed by Boyle
(1993) from his experience at the Asian Institute of Technology (AIT),
Bangkok. He cites cases where Asian students cannot attain the required
level of language proficiency in their own country, nor attend a pre-
sessional course. Yet they need to be able to follow lecture courses in

English at postgraduate level on arrival at AIT. One way to provide the necessary language preparation is by means of a distance learning listening package for the students to work on for up to three months before arrival. The package consists of specimen lectures (20–30 minutes) in their own subject area on audio-cassette, together with lecture instructions, visual aids, transcriptions, note-taking outlines and answer keys to the comprehension, note-taking and other exercises.

On an EAP course there are practical ways in which independent learning can be encouraged and developed: the longer the course, the more time there is to phase in the following. Possibilities for implementation are:

- negotiated elements in the syllabus;
- optional periods in the timetable (making choices);
- private study periods;
- one-to-one tutorials;
- personal projects;
- pair work/small group tasks/assignments;
- banks of self-access materials with keys (e.g. grammar, reading comprehension);
- self-monitoring in a language laboratory or on a computer;
- ESAP audio-tapes and video-cassettes: lectures/seminars – choices; self-access.

An example of learner autonomy being successfully developed on an EAP course in New Zealand is given in Cotterall (1995). Another viewpoint is put by Jones (1995) who discusses the establishment of a self-access centre at a university in Cambodia. He highlights the importance of being culturally sensitive to societies' different ways of learning. Learner autonomy comes 'laden with Western values' and needs to be adapted for different cultures. He then describes how the self-access centre can be used collaboratively and in groups, and the role of the teacher in this situation.

Movements towards independent learning require awareness-raising and learner training. These are looked at next.

7.8   Awareness-raising and learner training

In a thought-provoking article, Waters and Waters (1992) question the starting point for many EAP courses. It:

> needs to be the development of the learner's underlying study
> competence ... building up the cognitive and affective capacity of
> the learner for study.

They pose the question 'What does a successful student do that a less successful student does not do?' They answer it by reflecting on their own experience and comparing it with colleagues. They conclude that successful students typically:

- have a high degree of self-awareness;
- are good at critical questioning;
- tend to have an 'adult' approach to relations with their teachers;
- think clearly and logically;
- are self-confident;
- impose their own framework on study data;
- have a positive attitude to their studies;
- are willing and able to teach themselves;
- are intelligent, etc.

In other words, a successful student is 'a mature, balanced individual, possessing an open, questioning mind, and willing to adopt an active, independent approach to study'.

McDonough and Shaw (1993) report on research into the characteristics of good language learners. Among others, they include:

- understanding the organisation and function of language;
- evaluating progress;
- realising that hard work is involved;
- involving themselves actively in the target language;
- willing to experiment and practise;
- organising time and materials effectively.

In addition, other learner variables include: aptitude, motivation and personality. The notion of a good language learner is also examined by Rubin and Thompson (1983).

Bearing in mind the characteristics of successful students, Waters and Waters (1995) devised practice material that would attempt to encourage the development of these aspects. Students would then be in a better position to benefit from specific study skills materials. An example of the tasks is given below. Their book contains many activities to encourage students to think and discuss, and to take notes of answers, present their ideas clearly and logically and keep records of their progress.

The first ability of a successful student that was listed by Waters and Waters was self-awareness. Gibbs (1981) devised some exercises to help British mother-tongue students to learn. Basically, these are exercises designed to encourage students to discuss among themselves, comparing their experiences and thinking about their reasons for doing what they do. The purpose is to increase both self-awareness and self-confidence. Gibbs' approach is exemplified by an exercise on taking notes. Before the exercise, he explains in some detail to the tutor how to set up the session and what to say to the students. Suitably adapted, this kind of activity seems extremely relevant to the non-native speaker (see the example in Appendix 1.1).

Unit 1   How do I learn?

Task 2.1

Everyone is successful at some activities and less successful at others. Sometimes students do well in a subject one year but are less successful the next year. Other students may always do well in one subject but be very weak in another.

Think about any two things you have learnt successfully, and any two things you feel you have not learnt as successfully as you would have liked. Copy the table that follows into your notebook and complete it.

What did you learn successfully?	How did you learn it?	How did you know you were successful?	Why were you successful?	How did it make you feel?
1. 2.	1. 2.	1. 2.	1. 2.	1. 2.
What did you not learn successfully?	How did you try to learn it?	How did you know you failed?	Why did you fail?	How did it make you feel?
1. 2.	1. 2.	1. 2.	1. 2.	1. 2.

Task 2.2

The answers to these questions tell us a lot about how we learn. If we put all the answers together, we can form a picture of what usually leads to successful learning.

Compare your answers with those of two or three other students.
1 What contributed to the group's successes?
2 What contributed to the group's failures?
3 What are the general similarities in the answers?
4 Are there any major differences?

(From Waters 1995)

The raising of students' self-awareness of their learning styles and various methods of learning can be incorporated more systematically into a course under the heading of 'learner training'. This was referred to

119

in the last chapter in the context of learning styles and strategies. The purpose is to help the students to consider factors which may affect their language learning, and to enable them to become more effective and independent learners of English. The means employed are usually self-questioning, and activities involving discussion and sharing experiences with other students. Ellis and Sinclair (1989) have adopted this approach: their book covers the four traditional language skills together with grammar and vocabulary, and is intended to train students in the skills needed to learn English. Learner training is also addressed by Dickinson (1992).

As our students will probably have different learning strategies, it seems an excellent idea for them to discuss and compare methods of learning and to be aware of alternatives. It is also essential to remember that for the vast majority of students studying EAP, the language is a tool to be used with other subjects; it is not an end in itself. Consequently, motivation is important, especially for students who have learned English previously, perhaps imperfectly, and are often referred to as 'false beginners'. Motivation is often increased or improved by initial awareness-raising discussion activities.

An example of a straightforward initial self-awareness activity for study skills is given below. After students have completed it individually, they can compare and discuss with a partner. The tutor can then make a list involving the whole class.

A final example of an activity which can be used successfully for awareness-raising, and helping to develop self-confidence in talking in pairs and small groups, is a *'pyramid discussion'* (see Jordan 1990b for

STUDY SKILLS WORKSHOP

You have just registered for an eight-week pre-session English course. You will remember from the pre-session English course brochure that the main aim of the course is to: 'develop your ability to use English for study purposes at university level'. What do you think this will involve? In other words, what situations/activities do you expect the course to prepare you for? What study skills does each of these require?

Note down your thoughts using the table below.

Situation/activity	Study skills

Figure 17   Study skills: self-awareness table

research findings). This is described in Chapter 13, with further examples given in Chapter 17.

7.9   Team-teaching

Mention was made above of the desirability of team-teaching in the context of authenticity and, one could add, credibility. Team-teaching – the joint teaching, or sharing of teaching, by both the subject specialist and the English tutor – has added another dimension to the teaching of ESP/ESAP since the late 1970s. The specialists act as informants on what goes on in the subject discipline. This aspect is highly relevant to genre analysis, which is examined in Chapters 16 and 17. Although such joint ventures can be time-consuming, the benefits are shared by the tutors and the students.

There is an additional benefit: the students see that their subject tutors take the EAP/ESAP classes seriously. This can only be advantageous. Experiments in team-teaching, methods and materials, are well-documented (for example, see Dudley-Evans and Johns 1981; Dudley-Evans 1984a; Henderson and Skehan 1980; Johns and Dudley-Evans 1980; Skehan 1980).

A good example of collaboration between EAP and subject staff in civil engineering is contained in Gee *et al.* (1984). This account focuses on the writing of technical reports, essays, and essay-type exam answers, and discusses language support for the organisation and presentation of talks. The comment of the editor (Williams) on the paper summarises the essential elements needed for successful team-teaching:

- willingness to collaborate on the part of both sets of staff;
- clear demarcation as to where their respective responsibilities lie;
- awareness of each other's conceptual apparatus and teaching approach;
- the joint effort being viewed by the student as a complementary teaching situation.

It should be realised that it is not easy to set up team-teaching: there can be a number of very real obstacles, not the least of which may be a reluctance on the part of the subject department, for various reasons. However, other forms of useful co-operation with the department may be possible, even though they fall short of team-teaching. For example, tutors in the subject department may be willing to provide specimens of texts, vet materials that are produced, record short talks on audio- or video-cassette for use in a language laboratory or resource centre, give guest lectures on a course and so on. These are all very worthwhile and help to provide a link between subject and EAP tutors.

7.10 The role of the teacher

The role of the teacher will vary according to the type of syllabus and course, and which part of the world it takes place in. At one extreme, a full teacher-directed course will require a large direct input of teaching. At the other end of the spectrum, a fully learner-centred course or totally self-access course, will require managerial skills in addition to helping students to learn. This will be particularly so if you have to run a resource centre. A comprehensive discussion of the teacher's role in the learner-centred approach is contained in Tudor (1993). Most courses, however, are in between these extremes, with a mixture of direct teaching, managing pair and group work, and assisting students to learn by means of a variety of resources.

Robinson (1991) suggests that:

> the key quality needed by the ESP teacher is flexibility: the flexibility to change from being a general language teacher to being a specific purpose teacher, and the flexibility to cope with different groups of students, often at very short notice.

Jarvis (1983) encapsulated the overall *abilities needed* by an ESP teacher:

1. Analyse SP language and situations;
2. Evaluate textbooks and other sources;
3. Evaluate learner attainment;
4. Devise performance objectives for learners;
5. Design or interpret syllabuses;
6. Design or interpret schemes for work;
7. Devise teaching and learning strategies;
8. Devise individual but interrelated teaching/learning sessions;
9. Produce materials;
10. Organise teaching/learning sessions;
11. Assess achievement of objectives.

Kennedy and Bolitho (1984) also made a list of the 'likely requirements' of an ESP teacher:

- develop a working knowledge of the students' subject, for example, via team-teaching;
- deal with the pastoral problems of students a long way from homes and families;
- forge links with the institutions which the students will proceed to; and, sometimes, prepare the students for specific entry requirements of English language exams.

In the context of exploring the teacher's role, it is relevant to note problems that teachers have experienced. Johns, T. F. (1981) made an analysis of questionnaires from about 100 EAP teachers from all over the world. The problems, in rank order of importance, were:

1. Low priority in timetabling;
2. Lack of personal/professional contact with subject teachers;
3. Lower status/grade than subject teachers;
4. Isolation from other teachers of English doing similar work;
5. Lack of respect from students.

Wide-ranging discussions of the role of the ESP teacher are contained in: Robinson (1991), Hutchinson and Waters (1987), McDonough (1984), and Kennedy and Bolitho (1984). The whole issue of *ELT Documents: 112* (1981) is devoted to 'The ESP teacher: role, development and prospects', while *The ESP Journal*, Vol. 2 No. 1 (1983) is a special issue on ESP teacher-training, containing twenty articles.

7.11 Some pedagogical principles

Robinson (1991) stresses that:

> first and foremost, of course, the ESP teacher is a *teacher* and many writers agree that the qualities of good teaching generally, and of language teaching specifically, are also required for ESP.

Nunan (1991) reports on research into the length of time teachers wait for a response after asking a question. Apparently, even after specific training, 'some teachers never managed to extend their wait time beyond one or two seconds' before supplying the answer themselves or asking another student:

> In those classrooms where teachers did manage to extend their wait time from three to five seconds after asking a question, there was more participation by more students.

In particular, the following effects were observed:

1. There was an increase in the average length of student responses.
2. Unsolicited, but appropriate, student responses increased.
3. Failures to respond decreased.
4. There was an increase in speculative responses.
5. There was an increase in student-to-student comparisons of data.
6. Inferential statements increased.
7. Student-initiated questions increased.
8. Students generally made a greater variety of verbal contributions to the lesson.

Another interesting area in which we, as teachers, should question ourselves, is that of teacher talk. In other words, how far and in what ways do we modify/simplify our own speech when we are talking to, or teaching, students? If we are not aware of what we say and how we say it, we surely cannot be aware of the model that we give our students and the effect it has on them. For example, many years ago when I was giving a talk to overseas students on oral contractions and their use (e.g. *I'm, haven't*), a colleague told me afterwards that I did not use one natural contraction in the whole talk!

Chaudron (1988) gives a summary of research on teacher talk in language classrooms and notes the following modifications which occur 'concerning speech to lower-level NNSs':

1. Rates of speech appear to be slower.
2. Pauses, which may be evidence of the speaker planning more, are possibly more frequent and longer.
3. Pronunciation tends to be exaggerated and simplified.
4. Vocabulary use is more basic.
5. Degree of subordination is lower.
6. More declaratives and statements are used than questions.
7. Teachers may self-repeat more frequently.

Nunan (1991) comments that a better strategy for teachers might be:

> to build in redundancy through the use of repetition, paraphrase and rhetorical markers rather than simplifying their grammar and vocabulary.

7.12 Conclusion

It will be realised that although there are numerous views on the methodology appropriate to ESP (and therefore to EGAP and ESAP), nevertheless certain areas are almost always stressed as being of importance: for example, authenticity, problem-solving, communicative activities, learning by doing. It will also be appreciated that within the purview of EAP, not all the various organisational procedures, activities, tasks and exercises are appropriate or possible all the time. However, by having such a range of options available, it makes it possible to provide for a variety of circumstances and learning styles.

A synthesis of the methodological aspects is presented in Figure 18. It is not exhaustive, but covers the main aspects. It should be noted that different writers often use different terminology when discussing activities, tasks, exercises, techniques, etc. Consequently, at times it becomes confusing; it is not always easy, in any case, to make distinctions. Perhaps this is not important. In Figure 18 the intention is that activities may subsume tasks, exercises and techniques, or that exercises may be possible within an activity. It is fully realised that this may not always be the case.

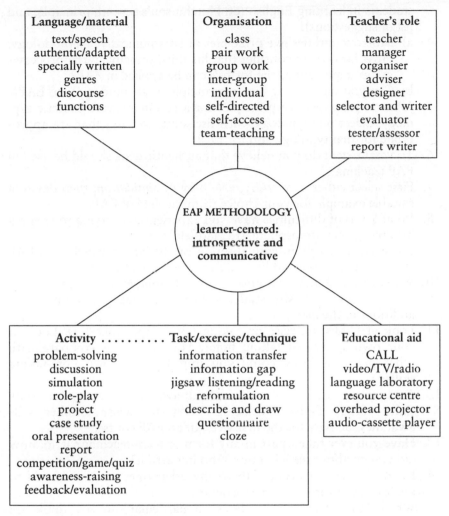

Language/material	Organisation	Teacher's role
text/speech	class	teacher
authentic/adapted	pair work	manager
specially written	group work	organiser
genres	inter-group	adviser
discourse	individual	designer
functions	self-directed	selector and writer
	self-access	evaluator
	team-teaching	tester/assessor
		report writer

EAP METHODOLOGY

learner-centred: introspective and communicative

Activity .... Task/exercise/technique		Educational aid
problem-solving	information transfer	CALL
discussion	information gap	video/TV/radio
simulation	jigsaw listening/reading	language laboratory
role-play	reformulation	resource centre
project	describe and draw	overhead projector
case study	questionnaire	audio-cassette player
oral presentation	cloze	
report		
competition/game/quiz		
awareness-raising		
feedback/evaluation		

Figure 18   EAP methodology

7.13 Introspect and discuss

1. Concerning the methodological principles proposed by Phillips, how important do you regard 'tolerance of error' in an EAP course?
2. Out of Hutchinson's nine fundamental principles of learning, which three would you consider to be the most important for an EAP teacher to remember?
3. Can you suggest any other ways to 'boost the positive emotions' of

     students in learning English (cf. Hutchinson's seventh principle, and list of suggestions)?

4. a) Morrow outlines five principles of communicative methodology. How far do you consider that his third principle ('The processes are as important as the forms') can be applied in EAP?

    b) Can you suggest any further principles that could apply to EAP?

5. Johnson proposes five principles for a communicative exercise typology. Select one typology, then list some exercises that are appropriate for that typology and for EAP.

6. To what extent do you believe that authentic texts should be used in EAP teaching?

7. First select either *case study*, *role-play* or *simulation*, then devise a suitable example for your choice from the field of EAP.

8. What kinds of difficulties have you experienced in trying to create a 'positive group atmosphere' (re Hadfield)?

9. List ways in which individualisation can be implemented in an EAP classroom or course (additional to the list provided).

10. Waters and Waters propose a list of abilities or characteristics possessed by successful students. Can you suggest any important additions to the list?

11. Look at Gibbs' exercise on taking notes (Appendix 1.1). Look at your own system of taking notes. How does this compare with other people's? How could you improve your own note-taking skills?

12. An example is given of an initial self-awareness activity for study skills ('Study Skills Workshop'). Try to devise another self-awareness activity for the first week of an EAP course.

13. Have you ever taken part in any form of team-teaching? If so, how did you go about setting it up? Who initiated it?

14. From your experience, are there any other roles you would add to the lists given for ESP/EAP teachers?

15. Which 'good teaching' qualities, in particular, do you think are most relevant in the EAP classroom?

16. Are you aware of any modifications that you make to your spoken language when teaching? What are they?

17. In Figure 18 an attempt is made to summarise the various aspects of EAP methodology. Are there any other items that you would add to the boxes? In particular, can you think of a clearer way of differentiating between activities, tasks, exercises and techniques? Which criteria would you use? Is it necessary or useful to differentiate in such a way?

8 Evaluating materials

Most courses use a mixture of published books and in-house produced material. Many books start their lives as in-house material, but here we are only concerned with published books – how to choose them. In reality, we may have no choice: the books may be bought by someone else, or they may be inherited. However, at some stage, we may be responsible for buying books, or recommending their purchase, or may be able to choose which to use from existing sets of books. These considerations apply as much to EAP/study skills books as to general ELT books. The following chapters will be looking at examples of study skills books. Our purpose, in this chapter, is to see how we can choose between them.

8.1 Choice of books

How do we, in fact, decide which books to use? What factors influence our choice? Is the decision completely subjective or are there external criteria that can be applied to enable us to make a more principled choice?

Before looking at possible yardsticks for making choices between books, let us first look at the subjective element. What attracts us to a book in the first place? In practice, it may be for a number or combination of reasons: an attractive, well-designed cover; the persuasive publisher's blurb; a list of contents that seems to cover everything that we want; the level seems appropriate for the students; a clearly set out text, and practice material that appears to be user-friendly; informative teacher's notes and key; a colleague recommended it; the size is convenient; the price is right; it is available; and so on.

Robinson (1991) has noted that 'No textbook is likely to be perfect, of course, and practical considerations, such as cost, may have to take precedence over pedagogic merit'. Sheldon (1988) had previously concluded that:

> it is clear that coursebook assessment is fundamentally a subjective, rule-of-thumb activity, and that no neat formula, grid or system will ever provide a definitive yardstick.

However, Sheldon has suggested a general set of criteria that can help to improve the selection process and which we shall look at shortly.

To counterbalance the possibly pessimistic tone conveyed by the above views, we can now turn to what is feasible. To enable us to compare books we can, at the very least, pose a number of questions, or provide a list of headings under which to make comparisons. Our comparison could take the form of a checklist of features, or a grid in which we can note the absence or presence of items. At its simplest level, we can simply note whether or not certain features exist or are covered in the book(s). The next stage could be to attach some value or weighting to the features so that one book will emerge in a more favourable light than the others. This was done, for example, by Hyland (1994) who compared 22 ESP and EAP writing textbooks for the inclusion of modal expressions in the context of 'hedging' (see Chapter 11): lexical verbs, and modal verbs, adverbs, adjectives and nouns. He used a three-point scale: no coverage, minimal coverage and fair-to-extensive coverage.

This points-system or scale could be arrived at by a consensus of a group of teachers: this would help to reduce some of the inevitable subjectivity. It might take the form of a *Which?*-style consumers' report and guide, with star ratings and comments. Some examples are included below to illustrate these different approaches.

8.2 Integrated study skills books: comparative contents

The first example lists, in date order, most of the major integrated study skills books that were available at the time of writing (see Figure 19). The books are integrated in the sense that a number of study skills areas are included in each: they do not focus on one or two skills only.

The various skills that the books might include are listed horizontally and their presence (✓) or absence (−) is noted. Additional aspects are noted in the last four columns. No attempt is made to evaluate the books: their comparative contents are simply noted objectively. This, at least, has the merit of enabling us to see if a book contains what we or our students want.

It can be seen from the table that the majority of the books are skills-based, only two selecting topics as the basis for practising study skills (e.g. Williams: population, resources, food, intermediate technology, pollution, etc., Forman *et al.*: help yourself, arresting stuff, a question of power, ringing the changes, food for thought, etc.). All the books contain a variety of practice in the form of exercises, tasks or activities. When further integrated skills books are published, they can be compared with these by checking their features against the headings in the grid. (Two of the books, those by Yorkey and Romanoff, are more suitable for use in North America.)

1. *Study Skills in English* – M. J. Wallace (1980)
2. *Study Skills for Students of English* – R. C. Yorkey (1982)
3. *Panorama* – R. Williams (1982)
4. *Study Skills for Higher Education* – J. Floyd (1984)
5. *A Study Skills Handbook* – M. and G. Smith (1990)
6. *Campus English* – D. Forman *et al.* (1990)
7. *Language and Study Skills for Learners of English* – M. R. Romanoff (1991)
8. *Learning to Study in English* – J. B. Heaton and D. Dunmore (1992)

The above titles all feature in Figure 19 in the same date order. Other titles that might still be used in some places are: Heaton (1975); Montgomery (1982); Salimbene (1985). These are not included in the table as they are out of print.

INTEGRATED STUDY SKILLS BOOKS

	Author(s)	Organising studies	Using dictionaries	Using a library; ref. skills	Reading efficiency; strategies	Making notes	Listening to lectures
1	Wallace (1980)	✓	–	✓	✓	✓	✓
2	Yorkey (1982)	✓	✓	✓	✓	✓	✓
3	Williams (1982)	–	✓	✓	✓	✓	✓
4	Floyd (1984)	✓	✓	✓	✓	✓	(some)
5	Smith and Smith (1990)	✓	✓	✓	✓	✓	–
6	Forman *et al.* (1990)	–	–	–	✓	✓	✓
7	Romanoff (1991)	✓	✓	✓	✓	✓	✓
8	Heaton and Dunmore (1992)	–	✓	✓	✓	✓	✓

✓ = included
– = not included

Figure 19 *Integrated study skills books* (continued overleaf)

	Writing	Discussion practice	Taking exams	Extra sections	Skills/ topics based	Also included	Level
1	✓	✓	✓	reading speed passages	skills	TCK	I+
2	✓	–	✓	vocabulary	skills	K index	I
3	✓	–	✓	data analysis; grammar revision	topics	TCK	I–A
4	✓	–	✓	reading speed passages	skills	TK index	I+
5	✓	–	✓	–	skills	index	I+
6	✓	✓	–	data analysis; numerous reading passages	topics	TCK	I–A
7	✓	–	✓	vocabulary	skills	K	LI
8	✓	✓	✓	data analysis; using grammar	skills	tapescript	I

KEY TO COLUMNS: *Also included*:
                              T = teacher's book; C = cassette(s); K = key/notes
                              Level:
(all levels are approx.)   LI = lower intermediate; I = intermediate;
                              I+ = intermediate plus; I–A = intermediate to advanced

8.3 Factors to compare

The next step, beyond listing specific content features, is to draw up a list of factors that you would wish to compare and evaluate. Sheldon (1988) has provided what he considers is a:

> summary of common-core factors that reviewers, administrators, teachers, learners and educational advisers most frequently use in deciding whether or not a textbook is chosen.

(Reproduced opposite). He adds a caveat, however:

> no one is really certain what criteria and constraints are actually operative in ELT contexts worldwide, and textbook criteria are emphatically local. Not all the criteria described would be deployed simultaneously, nor is the list definitive.

FACTUAL DETAILS

Title: . . . .
Author(s): . . . .
Publisher: . . . . Price: . . . .
ISBN: . . . . No. of Pages: . . . .
Components: SB/TB/WB/Tests/Cassettes/Video/CALL/Other . . . . .
Level: . . . . Physical size: . . . .
Length: . . . . . Units . . . . . Lessons/sections . . . . . Hours . . . . .
Target skills: . . . .
Target learners: . . . .
Target teachers . . . .

ASSESSMENT (*Poor   **Fair   ***Good   ****Excellent)

Factor	*Rating and comments*
Rationale	
Availability	
User definition	
Layout/graphics	
Accessibility	
Linkage	
Selection/grading	
Physical characteristics	
Appropriacy	
Authenticity	
Sufficiency	
Cultural bias	
Educational validity	
Stimulus/practice/revision	
Flexibility	
Guidance	
Overall value for money	

Textbook evaluation sheet

(Sheldon 1988)

131

8.4 Listening and note-taking

Hamp-Lyons (1983) drew up a list of criteria that she considered important in pre-judging an advanced course in listening and note-taking for possible adoption:

> appropriate level
> quality of tape production
> approximation of real lectures in the delivery
> relevance of content of the lectures to students' needs
> appropriacy of material (esp. culturally)
> course should teach, not only practice, skills
> teach note-taking techniques
> completeness (i.e. takes student from no note-taking ability re
>   lectures, to performative competence in one course)
> quality of text production
> pedagogic accuracy (does not teach what is not true)
> presence of answer key is a minimum
> teacher's book is a definite plus
> model notes (pref. several alternatives)
> transcript
> rationale for the course and method used
> suggestions for classroom activities
> student's book or worksheets
> pre/post tests
> sufficient practice material – this is partly a question of the number
>   of lessons, and partly a question of tape length
> reasonable price (this must be judged in relation to all the preceding
>   features)

Hamp-Lyons then surveyed eight published courses, putting her results into a matrix with scores 1–10 (1 = most negative) for the grading of the features (criteria listed vertically, against book titles listed horizontally). The total scores ranged from 73–165, out of a possible 180. Although such a matrix gives a semblance of objectivity, it is still, as Hamp-Lyons points out 'a personal matrix, using personal criteria on the vertical axis, and personal responses on the horizontal axis'. In other words, someone else might rate the criteria differently, or wish to include different criteria. One merit is that there could be internal consistency for the individual assessor.

8.5 Writing

The next example is taken from Hamp-Lyons and Heasley (1984) who tried out eight advanced level writing textbooks in classes and jointly evaluated them against their set of criteria. They first defined their own view of the process and product of writing as 'a communicative occurrence between a writer and an intended reader'. They then devised a list of seven standards of 'textuality' against which to measure the writing, as follows:

TABLE I: STANDARDS OF TEXTUALITY

Standard	Definition of scope	Possible realizations as syllabus items
1. Text-based		
Cohesion	The ways in which the components of the text are connected within a sequence	pro-forms; tense, aspect and junction; ellipsis, recurrence; lexical substitution
Coherence	The ways in which the configuration of concepts and relations which underlie the surface text are accessible and relevant	rhetorical acts (e.g. defining, classifying, exemplifying, etc.)
2. Discourse-based		
Intentionality	The manipulation of cohesion and coherence features to provide a text which can fulfil the writer's intentions	normal ordering strategies (e.g. natural time order, etc.); relevance; brevity; clarity
Acceptability	Awareness of reader's expectation that the text will possess certain features and will be of use and relevance	conventional textual features (e.g. instructions in recipes); aspects of text grammar (e.g. use of passives, articles, etc.)
Informativity	The extent to which the elements in the text are expected/unexpected, or known/unknown/uncertain	marked/unmarked sequences; given/new information; topic/comment; maintaining/breaking text conventions
Situationality	The ways in which a text is relevant to the situation in which it occurs	topic selection and development; situational constraints (e.g. formal letters, technical reports, etc.); exam questions
Intertextuality	The factors which make the accessibility of one text for a reader dependent upon knowledge of, or access to, other texts	use of source material; quotes; in-text references to other texts; bibliographies

Hamp-Lyons and Heasley constructed a matrix showing how the eight textbooks scored relative to their criteria of textuality. They used a modified star-rating, on a scale 1–3:

Key: ■ minimal coverage ■ ■ fair coverage   ■ ■ ■ wide coverage

Once again, the choice of criteria and the evaluation is subjective but, as the authors point out, 'it does provide a principled basis for evaluation which readers can adapt and develop for their situations'. It is clear from the list of 'standards of textuality', that the purpose and organisation of the book needs to be taken into account: otherwise it might perform poorly if its approach was contrary to that of the criteria.

8.6 Dictionaries

One way to eliminate some of the subjectivity from lists of criteria by which books are evaluated is for a number of teachers to agree on the items included. This was done by West (1987) with groups of in-service teachers from Britain and overseas:

> The object of the workshops was to look at the ever-increasing range of dictionaries that are available to English language learners and to select criteria by which comparisons could be made, then applying these criteria to the dictionaries on the market. The results were collated as a *Which?*-style consumers' guide with star ratings and comments.

West noted that 'everyone was concerned with classroom considerations and budget constraints, and it was these factors which determined recommendations'.

RATINGS

■ ■ ■ ■ Highly recommended   ■ ■ ■ Recommended
■ ■ Fair   □ Not recommended

There were 19 dictionaries in the survey, divided into four categories: those for advanced learners, those for lower-level learners, pocket dictionaries and ESP dictionaries. The list of criteria was as follows:

UK (or local) price
Date and format
Number of pages
Level/coverage
Workbook available? Quality?
Pronunciation system
Ease of use
Definitions

Grammatical assistance
Illustrations
Number of appendices
Comments

8.7 Evaluation: some questions

ELT Documents 126 (ed. Sheldon) devoted a whole issue to evaluation: '*ELT textbooks and materials: problems in evaluation and development*'. Several of the articles in it are directly relevant to our concerns; extracts from some are referred to below.

a) Breen and Candlin (1987) 'offer teachers a set of questions they can apply to any published or locally produced language teaching materials' based on their 'work with teachers from all over the world in materials design and evaluation workshops'.

They divide their guide into two phases: the first poses questions as to the usefulness of the materials (aims, content, requirements of learners and teacher, function); the second suggests criteria for the choice and use of the materials (covering learners' needs, interests and approaches to language learning; and the teaching/learning process used).

One of the most interesting sections is their questionnaire for discovering learners' criteria for good materials, in the belief that students' participation 'will help to establish accurately the criteria for selection'. They propose their questionnaire as a starting point for discovering learners' views and that it can be adapted and additional questions asked (reproduced below).

> *On the procedures for working with tasks and activities in the classroom*
>
> – What do you find are the most useful ways to learn a new language?
> – What are the best kinds of language learning tasks and activities? What are the reasons for your choice?
> – What can a teacher do which would help you most when you are learning a new language?
> – What can other learners in the class do which would help you most when you are learning a new language
> – What is your favourite kind of language lesson? What are the reasons for your choice?
> – What are the good things and the bad things about learning a language in a classroom?
> – What can materials best provide you with to help you learn a new language?
> – What are the best kinds of language learning materials? What do they look like? Why do you think they're best?

  – What is good and not so good about the materials you are working with now? What do you think is missing from them? What changes would you make to them?

. . . .?

. . . .?

b) Dudley-Evans and Bates (1987) look at the evaluation of one particular ESP textbook, their own, *Nucleus: General Science*. They are also concerned with learners' reactions to material. They discuss the use of the book 'in the upper secondary schools in Egypt, the methods used to evaluate the effectiveness of the book, and the resulting changes made' to the book. They used a combination of visits to schools, observations of classes, discussions with teachers and inspectors and questionnaires given to teachers using the book.

The questionnaires 'focused on the teachers and on student reaction to the material. In particular they asked what difficulties both had in using the book'. There was also a detailed questionnaire on each unit in the course given immediately after it had been taught. It concentrated on:

a) the learnability of the unit;
b) the workability of the unit and how long it took to teach;
c) the popularity of the unit with the students;
d) evidence of understanding on the part of the students.

c) Pilbeam (1987) addresses the question 'can published materials be used in ESP?' in view of the fact that learners' needs in ESP are usually highly specific. He poses some criteria by which an ESP book should be judged; they include the following:

1. Is it specific?
2. Is it appropriate?
3. Is it valid?
4. Is it flexible?
5. Is the approach suitable?

He concludes that, in general terms, 'published material can be widely used for ESP courses'.

d) An experienced EFL book reviewer, John Dougill (1987) 'lists the chief considerations a reviewer will bear in mind when looking at a book'. He groups his questions under the headings of: framework, units, subject-matter, form and components.

He comments that:

> while there may be no right way *per se*, there may be ways that tests, experience and consensus show to be better. For want of scientific evidence, value judgements have to be made.

Inevitably:

there is still very much a subjective element of likes and dislikes. What is appealing and motivating to one person can be turgid and deadly to another.

He acknowledges that one's teaching style and personal perceptions will necessarily play a key part in evaluation. He notes that it is the 'subjective elements that tend to prevail in teachers' preferences'. He illustrates this by showing the results of a small-scale survey he conducted among Oxford TEFL teachers into their reasons for liking or disliking a course book:

Survey of teachers in six Oxford Arels-Felco schools

Reasons for liking an EFL course	*Reasons for disliking an EFL course*
Interesting (referring to texts, activities or tapes)	Boring
Generates discussion and argument	Bland
Varied subject-matter	Badly developed
Contains useful further practice	Unclear direction, 'messy'
Has 'meaty' texts	Lack of continuity or further practice
Clear	Childish
Systematic approach	Lack of relevance
Attractive, well set-out	Repetitive
Useful teacher's book	

NB: The reasons are given in order of frequency. Only those reasons are included that appeared more than once.

8.8 Criteria: checklists

Checklists or evaluation criteria have been developed by several writers, among them Williams (1983) and Cunningsworth (1984). Cunningsworth, like other writers, acknowledges that the checklist:

> is not an automatic procedure ... [as] there are too many variables involved ... Professional judgement, founded on understanding of the rationale of language teaching and learning and backed up by practical experience, lies at the base of the evaluation procedure.

Cunningsworth and Kusel (1991) discuss the setting up of questions to form a set of criteria for evaluating teachers' guides to ELT materials.

They make a distinction between 'global appraisal' (the underlying approach of teachers' guides) and 'detailed evaluation' (dealing with the details of each unit of the book). They rightly point out that teachers' guides are, on the whole, a neglected area. Yet they are vitally important in countries:

> where English is being taught in a non-English-speaking environment and where teachers, for whatever reason, are heavily dependent on the TG for methodological guidance, for linguistic information, or for insights into cultural issues.

The principle of a two-stage appraisal is also adhered to by McDonough and Shaw (1993), though their approach is different from that above. They first utilise an 'external evaluation' (a brief 'overview' of the materials from the outside – cover, introduction, contents page), followed up by the 'internal evaluation' (a closer and more detailed appraisal). Their overall evaluation incorporates the following parameters:

1. The usability factor;
2. The generalisability factor;
3. The adaptability factor;
4. The flexibility factor.

They conclude by suggesting that:

> materials evaluation is one part of a complex process and that materials once selected can only be judged successful after classroom implementation and feedback.

Further discussions of materials evaluation are contained in Alderson (1985), Hutchinson and Waters (1987), Robinson (1991) and Nunan (1991).

8.9 Conclusion

We have read a variety of accounts of evaluation processes involving the compiling of checklists of headings or questions, sometimes designed by one person, sometimes by a group. What emerges is an acknowledgement of the subjectivity of the process, but also the desirability of counteracting this by means of a more principled approach through a set of criteria. It is also clear that feedback from both teachers and students is considered essential if the material is to achieve its true purpose, that is, to help learners to learn effectively. In this connection, it is sometimes forgotten that illustrations are often culture-bound and their point may be unclear to readers from very different cultural backgrounds. This is verified, to some extent, by research by Hewings (1991) among Vietnamese students in Britain.

It has been acknowledged that the professional judgement of teachers is at the root of evaluation, and that there will inevitably, be differences of opinion in the selection of materials. Consequently, we should be aware of our own preferences or prejudices in the matter of book selection so that we can guard against extremes of opinion.

Ultimately, you are the judge of what is best for you and your students: a book is needed that you all feel comfortable with. In other words, the style of the book should not clash with your teaching style. The book should allow you flexibility so that you can adapt it to suit your needs. It is worth remembering that there is no such thing as an ideal book for all teachers and all situations. This is why many teachers produce their own in-house material and, eventually, write their own books. However, it is uneconomic of time, effort and cost to do this for all teaching. Consequently, most teachers compromise by adapting books, using parts of them and supplementing them. In Chapter 18 we shall be looking at the design and production of our own materials for EAP situations.

A final point. Sometimes the problem with selecting a suitable book is that you are not aware of the whole range of books available because the local shop is poorly stocked or there is no access to an academic bookshop. To some extent, this can be overcome by obtaining ELT publishers' catalogues, and also those from ELT bookshops which can supply books by. In addition, survey reviews in journals, in which several books on the same theme are reviewed, are a source of useful comparative information (e.g. Jordan 1996b: books for study skills/ EAP).

8.10 Introspect and discuss

1. In the past, how have you decided which book to use on a course?
2. What attracts you to a book in the first place?
3. a) Figure 19 gives details of eight integrated study skills books. What other information about each book might you find useful?
   b) Suggest some suitable criteria (headings or questions) for evaluating the eight study skills books. Have you used any of the books in your teaching? With what effect?
4. Are there any criteria that you would like to change on the lists by Sheldon (1988) and Hamp-Lyons (1983)?
5. Hamp-Lyons and Heasley (1984) compare eight writing textbooks according to their criteria of 'textuality'. No criteria are suggested for teaching methodology, exercise types and other features. Suggest some criteria for these that you would find useful if you were comparing writing textbooks.

6. Analyse any two or more fairly recent dictionaries that are available, according to West's (1987) evaluation format. Add to the list any other useful bases for comparison.
7. Breen and Candlin (1987) suggest a questionnaire to discover learners' criteria for good materials. Devise a questionnaire that could be given to students to find out their views of a particular course book.
8. How would you evaluate teachers' guides for study skills course books?
9. What are your personal dislikes with regard to any aspect of EAP/study skills/ESP course books? Also include details such as the use of illustrations/diagrams, type-size, answer key, etc.
10. How would you describe your teaching style? What kind of course book do you feel comfortable with when teaching?
11. At the end of the chapter, reference is made to ELT publishers' catalogues. Design a set of criteria for evaluating such catalogues from the point of view of you, the teacher.

Part II   *Study skills and practice (EGAP)*

The purpose of Part II is to look in some detail at six main study skills areas: academic reading, with the addition, separately, of vocabulary development, which links reading and writing; academic writing; lectures and note-taking; speaking for academic purposes; reference/research skills; and examination skills. In each chapter, there are commentaries on the research in that field, usually taken from journal articles. In addition, there are references to appropriate books, showing different approaches, types of activity or exercise, etc. *Introspect and discuss*, with its questions and tasks, concludes each chapter.

Many of the books that are referred to in these chapters are, or have been, commonly used on EAP courses in the UK. A number of them are also used in other countries, both on short and long courses. The books are listed in Appendix 1.2: Selected study skills books. It should be noted that some of them are now out of print. As you look at the extracts (included in Appendix 1.1 in chapter order), it might be appropriate to think of some of the principles of evaluation suggested in the last chapter viz.

- Why do I like/dislike this extract?
- What is the purpose of the activity/exercise?
- Would this type of activity be appropriate for my students? (Why?/Why not?) etc.

Integrated study skills

There are several books available that integrate a number of study skills areas. Some advantages of such integration are that all the material is selected at approximately the same level, and is within the covers of one or two books (useful for tutors and students alike, and cheaper). A major advantage is that students can see the relationship between skills, which can serve as a model for their own studies and projects. Disadvantages are that less choice and control of material and methods are given to the tutors, although tutors may always supplement any course with their own material. Another disadvantage is that not all the skills may be needed: in that case, the separate skills books may be preferred. In the previous chapter, Figure 19 listed eight such books.

Extracts from some of these are referred to in the separate study skills sections that follow.

Before we look at the individual skills, let us take a brief look at the preliminary areas, sometimes included in the integrated skills books. Many students, just starting at university, need help to cope with their often newly-found independence. In this respect, the type of help that is provided in books referred to in Chapter 1 (for NS) is highly relevant. The areas that are particularly appropriate are:

- organising your studies
- establishing a routine
- planning your working week
- making a timetable
- being realistic over the use of time, etc.

Some books make use of checklists or grids to prompt students to question themselves. Others pose questions to initiate self-awareness and then proceed to discuss and compare. A good example of an initial awareness-raising activity is shown below: it encourages students to be realistic. It is within a unit on 'using your time'.

> Answer the following questions about yourself – truthfully! If you reply truthfully, you will have learned something about your work rhythm which will be useful when you come to plan your weekly study timetable.
> 1. How often in an hour do you feel the need to get up and stretch your legs while you are reading a textbook?
> 2. At what time of the day do you work best?
>   (a) morning
>   (b) afternoon
>   (c) evening
>   (d) late at night
> 3. Write down the hours when you can study *at the same time every day in the week* (meal times and travel times do not count!).
>
> Answer the following questions about things that affect your planning:
> 1. How long does it take you to read ten pages of a textbook?
> 2. How long does it take you to read ten pages of a novel?
> 3. How long does it take you to write a two-page class paper?
> Discuss your conclusions with a partner. Are you both being *realistic*? Are you being *honest*?
>
> (From *A Study Skills Handbook*, Smith and Smith 1990)

9 Academic reading

Reading, as a skill, is normally linked with writing. This is a fundamental characteristic of the target academic situation in which students are typically reading books and journals, noting, summarising, paraphrasing, and then writing essays, etc. In practice material for reading, the link with writing is normally included. Although the focus may be on various reading strategies and comprehension practice, the resultant exercises usually involve writing (apart from some multiple-choice questions and yes/no, true/false formats).

Reading for academic purposes is a multifaceted subject. However, there is one fundamental aspect which can be the starting point for other considerations. When students read, it is for a *purpose*. Clearly, students can have different purposes in their reading; these will include:

- to obtain information (facts, data, etc.)
- to understand ideas or theories, etc.
- to discover authors' viewpoints
- to seek evidence for their own point of view (and to quote) all of which may be needed for writing their essays, etc.

In the process of reading, students will be concerned with the *subject-content* of what they read and the *language* in which it is expressed. Both aspects involve *comprehension*, though of different kinds. Depending on the reading purpose, different reading *strategies* and *skills* will be involved; in turn, the skills can be divided into *sub-skills*. Some of these aspects were alluded to in Chapter 1 in the context of effective reading and using the method *SQ3R* for intensive reading.

9.1 Strategies and skills

Some of the main strategies, skills and sub-skills utilised in reading are as follows:

- prediction
- skimming (reading quickly for the main idea or gist)
- scanning (reading quickly for a specific piece of information)
- distinguishing between:
  - factual and non-factual information
  - important and less important items

- relevant and irrelevant information
- explicit and implicit information
- ideas and examples and opinions
- drawing inferences and conclusions
- deducing unknown words
- understanding graphic presentation (data, diagrams, etc.)
- understanding text organisation and linguistic/semantic aspects, e.g.
  - relationships between and within sentences (e.g. cohesion)
  - recognising discourse/semantic markers and their function.

All of them play a part in comprehension. (Fuller accounts are given by Munby 1978; Grellet 1981; and Nuttall 1996.)

The skills listed above are frequently taken as the basis for practice material in textbooks. Sometimes the skills are taken separately, or in combination, and used as the focus for the unit or exercise, but more frequently they are integrated within units in the form of activities/tasks/ problem-solving, which are topic- or content-based. The texts that are used as the basis for the practice are usually authentic, though possibly adapted or abridged, depending on the language level (see Chapter 7 regarding authenticity). Although the focus of the practice is on the reading skills, some exercises are usually included on the comprehension of certain aspects of the reading passage together with word study/ vocabulary practice and some relevant grammatical focus.

Most reading books are based on this combined/integrated strategies/ skills approach, e.g. Sim and Laufer-Dvorkin (1982), Forman *et al.* (1990), Glendinning and Holmström (1992), McGovern *et al.* (1994). Two extracts are shown in Appendix 1.1 from these last two books. They exemplify the approach of stating clear aims for the reading (i.e. providing a purpose), combined with activities/discussion as well as reading a text.

9.2 Categorising reading courses

Bloor (1985) has suggested an alternative approach to the consideration of reading courses: categorising them according to the philosophies adopted by the writers. In proposing this, Bloor acknowledges that individual books usually incorporate more than one of the underlying philosophies, usually combined with skills/strategies practice. Four main approaches have been identified: psychological, linguistic, content-orientated and pedagogically-oriented.

a) *Psychological*: this focuses on 'what takes place in the mind of the individual reader'. Such courses endeavour to practise the *processes* involved in reading, by means of exercises, often at two levels: the first is at the level of 'simple word recognition', while the second is at the level of 'interpretation'. Books following this approach are: University of Malaya (1980–81), Morrow (1980), and Moore (1979–80).

b) *Linguistic*: this focuses on the *words* and *sentences* of the text. 'The assumption is that if learners can handle linguistic features of the text efficiently, reading ability will be improved'. This approach is often present in a number of activities in many reading books. Overt grammatical exercises are included in books such as Sim and Laufer-Dvorkin (1982) and Glendinning and Holmström (1992).

c) *Content-orientated*: this approach is based on the view that if readers have, or are given, a specific purpose for their reading, efficiency will be improved. For example, the learner may be required to extract specific information from the text by means of pre-reading questions or tasks, as in Kaplan and Shaw (1983), Davies and Whitney (1984), and Holschuh and Kelley (1988). It is also assumed that if there are reading passages on topics related to students' specific areas of interest, their interest and involvement in reading will be stimulated. This is the basis for a number of books including a wide range of extracts from different disciplines, and topics that might have an international appeal, e.g. 'the individual and society', 'food for thought', 'pollution', 'language', 'academic success', etc.

d) *Pedagogically-orientated*: this approach is exemplified by 'those courses where learning theories are the prime motivation for the design of the *total course* rather than the design of individual exercises' (Bloor 1985). Self-access materials, from which students make their own choices and work at their own pace, exemplify this approach, with sets of reading cards as an example (Jolly 1982; and *SRA Reading laboratory* for NS).

Bloor points out that it is almost impossible to evaluate these four approaches as there are so many variables, a major one being the students' freedom of choice in reading. How far 'the learner is interested in the content of the reading passage would distort any results one might obtain'.

9.3 Reading for information

The reading purpose is clearly fundamental to all reading in EAP. In an important article, Johns and Davies (1983) maintain that in EAP a text is a 'vehicle for information' not a 'linguistic object'. They propose a methodology for studying written texts so that the focus is on the information in them. This involves the notion of *topic-types*, or conceptual frameworks, e.g. physical structure, process, characteristics, by which texts can be graded: from simple information structures to the more complex. An integral part of the approach is small-group work involved in puzzling out the meaning of the text.

Many reading skills books focus on reading for information; in doing so, they often give practice to various strategies, e.g. scanning, skimming, seeking the main idea, prediction (e.g. Jordan 1980; Wallace 1980).

9.4 Reading speed

As students need to read extensively as well as intensively, it is important that they are able to do so in the most efficient way possible. Efficiency is coupled with speed of reading, and it was noted in Chapter 3 that many students read slowly. It is for this reason that some reading courses include practice material aimed at increasing reading speed and comprehension rate.

It should be noted that there are two diametrically opposed points of view regarding reading speed. One is that because students have difficulties with reading comprehension, probably linked to a narrow range of vocabulary, they will naturally read slowly, and any attempt to increase reading speed before improving reading comprehension is misguided. The other point of view is that by improving reading speed, the student is able to see longer stretches of language with each fixation of the eyes and thus more easily contextualise unknown vocabulary and be able to achieve general understanding.

One well-tried method of increasing reading speed (Fry 1963a, 1963b) is for students to note the time they take to read a passage in words per minute (wpm) (see also Wallace 1980), and then to answer comprehension questions – often true/false or multiple-choice, noting their score. This information is then recorded in a progress chart (e.g. Abdulaziz and Stover 1989). Fry used reading passages divided into topics on public health and diseases: these were based on authentic language, simplified to a 2000-word vocabulary level. Morrow (1980) used extracts from the *New Scientist* as the basis for recognition, structuring and interpretation exercises, and also for reading speed and comprehension practice.

One book (Mosback and Mosback 1976) is devoted to giving practice in faster reading, with the material organised into topics. The speed reading technique is the same as Fry's, but the practice that follows is more extensive, consisting not only of comprehension exercises ('Ideas'), but also vocabulary (synonyms), paragraph topics and summary completion.

A useful analysis of, and commentary on, ways to improve reading speed is contained in Nuttall (1996); suggestions for preliminary exercises are made by Grellet (1981).

9.5 Reading comprehension and vocabulary

In reading their subject textbooks, students frequently meet unknown words and phrases. Hewings (1990) takes the example of texts concerned with theoretical model building in economics. She points out that various straightforward study skills techniques can help in different ways. For example, scanning headings and sub-headings, and skimming through text, can give an overview and set the scene. Using the index to a book and finding a word's initial occurrence could often lead to finding a definition or explanation. Failing that, the existence of suitable glossaries or subject dictionaries could be brought to the students' attention.

Bramki and Williams (1984) are concerned with strategies to help students use context clues to puzzle out the meaning of newly-introduced specialist vocabulary. They first analysed instances of intentional lexical familiarisation in an economics textbook and discovered that the most frequent categories, in descending order, were: exemplification, explanation, definition (these three together accounting for almost 90 per cent of all instances), stipulation, synonymy and non-verbal illustration. They then proposed strategies 'for capitalising on familiarisations deliberately implanted in text by the author, so that the reader can work out for himself the meanings of the terms concerned'. Initially, the teacher marks up a text – term, signalling and familiarisation – with coloured pens on the OHP, or by underlining, boxing, etc. on texts for photocopying or duplicating. This is to raise the students' awareness. The next stage is to mark up only one or two of the three elements in each case, with the student completing the marking up. The third stage is for an asterisk only to be placed in the margin where familiarisation occurs, and the students work in pairs to mark up the text themselves.

Calculating the meaning of vocabulary with the help of context clues is looked at in the next chapter.

9.6 Introspect and discuss

1. A list is given of the main reading strategies, skills and sub-skills. Which ones do you think would be the most difficult for students? Why?

2. Bloor distinguished four main categories of approach for reading materials (psychological, linguistic, content-orientated, and pedagogically-orientated). From a student's point of view, is any one approach preferable to another in EAP?
3. Reading for information is a common purpose in EAP. However, is 'information' homogeneous, or are there different types? Would this affect exercise types?
4. Do you have any views on the possibility of improving reading speed, and of ways of achieving it?
5. What would your ideal practice book on academic reading include? How would it be organised?

10 Vocabulary development

Although vocabulary development, as such, is not a specific study skill, but relates to all language learning, it is given separate attention here. The reason for this is twofold. Firstly, and perhaps most importantly, students usually want to increase their store of vocabulary, regarding it as a yardstick of their language improvement. 'Vocabulary knowledge is the single most important area of second language competence' regarding academic achievement (Saville-Troike 1984). Secondly, as it appears not to be a major area of concern in EAP courses (evidenced by the data in the survey looked at in Chapter 4), there is a tendency for it to become incidental to reading comprehension. The result is that it may be left to students' indirect learning, which may be inefficient.

Vocabulary development is of concern to all four language skills, but here it is treated as a link between reading and writing. This is partly for convenience, in that the printed word is more of a known quantity, and partly from convention, namely, that students and teachers are more familiar with its practice in the written mode. Clearly, however, there is transfer from one to the other. This chapter looks at some background studies and research into vocabulary acquisition, and explores the case for active involvement in vocabulary development.

Vocabulary learning and teaching relate to both reading, with its receptive understanding of language, and writing, with its productive use. This has been expressed by Nattinger (1988):

> comprehension of vocabulary relies on strategies that permit one to *understand* words and *store* them, to commit them to memory, that is, while production concerns strategies that activate one's storage by retrieving these words from memory, and by *using* them in appropriate situations. The priority this distinction assigns to comprehension is one of many reasons why a growing number of researchers believe that comprehension should precede production in language teaching.

In what follows, we will consider vocabulary from the point of view of the reading context but also look at ways of activating it.

Students often express a need to expand their vocabulary. Reference was made to this in Chapter 3 in a study of writing difficulties of overseas students: vocabulary emerged as the cause of most difficulties for the students (Jordan 1981). Specific difficulties referred to were:

using a word correctly; own lack of vocabulary; and confusion between similar sounding/looking words.

For a student to 'know' a word, it may mean the ability to:

a) recognise it in its spoken or written form;
b) recall it at will;
c) relate it to an appropriate object or concept;
d) use it in the appropriate grammatical form;
e) in speech, pronounce it in a recognisable way;
f) in writing, spell it correctly;
g) use it with the words it correctly goes with, i.e. in the correct collocation;
h) use it at the appropriate level of formality;
i) be aware of its connotations and associations.

(Wallace 1982)

With students of different language levels, background and specific subjects, attending EAP courses, an understandable emphasis may be placed on indirect learning, with an explanation to the student to infer the meaning from its context. This is then backed up by stressing the need to use a good learner's dictionary. In the case of subject-specific vocabulary, reference may be made to specialist dictionaries (see Appendix 1.2). This may be pragmatic but is it the most effective way for students to develop their vocabulary? In order to answer this question it is, first of all, necessary to ask and answer two further questions: *which* vocabulary should be taught/learned, and *how* should it be taught/learned?

10.1 Which vocabulary?

10.1.1 Core vocabulary

The vocabulary appropriate for students following EAP courses should clearly be more advanced than the core 2,000–3,000 words that provide the basis of about 80 per cent of the words likely to be encountered (Carter 1987). (Reference is made in Chapter 16 to word lists and frequency counts in the context of register analysis.) In general ELT terms, word lists have formed the basis of many courses, usually selected on account of their familiarity or usefulness. Sinclair and Renouf (1988) are more specific in the determination of criteria for lexical selection:

a) the commonest word forms in the language;
b) their central pattern of usage;
c) the combinations which they typically form.

Although they describe the Birmingham Corpus (based on the

COBUILD project), and give, as an example, the first 200 word forms ranked in order of frequency of occurrence, there are no real pointers for EAP in particular. The COBUILD project is a lexicographic research programme based in the Department of English Language and Literature at the University of Birmingham in association with William Collins, Publishers. The main contribution is 'the availability in machine-readable form of a concordance based on 7.3 million words' (Carter and McCarthy 1988; see also Willis 1990 for further details). We shall be looking at 'concordance' later in this chapter.

Carter (1988), in discussing core vocabulary in discourse, points out that:

> at least two broad distinctions have to be drawn. There is a level of core vocabulary which is 'core' as far as the organization of the lexicon as a whole is concerned; and there is a level of core vocabulary which is core to a particular field or subject. Subject-specific vocabulary will always be non-core as far as the language as a whole is concerned. This is because it is not neutral in field and is immediately associated with a specialized topic.

Thus we have 'core vocabulary', which 'will be neutral by not indicating degrees of intensity or formality', and 'subject-core vocabulary', which 'will be only expressive of a particular field'.

Carter also looks at discourse-genres that apply to writing in different subjects. His 'initial research suggests that the presence of *core, subject-core* and *non-core* lexical items can be connected with particular discourse-genres'. The following correlations between lexical coreness and genre can be observed:

Summary	} core	Instruction	
Explanation		Report	} subject core
		Recount	
Argumentation	} non-core		
Narrative			
Description			

10.1.2 Academic vocabulary

The idea of compiling word lists for academic vocabulary has been explored, and acted upon, by several researchers. An early list was compiled by Campion and Elley (1971), later modified by Nation (1986) to 'The University Word List'. Basically, there have been two types of frequency counts of university texts (summarised by Nation 1990). One type assumes a core vocabulary of about 2,000–3,000 words (e.g. Michael West's *General Service List*), and counts words outside this basic list. The other type counts only those words in the university texts that cause difficulties for overseas students. Nation (1990) reports on the compilation of four particular university word lists and how these were combined by Xue and Nation (1984) to form one University Word List of almost 740 headwords (Appendix 2 in Nation 1990). According to Nation, such specialised word lists can be used:

 – as a guide and focus for teachers in different activities;
 – as a checklist and aim for students.

Nation (1990) notes that 'technical words', or specialist vocabulary, are usually considered to be the responsibility of the subject teachers: the words are closely connected with learning the subject and may present conceptual difficulties. 'However, considering that large numbers occur in specialised texts, language teachers need to prepare learners to deal with them'. This is with the realisation that many of these difficult 'technical words' may be of low frequency. Consequently, 'the advice "Learn every word you meet that you don't know" would not result in too much wasted effort'. Nation then presents a decision chart for low-frequency words (Li 1983: an unpublished paper) to assist students in deciding which words to learn.

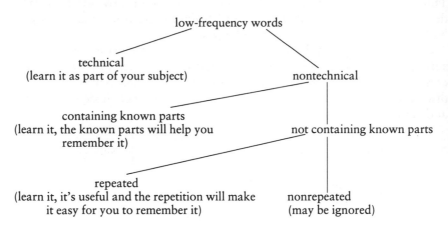

Decision chart for dealing with low-frequency words in specialized texts.

The next level of vocabulary below specialist words is variously called semi-technical, sub-technical or academic, and consists of words which occur across a number of disciplines. The inter-disciplinary nature of the academic vocabulary, as it relates to graduate research, is discussed by Martin (1976). She divides the academic vocabulary into three groups, appropriate for teaching/practising with research graduates: (a) the research process, (b) the vocabulary of analysis, and (c) the vocabulary of evaluation.

a) *The research process*: the vocabulary is primarily verbs and nouns and is 'presented in a context which discusses the five steps of research: formulating, investigating, analysing, drawing conclusions and reporting results'.

b) *The vocabulary of analysis*: it includes high-frequency and two-word verbs needed 'in order to present information in an organized sequence', e.g. consist of, group, result from, derive, base on, be noted for.
Verbs of analysis are grouped in a number of semantic sets, e.g. consist of, be composed of, contain, be made up of.

c) *The vocabulary of evaluation*: it includes adjectives and adverbs that occur in reviews, critiques and some reports, e.g. exhaustive, controversial, coherent, indispensable, comprehensive, distinctive, pervasive, substantive; objective–subjective, implicit–explicit, inductive–deductive, significant–insignificant.

Martin also gives examples of exercises appropriate for each of the areas of academic work.

Cowan (1974) identifies 'sub-technical vocabulary' as essential for university students' reading needs:

> context independent words which occur with high frequency across disciplines, e.g. function, inference, isolate, relation, basis, presuppose, simulate, approximately, etc.

Their importance has also been noted by Baker (1988) and King (1989). Baker examined certain lexical items performing specific rhetorical functions in medical journal articles. The data suggests that the items may be used in set patterns, which can be of use in teaching/learning. King analysed the use of certain nouns in project writing by engineering students: in nearly all cases they proved to be text-structuring words.

There can be different attitudes towards the teaching/learning of sub-technical vocabulary. One attitude is that students need to be aware of and learn the general meaning of the words – such as: function, factor, point – as they are more likely to know a specialist meaning from their own studies. The other approach is that the meaning/use of the word needs to be learned in its ESAP context as this is the most frequent need the students will have for using it. It can be argued that both approaches are valid: it will depend on the students' needs.

10.2 Second language vocabulary acquisition

The various ways in which we can help students to learn vocabulary have been influenced by research into second language acquisition and, more specifically, L2 vocabulary acquisition. There has been discussion

153

concerning the distinction between 'acquisition' and 'learning'. Here, it is sufficient to follow Channell (1988): 'Learning is the process, acquisition is the end result'. She considers this alongside the distinction between *productive* and *receptive* use of vocabulary, noting that 'learners gain receptive control of new words before active control'.

Channell discusses research into the speech errors of native speakers and compares it with that of second language learners. 'This research suggests that a learner's first and second vocabulary knowledge are linked together in their mental lexicon phonologically, semantically and associationally, and that learners can make conscious the links between them' (Nunan 1991). From this, Channell (1988) concludes that the main implications for classroom practice are:

1. Since the lexicon appears to be an independent entity in processing, there is justification for teaching approaches which make vocabulary work a separate learning activity. It is not essential always to integrate vocabulary with general communication.
2. Presentation of vocabulary should pay specific attention to pronunciation, in particular word stress. So visual presentation and reading may not be the best ways to introduce new vocabulary.
3. Learners should be encouraged to make their own lexical associations when they are actively learning new vocabulary. (However, at present we do not know which kind of associations are the most useful in aiding retention.)
4. Semantic links play an important role in production. This suggests the use of semantic field based presentation methods on the lines of that exemplified.

10.3 Semantic field theory and componential analysis

In order to have an active vocabulary, learners need to know about each new word:

1. How does it relate to other words with similar meaning?
2. Which other words can it be used with, and in which contexts?

Channell (1981) addresses these two questions in the context of semantic theory and its relevance to vocabulary learning. She regards *semantic field theory* and *componential analysis* as being potentially very useful.

10.3.1 Semantic field theory

The theory starts from the premise that the vocabulary of a language consists of 'many interrelating networks of relations between words', i.e.

154

semantic fields. In other words, words in the same network or field share some aspect of meaning and are part of a systematic structure; long random lists of words are ruled out. Channell refers to evidence which suggests that the mind uses semantic similarity in classifying words. Consequently, it makes sense to utilise this knowledge in vocabulary learning and therefore to incorporate semantic sets.

10.3.2 Componential analysis

Componential analysis provides a systematic way of describing the similarities and differences that exist between words in the same semantic field. 'It consists, simply, of breaking down the meaning of a word or words into different pieces known as semantic components' (Channell 1981), e.g.

walk: [+ move] [+ by feet] [+ on land] etc.
run: [+ move] [+ by feet] [+ on land] [+ quickly] etc.

Words in the same semantic field can be grouped together in a *grid* which indicates (+) if the component is part of the meaning of the marked word. The grid below (Channell 1981) for 'being surprised', illustrates this:

Being surprised

	affect with wonder	because unexpected	because difficult to believe	so as to cause confusion	so as to leave one helpless to act or think
surprise	+	+			
astonish	+		+		
amaze	+			+	
astound	+				+
flabbergast	+				+

Semantic grouping also makes it possible to show the contrast among words visually, on a scale or cline, with the words located according to their place between the extremes of the scale, e.g. good/bad, least/greatest, formal/slang.

In the second question that Channell posed above (Which other words can it be used with, and in which contexts?), there is a clear reference to collocations. It is important for the learner to see new words presented in example sentences and/or collocational grids, such as the following (Channell 1981):

	woman	man	child	dog	bird	flower	weather	landscape	view	house	furniture	bed	picture	dress	present	voice
handsome		+									+				+	
pretty	+		+	+	+	+		+	+	+		+	+	+		
charming	+	+								+				+		+
lovely	+		+	+	+	+	+	+	+	+	+	+	+	+	+	+

Although the examples above infer that grids and tables are ready-made, in fact they can be constructed by students working in pairs/groups and helped/advised by the teacher. In this way, students are more involved in the learning process. Some examples of this will be seen later, involving collocations and concordancing.

10.4 Teaching/learning vocabulary

10.4.1 Grids

An unusual vocabulary practice book exists in which the vocabulary is presented in semantic field tables and collocational grids, as described above (Rudzka *et al.* 1981). The words are shown in use in texts and sample sentences, and practice is given in a variety of exercises: blank-fill, synonyms, differences/similarities, extended writing, etc.

The idea of using grids in vocabulary teaching is also discussed by Stieglitz (1983). He refers to 'semantic feature analysis' rather than 'semantic field', and gives examples of food, animals, oral communication and positive feelings. Harvey (1983) uses grids in a wider sense, involving the students in devising the grid, deciding on categories and discussing the allocation of words to slots.

Harvey then looks at some of the advantages and uses of grids in vocabulary learning:

Some advantages

a. Organizing a system makes it less daunting for the student than a 'make a list of all the vocabulary relating to basketball' approach. It's also more fun.
b. Students (as well as teachers and linguists) *like* playing with words; it is not necessarily the negative activity it is often made out to be, particularly when organized on a thematic basis.

c. It seems likely that people generally find the use of grids and matrices psychologically satisfying.
d. It lends itself very easily to pair and group work.
e. Grids are very easy to construct; handouts can be used, or the grids can be done on the board.
f. The system can be used for personal reference and added to; it encourages the organization of study skills.
g. It provides excellent material for a number of exploitation and consolidation exercises. It increases variety.
h. As a system it is adaptable to various levels and skills.

Uses

Grids of this sort can be used in a large number of ways, either before or after contextualization. They can be exploited to help students see different elements and categories in vocabulary, and they lend themselves to a variety of consolidation exercises, for example:
– cloze exercises, blank filling, guessing games, spelling
– discussion and comparison of word formation, collocation, synonyms, etc.
– reference for reading or writing tasks, either intensive or extensive
– comprehension and memory activities

10.4.2 Word networks

The semantic grouping of words lends itself to the organisation of vocabulary teaching/learning into thematic webs or word networks. This is a visual approach to vocabulary presentation that can help students to associate words, remember them and extend the network themselves. These networks are used by Ellis and Sinclair (1989) as sensitising activities for extending vocabulary.

Jordan (1990a) also uses thematic webs for presenting vocabulary: the example in Appendix 1.1 shows vocabulary associated with universities, in a unit concerned with narrative description. In devising such networks, use can be made of various visual elements, e.g. circles, ovals or boxes; size of lettering: capitals or lower case; underlining; solid lines or broken; etc.

In spite of the above emphasis on the advantages of learning vocabulary in semantic groupings, word networks and the like, at times it is necessary to keep an open mind on the most beneficial approach for our students. One small-scale experiment in the USA (Tinkham 1993) found that 'new words ... are learned most easily if they are not grouped for presentation in prefabricated semantic clusters'. This, naturally, raises questions about the nature of the research and the students. However, it is possible to imagine students being confused by a number of similar or related words being presented for learning at the same time.

10.4.3 Context

Early in the chapter reference was made to inferring the meaning of a word from its context, the context normally being the stretch of language being read for a purpose. That aspect of vocabulary learning will now be considered.

After looking at various approaches for using context to assist in determining meaning, Kruse (1979) proposes a systematic strategy for learning vocabulary development skills. The basic aims are to teach word building skills and guessing word meanings from context clues. There is a progression from word building (suffixes, prefixes, roots) to definition clues (parentheses and footnotes, synonyms and antonyms) and then to inference clues, which require higher levels of analytical skills and practice (example, summary, experience).

Practice in inferring meaning from context is central to a number of course books aimed at developing reading skills, and supplementary practice books in vocabulary development (e.g. Sim and Laufer-Dvorkin, 1984). Typically, such practice books are organised according to topic or theme and begin with a reading passage in which the vocabulary for practice is contextualised. Exercises then follow, for example, on synonyms, matching phrases, blank-fill, comprehension, similar/confused words, word families, word building and grammatical features.

Dunmore (1989) examines five reading/vocabulary course books which contain exercises aiming to develop the skill of inferring meaning from context. He categorises the sixteen different exercise formats presented into four basic types:

1. The learner is required to match a given synonym with a word (presumed to be unknown) appearing in a text.
2. The learner is required to complete a blank space with a suitable word.
3. The learner discovers meaning by using contextual clues (basic awareness training).
4. The learner discovers meaning by exposure to various features of text.

Type 1 is the most popular type of exercise.

Dunmore concludes that there are two major criticisms of the exercise types:

> The first casts doubt on the ability of the exercises to achieve their aim; the second suggests that they promote an incomplete, if not misleading, view of lexical meaning.

Dunmore's evaluation:

> highlights the need for exercise types which teach rather than test the use of the strategies needed for readers to be successful in discovering the meaning of unknown words.

He then refers teachers and writers of teaching materials to two guidelines for the creation of exercises which display a more systematic approach – Clarke and Nation (1980), who provide a list of twelve useful conjunction relationships; and Grellet (1981), who, in a sensitising activity, provides a similar list of types of relation between the word and the context:

- equivalence: a synonym is mentioned in the text.
- contrast: the word means the contrary of another word or expression given in the text.
- cause: the meaning of the word can be guessed because it is the cause of something described in the text.
- consequence: the word describes or appears in the description of the consequence of something. If the cause is known, it may be possible to guess what the consequence is.
- purpose: the word applies to an object whose purpose is described in the text.
- explanation/illustration: the meaning of the word is explained or an example is given.
- generalization/specification: the word is just one specific instance of a more general thing or idea mentioned in the text, or, on the contrary, after a number of specific examples have been given, a generalization is made.

A useful overview of appropriate exercise types for practising inference from context is contained in Nuttall (1996).

The main concerns of vocabulary teaching since 1980 have been summarised by Carter and McCarthy (1988) (based on a paper given by D. Brown at RELC, Singapore) – 'seven Cs and a G':

1. collocation
2. clines (scales expressed diagrammatically)
3. clusters (similar to Halliday's 'sets', i.e. words linked conceptually without recourse to meaning)
4. cloze procedures (which reinforce clusters and collocations)
5. context (using, e.g. definition, word analysis, inference)
6. consultation (using dictionaries, etc.)
7. cards (keeping a card index of new vocabulary)
8. guessing (a skill to be learned).

10.5 Concordancing

Earlier, reference was made to collocations, i.e. 'the regular co-occurrence of two or more words within a given extent of text' (Levy 1990). In recent years, computer data corpuses have enabled lexicographers and researchers to have access to *concordances*, i.e. lists of words together with a list of the contexts in which each word occurs.

Johns, T. F. (1991, 1994) discusses classroom concordancing (or Data-driven Learning – DDL) in vocabulary and grammar learning for overseas postgraduate students attending EAP courses at Birmingham University. He stresses the overriding importance and advantages of having authentic text available in the form of concordances on computer printouts. Instead of the student being provided with sets of collocational rules, they are encouraged to develop their own discovery strategies – in pairs or groups, puzzling out the reasons why or why not certain words 'go together'. Clearly, for those with access to appropriate computers, data and programmes, this can be an invaluable learning resource. An example of part of a concordance is given below (from Johns 1994).

Make as many sentences (sensible or silly) as you can from the following table:

The girl over there	accept(s)		the weather will be even worse tomorrow
The Vice-Chancellor	consider(s)		we should all be given a long holiday
Tim Johns	think(s)		nothing is nicer than a cup of tea
Everyone in the room	know(s)	(that)	one day I shall become Prime Minister
Most experts	believe(s)		we have not been told the whole story
Some of my friends	realise(s)		students find grammar very boring
Overseas students	suspect(s)		the pubs close too early in England

Here, in citations from 'New Scientist' are some of the verbs we can use in this pattern: identify any verbs that you are interested in or that you are not sure of, and look at the contexts in which they are used.

1. t. Virtually all biologists now accept that evolution is a fact, and that natural and sexu
2. hing given away.' Ashagre acknowledges that this is too little. 'We had planned for 170,000
3. The pilot radioed his plight but added that he would try and land anyway. The scientists a
4. ear Regulatory Commission. GPU alleges that the commission failed to warn it about the saf
5. oyalties even after it has ascertained that a piece of Britain contains valuable metals. A
6. the safe side, it is better to assume that there is no 'no effect' level. And it backs in
7. ke regularly. Some 23 per cent believe that smoking keeps down weight. This may be another
8. ces, is at it again. But he is betting that the Department of Health will not prosecute hi
9. high-density chip alone. Intel boasts that CHMOS (complementary, high-performance, metalo
10. value of the wheat. Bowers calculates that, of the £5950 that the NCC pays, £500 goes in
11. this notion as 'silly', Regan cautions that 'silly sounding ideas sometimes turn out to be
12. m the House of Representatives charged that the EPA 'acted improperly or at a minimum crea
13. Rutherford Appleton Laboratory checked that the telescope was pointing correctly. One loo
14. rcles, and opponents of the work claim that the cycles are not statistically significant,
15. should be implemented. Hunt commented that his inquiry 'was not concerned with the techno
16. lin, NNC's managing director, conceded that the immediate export prospects were slim, howe
17. nstalled it would be wrong to conclude that the overall impact on jobs has been negative.
18. it. The Apollo missions have confirmed that the Moon is lifeless; all the hopes that Galil
19. the situation, however, I conjectured that in these times of diminishing reactor safety r
20. eim, however, saying that 'we consider that Heim acted in such a way as to reduce the cred
21. t out for themselves.' Marcus contends that responsible manufacturers are already dealing
22. to greater than 400°C, so they decided that they had better cool the reactor.' The cooling
23. tion. The incomparable Nature declared that his was 'a book fit for burning'. But we point
24. ion is poor. Kenneth Baker has decreed that all new cable systems must be compatible, so t
25. ends of the Earth has already demanded that the inquiry be adjourned until the NII has end

Other useful discussions of concordances are in: Johns 1986; Levy 1990; Butler 1990; Stevens 1991; Sinclair 1991.

10.6 Memory and mnemonics

At the beginning of the chapter, mention was made of memory and the storage of words. As memory here relates to any language learning, and not just to EAP, it will only be looked at briefly.

For the purpose of vocabulary learning (and any aspects of language), it is useful to remember that there are both *short-term* and *long-term* memories:

> Research in memory suggests that words are stored and remembered in a network of associations. These associations can be of many types and be linked in a number of ways. Words in our mental lexicon, for example, are tied to each other not only by meaning, form and sound, but also by sight.
>
> (Nattinger 1988)

> More meaningful tasks require learners to analyse and process language more deeply, which helps them to commit information to long term memory.
>
> (Gairns and Redman 1986)

The implication for teaching is clear: problem-solving and task-based activities help students to remember.

Hunter (1957/64) considered ways of lengthening the memory span. He discussed and exemplified several mnemonic or memory systems, all based on the principles of association and imagination, e.g. visual-symbol, successive-comparison, digit-letter systems. Perhaps the best known are rote learning (or learning by heart) and visual imagery. The latter involves the key word technique; this:

> consists of associating the target word with a word which is pronounced or spelt similarly in the mother tongue, but is not necessarily related in terms of meaning.
>
> (Gairns and Redman 1986)

Gairns and Redman, Meara (1980), Nattinger (1988), and O'Malley and Chamot (1990) contain discussions, with examples, of the different techniques. One of the best-known exponents of mnemonic systems is Buzan (1977b, 1981, 1982, 1986). His systems usually make use of key words or pegs, i.e. a special list of items which never changes and to which the items being remembered are joined or pegged, e.g. link, number-shape, number-rhyme, alphabet systems.

10.7 Conclusion

From the foregoing, it can be inferred that the most effective way for students to increase their active vocabulary store is for them to be centrally involved in the learning process. This may be under the direction of a teacher, working in groups with other students, or on a self-access basis. Initially, it will involve some kind of learner training. It is important that attention is drawn to the need to develop vocabulary in a systematic way rather than by incidental learning. The learning and practice could involve the use of collocations, semantic fields, networks, etc. It should also help students to develop their own strategies for inferring meaning from context and making effective use of dictionaries: thus becoming more independent learners.

10.8 Introspect and discuss

1. a) Have you actively taught vocabulary? If so, how did you teach it? Would you say it was successful?
   b) Have you found any difficulties in vocabulary teaching? What are they?
2. Regarding the compilation of a university word list, Nation (1990) refers to some of the values of such word counts.
   a) Can you suggest any other advantages to add to Nation's list?
   b) What are the disadvantages?
3. The following nineteen words appear under the letter 'L' in Appendix 2: A University Word List in *Teaching and Learning Vocabulary*, Nation (1990).

label	lecture	lens	locate
laboratory	legal	liable	locomotion
labour	legislate	liberate	logic
launch	legitimate	linguistic	luxury
layer	leisure	litigate	

   If you were going to teach vocabulary on an EAP course, which ten words from the list would you give priority to? Why?
4. Try to devise a *componential grid* for the following seven words, all from the same semantic field of 'friendship':
   friend, companion, partner, acquaintance, fellow, colleague, neighbour
   List appropriate semantic components as vertical headings in the grid, with the words above listed horizontally.
   a) Are any of these words unsuitable for the same grid?

b) Are there any additional words from the same semantic field that could be included in the grid?
5. Devise a suitable grid for the language associated with 'libraries'; carefully consider appropriate categories.
6. Harvey (1983) lists some of the advantages of using grids in vocabulary teaching. List and discuss some of the *disadvantages*.
7. An example is given of a *word network* or thematic web for describing 'universities' (in Appendix 1.1).
   a) Apart from the categories of words shown and listed, which other groups or categories could be added for 'universities'?
   b) Draw a suitable word network for 'Academic reading' and/or 'Lectures'.
8. A list of eight main concerns of vocabulary teaching since 1980 is given (Carter and McCarthy 1988). Which three aspects do you consider most important for the learner?
9. What views do you have on concordancing? Have you ever been involved in it in any way?
10. Have you ever employed any techniques for assisting the remembrance of vocabulary, either in teaching or in any language learning of your own? Which seemed to be the most helpful?

11 Academic writing

As academic writing is so important for students of all kinds, and as it is such a wide umbrella term, it is hardly surprising that there is range of approaches and types of practice for it. Sometimes these depend upon an underlying philosophy, sometimes upon the starting-point of the students, sometimes upon the purpose and type of writing, and sometimes simply on personal preference.

The different approaches in the USA are usefully summarised and put into context by Silva (1990). The starting-point was *controlled* or *guided composition*, with its emphasis on the manipulation of language structures and sentence patterns. In Britain, such an approach, based on substitution tables, stemmed from the work of F. G. French, and in New Zealand from H. V. George – both in the 1960s. This led, in general EFL, to books on composition writing making use of substitution tables or writing frames (e.g. Spencer 1967; Moody 1974).

The next major development in the USA was 'current traditional rhetoric', in which the central concern was the logical arrangement of discourse forms in the context of the paragraph (e.g. Imhoof and Hudson 1975, in the UK). In Britain, this approach is better known as *rhetorical-functional*, or simply the *functional approach*. From an initial concern with sentences and paragraphs, the focus switched to essay development with its structure of introduction, body and conclusion.

All the above approaches, and others to come later, can be subsumed under the umbrella term *product approach*. In a nutshell, the product approach is concerned with the finished product – the text. In the 1980s, especially in the USA, dissatisfaction was expressed with the limitations of this approach. It was suggested that with the provision of the aimed-for model, and practice that called for parallel writing, often to a 'template' design, students were restricted in what they could write or how they could write it.

As a reaction to the above, the *process approach* began to develop. This is concerned with the processes of writing that enable the product to be achieved. The processes involved match the mental processes inherent in writing in the mother tongue, namely, planning, drafting, re-thinking, revising, etc. They allow students to express themselves more as individuals.

This is an oversimplification of these two approaches, but it provides a starting-point for a more detailed consideration.

11.1 The product approach

11.1.1 Rhetorical-functional

In the product approach, a model is provided and various exercises undertaken to draw attention to its important features. Students are then required to produce a similar or parallel text.

Since 1976, when Wilkins's *Notional Syllabuses* was published, the product approach has often been combined with the functional approach so that *functional-product* might be a more apt description. If you examine books following a broadly product approach, published in Britain in the last fifteen years or so, you will find that they all contain practice in some of the main language functions commonly found in academic writing. In addition, attention is given to the organisation of writing, its structure, cohesion, various grammatical aspects and academic style; also, some incorporate elements of the process approach. Some of the books are organised into topics or themes, but most are organised according to language functions; the main ones are as follows:

– Description (including processes and sequencing)
– Narrative
– Instruction
– Explanation
– Definition
– Exemplification
– Classification
– Comparison and contrast
– Cause and effect
– Expressing: purpose, means, prediction, expectancy,
                reservation, result
– Generalisation and specificity
– Discussion and argumentation (problem and solution)
– Drawing conclusions.

An example of the product approach (slightly modified) is included in Appendix 1.1. It is by Jordan (1990) and shows part of a unit on *Classification*. The model text is given first; exercises then analyse its features and check comprehension. A further exercise in diagrammatic form draws attention to the classification criteria, after which students are asked to describe the information in the diagram. Finally, students are asked to provide a diagram and description based on their own country. A structure and vocabulary aid is provided at the end of each unit. Additional help is provided, as needed, by several appendices giving ready-to-hand information that students might require when writing, e.g. accuracy, comparisons, connectives, referencing, etc.

Other books that largely follow a functional-product approach are: Cooper (1979), Johnson (1981), Glendinning and Mantell (1983), Wong, Glendinning and Mantell (1987), Arnaudet and Barrett (1990). They are all *common core* in their approach: they contain language functions applicable across a range of disciplines.

An alternative to the above general approach is for books to be more *specific*, or restricted, in their focus. This leads into a consideration of academic genre.

11.1.2 Academic genres

It has been pointed out, by Silva (1990) among others, that writing in EAP must be acceptable to the host academic institution. In other words, the reader 'has well-developed schemata for academic discourse and clear and stable views of what is appropriate'. The primary focus should, thus, be on 'academic discourse genres and the range and nature of academic writing tasks, aimed at helping to socialise the student into the academic context'.

The types of genre that students are expected to become familiar with, and to produce, include the following: essays, reports, case studies, projects, literature reviews, exam answers, research papers/articles, dissertations and theses. Each of these will have its own content structure or format, style, and various conventions. O'Brien, T. (1988) compared the writing of native-speaking psychology undergraduates in course-work essays and in examinations. Her preliminary findings regarding style indicated that the language used in examinations contained more instances of informal language than that used in course-work essays.

James (1993) describes an interesting information-structuring exercise given to master's degree students as part of the preparation for special-subject essay writing. This combines a process and product approach, and focuses on the need for an adequate structuring and signalling of information content. Davies (1988) discusses the combination of both product and process in the creation of a genre-based syllabus for academic writing. In defining genre, she follows Swales:

> A genre is a recognised communicative event with a shared public purpose and with aims mutually understood by the participants in that event.

(A fuller discussion of genres is contained in Chapter 16.)

At the pinnacle, so to speak, of academic writing, are dissertations and theses. In their nature, as individual pieces of research and writing, help can usually best be given to students on a one-to-one basis. This was reported in Chapter 2 when looking at the case-study approach to thesis writing of James (1984a) and Dudley-Evans (1988b and 1991). However, it is possible to organise classes for research students. Swales (1987) instances a course utilising the literature: the sociology of science, citation analysis, technical writing and writing introductions.

Another example of a course for research students is described by Richards (1988). She organised a four-week, half-time, course for scientific thesis and dissertation writing at an American university. It was the result of co-operation between subject departments and an EAP tutor. Richards designed the learning-centred course using an 'interactive needs analysis model [which] defines the target outcome and course objectives as the course develops'. The 'total discourse-centred course' was based on a collection of examples of theses and dissertations written in, and recommended by, the subject departments. Richards focused on the standard genre of four sections: introduction, methods, results and discussion. The resulting course consisted of: lectures, individual assignments, class revision of the assignments, discussion of class assignments and individual revising sessions.

A good example of a genre-based writing course is that by Swales and Feak (1994) – shown in Appendix 1.1. It shows part of a unit concerned with *Constructing a research paper*, to help graduate students with writing up their own research. It begins by showing the overall design of a typical research paper and explaining its four main sections (introduction, methods, results and discussion). Some basic linguistic research relating to research papers is presented in a table; in addition, comments from a research article are provided. For a task, pairs of students are asked to make use of the information given and their own knowledge, and determine which of the four sections the comments are from. In other words, a miniature research and judgemental task.

Other practice books relating broadly to a genre approach are Weissberg and Buker (1990) which focuses on writing up research; Dudley-Evans (1985) on laboratory reports; Reid (1988), and Clanchy and Ballard (1992), on writing essays.

11.2 The process approach

This approach emphasises the composing processes which writers utilise, and thus puts meaning to the fore rather than form. The approach accords with the principles of learner-centredness, encouraging individuals to take more responsibility for their own learning. By means of discussion, tasks, drafting, feedback, revisions and informed choices, students can make clearer decisions about the direction of their writing.

Feedback is an essential element in the process approach to writing. Keh (1990) discusses three types of feedback: peer evaluation, conferences (i.e. teacher-student interaction) and written comments (by the teacher). She concludes that each type of feedback has its uses and advantages. Feedback will be examined in more detail shortly. From the point of view of academic writing, this approach has the advantage of drawing attention to the constant need to draft and revise; in other words, encouraging students to be responsible for making improvements themselves.

Perhaps the clearest exposition of what is entailed in process writing is contained in a resource book for teachers by White and Arndt (1991). They:

> see a process-focused approach to writing as an enabling approach
> ... the goal of this approach is to nurture the skills with which
> writers *work out their own solution to the problems they set
> themselves*, with which they shape their raw material into a
> coherent message, and with which they work towards an acceptable
> and appropriate form for expressing it.

This approach views writing as creative and the task of teachers as being to engage students in the creative process.

In discussing the advantages and disadvantages of the approaches, White (1988a) admits that:

> much EAP writing is very product-oriented, since the conventions
> governing the organization and expression of ideas are very tight.
> Thus the learner has to become thoroughly familiarized with these
> conventions and must learn to operate within them.

Much the same point is made by Horowitz (1986b). White points out, however, that 'above all else, academic writing involves the manipulation of ideas' and that this is best achieved through writing process activities.

Research has been conducted into examining the composing processes that students actually use or prefer while writing dissertations or research articles (Shaw 1991; St John 1987; Zamel 1983). Shaw (1991) conducted a survey of the composing techniques of overseas post-graduate research scientists at Newcastle University; this was achieved by means of structured interviews. Among a number of results, the following are of particular interest:

– the students 'could have benefited from practice in co-authoring' and 'from getting feedback from fellow members of the same discourse community';

- they would also have benefited from 'practice writing on their subject rather than more general topics'.

Some of the recommendations that Shaw made were:

- appropriate reading can serve as a model for appropriate style; awareness-raising can be helped by critical imitation of models and the collection of subject-specific lists of words and phrases; all this helps 'learners to assimilate the conventions of the genre and the register of their subject';
- exercises in paraphrase and synthesis are crucial in helping to avoid plagiarism;
- there is not enough collaboration and feedback: the formation of study groups and collaborative writing should be encouraged on EAP courses.

With the process approach, books are usually arranged according to the *stages* and *sequence* of writing. For example, variations on the following structure may be adopted: preliminary ideas, prewriting activities, the outline, getting started, the first paragraph, the first draft, revising, editing, proofreading, further drafts, etc.

Examples of books which generally follow this approach are: Hamp-Lyons and Heasley (1987); Schenck (1988); Kwan-Terry (1988); Leki (1989); Frank (1990).

The vast majority of the books are aimed at students, usually studying in a group or class (but with the product approach, sometimes working alone and, therefore, with answer key and notes). A few books, however, are aimed at teachers. An example is Brookes and Grundy (1990), which contains advice, suggestions and a variety of exercises for communicative practice among groups of students, with their interests remaining central.

For further discussion about 'product versus process' see the following publications which also carry extensive references to further books and articles: Robinson (1988) and Kroll (1990).

A good example of the process approach is by White and McGovern (1994) – shown in Appendix 1.1. A workshop approach is adopted in which students consider tasks and discuss common problems. Their writing is treated as a recursive process, i.e. revising and rewriting at each stage. They are encouraged to read their own writing critically, helped by means of evaluation checklists. The example shown is from a unit on *Comparing and contrasting cities*, and shows the tasks and steps involved in organising descriptions and determining categories. Typical writing tasks in White and McGovern have the following stages:

- discussion
- brainstorming

- self-evaluation
- planning
- peer evaluation
- writing the first draft
- self-evaluation
- peer evaluation
- revision/rewriting
- writing the second draft
- teacher evaluation and marking.

Note: Textbooks referred to in this chapter are listed in Appendix 1.2.

11.3 Summarising, paraphrasing and synthesising

Summary writing is an important aspect of academic writing, and is linked to academic reading by means of note-taking or note-making. Johns (1988b) argues that traditional approaches to summary writing often ignore the processes involved, and frequently overestimate the capabilities of the students, assuming that an instruction such as 'make the summary one-third the length of the text' is adequate. Johns outlines an approach which involves a consideration of the underlying structure of the text. She finds that this approach:

> results in a more accurate processing and written gist of the original text than does most of the surface script or rule-based instruction presently found.

She takes the example of the problem/solution text, fairly common in academic writing, with its four categories of topics – situation, problem, responses/solutions and evaluation. The students are instructed to draw four boxes, representing each of the categories. Starting with 'situation', in groups they analyse the text to find all the sentences that refer to it. They then describe the situation in their own words below the appropriate box; the same procedure is adopted for all four categories/boxes. Finally, the students produce their own summaries based on the box-diagram they have created.

Edge (1983) also emphasises the importance of summary writing. He demonstrates a procedure by which students work in pairs on a text, producing notes on each paragraph in turn, discussing areas of difficulty and agreement as they proceed. Finally, they reconstitute their notes into a one-paragraph summary of the original text. Useful practice is also given in Swales and Feak (1994) and Trzeciak and Mackay (1994).

An integral part of reading and summarising is paraphrasing – expressing someone else's ideas in your own words, structure and style. This difficult but essential skill is practised step by step in one popular American textbook (Arnaudet and Barrett 1984).

An aspect of academic writing that has received little attention is:

> the ability to integrate information from previous researchers in relevant areas of study. Even the most original academic paper integrates facts, ideas, concepts, and theories from other sources by means of quotations, paraphrases, summaries, and brief references.
>
> (Campbell 1990)

This integration or synthesising of others' writing has also been commented on by Leki and Carson (1994) who recommend that:

> EAP writing classes need to move away from writing tasks that require students only to tap their own opinions and experiences and toward work that encourages students to integrate those opinions and experiences with external sources of information and argument.

Campbell (1990) investigated how university students (NS and NNS) used information from background reading texts in their own academic writing. She concluded that the primary method of text integration was copying; references were given too infrequently (see the section on plagiarising in Chapter 6). She advocated training in the different ways of referring to sources. She also recommended that:

> writing instructors working with non-native speakers need to emphasize that source material is most often used as background and support for their own written ideas.

This is in order to discourage a tendency for the background text to govern rather than support the writer's content. Finally, Campbell considers that process-oriented writing is the most suitable means of developing an awareness of academic text and its various conventions.

In connection with aspects of the above, there are very strict academic conventions regarding the use and layout of references, which include quotations, footnotes and bibliographies. These will vary (in degree) from country to country, from institution to institution, and even from department to department. Students thus need to check the various conventions and styles carefully at their host institution. These conventions will be looked at generally in Chapter 14.

11.4   Feedback and evaluation

No matter which kind of academic writing students undertake, they will need feedback regarding its acceptability and accuracy. The feedback may take several forms, and is most often written by the teacher/tutor.

Some research has shown that overwhelmingly teachers:

> attend primarily to surface-level features of writing and seem to read and react to a text as a series of separate sentences or even clauses

> rather than as a whole unit of discourse. They are in fact so
> distracted by language-related local problems that they often correct
> these without realizing that a much larger meaning-related problem
> has totally escaped their notice
>
> (Zamel 1985)

Zamel noted that teachers frequently put generalised comments on students' writing. However, what was needed was more specific guidance to help students to understand how to revise their writing, and to lead them through 'cycles of revision'. There is some evidence that students do, in fact, find their teachers' feedback useful in helping them to improve their writing. The evidence indicates that students pay more attention if it is provided on preliminary drafts rather than final drafts (Ferris 1995).

11.4.1 Correcting codes

One typical method of correction of student writing is for the teacher to underline or cross out the errors and simply write in the correction (above it or in the margin). This may be done to save time or to ensure that students have a fully corrected version. However, there is some evidence to indicate that this is not an effective method as it does not actively involve the student and often does not prevent the mistake from being repeated. There is evidence, on the other hand, that shows that the use of teacher cues (e.g. underlining the error) assists students to engage actively in the process of self-correction, and is particularly effective with grammatical errors (Fathman and Whalley 1990; Makino 1993). Hamp-Lyons and Heasley (1987) give examples of, and discuss, different correcting procedures.

White and Arndt (1991) note that:

> Many teachers devise their own codes or sets of symbols for
> drawing attention to grammatical features, such as the following:
> S   = subject missing
> V   = verb form error
> A   = article error
> T   = tense error
> SV   = subject-verb concord error
> Adv = adverb order error, misplaced adverb or adverb missing
> Adj   = adjective order error, misplaced or missing adjective
> Prep = preposition error
> Such symbols can be written in the margin adjacent to the line in
> which the error occurs, and the student has to identify and correct
> the errors concerned.

It is generally recommended that not all errors are cued (the learner could be overwhelmed or discouraged). The emphasis should be on errors that interfere with communication and those that recur frequently. The main language areas that are likely to be concentrated on are organisation, style, grammar and vocabulary, together with the more mechanical aspects of spelling and punctuation.

An example of a list of symbols and their purpose as explained to students, appears in Appendix 1.1. It is important that the students have appropriate-level grammar books and a good monolingual learner's dictionary. The example refers to a 'grammar workshop': this aspect is looked at briefly below.

11.4.2 *Grammar*

Grammar, like vocabulary, is fundamental to all language learning. However, the reason for a short consideration of it is because of the importance it assumes to students. For example, Johns (1994), in the context of describing classroom concordancing or Data-driven Learning (see Chapter 10), notes the popularity of remedial grammar classes among overseas postgraduates at Birmingham University. He concludes that their preference for grammar is often 'a plea for help in overcoming confusion'. Support for this view is given by Leki and Carson (1994) who conducted a follow-up survey of NNS students at two American universities. They found that among the students who had attended EAP writing classes, there was 'a particular need for ... more language-related training focused especially on vocabulary and grammar'.

Many EAP courses attend to students' needs for grammatical help by the provision of grammar workshops in which common difficulties can be explained and practised. Another approach is by means of individual feedback and advice based on writing assignments. A resource centre, or self-access materials, may also provide help with a remedial grammar bank of exercises/practice based on accumulated experience of the type of help needed. The actual grammatical items to be practised will depend on the language level, difficulties and needs of the students. In general, however, most courses make use of grammar books: both reference grammars and student practice grammars.

11.4.3 *Student self-evaluation/-monitoring*

A scheme in which students tell the teacher the kind of help they want is referred to by White and Arndt (1991) (suggested by Coe), and illustrated below. The students put the code in the appropriate place in the margin of their writing.

R Please reply to content.

CM Please correct mistakes.

IM Please indicate (but don't correct) mistakes.

IMAC Indicate mistakes and add category (e.g. V for verb error, T for tense, etc.).

WUO Comment on words underlined only. (In this case, the student may be trying something out and may not be sure whether it is acceptable, appropriate or correct. The underlining of words or sections concerned encourages students to experiment and show that they are doing so.)

A similar 'self-monitoring' technique has been successfully developed by Charles (1990):

Students write the first draft of an assignment. They underline and number those parts of the text with which they are dissatisfied, either during the process of composing or on completion of the draft. They then annotate these problem areas with their queries, difficulties, comments, or judgements.

Charles notes four steps with this procedure:

1. Students draft and 'monitor' their texts.
2. Teacher/editor responds in writing to monitored comments.
3. Students respond to editorial comment and rewrite their drafts.
4. Teacher/editor responds to student comment and second draft.

Charles discusses the advantages of the technique noting, in particular, that as the students are actively involved in the process of correction, they are likely to be more receptive to the teacher's comments. A big advantage of the technique is that it reveals the concerns of the student, which may be very different from those of the teacher. (For another self-correction technique see Chandrasegaran 1986.)

11.4.4 Reformulation

In a discussion of mistake correction, Johnson (1988) firstly draws attention to the distinction made by Corder (1981) between *errors* and *mistakes*. Errors are a result of faulty knowledge (not knowing, or having the wrong idea), while mistakes are caused by a lack of processing ability (the knowledge is there, but there is a difficulty in applying it). Johnson suggests that there are four conditions necessary, on the part of the student, for *mistakes* to be eradicated:

a) The desire or need to eradicate the mistake.
b) An internal representation of what the correct behaviour looks like (i.e. the 'knowledge').
c) A realisation by the student that the performance given is flawed.
d) An opportunity to repractise in real conditions.

Johnson also highlights the difference between *reconstruction* and *reformulation*, as 'after the event' techniques:

> In *reconstruction*, errors and mistakes are simply corrected. The result will be sentences free from gross malformations, but ones which may not remotely resemble sentences a native speaker would produce to express the same content. Because reconstruction focuses on errors and mistakes, it may well provide the learner with information on where he or she went wrong.

Reformulation, of which there are several versions, consists, basically, of a native speaker rewriting a student's text, as far as possible retaining the intended meaning. Reformulation provides the student with information on how a native speaker would have written the same thing, i.e. a kind of model.

Allwright (1988) describes in detail the procedure for using reformulation in the writing class. The:

> rewriting may necessitate making changes of many kinds and at all levels, involving syntax, lexis, cohesion and discourse functions, but the point of any such changes must be to respect and bring out the original writer's probable intentions.

Allwright's aim is to help students to develop writer autonomy as quickly as possible; consequently, they 'have to be able to accept responsibility for editing, correcting and proof-reading their own texts'.

Allwright acknowledges that reformulation is, perhaps, ideal with a pairing system (one native-speaker writer for one student), but appreciates the virtual impossibility of such an arrangement in most teaching situations. She, therefore, developed the strategy of the class discussing one reformulation of one representative non-native text. Her strategy involves typing the original non-native version and the reformulation so that the anonymity of both writer and reformulator is preserved. First the non-native text is distributed to the class and they are asked to decide if the meaning is clear. Then the reformulation is circulated. The class is split into pairs/groups and asked to compare the two versions, noting similarities and differences, and discussing the probable reasons for the changes made. The students then report back in a plenary discussion session which Allwright considers to be 'the cornerstone of the whole reformulation strategy'.

Among other things, the:

> discussion is a consciousness-raising device which can help students and teacher to identify more clearly the features of a good text. As a result, clear and explicit criteria for editing and refining a text will eventually emerge.

These may involve the:

> more central issues of composition – overall organization,
> signposting, cohesion, information-packaging, and clarity of
> meaning (which) are too inconsistently dealt with by marginal notes
> on student texts – notes that are frequently too cryptic to be
> meaningful and helpful.

Further discussion of reformulation as a practical strategy for the teaching of academic writing is contained in Allwright, Woodley and Allwright (1988).

11.4.5 Peer-correction

Another approach to the correction of written work that ensures the active involvement of students is the correction of each other's writing, in pairs or groups, under the guidance of the teacher. Norrish (1983) describes the process as a stimulating and useful exercise for students as it encourages communication between them. Students can use a correcting code for the writing, similar to that described earlier. Such a procedure can save time, especially if writing needs to be checked in a sizeable class. It then allows the teacher to concentrate on major difficulties and to discuss aspects of them with the pairs/groups. Bartram and Walton (1991) show in diagrammatic form how peer-correction can operate in a large class, as well as discussing the merits of various correction techniques (see also Okoye 1994).

It is not always necessary (or perhaps desirable) for students actually to correct each other's writing. However, the opportunity to talk about their essays and discuss ideas with their peers gives valuable feedback as well as developing a sense of audience (Mendonca and Johnson 1994).

Finally, it should not be forgotten that students react to praise in a positive way. Cohen and Cavalcanti (1990) indicate that a balance between pointing out errors and praising what is correct may be the best means of encouraging improvements in writing. In their research studies they noted that 'students – especially the weak ones – are quite anxious to receive at least some feedback as to what they are doing right'.

11.5 Conclusion

From all that has been said above, it may be surmised that EAP courses should, as far as possible, combine both a process and a product approach to academic writing. While it is necessary for students to be aware of the processes involved in improving their writing, and actively to take part in developing those processes, it is also necessary for them to be aware of the target product. Their writing will need to conform to the requirements of their discipline and specific department, and the appropriate academic genre. Projects (in pairs or groups) are one way in which this integration can be achieved (see Chapter 4). Another is to undertake tasks of the type included in such books as Hamp-Lyons and Heasley (1987) and Brookes and Grundy (1990), which emphasise purposeful collaboration in the writing process.

Whichever approach to academic writing is adopted, it is useful to involve students in initial awareness-raising activities. For example, they can be provided with a list of academic writing skills and discuss their relative importance, and their own needs and difficulties, e.g. making an outline, describing tables and charts, being concise, summarising, etc. (see Waters and Waters 1995, page 91).

Finally, some other aspects of academic writing that have not been considered in this chapter, namely, style, 'hedging' and vague language, will be looked at in Chapter 16.

11.6 Introspect and discuss

1. Near the beginning of the chapter, a list is given of language functions commonly found in course books based on the *product approach*. From your experience, can you suggest further functions that should be added to the list for students attending EAP courses?
2. Three types of feedback are referred to in connection with the *process approach*. Keh (1990) concluded that each type has its uses and advantages. Suggest some of the advantages.
3. What do you consider to be the main advantages and disadvantages of both the product and the process approach, from the point of view of the teacher, and the student?
4. From your experience, what are the most effective types of practice for helping students to write summaries?
5. Which type of correction procedure have you found to be most effective with students? Is it one of those referred to in the chapter, or a different one?
6. If you have ever used a correcting code, is it the same as that illustrated in the chapter, or are there any big differences?
7. Within academic writing practice, which grammatical features have you found constantly cause difficulties for students? Which types of exercise and/or which grammar books have you found most useful in helping students to overcome the difficulties?
8. Imagine that you have just read a student's university-level essay in the social sciences. It contained the following types of error or mistake (some more frequently than others):
   a) singular/plural confusion, and lack of concord
   b) misuse or omission of articles

   c) wrong verb tenses and forms
   d) lack of punctuation
   e) misuse of prepositions
   f) wrong vocabulary
   g) lack, and misuse, of logical connectors
   h) spelling mistakes
   i) lack of appropriate paragraphing
   j) mixing formal and informal language
   k) inappropriate style
   l) seemingly unaware of referencing conventions.

   Note down which types of error/mistake you consider to be the most important and which the least important. Which correcting techniques seem most appropriate for the different types of error/mistake?

9. There appear to be considerable benefits for students from the techniques of self-monitoring and reformulation. Do you see any difficulties for teachers in implementing these techniques? How would you propose to overcome the difficulties?

10. a) Reference was made to praising what is correct. Simply writing 'good' in the margin is not very helpful as the students do not know what is good and why it is good. Can you suggest any more helpful way of giving praise?

    b) Can you devise a helpful 'praising code' of abbreviations/symbols for consistent use with good writing?

12 Lectures and note-taking

When students go to a lecture, they may already have some background knowledge of the subject and be able to predict a little of the content of the lecture, not least from its title. However, it is at this point that problems may develop. James (1977) summarises the main problems, within three broad areas:

1. decoding, i.e. recognising what has been said;
2. comprehending, i.e. understanding the main and subsidiary points;
3. taking notes, i.e. writing down quickly, briefly and clearly the important points for future use.

Expanding a little on these areas, we may see that the act of decoding involves not only recognising unit boundaries phonologically, but also the recognition of 'irregular pausing, false starts, hesitations, stress and intonation patterns' (Flowerdew 1994). The problem will be exacerbated for NNS who lack familiarity with spoken discourse structure, various styles of delivery and the accent and speed of speaking of the lecturer. Students may be inexperienced in listening to fluent, native-speaker spoken English together with its colloquialisms and idiomatic expressions, apart from probable difficulties caused by the use of weak forms and contractions. Comprehension difficulties may be compounded by insufficient knowledge of the specialist subject.

The lecture genre itself (discussed in Benson 1994) brings its own particular and potential areas of difficulty. Especially problematic is:

> the requirement to be able to concentrate on and understand long stretches of talk without the opportunity of engaging in the facilitating functions of interactive discourse, such as asking for a repetition, negotiating meaning.
>
> (Flowerdew 1994)

In addition, students may be expected to combine the spoken input with input from other sources, e.g. handouts, black/white-board displays, slides, overhead projector transparencies or video.

Note-taking can also cause problems. As a skill, it involves several processes, among which are:

– the ability to distinguish between important and less important information;

- deciding when to record the points (so that other important points are not missed while writing);
- the ability to write concisely and clearly in a kind of personal shorthand which will probably make use of various devices, e.g. abbreviations, symbols, etc.;
- the ability to decipher one's own notes at a later date and to recall the essence of the lecture.

In this chapter, we shall be looking at various investigations that have been conducted into lecturing styles, the structuring of lectures, the signalling devices used by lecturers and note-taking. Combined with these, we shall also look at some examples of published material for lectures and note-taking.

Richards (1983) has neatly summarised the range of topics associated with research into lectures by constructing a taxonomy of micro-skills needed for academic listening (listed below). Features of the language itself may cause difficulties for students as well as the way in which the lecture is delivered.

Micro-Skills: Academic Listening (Listening to Lectures)
1. ability to identify purpose and scope of lecture
2. ability to identify topic of lecture and follow topic development
3. ability to identify relationships among units within discourse (e.g. major ideas, generalizations, hypotheses, supporting ideas, examples)
4. ability to identify role of discourse markers in signalling structure of a lecture (e.g. conjunctions, adverbs, gambits, routines)
5. ability to infer relationships (e.g. cause, effect, conclusion)
6. ability to recognize key lexical items related to subject/topic
7. ability to deduce meanings of words from context
8. ability to recognize markers of cohesion
9. ability to recognize function of intonation to signal information structure (e.g. pitch, volume, pace, key)
10. ability to detect attitude of speaker toward subject matter
11. ability to follow different modes of lecturing: spoken, audio, audio-visual
12. ability to follow lecture despite differences in accent and speed
13. familiarity with different styles of lecturing: formal, conversational, read, unplanned
14. familiarity with different registers: written versus colloquial
15. ability to recognize irrelevant matter: jokes, digressions, meanderings
16. ability to recognize function of non-verbal cues as markers of emphasis and attitude
17. knowledge of classroom conventions (e.g. turn taking, clarification requests)

18. ability to recognize instructional/learner tasks (e.g. warnings, suggestions, recommendations, advice, instructions)

A dimension often missing from research into lectures is that of their cultural features. Flowerdew and Miller (1995) conducted a three-year study of lecturers given in areas of science, social sciences, business and law by NS lecturers to NNS students at the City University of Hong Kong. They devised a cultural framework for the analysis of lectures which had four dimensions: ethnic, local, academic and disciplinary cultures. To take one example, disciplinary culture: they observed a considerable variation in discourse structure across disciplines. In law, the lecture discourse was often structured around a series of problem-solving tasks illustrating a certain legal concept. In computer science, lectures typically followed a problem-solution pattern. In economics, they were sometimes structured around a series of related concepts, with examples. In public and social administration, they took the form of a comparison between different models or systems.

There are important consequences for EAP staff. As Flowerdew and Miller conclude, they 'need to sensitise their students to the culture of lectures being delivered in English by Western lecturers'. Tutors can help their students to understand the cultural aspects of lectures 'by discussing such things as students' cultural assumptions about lectures and comparing and contrasting these with the objectives and underlying assumptions of the Western lecturers'.

12.1 Lecturing styles and lecture structure

Morrison (1974) analysed science lectures and divided them into two kinds: *formal* ('formal register, and close to spoken prose') and *informal* ('high informational content but not necessarily in highly formal register'). He noted that students had greater difficulty understanding informal lectures than formal ones. This may be regarded as a basic division for most lectures.

Dudley-Evans and Johns (1981) analysed lectures in transportation, plant biology and minerals engineering, and identified three styles of lecturing:

A. *Reading Style*: the lecturer reads from notes (or sounds as if he is so doing); characterised by short tone-groups, and narrowness of intonational range; a falling tone predominates.
B. *Conversational Style*: the lecturer speaks informally, with or without notes; characterised by longer tone-groups and key-sequences from high to low.
C. *Rhetorical Style*: the lecturer as performer; characterised by wide

intonational range; often exploiting high key; frequent asides and digressions.

Other analyses of lecture modes have used different terms to indicate the essence of the mode. Two examples are given from Flowerdew (1994):

1. Goffman (1981, reported in Flowerdew):
   – *memorization*
   – *aloud reading*
   – *fresh talk*
2. Mason (1994):
   – *talk-and-chalk* (the blackboard is the main visual aid)
   – *give-and-take* (material is presented by the lecturer to encourage discussion, questions and comments)
   – *report-and-discuss* (topics are allocated by the lecturer for study, presentation and discussion in the class; the students' participation is integral).

Flowerdew (1994) comments that there is an increasing use of the informal, conversational style, based on notes or handouts. In the USA at least, there is more interaction between lecturer and students; in itself, this might cause problems for NNS from backgrounds where the lecturing style is the more traditional monologue.

12.1.1 Structure: information versus ideas

Another aspect of lectures to consider, in analysing features to assist students, is the type of lecture and its purpose. Olsen and Huckin (1990) analysed the written responses of students to a task set for a mechanical engineering lecture. They concluded that many students were not aware of the distinction between: (1) lectures giving information, and (2) those developing an argument, point by point, with a discussion of ideas and in a problem-solving framework. In the former, an 'information-driven' listening strategy is needed, whereby facts can be absorbed. In the latter, a 'point-driven' listening strategy is needed with which listeners can 'take a broader view [of] ... the larger situation of which the discourse is part'. In effect, this involves 'the discourse as having a single overriding main point and a number of subordinate points supporting it'. Students will also need to infer the speaker's intentions and goals.

Further research by Tauroza and Allison (1994), among first year science undergraduates in Hong Kong, complemented Olsen's and Huckin's findings in several respects, especially in showing that 'L2 listeners have difficulties following argumentation that is developed in more complex discourse structures than they are used to'. However, Tauroza and Allison found that their students had few difficulties understanding the lecturer's main points, 'except when one such point was introduced in a manner which they did not expect'. Later, Allison and Tauroza (1995) replicated their experiment among L1 students. They found that both groups of students have similar problems in understanding lectures when complex discourse patterns beyond the most basic problem-solution pattern are used.

Dudley-Evans (1994) investigated lectures in highway engineering and plant biology and agreed to a considerable extent with Olsen and Huckin that the point-driven strategy is needed to understand the 'problem-solution' lecture framework. Dudley-Evans concluded by considering the implications for teaching listening comprehension on an EAP course. He recommends that as well as common-core listening strategies (EGAP), students 'will need to be made aware of the particular features that distinguish the practices of the discourse community they wish to become members of' (ESAP).

Practice books and tapes for students in listening and note-taking have mainly focused on two styles of lecture delivery: the 'reading style', exemplified by James *et al.* (1979/91); and the 'conversational style', exemplified by McDonough (1978a), Mason (1983), and Lynch (1983). Often the talks or extracts increase in length during the course, and control may be gradually removed from the note-taking exercises. Additional grading may be provided by increasing the complexity of the listening tasks. The principle of moving from 'small' to 'big' may be extended to the listening, for example, from 'localised' (individual items and small segments) to 'global' ('semantic' or whole meaning). Some of these books will be looked at shortly.

12.2 Listening cues

Whichever style of lecturing is adopted, the lecturer will normally make use of various devices in order to indicate to listeners the relative importance of the ideas and information contained in the talk. These devices, or cues, are usually of three types (Tyler *et al.* 1988):

- prosodic features (stress, intonation, pauses);
- subordinating syntactic structures (e.g. relative clauses, noun complements, other subordinate clauses);
- lexical discourse markers (e.g. logical connectors, number and other phrases).

In addition, there can be 'vocal underlining':

> varying the pace, pitch, and volume of . . . speech to emphasise
> particular ideas . . . A lecturer's voice can signal meanings as
> effectively as words can.
>
> (Yorkey 1982)

The body can also be used to emphasise various points, in particular, the use of hand gestures. Other non-verbal cues are referred to by Brown (1978). It is for these reasons that it is important for students to experience either live lectures, or lectures on video, in their EAP courses.

In an investigation of 'how different categories of discourse markers affect the degree to which foreign students understand university lectures', Chaudron and Richards (1986) concentrated primarily on lectures in the reading style. They divided the markers into two types: macro-markers and micro-markers. *Macro-markers* are 'higher-order discourse markers signalling major transitions and emphasis in the lectures'; *micro-markers* are 'lower-order markers of segmentation and intersentential connections'. Chaudron and Richards list the markers used in their research: these are reproduced below. They found that:

> a lecture read from a written text will usually lack the kinds of
> macro-markers found in the more conversational style of teaching.
> A lecture which uses more macro-markers is likely to be easier to
> follow. On the other hand, an over-use of micro-markers possibly
> detracts from the overall coherence of the lecture. For the
> curriculum and materials developer, and for L2 teachers, the macro-
> markers probably constitute a relevant focus for second-language
> classroom activities and instructional materials.

Micro-Markers

Segmentation	Temporal	Causal	Contrast	Emphasis
Well	*At that time*	*So*	*Both*	*Of course*
OK	*And*	*Then*	*But*	*You can see*
Now	*After this*	*Because*	*Only*	*You see*
And	*For the moment*		*On the other hand*	*Actually*
Right	*Eventually*			*Obviously*
All right				*Unbelievably*
				As you know
				In fact
				Naturally

Macro-Markers

What I'm going to talk about today is something
you probably know something about already –
What [had] happened [then/after that] was [that]
We'll see that
That/this is why
To begin with

Another interesting development was
You probably know that
The surprising thing is
As you may have heard
Now where are we
This is how it came about

The problem [here] was that	*You can imagine what happened next*
This/that was how	*In this way*
The next thing was	*It's really very interesting that*
This meant that	*This is not the end of the story*
One of the problems was	*Our story doesn't finish there*
Here was a big problem	*And that's all we'll talk about today*
What we've come to by now was that	

DeCarrico and Nattinger (1988) built on the research by Chaudron and Richards and investigated lectures from a variety of disciplines and delivered in all three styles (re Dudley-Evans and Johns), though the main focus was on the conversational style. They used an informal lexical phrase approach (i.e. ' "chunks" of language of varying length, phrases like *as it were, that goes without saying ...* ') and confined their study to macro-markers, or 'macro-organizers' as they preferred to call them. The macro-organizers 'function rather as important directional signals ... and so indicate how the information in the lecture is organised'.

DeCarrico and Nattinger divided the macro-organizers into eight main functional categories: topic markers, topic shifters, summarizers, exemplifiers, relators, evaluators, qualifiers and aside markers. They further divided these functional categories into:

> (a) global macro-organizers [the first three in their list above] – those that indicate the overall organization of the lecture – and (b), local macro-organizers [the last five in the list above] – those that also highlight sequencing or importance of information, but do so at specific points *within* the overall framework set by the global organizers.

DeCarrico and Nattinger concluded that foreign students:

> would not be expected to know that these lexical phrase macro-organizers are signalling important functions in the lecture discourse.

Consequently, they suggest that more emphasis needs to be placed on teaching these markers.

Yorkey (1982) focused on recognising and understanding the function of the various markers by categorising a lengthy list of examples of 'Note-making Cues'. They were divided into:

Introduction to an idea
Development of an idea
Contrast of several ideas
Results of ideas
Transition of ideas
Chronology of ideas
Emphasis of an idea
Summary of ideas.

However, no listening practice was provided.

Now follow two examples from published materials showing the different approaches to giving practice in markers. In the first example, Lynch (1983) looks at three types of importance markers, and gives practice in recognising them and noting the importance points that follow. The practice consists of the following stages: exemplification/recognition; identification and discussion; listening and recognition; listening and writing. An example from Lynch is given in Appendix 1.1. The second example, from Williams (1982), draws attention to markers that have already been heard in a talk and questions their significance (also in Appendix 1.1).

12.3 Informal language

In a description of a team-teaching experiment involving lecture comprehension, Johns and Dudley-Evans (1980) touch on the problems created by the lecturers' use of colloquial words and phrases – 'most of whom do not realise how many colloquialisms they use': for example, 'This is *pretty* difficult', 'We'll need to *jack up* the figures'. Johns and Dudley-Evans devised practice material in which students were asked to guess the meaning of colloquialisms and to find equivalents in formal written English.

This use of colloquial language was also noted by Jackson and Bilton (1994) who investigated geology lectures given in English by NS to NNS students in the Sultanate of Oman, at Sultan Qaboos University (SQU). They observed that the lecturers sometimes used analogies to explain certain concepts

> during which they often moved from the scientific world into the everyday one. However, not everyone shares the same everyday world ... Moreover, the lecturers' shift to a colloquial register when using analogies may have disconcerted the SQU students, whose exposure to English had been restricted to a formal classroom setting.

Strodt-Lopez (1991), in an investigation of American university lectures, found that some of the structural features of everyday conversation are carried over into lectures, though usually fulfilling a different role. She found that 'asides' (e.g. 'by the way') are one such structure. An aside is simply talking about something other than 'topic'. Strodt-Lopez shows that asides contribute to the global unity of the lecture, for example, by enabling the speaker 'to forestall or repair the apparent contradiction' that has arisen in the main line of argument. She concludes that detailed analyses of lectures are the most fruitful way for students to observe their structure; too often teaching materials 'focus on one hierarchical structure and markers of it'.

An analysis of lecture transcripts with students is described by Lebauer (1984); the analysis draws attention to cues, references, repetition, etc. By means of cloze-type exercises, the students are introduced to concepts of cues, organisational patterns, redundancy, expansion and paraphrase. At a later stage, they make predictions about the discourse direction. Finally, note-taking is practised.

12.4 Taking notes

A distinction is sometimes made between note-*taking* and note-*making*. *Note-taking* is the straightforward writing down of whatever is said or written on a board, etc. It may not require much thought. *Note-making*, on the other hand, is the creation of your *own* notes, which may involve summarising, paraphrasing, putting question marks against some items (to query, check or comment on at a later stage), and making important elements stand out by visual means. For convenience here, however, the more generally used term *note-taking* will be used for both.

The importance of note-taking in the lecture comprehension process has been observed by several researchers in Flowerdew (1994). In particular, the quality of notes and training in note-taking were looked at as an aspect of successful recall of lecture information by students at a later time (Chaudron, Loschky and Cook 1994).

Rost (1990) provides a list of types of note-taking (reproduced below). Many of the aspects and items listed are practised on EAP courses and in listening and note-taking books, which will be looked at shortly.

> *Topic-relation notes:*
> 1. Topicalizing – writing down a word or phrase to represent a section of the text
> 2. Translating – writing down L1 equivalent of topic
> 3. Copying – writing down verbatim what the lecturer has written on the blackboard (overhead projector, etc.)
> 4. Transcribing – writing down verbatim what the lecturer has said
> 5. Schematizing – inserting graphics (e.g. diagrams) to organize or represent a topic or relationship
>
> *Concept-ordering notes:*
> 1. Sequence cuing – listing topics in order, numbering
> 2. Hierarchy cuing – labelling notes as main point (key finding, conclusion, etc.) or example (quote, anecdote, etc.)
> 3. Relation ordering – left-to-right indenting, using arrows, dashes, semi-circles, or = signs to indicate relation among topics

Focusing notes:
1. Highlighting – underlining, placing a dot or arrow in front of a topic, circling a topic word
2. De-highlighting – writing in smaller letters or placing topic inside parentheses

Revising notes:
1. Inserting – drawing arrow back to earlier note, inserting with caret
2. Erasing – crossing out old note.

Types of correspondences between listener notes and lecture texts

(From Rost 1990)

Dunkel and Davy (1989) investigated note-taking in lectures. The main reasons given by students for the importance of note-taking were:
– as a mnemonic device;
– to prepare for exams;
– to reinforce or compare information contained in the textbook and the lecture;
– to increase attention during the lecture.

A comparison was made by Clerehan (1995) of L1 and L2 undergraduate notes in the same commercial law lecture at Monash University, Australia. The biggest differences were in the students' noting of the hierarchical structure of the lecture, where L1 students recorded almost 100 per cent of the main elements. On the other hand, the L2 students omitted an average of 19 per cent of major headings, 34 per cent of sub-headings, and 40 per cent of legal cases.

Murphy (1980) describes an interesting dimension to devising self-access note-taking tasks for a tape-slide programme, in a resource centre, based on recorded lectures. He collected sets of notes from NS students of engineering after a lecture, and examined them with the lecturer. 'They were all considered to be adequate in his view, and two sets were singled out as being "very good".' Clearly, notes are personal to each student, and each student may be idiosyncratic in the way that the notes are taken. However, for the non-specialist EAP teacher, the potential use of subject-specialist students' notes may be invaluable as an aid to devising practice material, especially if done with the co-operation of the specialist department. For example, the outline, hierarchy of main points, and use of some of the content, may help in constructing guided note-taking worksheets (based on a recorded lecture or talk).

Note-taking as a skill is not easy in one's own language; in a foreign language, the difficulties can become very serious. For this reason, considerable help may be needed, which may take several forms. Some of these forms are now looked at in the context of some of the books that give note-taking practice.

Help may be provided by supplying the overall framework or structure of a talk (with numbered sections, points, etc.) and/or giving semantic or discourse markers or cues. In the early stages, and at lower language levels, it may be necessary for students to have practice in writing down the words that they hear in the order that they hear them (similar to a dictation). Once they have increased their ability and confidence, they can try to take notes with the use of discourse markers, and later to try to paraphrase as they listen and write (a very demanding task). By using standard and personal abbreviations and symbols, they can save some time in writing (see the example in Appendix 1.1 from James *et al.* 1991). A preliminary activity that has been found useful in helping students to transfer information from the spoken word to paper, is the provision of a table or chart which must be completed while listening to a talk.

Probably the vast majority of students are only aware of the note-taking system that they have used in their mother tongue; in all probability, this will be a linear system, involving the vertical listing of items and points. Very often this system is not as developed as it might be for the purposes of clarity. It can often be improved by showing the use of numbers and letters to separate sections and sub-sections, and the use of space and indentations for the layout. In addition, the use of capital letters and underlining, as well as boxing and the possible use of colour, can increase the impact.

Although a linear system may be perfectly satisfactory, or even the best for the purpose, it is useful for students to be aware of alternative systems. They can then compare and discuss the relative merits. One that is sometimes used or demonstrated is the *branching system*: it may be referred to by other names, e.g. diagramming, web, mapping, or a variant – mind or concept map. In its basic form, it consists of a central topic (centralised on the page and boxed or ringed) from which the points emanate, like the spokes of a wheel. The use of lines, arrows, and boxes is important for providing the linking. The system is essentially visual, and for some people it makes it easier to remember its content.

Some examples of *guided note-taking* are included in Appendix 1.1. The first is from Heaton and Dunmore (1992) which shows a task which concentrates on the use of *space and clear organisation*. The second extract (James *et al.* 1991) consists of two parts. The first part (from the beginning of a talk) shows the use of *word cues* to prompt the writing of the information and ideas that follow. This lower-level task is devised to help students to write the exact words that they hear, in the same sequence. It is an expanded blank-fill exercise. The second part shows alternative guidance for the same section of the talk; this time *discourse markers* are used as prompts for the more advanced note-taking. The third extract shows the use of *branching notes* (from Wallace 1980). In some respects, 'mind maps' are similar in that they also depend on a visual layout, showing points being linked in various ways (see Forman *et al.* 1990).

12.5 Lecture length

To the problems facing students taking notes in lectures can be added one more item: the sheer length of a lecture, usually 45–60 minutes. Students need help in building up their ability to concentrate and take notes for such a lengthy period. For this reason, some course books give note-taking practice in steps. For example, Lynch (1983) develops students' understanding of the way English is used in lectures (and seminars) through four *phases*. The first helps to find 'important information *within* sentences; the second, to recognise logical connections *between* sentences; the third deals with *sections* of a talk'; and the fourth looks at *complete* talks.

James *et al.* (1991) makes use of three *stages* for each unit. The first stage, less than one minute, provides a brief introduction to the lecture: it can be used as discussion input. The second stage, up to $3\frac{1}{2}$ minutes, contains an intermediate version of the lecture, with a listening and blank-fill exercise. Stage three, up to $10\frac{1}{2}$ minutes, gives the full version of the talk, with guided note-taking in two versions, one more difficult than the other.

To assist the understanding of lectures and the development of note-taking on EAP courses, there is often an increase in difficulty, complexity, length of talk and variety of delivery throughout the course. For example, a course may begin with very short (2–3 minutes) talks by a tutor to a group, or by using an audio-cassette with one of the course books already referred to. The tutor may then give longer talks (perhaps 10–15 minutes) in a seminar mode. Finally, course tutors initially, and then guest lecturers, may give plenary talks (perhaps 30–45 minutes), followed by seminars/discussions.

12.6 Conclusion

Many EAP tutors, over the years, have remarked that students' tasks in understanding lectures would be considerably eased if lecturers clearly structured and delivered their talks (e.g. Tauroza and Allison 1994). Many universities organise some kind of staff training sessions but these rarely prepare lecturers for the specific difficulties of NNS.

Even less does the training include reference to the cross-cultural aspects of lectures and how these might affect students (Flowerdew and

Miller 1995). The number of NNS students at British, American, etc. universities has been increasing in recent years, and in this context Lynch (1994) discusses ways in which lecturers could be more effectively trained. He summarises a set of recommendations widely cited in the literature relating to UK lecture methodology:

1. Speak loudly, and clearly ... don't go too fast.
2. Plan, prepare, structure every lecture.
3. Make it understandable – explain, emphasise, recap, repeat and summarise main points and relate to current examples and applications.
4. Watch out for reaction and feedback, invite questions and ask questions, encourage participation, involve your audience.
5. Be adequate, do not try to cover everything.
6. Know your subject.
7. Keep time.
8. Look at the audience.
9. Assemble ... materials to which the students won't have easy access.
10. Don't read from your notes.
11. Be interesting and humorous but not too much.
12. Prepare handouts.

Lynch stresses the need to raise lecturers' 'awareness of the benefits of allowing *input from the students*, in the form of clarifying questions'. Support for this approach is also given by Rost (1990):

> in lecture-type settings, it is important to create opportunities for clarification and questioning in order to assure that learners are indeed actively engaged in listening.

The need to give students practice in this type of questioning on EAP courses is also stressed by Jackson and Bilton (1994). There is sufficient evidence to push for the kind of change advocated by Lynch (1994). The best way to attempt to implement it is an open question and is outside the scope of this book. However, 'questioning' leads us into the next chapter.

12.7 Introspect and discuss

1. Of the 18 micro-skills needed for listening to lectures (Richards 1983), which do you consider are (a) the most important, and (b) the most difficult, for students to master?
2. Dudley-Evans and Johns (1981) identified three styles of lecturing. Which do you think is the most difficult for students to understand, and why?

3. What differences would you expect to find in the lecture structure and use of markers in an 'information-driven' lecture compared with a 'point-driven' lecture?
4. Several different ways of giving practice in understanding the use of markers are shown. Can you suggest any further ways?
5. From your experience, what is the biggest difficulty that students have when listening to informal/colloquial language?
6. If possible, discuss and compare with colleagues your own system of note-taking: compare its organisation, numbering system and use of abbreviations and symbols. Has anyone used a branching system? Would this be a good awareness-raising activity for students?
7. What do you think are the main advantages and disadvantages of both the linear and branching systems of note-taking?
8. What kind of note-taking practice do you think is the most helpful for students?
9. At the end of the chapter, some examples are given of ways in which students can be gradually helped to cope with taking notes in a full-length lecture. Can you suggest any other ways?

13 Speaking for academic purposes

Speaking for academic purposes is an overall term used to describe spoken language in various academic settings. In addition, it suggests that the language used is normally formal or neutral, and obeys the conventions associated with the genre or activity. Typically, situations or activities covered are:

- asking questions in *lectures*;
- participation in *seminars*/discussions;
- making *oral presentations*; answering ensuing questions/points;
- *verbalising data*, and giving oral instructions, in seminars/workshops/ laboratories.

Individual tutorials and supervisions, although different in structure and purpose to the above, nevertheless seemingly need many of the same skills as those required in seminar discussions. Unfortunately, there is a shortage of data on tutorials: consequently, they will not be commented on separately here. Discussions with fellow-students about aspects of studies are relevant but are excluded, as the language is likely to be informal/colloquial and the situations varied.

The situations outlined above will be looked at in this chapter; appropriate teaching materials will also be included. At the end of the chapter, reference will be made to individual speech difficulties.

13.1 Lectures

Various surveys, referred to in Chapter 3, have shown that one of the biggest difficulties for students is expressing themselves in speech. Although this mostly applied to speaking in seminars, it is also relevant to asking questions in lectures.

McKenna (1987) analysed the questions asked in 33 lectures on general phonetics at the University of Michigan. She observed that most questions occurred 'during review sessions at the end of each major division of the topic'. She also noted that 'as in most classroom communities, students could signal that they wanted a turn to talk but had to wait to be recognized by the lecturer. There were contextual constraints in this community on the process of getting the floor'. Constraints in turn-taking were as follows:

1. Signal to open channels.
2. Wait for go-ahead signal.
3. Defer question if not given go-ahead.
4. Defer question if topic change is signalled.
5. Apologize if summoning the lecturer.
6. Alert lecturer to shift back after topic change.

From her observations, McKenna was able to categorise the questions into four main types:

1. *Clarification*
   a) requesting repeated information
   b) requesting additional information
2. *Interpretation check*
   a) rephrasing information (interpreting the speaker's words)
   b) illustrating given information (using an example as a check)
3. *Digression*
4. *Challenge*
   querying something the speaker said.

McKenna points out the dangers of encouraging students on EAP courses to ask questions in lectures. She observed that most of the questions from NS were not seeking information but contributing to the flow of discourse. She recommended showing short video-lectures to give students practice in preparing appropriate questions. However, McKenna's observation regarding asking questions and the behaviour of NS, needs to be tempered with the reality of NNS's requirements. The last chapter ended with a strong recommendation for asking questions for clarification purposes in lectures. In this respect, NNS are likely to need more help than NS and thus need to be given practice in asking appropriate questions. This aspect will be included in the following section on seminars.

Questions may also be asked in lectures by the lecturers: the purpose may be to draw attention to certain aspects of the content of the talk.

Houghton and King (1990) describe an analysis and experiment that they carried out with students of development economics. Their aim was to help students to focus on the importance of questions as a key to the concerns of a particular discipline – the kinds of questions that 'the lecturer used in working through the data (frequently numerical) on which his lectures were based, in particular focusing on his more abstract questions'. The main types of question that Houghton and King identified were:

a) A group of relatively straightforward questions where there was generally a 'correct' answer.
b) Questions asking for causes or reason why.
c) Questions requiring some kind of inference before an answer could be attempted.
d) Questions inviting the making of a case or argument from existing information.
(plus two less important categories)

Houghton and King then suggest some types of practice that can help students, beginning with the importance of stressing to students that 'society ... gives a positive value to the notion of the person who asks questions'. By listening to taped lectures, students can be sensitised to the importance of questions, their place in the discourse, and the types of answer the lecturer is looking for. In addition, the students may have difficulty with the syntax of questions and can be helped. Also, 'asking questions related to particular pieces of numerical information may be more difficult for students than asking about more general issues'. Therefore, guidance and practice in this area is needed (verbalising data is discussed later).

13.2 Seminars

13.2.1 Form

It was noted in Chapter 1 that the term 'group discussion' was preferable to 'seminar/tutorial' as there was disagreement as to what constituted a seminar. However, in this chapter I shall retain the label 'seminar' as that is the one most usually employed in higher education.

The variety of form of seminars, and their differing objectives, was discussed in detail in Johns and Johns (1977). Further investigations were reported in Johns (1978). She points out that the variety of forms seems to be determined by the differing academic traditions of the various disciplines. She gives an example of one faculty in which seminars consist entirely of monologue without any student–student exchange; occasionally one student answers a tutor's question, or there are a number of questions from the tutor and different students answer:

> The typical 'seminar' at postgraduate level seems to be more of a teaching situation (viz. sciences and management) than a discussion situation: it is not an inward-facing circle (viz. humanities) in which free address is the norm ...

Further investigations into the nature of seminars are reported by

Furneaux *et al.* (1991). In reply to their questionnaires to lecturers and students at the University of Reading, Furneaux *et al.* noted that:

> 67 per cent of respondents defined a 'seminar' as involving some form of student discussion or interaction. However, as many as 28 per cent excluded discussion and interaction from their definitions.

The main seminar purposes emerged as opportunities to ask questions and to give new information. The lecturer's chief role is to guide the discussion, which is seen to be the most important student role, followed by listening and note-taking.

Furneaux *et al.* observed four main types of 'seminar' (with some overlap between them):

1. *student group work*: e.g. a problem-solving exercise;
2. *the lesson*: nominated students go over prepared answers to case studies;
3. *discussion*: e.g. of material previously read by the whole group;
4. *presentation*: e.g. class members reporting on reading they had done or research students presenting research to date.

The conclusion of the Furneaux *et al.* investigation is clear:

> EAP course organisers need to check carefully on the types of seminar held by receiving departments ... having established the nature of the seminars that EAP course 'graduates' are likely to encounter, EAP teachers should actually *tell* their students what to expect, and what is expected of them.

Furneaux *et al.* also recommend advising students of:

> the value of listening to other students, of being more selective in note-taking, and of being prepared to ask questions of other students and staff during seminars.

They suggest that practice in 'breaking into the discussion' will be a waste of time as very few students will want to do this. In this connection, it is interesting to note that Lynch and Anderson (1991) found no cases of 'interruption' by NS in their observations of seminars. However, the needs of NNS must be borne in mind with regard to asking questions for clarification purposes.

Both the investigations of Furneaux *et al.* (1991) into seminars, and McKenna (1987) into lectures, involve not simply observations of language difficulties, but of whole language use and the relationships of the participants in establishing socio-academic parameters. In other words, the research is ethnographic and is concerned with the nature of the 'discourse communities' (these will be looked at further in Chapter 16). It is of interest to note that in the investigation by Furneaux *et al.*, the greatest area of dissatisfaction by NNS students with their own performance was because of lack of knowledge of the topic.

Tomlins (1993), in observing three social science seminars, noted that there were two distinct purposes. In an education seminar 'the students were engaged in problem-solving activities where a convergence of opinion was important'. In two sociology seminars 'most of the time was spent on discussing issues where a divergence of opinion was primary'. This would indicate a need for practising the language and conventions appropriate for agreeing and disagreeing. Tomlins also observed that within the category of clarification, students used four related strategies: asking for repetition, getting confirmation, correcting misunderstanding and rephrasing. This matches the observations made by McKenna in lectures, noted above.

Some of the difficulties that students experience in seminars were noted in Chapter 3. To these may be added others, listed by Lynch and Anderson (1991):

- the publicness of the performance;
- the need to think on your feet;
- the requirement to call up relevant subject knowledge;
- the need to present logically ordered arguments;
- the fact that you may be being assessed academically on the basis of your contribution.

McDonough (1984) reports an additional difficulty, claimed by Slater: it is not use of appropriate language, but speed of reaction that causes the most serious problem. Slater then devised a set of language laboratory-based tasks where precisely this could be practised.

13.2.2 Language

In an analysis of turn-taking and how a move in discourse is realised, Johns and Johns (1977) comment that, apart from language use, the bid for permission to speak may take a subtle form, 'such as a breath intake, a worried facial expression, eye-contact with the tutor, a filler such as "er" or "um", or all of these simultaneously'. Among other move types, Johns and Johns look at how speakers signal that they intend to continue speaking. In addition, in noting that there are probably culturally different conventions for interrupting, they look at how entry in a discussion is effected. Typically, it is effected by use of short, monosyllabic utterances, such as 'Yes ...', 'But ...', or 'No ...'. A common device is to appear to agree with a previous speaker ('Yes ...') and then to use the entry allowed for agreement to embellish or even partially contradict. Other entry prefaces include (Johns and Johns, 1977):

- If I can just come in here ...
- Can I just come in at this point ...?
- Can I just make a comment about that ...?
- ... ah yes, and ...
- ... ah yes, but ...

Lynch and Anderson (1991) were also interested to note entry prefaces. In their list below, half of the utterances were produced by native speakers and half by non-native students. Which do you think are which?

1. Can I ask a few questions of you?
2. From your introduction I perceive that ...
3. Do you have that answered?
4. Excuse me! (=bidding for a turn)
5. Can you give me an example of this?
6. Can you clarify, are the ...?
7. Would you care to put the first slide on and comment on ...?
8. I just want to comment a little bit on what you said ...
9. Problem is that it's in this sort of ...
10. Just in this regard I was wondering ...

As is often the case, what we found was rather different to what we expected. (Prefaces 1, 3, 5, 6 and 10 were uttered by native participants.) In fact, our observations of the relative frequency of explicit prefacing markers brought very little enlightenment – except for the mere fact that there was no clear difference in their use by native and non-native students.

In many seminars of the discussion or problem-solving type, in which exchanges of views are encouraged or expected, an analysis of the language functions employed reveals the following (Tomlins 1993, using the term 'strategies'):

disagreeing, agreeing, expressing an opinion, persuading, stating a criticism, giving an example, introducing, giving a reason, commenting ...

Earlier, Price (1977) had found that the following language functions were needed in seminars:

interrupting; asking questions; expressing general comments; agreeing; disagreeing; expressing criticism, objections, and doubt; making suggestions.

Price (1978) took two of these for inclusion in her discussion practice teaching material. She divided *agreement* into *full* agreement ('I fully support what you say') and *partial* agreement ('I agree with you to a certain extent, but ...'); and *disagreement* into '*soft type*' ('I think you may be wrong') and '*hard type*' ('I disagree with you').

Most of the communicative functions listed above can be subsumed in

198

Wilkins's categories of argument, rational enquiry and exposition, and suasion (1976). These categories featured frequently in an analysis of language used by students when involved in a pyramid discussion. Jordan (1990b) found that out of the total utterances in the discussion:

a) 20 per cent were of rational enquiry and exposition
b) 14 per cent were of argument
c) 5.5 per cent were of suasion

while 18 per cent were questions of all types.

Examples of the language used in the above categories were:

a) – statements of necessary conditions
    – explanation
    – questions seeking: agreement, opinions, information, clarification
b) statements of: agreement, partial/qualified agreement, disagreement
c) proposals (personal and impersonal).

Lynch and Anderson (1991) had noted that there can seem to be a 'lack of congruence between the language classroom and the world outside'; that there may be a 'divergence essentially between what is preached and what is practised'. It is clear that the more investigations there are into what seminars are really like, in all respects, the better it will eventually be for EAP students.

. Some of the authors above describe how they organise their teaching of seminar skills or make suggestions for areas of focus. For example, Lynch and Anderson describe how they divide the materials and teaching of seminar skills at Edinburgh into two types: presentation skills and participation skills:

SEMINAR SKILLS

presentation (as main speaker)	*participation* ('audience')
– sequencing – signposting – delivery (speed/clarity) – visual aids – body language – concluding	– indicating non-comprehension – asking for clarification – questioning – disagreeing

Furneaux *et al.* (1991) suggest that for preparation for seminar participation it would seem worthwhile to focus on the following:

1. listening skills, with special emphasis on picking up those

'throw-away' instructions by a lecturer at the end of a seminar regarding reading for the next one;

2. oral presentation skills, with special emphasis on conciseness, and intelligibility to a non-specialist audience;
3. asking questions; and
4. problem-solving, of the collaborative case-study sort, where a clear product, often on an overhead transparency, will be required at the end of a fixed time period.

13.2.3 Questions

Both in lectures and in seminars it may be necessary for students to ask questions for purposes of repetition (perhaps they did not hear something, or fully catch a reference, etc.), or clarification (perhaps they did not (fully) understand the point), or for further information. These need not be interruptions but straightforward requests at appropriate breaks in the monologue/presentation/discussion. Cawood (1978) gave the sequence for a request for repetition practised on a pre-sessional EAP course; he noted that the question would need to be concise and clear, e.g. *'Excuse me,'* followed by the polite request: *'please could you'*; this would then be followed by the required action: *'repeat'*, and then the required item: *'the last sentence'*. He then described the activity to practise this: a taped talk in which the information was masked at certain vital points by coughs, indistinct words, etc. The students were then shown how to obtain the necessary information by appropriate questions, and given practice in doing so in a follow-up talk. An example of material to practise this aspect is given in Appendix 1.1, by Lynch and Anderson (1992).

13.2.4 Discussions

In a seminar, the discussion that may take place normally evolves around the topic that has been nominated as the theme for the session. After noting that a topic may be expressed in the form of a statement or question, Wallace (1980) analysed the various forms of the topic subject matter and observed that the most common were:

1. Fact
2. Personal feeling
3. Opinion
4. Action

He then suggested how these might be approached in discussions.

Some examples of practice material for discussions, giving varying degrees of guidance in using appropriate language for agreement and disagreement are shown in Appendix 1.1.

Suggested ways of handling four different kinds of topics

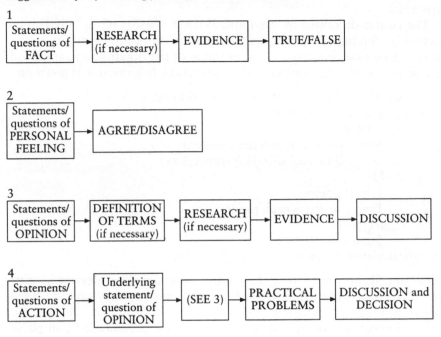

(From Wallace 1980)

13.3 Oral presentations

Often in seminars, and certainly among postgraduate students involved in research, students will be asked to give a short talk on some aspect of their studies or research. Price (1977) proposed teaching the language appropriate for ordering and sequencing ideas and information. She identified five possible stages in the presentation of a topic:

1. general introduction
2. statement of intention
3. information in detail
4. conclusion
5. invitation to discuss.

Nesi and Skelton (1987) stress the need for the careful organisation of material in oral presentations. They describe a course in which students are helped to 'present information (and ideas) in an organised and lucid fashion. This is a communication skill, not a language skill'. They are not concerned with total accuracy or fluency; in fact, Nesi and Skelton's

201

strategies can be used with students from lower-intermediate level upwards.

The course described by Nesi and Skelton consists of an initial short lecture by the tutor, which gives information on oral presentations and, at the same time, sets itself as an example of the organisation, style and use of aids needed for a successful presentation. Information is given on:

a) *logistical problems*, e.g. standing, positioning, looking
b) *structuring and signalling*:
    1. *Introduction*
        State: *what* you will do (content)
             how you will do it (procedure)
    2. *Body*
        List of points
        Frame or focus each point
    3. *Conclusion*
        Summarise
c) *visual material*: especially use of the OHP.

Nesi and Skelton insist that the students use signalling devices in their seven minutes' talk: it helps them to organise what they say and helps the audience to follow.

The importance of signalling devices in oral presentations, in particular, lexical signals, is noted by Boyle (1996). He discusses how the use of an algorithm based on the problem-solution pattern can help to provide a framework for students' 10–15-minute talks, 'while the clause relations and the lexical signals can help them to project their intentions clearly'.

Shorter talks, as a technique for developing confidence in speaking and improving speaking fluency, are described by Nation (1990). He describes the '4/3/2 Technique' which has the following steps. A student spends a few minutes preparing a talk without notes, on a given topic. Paired up with another student, the first student talks on the topic for *four minutes* – without interruption or questions, i.e. just listening. Partners are then changed. The speaker then talks again on the same topic to another student, giving the same information, but this time for only *three minutes*. Then follows another change of partners and the talk is given for a third time, but this time in only *two minutes*.

The features of the technique are thus: a different audience each time the talk is given; the talk is repeated; the time is reduced on each occasion. Nation found that confidence and fluency develop with the repetition. This would seem to be a useful technique for practice in giving oral presentations and taking part in seminars.

Self-confidence can be a big factor concerning students' willingness to speak in seminars. To assist in this, Jordan (1990b) developed problem-solving discussion activities, with a minimum of teacher-participation, known as 'pyramid discussions'. These involve students making choices from a list of items within a given theme or subject. It is an ideal activity for practising spoken language in any academic discipline, and helps to develop self-confidence and fluency (see also Chapters 7 and 17). An example is included in Appendix 1.1.

It may be that students are not sufficiently advanced in speaking skills to embark on a full-scale oral presentation. Their lack of core fluency may cause a communication breakdown. Chirnside (1986) describes core fluency as:

> the ability to compose comprehensible utterances by manipulating such linguistic micro skills as subject-verb concord, tense harmony, post-modification, clause linkage and basic intonation features.

Where students' spoken language skills are insufficient to give a meaningful talk, some of the techniques described above might be tried, possibly adapted. In some cases, students will need individual help with speech difficulties. This aspect is considered shortly.

An example of preparation for a short talk is given in Appendix 1.1 from Forman *et al.* (1990). Practical suggestions for the preparation of a talk and the use of visual aids are contained in Wright (1993).

A way of helping both the audience and the speaker to improve oral presentations is outlined by Lynch (1988a). He describes the use of peer evaluation in which everyone listening to the presentation completes an evaluation sheet which is used for feedback purposes (this is reproduced in Appendix 1.1). Lynch summarises the reasons for using peer evaluation:

- to stress the value of communication between and among students;
- to draw attention to the necessity for understanding and being understood by other NNS;
- to get feedback for the speaker on what the audience has understood;
- to obtain a wider sample of opinions than just one, regarding oral assessment.

Lynch has found that such peer evaluation 'has a marked effect on the extent to which speakers take their audience into account'.

Mason (1995) describes the procedure for a teacher to evaluate each student quickly during an oral presentation, and then to give the feedback to the student very soon afterwards. Mason's evaluation form (reproduced in Appendix 1.1) gives a checklist of points to look for; the yes/no answers to questions can be quickly circled. She also comments that class evaluation can be encouraged. Basically, the three main areas to consider in an evaluation are the content, the language used and the delivery – all from several points of view.

Research is ongoing into methods of assessing student presentations. Khidhayir and Du Boulay (1994) have described and discussed the criteria for oral assessment on their pre-sessional EAP courses at Sussex University. They are concerned to discover the degree of agreement between EAP teachers and subject tutors in their assessment of students' spoken performance. The assessment criteria are covered by the following headings: appropriacy, evidence of preparation, use of aids, delivery (style/expression), structure of talk and handling of questions at the end.

13.4 Verbalising data

An area of difficulty for many students is verbalising data. Usually there are few problems in reading and writing; they emerge in listening and understanding, and speaking. Students in the arts and humanities may need little help, apart from some practice with larger numbers and dates, but students in the social sciences (noted by Fisher 1990 in economics), sciences and technology may need considerable help. They often need to understand various forms of data, including equations and formulae, in lectures and seminars, and they sometimes need to verbalise data themselves, either in asking questions or in giving talks.

Depending on the students' needs, practice can be given in the following areas:

> cardinal and ordinal numbers, fractions, decimals, percentages, formulae and equations, measures, dates, time, money.

Similarly, some of the above may need to be practised in:

> graphs, tables, histograms, diagrams, charts, plans, maps.

An example from Elsworth (1982) is given in Appendix 1.1; similar practice is contained in Fletcher and Hargreaves (1980).

Jordan (1982) also gave practice in verbalising data: he concentrated on shapes, various types of data presentation, and maps and plans. He used the technique of 'describe and draw' as a pair work activity to give practice in clear, accurate description, combined with instructions and precise questioning (the procedure is described in Chapter 18). The technique of describe and draw can also be utilised to give practice for instructions, etc. in workshops and laboratories, with the resulting drawing as the check on accuracy.

The need for practice in using mathematical formulae and equations for economists had been noted by Jordan (1984): frequently the formulae involved using the letters of the Greek alphabet. Suggestions for pair work or group practice were given in Jordan and Nixson (1986). For example, a list of Greek letters and equations is given to one student/ group while another student/group has the same, but expressed in words. Group 1 can try to read the equations to Group 2, who can check the accuracy. An alternative method is for Group 2 to read out the equations, and Group 1 to try to write them down in the form of letters and symbols. They can check against an answer key. The same activity can be put onto tape, with worksheets, for use in a language laboratory or resource centre.

13.5 Individual speech difficulties

In the last resort, difficulty in speaking in a discussion may be caused by shyness or personality factors which are independent of the language being used. There is, of course, another important factor: many students have individual difficulties with pronunciation, stress, intonation or overall rhythm. At times, their speech may be virtually unintelligible to other students or the tutor. In these cases, some kind of individual tuition and/or self-access help will be needed. This can be partly achieved by working independently in a language laboratory or resource centre. In this case, the students will need to be trained to be self-critical and to monitor themselves (see Appendix 2).

Hewings (1988) acknowledges that some sort of individualised scheme for speech improvement is needed on EAP courses. He describes strategies for the diagnosis of problems and remedial work, involving two main areas of difficulty: word pronunciation and word stress. Within word pronunciation, he concentrates on sound-symbol correspondence and 'problem sounds'. Within word stress, the main concern is:

> primary stress placement, a frequent source of difficulty, it seems, in technical and semi-technical vocabulary. Attention is also given to shifts of stress in words when used in context.

The two strategies that Hewings has developed involve students reading from a selected text which they record in a language laboratory. The tutor then circles on a copy of the text the places where major errors occur (but not indicating the nature of the error). In groups, students then listen to the appropriate recordings, look at the circled text, and identify the nature of the errors. A student who can correct the error then shows the others how to produce the correct version. Hewings found a high motivation for this *peer group teaching*. The second strategy, *a tape exchange scheme*, is more individualised in that the tutor gives each student a circled text of the errors in his/her recording, and records a model version for the student to listen to in the language laboratory. The method is effective but Hewings admits that it can be time-consuming, particularly in the early stages. Practice appropriate for individual or class use, covering all aspects of pronunciation, stress and intonation, is contained in Hewings (1993a).

13.6 Conclusion

We had noted in Chapter 3, in looking at surveys of students' difficulties, that seminars were an area of major difficulty. We have seen in this chapter that seminars may take a variety of forms. The advice of Furneaux *et al.* (1991) is highly relevant: that EAP course directors need to find out the types of seminar that their students are likely to meet, and then to tell them what to expect. This is reinforced by Lynch and Anderson (1991) who recommended that subject lecturers should 'explain to their students in some detail exactly what they expect from seminar participants'. Lynch and Anderson propose something that has been long overdue in EAP courses – showing videotapes of actual seminars in progress. This would be the best way to demonstrate what really happens.

13.7 Introspect and discuss

1. Reference has been made to turn-taking in speaking at the end of lectures (or major divisions thereof). What kind of signals have you noticed being used in turn-taking in your country?
2. From your experience of lectures, have you noticed that questions tend to fall into the four main types categorised by McKenna (1987)? Which type have you found to be the most common?
3. Some of the difficulties that students experience in seminars were noted by Lynch and Anderson (1991). Are there any others that you can add from your experience?
4. Which 'entry prefaces' (Johns and Johns 1977) have you noticed being used in seminars that you have experience of?
5. An example is given in Appendix 1.1 of an extract from a book giving practice in asking questions for clarification. Look at the extract and then propose an alternative way to practise such questions.
6. Some examples of practice material for discussion are given in Appendix 1.1. Which type of practice do you prefer, and why? Suggest an alternative type.

7. Oral presentations are looked at from various aspects. List the features of a talk and its presentation that can help to make it interesting for listeners.
8. In giving a talk, there are at least three aspects of spoken language that can cause comprehension difficulties for listeners: pronunciation, stress and speed of speaking. Suggest other aspects that can cause difficulties.
9. In Appendix 1.1, two examples are given of evaluation forms for use in oral presentations – one for students to use (peer evaluation), and one for teachers. Compare the two forms and suggest other items that you might wish to include, or alternative ways of evaluating.
10. If you can speak a foreign language, or if English is a foreign language for you, which types of data do you find it most difficult to understand easily in speech, and to verbalise yourself?
11. Devise a suitable 'describe and draw' activity that would enable you to practise, with a partner, the forms of data that you find it difficult to verbalise (see 10 above).
12. An example of a pyramid discussion, on the theme of 'developing study skills', is shown in Appendix 1.1. Taking the theme of 'Developing seminar strategies', devise a suitable list of at least 15 items (max. 20) from which students could choose, for a pyramid discussion.
13. Hewings refers to two types of individualised spoken language practice that can be incorporated in an EAP course. Can you suggest any others that are suitable?

14   Reference/research skills

Reference skills is an umbrella term that comprises a range of sub-skills relating to various types of reference materials. Sometimes the reference skills are sub-divided into language reference skills, which include the efficient use of dictionaries and books, and academic reference skills, which include library use, and giving references in dissertations and theses. Sometimes the label 'research skills' is used instead of 'academic reference skills': it might also include the keeping of record cards (or information on computer), on which to note books, journals and articles referred to, and the layout of research papers. Occasionally the term 'study skills' is used to refer to some of the more mechanical aspects of the above, but this is to be discouraged as it can be confusing. It will be seen that using a dictionary and the library are, in any case, far from being 'mechanical skills'.

14.1   Dictionaries

Dictionaries may be *monolingual* or *bilingual*. Many students use *bilingual* or translating dictionaries, at least in the early stages of their studies; this is understandable. However, they will need to use monolingual dictionaries if they are to be advanced users of the language. The reason for this is that bilingual dictionaries often give a number of synonyms, and it may not be easy to select the most appropriate one. Good monolingual dictionaries give guidance on usage, style, and context of use.
Monolingual dictionaries may be of several kinds:

– learner's dictionaries;
– native speaker's dictionaries;
– pronouncing dictionaries;
– specialist subject dictionaries;
– thesaurus (a virtual dictionary of synonyms).

Our main concern is with the first type above. However, before considering them in some detail, we shall look briefly at the other monolingual dictionaries. Some of the better known ones are listed in Appendix 1.2.

208

a) *Native speaker's dictionaries*

They are primarily designed to provide decoding information. The kinds of encoding information that a foreign learner would need are not included. They would only be of use to an advanced student in need of a wider range of entries than in a learner's dictionary.

b) *Pronouncing dictionaries*

They give the standard pronunciation, in phonetic symbols, of not only the headwords (as in a learner's dictionary), but all word forms (e.g. plurals, verb forms, etc.). This could be useful, especially for a teacher of English who might be uncertain of some pronunciations.

c) *Specialist subject dictionaries*

They can be very useful for both students and teachers of ESAP. Further reference is made to them in Chapter 17.

d) *Thesaurus*

They contain synonyms grouped according to their meanings, and usually give no indication of usage, collocation or style. They can only be recommended for advanced students.

14.4.1 *Monolingual learner's dictionaries*

We shall only consider the general English language dictionaries and make no comment on picture dictionaries or the various dictionaries on aspects of language, viz. English idioms and phrasal verbs (useful though these may be). Reference has already been made to a *Which?*-style guide to learners' dictionaries in Chapter 8 (West 1987); some of these are listed in Appendix 1.2.

The following seven examples of the entry 'ambiguous' are taken from learners' and native speakers' dictionaries, and illustrate the differences between the dictionaries.

1. **am-bigu-ous** /æm'bɪgjuəs/ *adj* 1 having more than one possible meaning: *'Look at those pretty little girls' dresses' is ambiguous, because it is not clear whether the girls or the dresses are 'pretty'.* 2 uncertain in meaning or intention: *an ambiguous smile, glance, gesture, etc.* ▷ **am-bigu-ously** *adv.* **am-bigu-ous-ness** n[U].
   (*Oxford Advanced Learner's Dictionary of Current English* – 4th edition, 1989)

2. **am-big-u-ous** /æm'bɪgjuəs/ *adj* having more than one possible meaning or INTERPRETATION; unclear: *an ambiguous reply/attitude* – opposite **unambiguous**; compare AMBIVALENT – ~**ly** *adv* – **guity** / 'æmbɪ'gjuːɪti/ n [C;U]: *You should avoid ambiguity in your writing. /His reply was full of ambiguities.*
   (*Longman Dictionary of Contemporary English*, 1987)

3. **ambiguous** /æmbɪgjuəs/   ◆◇◇◇◇
   1 If you describe something as **ambiguous**, you mean that it is   ADJ-GRADED
   unclear or confusing because it can be understood in more   = vague

than one way. *This agreement is very ambiguous and open to various interpretations ... The Foreign Secretary's remarks clarify an ambiguous statement issued earlier this week.*

≠ obvious, clear

♦ **ambiguously** *Zaire's national conference on democracy ended ambiguously.*

ADV-GRADED: usu ADV with v, also ADV adj

2 If you describe something as **ambiguous**, you mean that it contains several different ideas or attitudes that do not fit well together. *Students have ambiguous feelings about their role in the world.*

ADJ-GRADED

(*Collins COBUILD English Language Dictionary*, 1995)

4. **am-bi-gu-ous** /æmˈbɪg-ju-əs/ *adj* having or expressing more than one possible meaning, sometimes intentionally
 • *It was hoped that he would clarify the ambiguous remarks he made earlier.*
 • *The government has been ambiguous on this issue.* • *Her speech was* **deliberately** *ambiguous to avoid offending either side.* • *His reply to my question was* **somewhat** *ambiguous.* • *The* **wording** *of the agreement is ambiguous, so both interpretations are valid.* • *They've always had ambiguous (=uncertain)* **feelings** *about whether or not they should have childen.*
 (*Cambridge International Dictionary of English*, 1995)

5. **ambiguous**, **-ly**, **-ness** æmˈbɪgjʊəs/ *adj*. 1 having an obscure or double meaning. 2 difficult to classify. □□ **ambiguously** *adv*. **ambiguousness** n. [L *ambiguus* doubtful f. *ambigere* f. *ambi* – both ways + *agere* drive]
 (*The Concise Oxford Dictionary of Current English* – 8th edition, 1990)

6. **ambiguous**, æmˈbɪg-ju-əs **-ly** -li **-ness** -nəs, -nɪs
 (*English Pronouncing Dictionary*, Daniel Jones –15th edition, 1996)

7. **ambiguous** *adj*. 1 ˈequivocal, amphibological, amphibolic or amphibolous; misleading: *If one says 'Taylor saw Tyler drunk', which one was drunk is ambiguous.* 2 ˈdoubtful, dubious, ˈquestionable, ˈobscure, ˈindistinct, unclear, ˈindefinite, indeterminate, ˈuncertain, undefined, ˈinconclusive, uncertain, ˈvague, ˈmisty, foggy; ˈcryptic, Delphic enigmatic(al), oracular, ˈmysterious, ˈpuzzling; confusable: *The soothsayer's prophecies were sufficiently ambiguous to allow for several conflicting interpretations.* 3 ˈunreliable, undependable: *How can the doctor decide on a correct diagnosis when the symptoms are ambiguous?*
 (*The Oxford Thesaurus* (An A–Z Dictionary of Synonyms), 1991)

'Dictionaries have a good image. Almost every learner or user of English as a second or foreign language owns one; and it is probably one of the few books which are retained after following a language course' (Carter 1987). It is a pity then that 'training in dictionary skills is less common in ELT ... as teachers assume such training has already been given for the mother tongue' (Summers 1988). From her research, Summers noted that:

> although the dictionary can 'put the student in charge', teachers often do not train their students in how to use the dictionary to best advantage.

Perhaps one of the reasons for this, in the EAP context, is that:

even though many students have very poor skills in dictionary use, there is only a limited amount of work that can be done with dictionaries without antagonising large numbers of students.

(Blue 1993)

Most would agree that there is a need to be sensitive to students' feelings regarding dictionary work. Perhaps the solution is first to discuss with the students the advantages of using a monolingual dictionary efficiently (these are noted by Underhill 1985) which, in turn, entails a consideration of the main uses of the dictionary.

Studies have shown (Carter 1987) that the main reasons learners use dictionaries are:

> for looking for meanings and synonyms (especially low-frequency specialist terms), for checking spellings and for decoding activities in the written medium such as translation and reading.

To these may be added: word pronunciation and stress, differences between confused words, and information about grammar, collocation and style. For whatever reason a dictionary is used, advice from a teacher to 'look it up in the dictionary' is not very helpful:

> Looking a word up in a dictionary requires that certain skills be applied in a systematic way; it requires a strategy.

(Scholfield 1982)

Scholfield then describes seven steps that can be involved in using the dictionary for comprehension purposes. These range from possible problems in actually locating the word, to selecting the correct explanation and understanding it. For the inexperienced dictionary user, the steps are far from simple, and may be difficult to follow quickly.

Just as students vary in their language level and needs, so dictionaries are different in their coverage. Consequently, students may need advice as to the most appropriate dictionary for their needs. Cambridge University Press (1995) pose some questions in the form of a guide to assist students in choosing a dictionary:

1. Is it written for native English speakers, or for people whose first language is not English?
2. Does it cover enough English?
3. Does it cover American English, British English or both?
4. Is it up-to-date?
5. Does it help me use and understand English?
6. Does the dictionary use 'labels' to help you?
7. Can I understand the definitions?
8. How do I find the meaning I'm looking for if the word has many meanings?

9. Can I find my way around the dictionary?
10. Was the dictionary designed for speakers of my language?
11. Does the dictionary use illustrations?
12. Why should I use a monolingual dictionary?

Additional information about appropriate dictionaries can sometimes be obtained from reviews that appear in journals, e.g. *ELT Journal*. A survey of five up-to-date dictionaries was published in 1995 in *EFL Gazette* (see Appendix 1.2).

14.1.2 Dictionary practice

A basic requirement is for students to be familiar with the alphabetical order of entries, which means they must know the English alphabet backwards, so to speak. If a student's mother tongue is Arabic, Chinese, Hindi, Japanese, etc., in other words, involving a totally different writing system, this is not an easy task. An example of exercises to improve alphabetical ordering and using the dictionary quickly is given in Appendix 1.2 from O'Brien and Jordan (1985). Similar exercises can be constructed for giving practice in arranging authors' surnames and initials in strict alphabetical order, preparatory to using the library catalogues.

The main uses of the dictionary need to be practised. Exercises for this purpose are contained in the following: Williams (1982), O'Brien and Jordan (1985), Smith and Smith (1990), Heaton and Dunmore (1992). In addition, some of the learners' dictionaries have accompanying work-books that give practice in the following areas:

> finding words and meanings; spelling; abbreviations; pronunciation, with phonetic symbols; usage and style; grammatical information; learning and extending vocabulary.

In general, students are probably more successful in using dictionaries for comprehension purposes than for production. Consequently, it is to their advantage if they can be shown how useful some of the information can be for their writing, e.g. verb pattern codes, the use of prepositions, phrasal verbs, (un)countable nouns, through examples and the explanations in usage notes (Huang 1985).

14.2 Books

Useful practice can be given in using the *contents page* and the *index* to books. It should be remembered that different cultures locate them in different places in books. Students need to be aware that they convey different kinds of information and that cross-referencing can often help in tracing an item. Other features of a book may need pointing out, e.g. date of publication, edition number, etc. A number of the integrated study skills books give practice in this.

14.3 Using the library

One of the surveys in Chapter 3 (at Manchester University in 1988) analysed students' experience in using libraries in their own countries. It reported that 40 per cent of those students used a closed-access library, and 49 per cent had received no formal instruction in using the library. Closed-access libraries require students to fill in request forms for books, which are later brought to them (or they collect at a later time). Students do not have the facility to look along bookshelves themselves to find their own books. This means that a sizeable proportion of students are likely to have some difficulty in using open-access libraries, in which they have to locate books and journals themselves.

Primrose (1993) surveys, from the point of view of an academic librarian (Glasgow University Library), the difficulties of overseas students coming to terms with a large academic library. Her article should be required reading for anyone who wants to catch a glimpse of the real difficulties facing overseas students. Primrose describes four categories of problems: communication, culture, library use and the handling of information. Some of the problems that Primrose comments on include difficulty in recognising surnames, and inhibitions in asking questions or indicating ignorance:

> The function of library staff is often misunderstood: some see us as too remote or exalted to approach at all; others see us as menials ... others again see us as universal aunts ...

The major problem of coping with the wide range of information is highlighted by Primrose. It:

> comes in a variety of formats ... film and microfiche, magnetic tape, compact discs, CD-ROM and electronic data, all of which require varying levels of technical expertise. To gain access to this information, students must know, or learn, how to use catalogues, bibliographies, abstracting and indexing journals and on-line networks. To make use of it, they must know how to conduct a literature search, defining and refining their search procedures as they go, and they must have some concept of choice, of how to evaluate and select from the references they retrieve. These are advanced and sophisticated skills, and the overseas student is by no means alone in having to learn them from scratch ...

Some students may have their own, or access to a personal computer. Just as with computers in libraries, they may be able to access databases and pick up references from searches, of dissertation abstracts, for example, on CD-ROM. They may also be able to use 'Internet' – the large system of connected computers around the world used by groups to communicate with each other. Through 'Internet', students may be able to key in to groups of people with similar research interests.

Primrose has produced a *Study Guide for Overseas Students* which includes information on using the University Library. Probably all university libraries issue their own guide to library services. However, these may not always indicate what many overseas students need help with viz.:

– a description of the library classification system: in the UK it is likely to be the *Dewey Decimal Classification*; in the USA it is likely to be the *Library of Congress Classification* (these are shown in Appendix 1.1);
– understanding book and journal references;
– using the different library *catalogues*: whether the card-index type – mainly *author/name* and *subject*, and the *periodicals list* – or *computer*, with its *on-line catalogue* available at catalogue terminals;
– locating books and journals on shelves in the library;
– using other library services and facilities, e.g. inter-library loans.

Because of the importance of the library in students' studies, many EAP courses include library familiarisation tasks in their introductory sessions. Tadros (1984) describes training exercises for law students at Khartoum University. Similar exercises are found in most of the integrated study skills books already referred to. An example of a library project is shown in Appendix 1.1 (re Chapter 4). See also Appendix 1.1 for an example of a practical exercise in library use from Williams (1982).

14.4   References

There are various academic conventions that govern the different forms of making *references* or *citations*. It is necessary for students to become familiar with those that are appropriate for their subject and the type of academic writing they embark upon. Basically, referencing falls into three types: quotations, footnotes and reference lists or bibliographies. We will look briefly at each in turn.

Students need to be informed of the value of *citation indexes* available in academic libraries. They can enable students to follow up the references/citations given in papers which are of interest to them. They are based on the assumption that if one author cites another, there must be some relationship between their work. They are also useful as up-to-date subject indexes, and are available for the main subject areas – science, arts and humanities, 'compumath', and social sciences.

14.4.1 Quotations

Quotations may be divided into two types: indirect and direct. *Indirect quotations involve summarising* a writer's ideas and putting them into your own words, in other words, *paraphrasing*. When information from two or more sources is combined, then students need practice in *synthesising*. These aspects were referred to in Chapter 11.

It is essential that students are informed of the importance of acknowledging sources of information, ideas, quotations, etc. otherwise they may be accused of *plagiarism* (referred to in Chapter 6), which is viewed very strictly in Western academic circles. Students then need to be shown the different methods of acknowledging the sources (see below).

Direct quotations involve using the actual words of the writer. In analysing economics articles, Jordan (1990c) looked at the main methods of incorporating quotations within a text: the most common lead-in for a quotation was by using 'as' (e.g. 'As X has noted ...'). There were six main purposes or functions of the quotations within a text:

support, exemplification, introduction, conclusion, explanation and definition.

By far the biggest category was '*support*' which was fairly wide-ranging but basically gave support for the point being made by the writer, or to provide authority for his/her viewpoint: in other words, to establish academic credentials.

Thompson and Ye (1991) investigated the reporting verbs used in citations in the introductions to about 100 academic papers from a diversity of journals: they found more than 400 verbs being used. They classified the verbs into two main categories. The first, and larger group, are directly attributable to the author of an initial article, and include three groups of processes: textual, mental and research. The second group of verbs relate to attitudes of a reporting writer who refers to other authors: these are divided into comparing and theorising verbs.

Swales and Feak (1994) also refer to the reporting verbs used in reviewing previous research. They infer that 'at least two-thirds of all citing statements fall into one of ... three major patterns'. Briefly, the patterns are:

1. *Past*: reference to single studies ('researcher activity as agent'): e.g. Smith (1981) *investigated* the causes of poverty.

2. *Present perfect*: reference to areas of inquiry ('research activity not as agent'): e.g. The causes of poverty *have been* widely *investigated* (Smith 1981; Jones 1987; Brown 1992).
3. *Present*: reference to state of current knowledge ('no reference to researcher activity'): e.g. The causes of poverty *are* complex (Smith 1981; Jones 1987; Brown 1992).

14.4.2 Footnotes

Footnotes are frequently used in articles to give reference to a source referred to in the body of the text. Although students may not need to use them in their own writing, they should at least be familiar with them and some of their conventions, as they will meet them in their reading. Often abbreviations, particularly of Latin words, may be used in footnotes: these can cause difficulty at first, viz. *et al.*, *ibid.*, *op. cit.*, and *passim*. An example of an exercise to practise the understanding of footnotes in journals/books is given in Appendix 1.1 from Smith and Smith (1990).

14.4.4 Bibliographies

In drawing up a reference list or bibliography for an essay, dissertation or thesis, students need to obey strict conventions for the layout and sequencing of references. In particular, there are differences in the way that book and journal references are set out and which part is underlined or printed in italics. In addition, there can be slight differences between disciplines in the sequencing of items. When listing authors' names, students need to be aware of possible inconsistencies in the use of authors' forenames or initials, which can, at times, cause complications or confusion (see Jordan 1997).

There are two main methods of referencing that students need to be familiar with: the Numeric System, and the Harvard Method. The *Numeric System* involves putting a small number in the text next to the quotation, etc. The full reference is then given as a *footnote* at the bottom of the page, or at the end of the essay, article, chapter or book – in numerical sequence. The *Harvard Method*, which is probably more popular, avoids the use of numbers/footnotes by putting a short reference in the text next to the quotation, paraphrase, etc. Typically, this is the author's surname, followed by the year of publication, one or both items being inside brackets. The full references are then given at the end of the essay, article, etc. This is the method used in this book.

Practice can be given to students on EAP courses in drawing up correctly referenced bibliographies. Lynch and McGrath (1993) describe the need for such practice and also outline the workshop sessions in which students are given help. Lynch and McGrath discern several underlying guiding principles to the construction of bibliographies, which they call 'The Five Cs':

Completeness
Clarity
Consistency
eConomy
Care

They also drew up a list of important bibliographic features that students need to be aware of, and to obtain practice in. These are reproduced below. Finally, they emphasise the need for postgraduates, especially, to be familiar with the conventions that apply across disciplines, and those that are localised to a particular subject, department, etc. An example of their list of references is included in Appendix 1.1.

Important Bibliographic Features

a) alphabetical ordering of items
b) title of article in collection
c) author's initial
d) volume number (journal)
e) date of publication (book)
f) distinction between book and article titles
g) editor's name (collection)
h) publisher's name (book)
i) editor's initial
j) distinction between items by author in same year
k) spelling
l) date of collection where cited item appears
m) issue number (journal)

(from Lynch and McGrath 1993)

Practice in different aspects of referencing is contained in: Wallace (1980), Williams (1982), Hamp-Lyons and Courter (1984), O'Brien and Jordan (1985), Smith and Smith (1990), Heaton and Dunmore (1992), Trzeciak and Mackay (1994), Swales and Feak (1994). A common type of exercise is for some of the different elements in a reference to be put incorrectly for students to rectify.

14.5 Conclusion

A final note can be added regarding the importance for students of keeping records of the readings that they have done from books and journals. This is best done on index cards: one side can be used for noting the details of the source, while the other could be used for notes or quotations from the source itself. The advantage of using cards is that they can be kept in alphabetical order and are ready to hand for providing a reference list or bibliography at the end of the academic writing. Clearly, the same principle can apply to keeping the information on a personal computer.

14.6 Introspect and discuss

1. What are some of the disadvantages of using only a bilingual dictionary?
2. What kinds of *encoding* information in a dictionary are useful for a foreign learner?
3. a) Entries from seven dictionaries are shown for the word 'ambiguous'. What are the main ways in which the entries differ?
   b) Four of the entries are from learners' dictionaries. Which entry do you prefer, and why?
4. What are some of the advantages of using a monolingual learner's dictionary, apart from the brief reasons given?
5. Which monolingual learners' dictionary, out of all those published, do you prefer? Why?
6. Which different kinds of information are conveyed by the contents page and the index of a book? How can cross-referencing between the two help to trace an item?
7. Does your experience of using an academic library match that of overseas students as observed by Primrose (1993)? If not, in which ways does it differ?
8. Look at the exercise in Appendix 1.1 on '*Practical work in the library*' by Williams (1982). Suggest another kind of library familiarisation task that you would include in a short EAP course.
9. If you were devising a questionnaire to check on students' ability to use the library and awareness of its services and facilities, which features would you ask questions about?
10. Suggest a suitable exercise to give practice in using direct quotations.
11. Look in Appendix 1.1 at 'Putting Principles into Practice: Examples of References' by Lynch and McGrath (1993). Devise an appropriate exercise based on this that would help students to become more aware of the conventions involved in making references.

15 Examination skills

After students have started their subject-specific courses, one of their biggest anxieties is the prospect of taking an examination in English; this may be for a degree or other academic qualification. All kinds of pressures build up on the students at the same time: requirements of knowledge, memory, time, writing skills, understanding the question, etc. One of the perceived needs of students is to practise for this traumatic event: not only practice in analysing the question and structuring a possible answer, but also practice in writing an answer 'against the clock', e.g. one question in an hour, four questions in three hours, etc.

In all the above respects, NNS students are similar to NS students, who are well catered for with study skills books that give advice, examples, and practice (e.g. Northedge 1990; Montgomery 1991; McIlroy and Jones 1993). The overall advice to NS students is based on:

- *revision*: planning and adequate time;
- *questions*: analyse previous exam papers – become familiar with the layout, instructions, and content and form of questions;
- *the exam*: allocate time among the questions; answer the question; ensure clear presentation and legible writing.

For NNS students, the situation can be more difficult and challenging because they may not have taken a specialist subject exam in English before. In addition, if they are studying in another country, the exam procedures and conventions may be different from those in their own country.

15.1 Question analysis

The starting point for assisting students is to make an analysis of exam questions. Friederichs and Pierson (1981) analysed questions occurring in science examination papers for first year undergraduates in Hong Kong. They classified them according to 27 categories, e.g. enumerate, state purpose, explain, conclude. They then conducted a frequency count and found that the eight most common types were (% of total):

1. discuss (13.2%)	5. show (6%)
2. explain (12.5%)	6. give reasons (5.3%)
3. describe (12.4%)	7. define (5%)
4. list (10.5%)	8. compare/contrast (4.4%)

Swales (1982) also analysed questions in the sciences (chemistry and biochemistry), at Aston University. He found that the instructional verbs could be subsumed within seven categories. In rank order they were:

1. describe (most common)	5. discuss and compare
2. define	6. calculate
3. explain	7. list
4. draw	

Although the order is not exactly the same in the two lists, there is sufficient similarity for them to be used as the basis for local modification in the sciences ('draw' and 'calculate' do not appear in the first list).

Swales' method of analysis was followed by Horowitz (1986a) who presented a typology of examination questions from across the disciplines. Basically, 'there are four tasks that an essay prompt can require a student to perform': display familiarity with:

1. a concept;
2. the relation between/among concepts;
3. a process;
4. argumentation.

An analysis of 'Discuss' questions in MSc papers in plant biology was made by Dudley-Evans (1988a). He found that there is a wide range of meaning for 'discuss':

> There seem to be three types of 'discuss' questions. The first type requires the writer to present various opposing points of view and to conclude by giving his own opinion. At the other extreme certain 'discuss' questions require the writer only to describe a theory, or process, and give some further explanation ... The third type of 'discuss' question has a meaning which lies between the first two. It requires the writer to present points in favour of the argument and points against ... there will be no room for personal opinion.

The rhetorical structure of the essay test question was analysed by Hamp-Lyons (1988), based on a wide range of actual essay test questions at Edinburgh University from both subject specialists and EAP/ESP sources. Acknowledging that the essay test is a product-oriented activity, Hamp-Lyons developed a model that focused on: topic, comment, focus and perspective. It is exemplified as follows:

Example question	Components
DISCUSS	2. comment
THE USE OF	3. focus
NUCLEAR ENERGY	1. topic
TO BENEFIT MANKIND	4. perspective

The 'perspective' 'determines viewpoint to be taken; defines what can be accepted as "true" by each participant in the discourse exchange'. Hamp-Lyons noted that it is the perspective of the academic essay test question that can cause real problems for the student – the 'perspective' is that of the question-setter.

15.2   Writing practice

If a class can be formed of students from the same subject area, it would be useful to obtain copies of past exam papers from the appropriate department. The type of question paper should be noted: *objective* – multiple-choice questions (which can take several forms); *subjective* – essay-type questions. The questions can then be analysed with the students, noting, in particular, the ones that appear frequently. Using that as a basis, the students could compile a glossary of question-words for their own subject. If the class is mixed, students could be asked to bring copies of their own subject exam papers. Initially, the questions could be analysed in a general way, and a consensus reached among scientists, social scientists, arts students and so on. Multi-disciplinary glossaries of question words are contained in Howe (1983) and Jordan (1990a).

Many EAP centres organise sessions in writing practice for exams. Lynch (1988b) describes one such course at Edinburgh which was based on the examination instruction types contained in Williams (1982).

Schedule for *Writing Examination Answers* (WEA)

Session 1   General advice:
  The 'rules of the game'
  The components of a question
  The instruction *describe*
Session 2   The instruction *discuss*
Session 3   The instruction *contrast*
Session 4   The instruction *to what extent*
Session 5   The instruction *outline*
Session 6   The instruction *compare*
Session 7   The instruction *write notes*
Session 8   Writing under examination conditions.
  General discussion on exam techniques.

Lynch summarised the different levels of the WEA component as follows:

> CULTURAL
> interpretation of academic conventions, e.g. the question-instruction 'code'
> assumed value of intellectual synthesis and abstraction, rather than reproduction of rote-learned answers
> SUBJECT-SPECIFIC/COGNITIVE
> judgment as to what constitutes a valid and sufficient answer
> application/presentation of relevant knowledge from course
> RHETORICAL
> conformity to patterns of factual presentation and logical argument; development of writing 'flow'
> LINGUISTIC
> mechanics of formal accuracy (grammar and spelling)
> sentence/paragraph-level focus

Howe (1988) stresses the advantages of giving practice in writing for exams:

> The first of course is that the student benefits from being reminded, or taught, the importance of obeying the rubric, allotting time wisely, understanding the vocabulary of the questions and so on, and this is valuable, necessary help which should not be underestimated. But the second major effect is the reduction of anxiety or if you wish to name it so – the placebo effect.

An example of an activity focusing on the need to read instructions carefully is contained in Appendix 1.1, from Heaton and Dunmore (1992).

Most EAP courses contain students from a variety of disciplines. One problem, therefore, is how to give practice in:

> the task of composing the whole of a viable answer to a relevant question in their chosen field of study, and of writing at sufficient length to be able to do justice to their knowledge.
>
> (McDonough 1985)

McDonough discusses one approach that avoids some of the problems inherent in a mixed discipline class with a non-specialist EAP teacher. First, the students

> are asked to write five questions which raise typical problems in their subject areas. This immediately gives the teacher a selection of relevant topics to ask them to write about. Then, after various kinds of preparatory work, they write the answers in one-hour periods under simulated examination conditions. The advantages of this system are that the teacher does not have to invent or research questions for which he or she has no professional training, and that

most likely the students will suggest questions that they would quite like to answer.

Another approach to giving some practice in answering questions, as part of the revision process, is suggested by Howe (1983) in the following exercise.

A relevance exercise for your own subject

It is useful and stimulating to do part of your revision for an examination by working with a friend. An exercise on 'relevance' is an especially useful way of checking the way you answer as well as the material learnt.
1. Agree with your friend to test a particular part of your subject, perhaps the contents of a lecture or a chapter of a book.
2. Write down 5 to 10 questions to ask your friend on the first half.
3. Let your friend write down 5 to 10 questions to ask you on the second half.
4. Answer each other's questions.
5. Carefully correct the questions that were wrong.
6. Decide why they were wrong:
   Were the facts wrong?
   Did you answer with irrelevant memorised facts?
   Did you listen to only part of the question?
   Did you give only part of the answer?
7. Give yourself and your friend marks for your answers. At the next revision meeting try to improve the marks.

Jordan (1984) describes the practice in exam writing that he gave to a group of 10–15 economists each year.

Practice for examinations

In the second term, every other week is devoted to discussing and answering examination questions. The questions are supplied by the Department of Economics and are relevant to the students' studies and useful for revision purposes. It is soon apparent that it is not only knowledge of the subject matter that is required but a complete understanding of the question: interpreting it correctly, judging where the main emphasis should be, etc. In addition to this, there is the matter of structuring the answer coherently, writing legibly (for some, a problem!), and writing sufficient to develop the answer in the available time.

The students need to decide what kind of question they are dealing with. In a collection of 11 questions received for practice purposes, three consisted of quotations followed by the word *discuss*; five consisted of opening statement-instructions:

Examine the view that ...
Evaluate the contribution that ...
Discuss the proposition that ...

> *Explain why ...*
> *Outline the circumstances ... ;*
>
> three were direct questions:
>
> *Under what circumstances ... ?*
> *What policies would you ... ?*
> *Can the T.N.C. be regarded as ... ?*
>
> Our two-hour period is normally structured as follows: we discuss
> the question, agree on the emphasis, and organise the answer by
> means of notes on the blackboard. After a short break the students
> have one hour to write an answer: at the beginning of term the notes
> are left on the board as an aid; later on they are removed before the
> writing commences. The following week, I see each student
> individually and discuss the writing with him/her, returning the
> answer which contains comments and a list of specific areas of
> difficulty to focus on. For specific grammatical difficulties s/he is
> either provided with a worksheet from a supporting remedial
> grammar bank (e.g. the frequently confused differences in use
> between *raise/rise/increase*), or referred to the appropriate section
> of a practice book. Towards the end of term the preliminary
> discussion and notes are omitted and the practice is with
> unprepared questions.

If there is a group of students from the same discipline and following the
same subject course, then team-teaching of the writing practice would be
ideal. Dudley-Evans (1988a) describes such an approach involving
students doing an MSc by coursework who are taught jointly by a
language teacher and a member of the subject department. He summarises the procedure as follows:

Stage 1 (before class)	The subject teacher selects an examination question.
Stage 2 (before class)	The subject teacher and the language teacher discuss the meaning of the question and the expected answer.
Stage 3 (in class)	Students discuss the meaning of the question prompted by the language teacher. The subject teacher comments.
Stage 4 (in class)	Students suggest a plan for the answer prompted by the language teacher. The subject teacher comments.
Stage 5 (in class)	Students write an answer based on the plan.
Stage 6 (in class)	Both the subject teacher and the language teacher mark the answer.

Another important part of exam writing practice is learning to structure
an answer appropriately. To this end, discussion with the students can
determine the division of an answer into its introduction, main body/

development and conclusion. Attention can be drawn to some of the main language functions needed, e.g. definitions, assumptions, description, exemplification, inference; and the language forms necessary to realise them, e.g. verb tenses (present, future and past simple; conditional), and connectives (for enumeration, result, contrast), as well as the use of 'vague' language.

One of the main difficulties in writing is the actual process of 'getting started'. For NS of English, writing the first paragraph is the main source of difficulty in academic writing (Hartley and Knapper 1984). For NNS the problem is larger still. Jordan (1988a) gave an example of the expectations of a tutor in economics of the introductory paragraph. His requirements were precise:

> – It should indicate that the student has understood the question and that he/she can interpret it.
> – It should indicate the structure of the answer.
> – It should indicate the way that it is to be answered with regard to content (and possibly some indication of the conclusion).
> – It should be not more than 4–5 sentences long, about 15 lines maximum. (In the examination students have one hour to write each question. The students' essays are similarly short as they are geared to match the examination answers.)

In addition to giving practice in writing an introduction (vitally important for the first impression that it creates in the mind of the reader), it is also necessary to focus on the conclusion. Too often it may contain repetitions, non-sequiturs, irrelevancies, lengthy summaries, unnecessary new information and inappropriate quotations.

15.3 Revision

An essential requirement for students faced with exams is revision. This needs to be planned and undertaken long before exams begin. Wallace (1980) refers to the 'Ebbinghaus forgetting curve' which shows the rate at which people forget. In fact, most items are forgotten 1–2 days after reading/listening unless there are deliberate attempts to remember (Wallace (1980) suggests some memorisation techniques or mnemonics). Howe (1983) neatly summarises revision techniques that can be practised by students (shown overleaf).

15.4 Conclusion

Some students may have to take oral exams or some kind of interview as part of the assessment procedure. These situations would need to be

A spider diagram of revision techniques

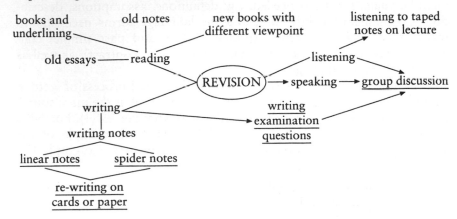

The most useful methods of revision are <u>underlined</u>.

(From Howe 1983)

analysed and the students informed of the structure of the event. General advice can be given to a group, but practice would need to be given on a one-to-one basis, in some kind of question and answer format. Pair work activities could form part of the practice, as could interviews by pairs of students.

Finally, many students would benefit from seeing a specimen or model exam answer, provided by the specialist department, preferably commented on by the department. In this way, there need be no false expectations, either by the students or the subject staff.

Books giving various kinds of practice for exams are: Wallace 1980; Williams 1982; Howe 1983; Jordan 1990a; Smith and Smith 1990; Heaton and Dunmore 1992.

15.5 Introspect and discuss

1. From your experience, which question types (e.g. discuss, explain, etc.) cause students the most problems? What is the nature of the difficulty?
2. The following is an example of an essay test question:
   'Discuss the role of higher education in the development of a country's economy'.
   How would you structure an answer on this topic, and how would you give students appropriate practice in writing this kind of essay answer?

3. Apart from the examples given, have you any suggestions for exam practice in mixed discipline classes?
4. 'Getting started' was referred to as one of the main difficulties in writing. From your experience, have you found any techniques that can help students with this widespread problem?
5. What kinds of exercises/activities can you suggest for practising the writing of introductions and conclusions to essay test questions?
6. From the revision techniques shown in the diagram, which do you think are the most effective? Can you suggest any further ones to add to the diagram?

Part III *English for Specific Academic Purposes*

16 Academic discourse and style

This chapter is concerned with the different features and aspects of language that contribute to what we know as 'academic style'. We will consider this at different levels through different forms of analysis. We shall then look at a feature of academic language – cautious language, covered by 'hedging' or 'vague language'. Finally, we shall look at more general aspects of style, and some implications for teaching.

Subject-specific language, and its organisation, has been subjected to various types of analysis over a long period of time, starting with register analysis, followed by discourse analysis and, more recently, genre analysis. These will now be looked at in turn.

16.1 Register analysis

In the 1960s, the focus was on *register analysis*, whereby statistical analyses were conducted into, for example, verb tense frequencies and vocabulary frequencies for different subjects (ESP) in order to provide grammar registers and lexicons of those subjects.

The names of Halliday, McIntosh and Strevens (1964) are usually associated with the concept of register in ESP. However, Michael West was, perhaps, the true originator of register analysis in 1936 with his count of the frequency of the occurrence of the meanings and uses of words in a study of five million running words. This was reprinted as *A General Service List of English Words* (Longman 1953), and presented a list of 2000 of the most common words 'considered suitable as the basis of vocabulary for learning English as a foreign language'. It included a supplementary word list for the writing of 'popular science and technology'.

One of the first ESP books, and one which took a register analysis approach, was Herbert (1965). The technical passages in his book were 'specially written to illustrate features of technical style' which consisted of both lexical and structural features. Perhaps the best-known ESP book of the same decade, and one that was based on a register analysis of scientific texts, was Ewer and Latorre (1969). Their preliminary research involved a register analysis based on a frequency count of a three-million word corpus of scientific texts. This analysis revealed a number of grammatical and lexical features which were essential to basic scientific English but which were mainly excluded from common-core English language course books at the time. These items were listed as follows (Ewer and Hughes-Davies 1971):

-*ing* forms replacing a relative;
infinitive as substitute for longer phrases;
words similar in form but with different meanings for the same function;
most prefixes and suffixes;
most structural and qualifying words and phrases;
compound nouns;
passives;
conditionals;
anomalous finites;
cause-and-result constructions;
words similar in form but with different functions;
past participle usage;
the prepositional (two-part) verbs common in scientific English.

Swales (1985) provides a useful overview of the various types of linguistic analysis for ESP.

16.2 Discourse analysis

Register analysis operated almost entirely at the word and sentence level. Consequently, one needed to look elsewhere for information about the structuring of longer stretches of speech or text. This need led to a different approach in the 1970s – *discourse analysis*, or a rhetorical approach.

Discourse analysis is concerned with describing the language and its structure that is used in speech or text that is longer than the sentence, e.g. conversations, paragraphs, complete texts. It examines the communicative contexts that affect language use, for example, in social transactions, the relationship between the discourse and the speakers and listeners. It looks at how, for example, the choice of verb tenses or other grammatical features affect the structure of the discourse. The analysis also looks at the relationship between utterances, for example, aspects of cohesion, and the discourse markers or cohesive devices that are employed.

Recurring patterns and text organisation are involved in the analysis, which attempts to develop a framework for the data. For example, a common pattern to be found in texts is – situation, problem, response, evaluation: this is usually called a *problem-solution* pattern. This pattern is highly relevant for academic texts. For full discussions of discourse analysis see McCarthy (1991), Nunan (1993), and McCarthy and Carter (1994).

Within ESP the most influential names associated with discourse analysis approaches have been Widdowson, especially for the *English in Focus* series (with Allen, 1973–78), and for his emphasis on rhetorical functions and information transfer (Widdowson 1979); Candlin *et al.* (1977) for 'DOPACS' and speech functions ('Doctor-Patient Communication Skills'); and Bates and Dudley-Evans for the *Nucleus* series (1976–85). At the same time, in the field of general and applied linguistics, parallel developments were taking place, involving discourse analysis (Sinclair and Coulthard 1975) and communicative language functions (Wilkins 1976). See also Selinker *et al.* (1981) and Robinson (1991).

16.3 Genre analysis

16.3.1 Definition

One fruitful area of research in the 1980s, continuing into the 1990s, is *genre analysis*. Since being closely involved in a number of genre-based research investigations, some of which will be noted shortly, Swales (1990) has elaborated his earlier working definition of genre (Swales 1981) to the following:

Genre defined

A genre comprises a class of communicative events, the members of which share some set of communicative purposes. These purposes are recognized by the expert members of the parent discourse community, and thereby constitute the rationale for the genre. This rationale shapes the schematic structure of the discourse and influences and constrains choice of content and style. Communicative purpose is both a privileged criterion and one that operates to keep the scope of a genre as here conceived narrowly focused on comparable rhetorical action. In addition to purpose, exemplars of a genre exhibit various patterns of similarity in terms of structure, style, content and intended audience. If all high probability expectations are realized, the exemplar will be viewed as prototypical by the parent discourse community. The genre names inherited and produced by discourse communities and imported by others constitute valuable ethnographic communication, but typically need further validation.

In a nutshell, the study of how language is used within a particular setting, i.e. from our point of view, ESAP.

Examples of genres in academic written English are: research articles or papers (especially their introductions), abstracts, theses and dissertations (and their titles – see Dudley-Evans 1984b) and textbooks. Most of the research to date has concentrated on academic text, research articles in particular, but genre analysis does not exclude the spoken form: this will be seen shortly.

Dudley-Evans (1987) provides a clear introduction to genre analysis:

> it has characteristic features of style and form that are recognised, either overtly or covertly, by those who use the genre. Thus, for example, the research article has a known public purpose, and has conventions about layout, form and style that are to a large degree standardised.

Dudley-Evans also relates genre analysis to register analysis and discourse analysis. The essential difference between discourse and genre analysis:

> seems to be that discourse analysis ... seeks to describe relations that are in all texts. It is concerned with the similarities between texts ... Genre analysis claims only to be able to say something about individual texts

(or, perhaps, types of text).

Swales (1990) proposes three key concepts in genre analysis: discourse community, genre and language-learning task. Discourse community is central to an explanation of genre. Swales summarises six defining criteria for discourse community thus:

> there are common goals, participatory mechanisms, information exchange, community specific genres, a highly specialized terminology and a high general level of expertise.

He later adds that:

> genres are neither simply texts, nor discourse communities simply groups of individuals who share attitudes, beliefs and expectations.

The implication here is that a study of institutional culture is involved. Swales neatly summarises in the following diagram the various influences on a genre-based approach to language use, analysis and teaching.

16.3.2 Research

A) WRITING

Swales (1981, 1983, 1984) analysed the introductions to 48 academic articles: 16 from the 'hard' sciences, 16 from biology/medicine and 16 from the social sciences. He found that the majority of the short

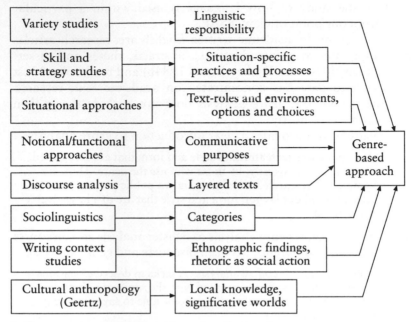

Influences on a genre-based approach (Swales 1990)

introductions investigated followed a four-move pattern. After further research into longer introductions, and because of the difficulty of separating his first two moves, Swales (1990) modified his framework to include three moves – the *Create a Research Space* (CARS) model, reproduced overleaf.

Hopkins and Dudley-Evans (1988) extended Swales' approach to the discussion sections of MSc dissertations in biology, and articles on irrigation and drainage. What emerges is a 'clear cyclical patterning in the writer's choice of moves'. A pedagogically useful set of moves is as follows:

1. Background information
2. Statement of result
3. (Un)expected outcome
4. Reference to previous research (comparison)
5. Explanation of unsatisfactory result
6. Exemplification
7. Deduction
8. Hypothesis
9. Reference to previous research (support)
10. Recommendation
11. Justification

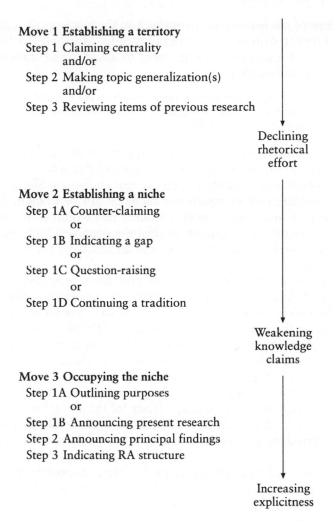

Move 1 Establishing a territory
  Step 1 Claiming centrality
          and/or
  Step 2 Making topic generalization(s)
          and/or
  Step 3 Reviewing items of previous research

Declining
rhetorical
effort

Move 2 Establishing a niche
  Step 1A Counter-claiming
          or
  Step 1B Indicating a gap
          or
  Step 1C Question-raising
          or
  Step 1D Continuing a tradition

Weakening
knowledge
claims

Move 3 Occupying the niche
  Step 1A Outlining purposes
          or
  Step 1B Announcing present research
  Step 2 Announcing principal findings
  Step 3 Indicating RA structure

Increasing
explicitness

A CARS model for article introductions (Swales 1990)

Brett (1994) looked at the results section of sociology articles and found that the categories were similar to those described by Hopkins and Dudley-Evans (1988) in discussion sections. He concluded that:

> the material and tasks used to increase learners' comprehension and production of such texts should be authentic and disciplinarily appropriate.

The application of the genre-based approach in the teaching of scientific and technical report-writing has been examined by Marshall (1991). He explains the use of a computer programme to assist in the marking of students' reports, adding that:

> the teacher must examine the extent to which the student is able to utilize these (schematic) structures to communicate his or her scientific/engineering thinking.

Communication implies that there is a recipient for the writing. Johns (1993) looks at ways in which teachers can give students the experience of writing authentic argumentative texts for real audiences. She gives an example of a writing task in which the audience can be known. In her situation, it was an announcement that student fees would be increased. This was utilised to write arguments against the proposed increase. The tasks will depend on local circumstances and an ability by the teacher to exploit a situation.

Various aspects of academic research writing have been investigated. Dudley-Evans (1984b) looked at the writing of dissertation titles and found that discussing the title with students led to a 'clarification of the students' aims in their project work'. Hewings (1993b) examined the opposite end of the spectrum, so to speak. He investigated the conclusions of a number of MBA dissertations and found that they 'contained elements which had three broadly identifiable functions: to report, to "comment" ..., and to suggest'. Another detailed area that has been considered is citation analysis, that is, a study 'of the citing behaviour of researchers and scholars in their construction of academic text – and sometimes referred to as "content citation analysis" (CCA)' (Swales 1986).

A different approach to analysing genre has been adopted by Paltridge (1995). He discusses an approach 'which aims to complement existing descriptions of genres by focusing on semantic relationships between structural elements in texts'. This area has previously received little attention. Paltridge divides the semantic relations into three broad categories: (1) associative (e.g. statement-amplification) (2) logico-deductive (e.g. reason-result) (3) tempero-contingual (e.g. chronological sequence).

Narrative analysis is rarely referred to in research, yet, as Cortazzi (1994) observes, narrative structure is common in many branches of learning, e.g. law cases, research interviews, occupational narrative, and in the social sciences and education generally. 'Narrative analysis helps teachers to choose optimum points for text breaks for prediction, sequencing, gap filling, editing and story completion tasks'. Cortazzi, in his comprehensive state-of-the-art article, refers to one model for analysing oral narrative structure, in which the main components are:

abstract, orientation, complication, evaluation, and result. These can be in various sequences and combinations.

Finally, in this section on writing, we can note that Swales (1995) argues for the inclusion of advanced writing textbooks as a genre that can inform academic writing. Such books can be seen as hybrid genres: 'they may consolidate and apply recent scholarship, incorporate new research findings and generate interesting new topics worth further study' as well as teach writing skills to students. Swales backs up his argument with examples from his own writing textbook (Swales and Feak 1994) in which graduate students are given practice in constructing a research paper.

B) SPEECH

Spoken language has received much less attention than written. However, an investigation of the graduate seminar in the USA has been made by Weissberg (1993). He observed ten seminars in animal science and agronomy and noted that there appeared to be four subgenres: proposals, in-progress reports, preliminary literature reviews and completed research reports. This last group matched the 'Introduction – Methods – Results – Discussion sections of the R(esearch) A(rticle) ... summarised by Swales (1990)'.

Weissberg concluded by examining the implications for teaching. He suggested that on a course devoted to academic speaking, a:

> full seminar presentation might be the culminating activity in a
> graded sequence of shorter speaking tasks, for example:
> 1. giving a professional autobiography
> 2. introducing a speaker;
> 3. profiling an academic department and its research interests;
> 4. delimiting an area of research, citing key references;
> 5. discussing a specific research problem or controversy;
> 6. describing in detail a single experiment from the literature or
>   from personal experience;
> 7. presenting experimental data with slides/transparencies;
> 8. giving a full seminar.

On a broader front, and of potential interest to a wider audience, Thompson (1994) has analysed the introductions to lectures. The analysis was based on eighteen lecture introductions from a range of disciplines, including applied linguistics, engineering and medicine. Thompson analysed the introductions for their rhetorical functions, which 'were identified in terms of the lecturer's overall goals and communicative aims'. She highlights the difficulties inherent in trying to identify a straightforward pedagogic model 'because of the structural heterogeneity of lectures'. There were problems in 'identifying a generically approved order of units' and in disentangling one sub-function from another.

Thompson gives an example of the structure of a lecture introduction (LI):

> Announce topic
> Indicate scope
> Announce topic
> Outline structure
> Show importance/relevance of topic
> Relate new to given
> Refer to earlier lecture
> Relate new to given.

The importance of LIs are stressed as an aid to listeners to help them process dense information delivered at a fast rate. The LI gives the audience a *'framework* for listening to the lecture and a *context* within which to place the new topics'. Thompson proposes some awareness-raising activities for students which include listening to examples of authentic lecture introductions to identify the functions and sub-functions which indicate the lecture content. Note-taking activities focus on including information in 'Announce topic' and 'Outline structure' so that students will have a framework for reference during the rest of the lecture.

Still within the domain of lectures, but on a much narrower front, Shalom (1993) investigated the structure and moves involved in plenary lecture and poster session discussions at academic conferences. She noted the opening, discussion and closing phases, and the central role of the chairperson in controlling the phases and moves. The plenary lecture discussion had a much clearer framework than the poster session discussion, which seemed not yet to have defined itself.

c) SPECIFIC SUBJECTS: ECONOMICS AND LAW

Economics is a discipline that has attracted a number of genre-researchers. Hewings and Henderson (1987) consider and compare economics textbooks and articles in bank reviews. Jordan (1988a) looks at the structure of introductory paragraphs in economics essays. He also analyses the ways in which quotations in economics articles are presented (Jordan 1990c). Economics articles are also analysed by Dudley-Evans and Henderson (1990b), who focus on the introductions to articles over a long period of time and, using Swales' model for article introductions, study the evolution of academic writing in economics.

Another specialised area of investigation is the language and structure of the 'problem question' in law. The 'problem question' is a highly specialised genre and very different from the essay in its structure. Howe (1990; 1993) analysed the features of 20 scripts from criminal law, public law, contract law and tort. She constructed a schema consisting of eight basic units of discourse:

1. the situation
2. the instruction } = the question, written by the teacher/examiner
3. the forecast
4. the issue
5. the law
6. its authority } written by the student
7. the application of the facts
8. opinion (and advice)

Howe (1993) also noted the areas of legal language that cause particular difficulty for students:

> Students ... must be able to switch tenses from sentence to sentence ... [as in a] legal argument .. the time reference may change several times in a paragraph.

Other areas to consider are:

> the great number of legal collocations, other technical vocabulary, the importance of general academic vocabulary (e.g. hypothesis, analogy, assertion)

Legal language has been researched and reported on over the years: a very useful account and bibliography is contained in Bhatia (1987).

The examination of genres within one discipline, as exemplified by economics, seems justified according to the concern expressed by Johns (1988a), who comments that:

> we are still having difficulty identifying the skills which are actually transferable to a variety of academic contexts ... [and] though some generalizations can be made about the conventions and skills in academia, the differences among them may be greater than the similarities; for discipline, audience, and context significantly influence the language required.

Dudley-Evans (1993) also questions the 'common-core' teaching approach in EAP. From his experience of comparing dissertations in two science disciplines he supports Johns' view. He finds, in particular, that the discussion sections in plant biology are not only significantly longer than those in highway engineering, but also contain 'significant differences in the ways that they are structured'.

Kusel (1992) made a study of the structuring of essay introductions and endings across six subject departments. The results suggest that the rhetorical organisation of these sections of essays is influenced significantly by the conventions adopted by the subject departments.

Robinson (1991) has observed that:

> there is a greater interest in the content with which ESP must be involved – the subject matter which ESP students have to study and work with through English.

In other words, the actual subjects that students study (economics, etc.) are being analysed more, from the point of view of the language used, its structure, particular genres, and associated academic conventions.

This tendency has been observed in the USA, Canada and Britain. In a sense, a dichotomy has been created which hinges on the strengths and weaknesses of genre analysis:

> The weakness of the approach is that it is of limited generalisability. Its strength is that it provides a model that is likely to be of use to students
>
> (Henderson and Dudley-Evans 1990)

16.3.3   Implications for teaching

Some of the practical implications for teaching, linked to a genre-analysis approach, have already been referred to above (e.g. Weissberg 1993; Johns 1993; Thompson 1994). Swales (1983, 1984) listed some class activities and exercise types appropriate for academic writing as a follow-up to his investigation into article introductions. Among several activities mentioned are:

- *colour-coding*: using sets of marker-pens (different colours for the moves) for categorising the structure of article introductions.
- *jumbled introductions*: a reassembly exercise – initially with the *moves* out of order, subsequently with the individual sentences on separate slips of paper in random order.
- *writing scholarly introductions*: cloze exercises on whole introductions; inserting references into introductory arguments; the writing of introductions based on library research cards plus title or abstract.

Swales (1990) adds to his previous proposals in a number of ways. He suggests that students could be sensitised to:

> rhetorical effects and to the rhetorical structures that tend to recur in genre-specific texts ... [and] that students are helped if they can also schematize the structures of the sections [in an academic paper] themselves and so further develop an understanding of what it is that allows them to recognize a section as Method or Discussion, and what it is that allows them to argue that one section is more or less effective than another.

In proposing activities in a research-process course, Swales acknowledges that the 'problem' of content may loom large. The different ways of coping with this will depend on whether the class is homogeneous in disciplinary interest or is multi-disciplinary. One suggestion, among several, is that students could individually analyse a research article from their own discipline and compare with others and note similarities and differences. A common denominator might be to explore research into higher education 'if only because *all* participants in the course will be currently engaged in that process'. Finally, Swales makes some suggestions for activities involving research titles, suggestions for further research, and course descriptions.

Although his interest is in the teaching of professional/business genres, Flowerdew (1993) makes out a case for an educational, or process, approach to the teaching of genres which has wider implications. He proposes six types of activity:

1. using the results of genre analysis (i.e. the techniques of the analysis);
2. 'metacommunicating' (talking about instances of genres);
3. learners doing their own genre analysis;
4. concordancing;
5. 'on-line' genre analysis by learners as an aid in creating their own texts;
6. translation based on a sample of instances of a given genre.

By these means, 'learners can be taught to approach, adapt to, and ultimately acquire new genres'.

In order to avoid any 'potential mismatch between the longer term goals of the student and the goals of the language teacher', Davies (1988) proposes a genre-based syllabus, that is, one 'which is founded on the identification and analysis of the specific genres that students are required to read and write in their subject-based studies'. She is particularly concerned with the genres that students are expected to produce and which can be difficult to access or to study, namely, exam answers, essays, laboratory reports, dissertations and theses. She is not only concerned with developing an awareness of different genres, but also in developing 'student awareness of the strategies which can be deployed in learning to write for academic purposes'.

Other suggestions for activities/tasks for raising awareness of genres among students are contained in Kusel (1992), and Bhatia (1993) who considers a wide range of genres, both academic and professional.

In concluding this section, we can note Swales' prediction (Swales 1994), made in his valedictory comments as retiring editor of *English for Specific Purposes*:

there will be less exclusive attention on the 'high' genres such as the research article, and more interest in 'homely' or 'low' genres.

This will be welcomed by most EAP teachers.

16.4   Hedging/vague language

A feature of academic writing is the need to be cautious in one's claims or statements. In other words, you may indicate your certainty or commitment in varying degrees. The concept of cautious language was first termed 'hedging' in 1972 and 1973 by George Lakoff when he spoke of 'words whose job it is to make things fuzzier or less fuzzy'.

Selinker (1979) noted that hedging was:

> an important and necessary feature of EST/EAP writing ... The well-known practice of hedging in scientific writing is due to the fact that every attempt to explain a given phenomenon in a particular manner is open to an alternative explanation – generally introduced by the phrase 'but maybe'.

In an examination of forecasting in economics reports, Makaya and Bloor (1987) note that:

> authors need to be cautious in their claims, and it is a common weakness of inexperienced writers, in particular non-native speakers, to fail to modulate their utterances appropriately.

Makaya and Bloor analysed three ways in which economics forecasters modify their commitment to a prediction:

– by *hedging*: e.g. using modal verbs (may, might, etc.);
　　　　　　some adverbs (possibly, perhaps, etc.);
　　　　　　some adjectives (likely, probable, etc.);
　　　　　　impersonal verb forms (suggest, seem, etc.);
– by *attribution*: e.g. X expects y ...
　　　　　　According to X, the y ...
– by *specifying conditions*: e.g. X will happen if ...

Salager-Meyer (1994) found that the discussion and comment sections of medical journal articles are the most heavily hedged sections. She adopted the following taxonomy of hedges and observed that both *shields* and *compound hedges* are the most frequently encountered hedging devices in the two sections referred to.

1. *Shields*, e.g. all modal verbs expressing possibility; semi-auxiliaries like: to appear, to seem; probability adverbs like: probably, likely;
2. *Approximators*, e.g. of quantity, degree, frequency and time viz. approximately, roughly, often;

3. Expressions such as 'I believe', 'to our knowledge', etc. which express the *author's personal doubt and direct involvement*;
4. *Emotionally-charged intensifiers*, such as: extremely interesting, particularly encouraging, unexpectedly;
5. *Compound hedges*, i.e. the juxtaposition of several hedges, e.g. It may suggest that . . ., it seems reasonable to assume . . , etc.

Salager-Meyer concludes that hedging is a necessary and vitally important skill; consequently, she proposes some types of exercise to raise students' awareness of the various hedging techniques. She suggests sensitisation and translation exercises, and rewriting exercises (e.g. rewriting a popularised article with 'hedges' to make it more academically acceptable).

'Hedging' is examined in detail by Skelton (1988a):

> It is by means of the hedging system of a language that a user distinguishes between what s/he says and what s/he thinks about what s/he says. Without hedging, the world is purely propositional . . . With a hedging system, language is rendered more flexible and the world more subtle'.

As Skelton points out, 'there are a very large number of ways in which one can hedge in English'. Skelton notes that 'hedging' is a pejorative term and for it substitutes the word 'comment': it is the role of comment to modulate. It is important, as Skelton stresses, for students to be taught the relationship between proposition and comment.

Skelton (1988b) further investigated commentative language by analysing 40 journal articles from the sciences and humanities: he identified three main comment types which cover the language forms noted above. He also quantified the data and discovered that commentative language is about equally common in arts and science:

> Comments . . . certainly appear to occur, overall, in between one third and one half of all sentences . . . they are a much more common feature of academic writing than, say, most verb tenses.

The advantage of teaching the commentative system to students is that it enables them to 'achieve greater delicacy of meaning'.

Twenty-two textbooks for ESP and EAP were analysed and compared by Hyland (1994) to see the coverage given to hedging. He noted that the EAP writing textbooks were more comprehensive in their coverage than the ESP books, but they still needed to devote more attention to 'this important interpersonal strategy'. Hyland observed that very little attention was paid to the use of modal nouns. The main modal expressions used, in descending order, were:

– modal verbs (e.g. would, could, may);
– lexical verbs (e.g. seem, appear, suggest);
– modal adverbs (e.g. probably, possibly, apparently);

– modal adjectives (e.g. certain, probable, undoubted);
– modal nouns (e.g. assumption, possibility, estimate).

The frequency of occurrence of 'vague language' is noted by Channell (1994), who quotes research into the spoken language of doctors working in a hospital where the instances of vague language were found to be about one every fifteen seconds! Channell denotes an expression or word as being vague if:

– it can be contrasted with a precise way of rendering the same proposition:
– it is 'purposely and unabashedly vague';
– its meaning arises from 'intrinsic uncertainty' (caused by the speaker's habits of language being indeterminate).

In her study of vague language, Channell looks in detail at approximating quantities with:

– *numbers and approximators*, e.g. about, around, approximately;
– *round numbers*, e.g. ninety-nine per cent (in some situations), a couple of;
– *non-numerical vague quantifiers*, e.g. lots of, a bit of, several.

Channell considers the various uses of vague language over a wide-ranging field, including such colloquialisms as 'thingy', 'whatsisname', and 'whatsit'. She concludes by noting that:

> learners of English need to gain an understanding of how vagueness expresses politeness, both so that they can produce appropriately polite language, and so that they can correctly interpret the politeness strategies they hear used by others.

She also makes some suggestions for giving students practice in using vague language, e.g. in a text, locate all the vague words and explain their meaning; then note the changes to the text by substituting precise words for each vague occurrence.

Two examples are shown below of the type of practice that can be given in hedging/vague language.

> A feature of written academic English is the need to be careful (i.e. to indicate 'less than one hundred per cent certainty'). The purpose of such writing is to show that one is generalising or desires to be cautious, or even that one *might possibly* be wrong (though it is not *likely*!).
> Note:
> The three preceding words in italics are examples of such language in use.
>
> The most usual ways of expressing caution or lack of certainty are by means of verbs (e.g. appears to/seems to/tends to/may/might) and

adverbs (e.g. perhaps/possibly/probably/apparently). For an explanation of this see Unit 10 (page 62).
a) The following sentence is a *definite statement*:
   Industrialisation is viewed as a superior way of life.
b) To make it more *tentative* or *cautious* we can change or add some words:
   Industrialisation *tends* to be viewed as a superior way of life.

Exercise
Now look at the following sentences taken from an economics book:
a) It *is* also *likely to* appear in the development of institutions ...
b) The ideal of economic development *tends* to be associated with different policy goals ...
c) *Perhaps* greater clarity can be brought to the meaning of economic development ...
   How would the above three sentences be written if we wanted to make them *definite* and *not* tentative?

(Jordan 1990a)

A similar exercise to the above can be given in reverse, i.e. give a series of definite statements and ask students to make them more cautious, in different ways.

a) Decide on an order for the sentences below, starting with the one which shows the most commitment to the statement and ending with the one which shows the least commitment.
   i)   The earth is probably round.
   ii) The earth is possibly round.
   iii) The earth is round.
   iv) Perhaps the earth is round.
   v)   The earth undoubtedly is round.
   vi) It is said that the earth is round.
b) One of the sentences above uses a different method to reduce the degree of commitment to the truth of the statement. Which one? Explain how it is different.

(Hamp-Lyons and Heasley 1987)

16.5 Appropriacy

The purpose of this section is to look at language from the viewpoint of students who need, initially, a more global approach to raise their awareness of differences between academic and general language. This section also looks at some practical examples for teaching.

Not only do students need to distinguish between a formal, or academic, style and an informal one, but they also have to understand differences between what is acceptable in spoken language and what is appropriate in writing. Appropriacy may be difficult to transfer from one culture to another: it takes time and experience to develop.

The question of what is appropriate in academic writing is well illustrated by the following anecdote. An overseas student, visiting Britain, wrote a university essay on economics. In general, his language use was very good. However, the final paragraph of the essay included the following:

> That's all I can think of to write now. Goodbye.

There are no errors in the language use, though one would discourage using the contraction at the beginning. The point is that it is totally out of place in an academic essay: it is inappropriate. It would, however, be perfectly suitable at the end of an informal letter to a friend.

Students who go to study in English-speaking countries first have to come to terms with the conventions of informal, spoken language, with all its features, including, for example, the use of colloquialisms, slang and contracted forms. Then they have to adjust to the requirements of a formal written style for their studies. It is not surprising then that there may be confusion in the students' language use, jumping from informal speech to formal writing. The result is that the writing often contains features of the spoken language which are not appropriate. Useful preliminary practice, to assist in overcoming this problem is, for example, contained in the section 'Looking at Style and Usage' in the worksheets accompanying the *Oxford Advanced Leaner's Dictionary*.

Discussing and analysing an academic text with students can help to draw attention to the features that, when combined, determine that the discourse is formal and academic. Such an analysis may reveal certain characteristics (Clanchy and Ballard (1992):

The academic writer's *approach* to his or her material is:

analytical		impressionistic
objective	*rather than*	subjective
intellectual		emotional
rational		polemical

The academic writer's *tone* is:

serious		conversational
impersonal	*rather than*	personal
formal		colloquial

The academic writer makes frequent use of:
    passive forms of the verb
    impersonal pronouns and phrases
    qualifying words and phrases
    complex sentence structures
    specialised vocabulary

The analysis will involve looking at: the writer's purpose, the content and the reader's expectations. The overall impression created by the text may be of a piece of detached writing, cautiously phrased, seeking justification for its point of view by making references to other writers. In addition, it would probably present a balanced viewpoint, avoiding heavy bias or prejudice. The actual content and vocabulary will determine which particular discipline it belongs to. Vocabulary selection is linked to Halliday's (1978) key components of *field* (subject matter and purpose of message), *tenor* (relationship between sender and receiver), and *mode* (the channel of communication). An analysis of the whole text, which includes an examination of communicative purpose, will involve an analysis of genre.

After looking at some texts with students, various lexical characteristics can be examined. Often these are expressed in terms of avoidance. Thus, for example, *avoid using*:

a) contractions (e.g. it's, hasn't; *do use*: it is, has not)
b) many phrasal verbs (e.g. look into, find out; *do use*: investigate, discover)
c) colloquialisms/slang (e.g. you know, lots, kid – *omit these*)
d) personal pronouns (e.g. I, you; *do use*: it, there, one + passive verb forms. However, 'I' will sometimes be appropriate: it depends on the subject/situation, e.g. in literary criticism, and where personal opinions or the writer's own attitude are required)
e) vagueness in word choice (e.g. thing; *be explicit/specific*)

Do use: appropriate punctuation (e.g. become familiar with: commas, colons, semi-colons).

Practice can be given in recognising formal, academic writing, initially in sentences.

Exercise

The following sentences are mixed *formal* and *informal*. Write F (formal) or I (informal) in the brackets after each sentence.
a) The project will be completed next year.   ( )
b) I showed that his arguments did not hold water.   ( )
c) I wonder why he put up with those terrible conditions
   for so long.   ( )
d) Five more tests will be necessary before the experiment
   can be concluded.   ( )
e) It is possible to consider the results from a different
   viewpoint   ( )
f) It has been proved that the arguments so far are without
   foundation.   ( )
g) He'll have to do another five tests before he can stop the
   experiment.   ( )
h) It is not clear why such terrible conditions were tolerated
   for so long.   ( )

    i) There are a number of reasons why the questionnaire
        should be revised.   ( )
    j) We'll finish the job next year.   ( )

(Jordan 1990a)

A next step could be to list further sentences and ask students which ones they would expect to find in an academic text, and why. This would lead to a useful discussion.

A group activity can evolve around the study of a serious newspaper/magazine report, in which there is the need to engage the interest of the reader, and the use of appropriate language to do that. Academic writing would avoid emotive language; journalese and sensationalism are also out of place. The discussion might consider the most important pieces of information in the report. A task could then be set: to convert the report into an academic account, using a general-specific structure. Alternatively, the students could be asked to suggest the source of the text, and identify the characteristic features of that source. They could then propose changes so that it became an academic report: in other words, a register transfer exercise. An example of the first type of activity is in Appendix 1.1 from Hamp-Lyons and Heasley (1987).

Two other activities to develop awareness and recognition of features of academic style are as follows. Firstly, provide a selection of paragraphs or short texts from mixed sources, e.g. an academic textbook, an academic journal, an encyclopedia entry, a serious magazine and a quality newspaper. The students can be asked to identify the type of source and explain the differences. Their attention can be drawn to a number of items, e.g. length of sentences, verbs and tenses used, use of hedging, etc. Secondly, a similar activity, but this time all the extracts are written by specialists in the same subject area, e.g. academic textbooks (both introductory and advanced), an academic journal, a conference paper, a lecture transcript. The students can discuss the extracts and try to ascertain the type of writing and for whom it was written.

Although a consideration of academic style usually involves writing, there is no reason why it should not extend to speech.

> Learners need to develop a sensitivity to stylistic variation in order to participate effectively in conversation ... there should be an awareness of the difference between informal, neutral and formal styles ...
>
> (Cunningsworth 1987)

Cunningsworth notes that:

> the most important variables in the speech situation are the physical context (setting), the social roles of the participants in that context and the goals of the participants.

This is clearly of importance in the context of the seminar and students' meetings with their supervisor or tutor. Cunningsworth stresses the need for:

> teaching materials to present exponents of language on a formality/ politeness scale ... [and we should see] some sensitisation of learners to why some forms are more or less formal or polite than others.

A number of books contain exercises in the use of formal style, sometimes referred to as objective or impersonal writing (e.g. Jordan 1990a; Montgomery 1982; Hamp-Lyons and Courter 1984; Smith and Smith 1990; Brookes and Grundy 1990; Heaton and Dunmore, 1992; *Photocopiable Worksheets*, OUP; Swales and Feak 1994).

Conclusion

One of the best pieces of advice that can be given to students about to begin academic writing, and who are uncertain about the style and conventions of their specialist subject, is for them to ask in the subject department to see good examples of appropriate writing. Reports, dissertations and theses may be available in departmental or university libraries. It may be more difficult to see an essay, but persistence can pay dividends. For the larger subject groups, EAP course directors should be able to obtain good specimens of subject-writing to analyse and show students attending courses. Appropriate academic journals can also be useful in illustrating style and various conventions, e.g. quotations, footnotes, references and bibliographies.

16.7 Introspect and discuss

1. Johns (1993) refers to writing tasks to give students the experience of writing authentic argumentative texts for real audiences. Can you suggest any appropriate activities?
2. In the context of genre analysis, very little research has been done on essays. Try to analyse the overall structure of one essay so that the analysis would be of practical use to students who have to write essays.
3. Swales has mentioned the possible 'problem' of *content* in a research-process course. List appropriate classroom activities for students who are (a) of homogeneous disciplines, and (b) from heterogeneous disciplines.
4. Using an article, or section from a textbook, note any instances of hedging or vague language that you see. How would you categorise them? How would you raise students' awareness of their use?

5. Try to note examples of hedging/vague language that you commonly hear, compared with those that you commonly see in academic writing. Are there any differences? If so, of what type? How would you draw students' attention to the differences?

6. A list of language features to be avoided in academic writing is given in the last section ('Appropriacy'); five categories are shown. From your experience, can you add:
   a) further items that you have noticed being misused;
   b) further categories?

7. Some exercise-types are shown for recognising and practising the differences between non-academic and academic written language. Try to devise further exercise-types.

8. The following is an activity that can be developed in order to raise students' awareness of differences in style, genre, etc. Take a general topic, such as 'democracy' or 'death'. Then pose the question 'What is democracy?' or 'What is death?' Try to list as many definitions from as many varied sources as you can, e.g. informal spoken, informal written, journalism, encyclopedia, dictionary, subject-specialist dictionary, academic textbook, subject specialist department, etc. Number the definitions (but do not give the source) and see if students can identify them and justify their answers.

17 Subject-specific language

We must not lose sight of the fact that students do not study EAP for general purposes but to equip themselves with the necessary tools to study specific academic subjects. They may be studying one discipline or, more likely, combined subjects: they will, thus, encounter a variety of academic sub-genres. It is for this reason that there are often specific components or options within an EAP course, or even the entire course, devoted to particular disciplines or subjects.

The purpose of this chapter is to draw some threads together that have been referred to in earlier chapters that relate to ESAP: in particular, how aspects of ESAP may be taught by EAP teachers, and the kinds of activities that are feasible. We must bear in mind that on EAP courses time is limited, i.e. what is the most efficient way to utilise the time? How can students be helped best? What are teachers capable of achieving? What considerations need to be addressed?

Regarding a possible conflict of interests between EGAP and ESAP, Johns' (1988a) observation is relevant:

> the differences between the skills and conventions needed in
> academia may be greater than the similarities; for discipline,
> audience and context significantly influence the language required.
> Students must therefore readjust somewhat to each academic
> discipline they encounter.

The situation, as it affects teachers and students, can be summarised diagrammatically, with EGAP as the base and ESAP the pinnacle (see Figure 20).

It seems appropriate to ask what exactly it is that distinguishes one discipline from another. The answer is not clear-cut. The subject content will be one difference. This will lead to the technical or specialist vocabulary which may show significant variations between disciplines (but it may not between subjects within discipline groups). Structural, general or sub-technical vocabulary may show few or no differences. If we look at the grammatical system, we may find that some subjects, in the sciences and technology, have a tendency to use verb tenses in the passive and nominal compounds more frequently than other subjects.

However, once we embark on genre analysis, we may find that differences start to emerge between disciplines in, for example, rhetorical

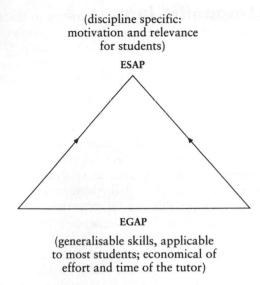

(discipline specific:
motivation and relevance
for students)

ESAP

EGAP

(generalisable skills, applicable
to most students; economical of
effort and time of the tutor)

Figure 20   EGAP → ESAP

organisation (see the previous chapter). Differences also exist in the underlying conceptual approach to the subject. This is part of the difference that is expressed through the disciplinary culture, of which specific expectations and conventions are an integral part (see Chapter 6).

Students usually prefer to devote time to studying texts and topics related to their particular discipline. This at least gives face validity, and is also valuable as a familiarisation activity. Consequently, there may be whole courses devoted to the language and genres of specific disciplines – in situations where all the students will be going on to the same subject-course after completing the EAP course (e.g. English for Academic Legal Purposes, described by Howe 1993). At the other extreme, there may be individualised tuition in writing subject-specific essays within the framework of an EGAP course (e.g. Blue 1988a).

We will now turn to some of the problems or issues that relate to ESAP.

17.1   Students' inadequacy in the specialist subject

It sometimes happens that a student is not only weak in the language of the specialist subject, but weak also in the subject itself. There may be an inadequate background in the subject, or the level at which it was previously studied may be too low to cope with the demands of higher education. If this is so, the EAP tutor should *not* try to teach the subject itself (he/she would probably not be able to anyway), but should strongly advise the student to discuss the matter with his/her subject tutor. If necessary, it may be helpful for the EAP tutor to discuss the difficulties with the department. It may be that the student has been placed on the wrong course and a change can be made.

17.2   The EAP tutor and the subject specialism

'It is not the job of the English teacher to teach technical vocabulary; it consumes too much time, and he will probably not do it well' (Higgins 1966). Some years later, Strevens (1977) noted some of the problems facing the ESP tutor:

> teachers are faced (a) by the task of meeting the needs of scientists
> without themselves understanding or having experience of what
> these needs actually are, and (b) by the task of teaching the language
> used in a particular subject (electronics, computer programming,
> tropical agriculture, jet engine maintenance, navigation, textile
> engineering, etc.) with which they are totally unfamiliar, to the
> extent that the very teaching texts they will need to use are
> meaningless, incomprehensible and daunting to them.

To these problems could have been added the resultant lack of self-confidence combined with a lack of suitable teaching materials. Fortunately, this last problem has, to some extent, been solved.

Spack (1988) has pointed out the dangers of basing a writing course in specialised disciplines. EAP tutors:

> even when they collaborate with content teachers, find they have
> little basis for dealing with the content. They therefore find
> themselves in the uncomfortable position of being less
> knowledgeable than their students.

Some of the tutors' problems are encapsulated in the following anecdote (Howe 1993):

> Several years ago I tried to give in-sessional reading classes to
> overseas students in the University's Law School. The reading
> classes were well attended and I wrote further exercises to help
> students find their way through difficult texts. When the reading
> exercises found their way into a law tutor's hand, I was in trouble.
> His comments, in writing, to another law lecturer were kindly
> passed on to me. 'Of immemorial antiquity' does not mean 'older
> than any person's memory', as I had suggested; it means 'before
> 1189'. Of course! My friend had written a long list of criticisms of
> my well-intentioned efforts and it all ended in my being asked to see
> the Professor of Law. He gently beetled his brows at me from

behind the desk and said: 'You teach them the English, Mrs Howe, and we'll teach them the law.'

The clear inference from all the above comments seems to be: danger – keep away! This would suggest confining the language teaching to EGAP, i.e. study skills etc., and not being involved in ESAP. In itself, this poses some dichotomies.

Research has shown, through genre analysis as well as by other means, that the more content-specific the course, the more students will find it useful and be motivated. However, if we adopt this approach, how do we reconcile it with the desire to appeal to students from the wide range of disciplines to be found on most EAP courses? In other words, how do we reconcile the common denominator or 'common core' (wide angle) approach with the attractions to the student of a subject-specific approach (narrow angle)? At first glance, there might appear to be a conflict between research findings and their implementation, involving organisation and teaching.

17.3 Other concerns

There are other areas of concern: these will be noted briefly before turning to look at some suggestions for teaching ESAP.

1. Is there a methodology which is specific to, or appropriate for, ESAP/ ESP? This has been commented on in Chapter 7 when considering collaboration between EAP tutors and subject tutors and the development of team-teaching. In this connection, task-based or problem-solving activities are highly relevant.
2. Should ESAP courses focus on one particular skill, for example, reading, or should the four skills always be integrated? In raising this question, Johns and Dudley-Evans (1991) comment that specialised reading courses have been organised in a number of countries and have proved to be popular. A common-sense approach would indicate that it depends on needs and local circumstances.
3. Flowerdew (1990) raised the question of the use of authentic as opposed to simplified texts in ESP. Authenticity was discussed in Chapter 7. Aspects of it will be considered in the next section in the context of teaching ESAP.

17.4 Suggestions for teaching

It was suggested in the previous section that the EAP tutor's ignorance of the specialist subject might be a barrier to teaching ESAP. This needs to be put into context and into perspective. Probably very few NS EAP tutors have a straight English degree as their first or main academic qualification. Many more will have a modern languages degree. Others will have a variety of academic backgrounds, for example, economics, history, law, chemistry, etc. To put it another way, not all tutors are necessarily ignorant of the subject concepts or content. However, for our purposes here, we will assume that the tutor has no previous training in the subject. What can be done?

17.4.1 Asking questions

Hutchinson and Waters (1987) provide part of the answer.

> ESP teachers do not need to learn specialist subject knowledge. They require three things only:
> i)   a positive attitude towards the ESP content;
> ii) a knowledge of the fundamental principles of the subject area;
> iii) an awareness of how much they probably already know.
> This can be summed up as 'the ability to ask intelligent questions'. ... In other words, the ESP teacher should not become a teacher of the subject matter, but rather an interested student of the subject matter.

This approach is reinforced by McDonough (1984):

> The teacher, recognising that the learners are specialists in a different area from himself/herself, can capitalise on this by asking for information which the teacher genuinely does not possess ... for instance, the teacher might ask for clarification of terminology and definitions of key concepts.

Clearly, this has to be undertaken in moderation. Nothing would be achieved by asking students to define and explain almost everything they said or wrote – except alienation! Nevertheless, used judiciously, the approach has merit.

17.4.2 Team-teaching

This has already been discussed in Chapter 7: references were given to papers which report examples of departmental collaboration. There may be varying degrees of co-operation:

- the provision of information including description of target situation, and identification of problem areas;
- providing reading lists, recommended journals, timetables, etc.;
- assistance with writing or vetting teaching materials;
- recording short talks on audio-/video-cassette for teaching and self-access purposes;

- guest lectures on EAP courses and follow-up seminars for subject-specialist students;
- full-scale sharing of some other lecturing/teaching sessions.

17.4.3 Discipline-specific topics/texts

If a class consists of students from one discipline, appropriate texts/topics may be used as part of the teaching process. Perhaps these will be in EAP/ESAP books (see the next section) or provided by departments. If, however, students are from several disciplines, it may be possible to group them along broad subject lines, e.g. social sciences, physical sciences, natural sciences, medicine, etc. In this case, topics/texts will need to be broader based. One possible solution is to select a topic which may be approached in different ways by a number of disciplines:

> Take pumps as a simple example: pumps are found in the body (the heart), in houses (central heating systems), in engines (petrol pumps), in hospitals (peristaltic pumps in heart-lung machines), etc. Using topics like this, learners can apply the ideas and language of a core text to their own specialist field.

(Hutchinson and Waters 1987)

An example of another topic that could be treated in a similar way is 'traffic problems in a city'. A simple research task, based on the use of texts and data, observations, interviews, questionnaires and surveys, could enable students from a number of disciplines to be involved, e.g. economics, statistics, sociology, law, politics, pollution control, architecture, engineering. This approach may be used with topics/texts/data which are not discipline-based but which are of general current concern or of international significance.

The place of projects, simulations, role plays and pyramid discussions has been referred to in Chapter 7. It is worth pointing out that an activity such as pyramid discussion can be utilised in a class in spite of the teacher knowing little of the subject or discipline. Students can suggest appropriate important or controversial topics, and they can also propose the necessary 15–20 items that comprise the list of choices. As they will then be considering the list individually, and then discussing in pairs and groups, the teacher is employed as an organiser and language adviser (if necessary), not as a subject specialist.

17.4.4 Individualisation/self-access

Even if there are not enough students of a subject to justify the setting up of a special group, it may still be possible to provide practice in the language of a specific subject in several ways.

1. By means of an *individual project*, selected by the students from their own subject area. It will usually be written, and may incorporate data and visual material as appropriate. An oral summary can be required, thus providing the opportunity to practise the spoken language as well.

   Blue (1988a) provides an example of essay writing, rather than a project, on a pre-sessional EAP course. 'The essay titles are set either by or in conjunction with the receiving departments'. He discusses the difficulties and advantages and concludes that it is very worthwhile: it 'is by far the most popular component of the pre-sessional course'.

   Peretz (1988) describes, in some detail, a project-oriented course for students of science and technology in which the students decide which academic articles to read in preparation for giving a fifteen-minute oral presentation. Peretz also discusses the distinct advantages that accrue to the students from adopting such an approach. It is assumed that the teacher is not a specialist in the subject areas.

2. By the provision of a selection of *audio-/video-cassettes* on different subjects, available in the language laboratory or resource centre for individual/library use. These may be a mixture of published material and teacher-recorded talks. The recordings may be provided by different academic departments (e.g. introductory talks of 10–15 minutes on a variety of topics) and different members of staff. The advantage is that students may have the opportunity to listen to the voices of lecturers they will meet later in their departments. The EAP tutor can devise appropriate exercises, in the form of (self-access) worksheets, based on the talks. Alternatively, recordings may be made of live lectures/seminars, though this may present additional listening problems for some students, coupled with the fact that such sessions are invariably lengthy viz. 45–60 minutes. These can, of course, be broken down into manageable units.

3. By the establishment of a *small library* of textbooks and specimen journals from some of the subject areas so that students may develop some familiarity with them. Optional reading/writing tasks could be provided on an individual basis, perhaps self-access, and perhaps guided by subject departments for reading purpose and type of task.

The complete opposite of an individualised approach to ESAP within the framework of an EGAP course, is described by Howe (1993). She describes and discusses the planning and preparation needed for a whole ESAP course in law. She admits that 'ideally, the language teacher should take the first year law course' (Howe 1990)! As this will be beyond the resources of almost all EAP tutors, she continues:

failing that, an interest in the law is essential, together with the help of colleagues from the law school to suggest teaching materials and to check those that have been written. For the lexis and syntax of legal language cannot be separated from its concepts and discourse.

17.5 ESAP books

If a subject-specific class is formed, it is likely that a book will be used as the basis for some of the practice. Care needs to be taken over the choice of book, not only for the *appropriacy* and *level of subject content* (e.g. Is a general engineering book really appropriate? Or are the students too specialised to obtain much benefit or motivation from it?), but also for the *level of language* being practised. A book with useful language practice will be a failure with a group of postgraduates if the subject content is of a pre-university level. If it is necessary to devise your own material or exercises, some suggestions are made in the next chapter.

Common features of much of the published material are as follows:

authentic text, comprehension checks/questions, grammar practice, vocabulary study, summarising, writing tasks, pair work/group discussions, listening to a talk on cassette, note-taking and other listening activities and a glossary of specialist terms.

The different language and study skills involved in using subject-specific material are often specialist versions of general study skills practice. Language functions and notions were defined and exemplified by Wilkins (1976). His notional category of rational enquiry and exposition contains a number of functions common to most, if not all, academic subjects. For example, assumption and hypothesis are usually associated with the present and future simple verb tenses, and conditionals (if ..., then ..., although ...); and present simple passive, and allied syntactical features, e.g. on the one hand ..., on the other hand ... In addition, the language functions of defining, classifying, cause and effect, etc. can be used in writing for most subjects. Similarly, commenting on data can be adapted to suit most disciplines. Frequently, the changes that will need to be made are ones of vocabulary (lexis) and grammatical structure (syntax), according to the style, conventions and organisation of the written mode of the subject.

A basic difference between general EAP books, especially academic writing, and subject-specific books, is in the organisation of the contents. Most of the EAP books are arranged in terms of language functions or individual study skills. Most, if not all, subject-specific books are organised according to theme or topic, with integrated practice in the functions and skills.

Some appropriate ESAP books for teaching, and specialised diction-aries, are listed in Appendix 1.3, together with recommended surveys/overviews of ESAP, and state-of-the-art articles. Publishers' catalogues will list more up-to-date books.

17.6 Example of economics

A brief look at the subject economics will help to illustrate some of the points already referred to. Some examples are taken from Jordan and Nixson (1986) and are in Appendix 1.1.

As vocabulary is an area of concern for many students, almost all ESAP books contain exercises in it. It is often practised in stages – recognition/identification (i.e. receptive), and open (i.e. productive). Receptive prac-tice may take the form of, for example, making correct choices from a given list, selecting appropriate synonyms or blank-filling in sentences/paragraphs. In order to create more of a problem-solving task, vocabu-lary practice may be combined with information transfer activities.

From economics, *general lexis* (e.g. verbs) might include: raise, rise, increase, fall, reduce, lower, decrease; *specific lexis* might include: supply of, demand for – goods/products/services, balance of payments, terms of trade, developed, developing, underdeveloped, less developed, least developed – countries.

Writing and discussion activities in ESAP often stem from reading passages, combined with giving scope to students to make use of their knowledge and experience – of the subject, the world in general and their own country in particular. Role-play and problem-solving activities are often motivating and successful (see Jordan 1978a and 1984), and can be integrated with speaking and writing. Two examples are given in Appendix 1.1.

Perhaps some of the exercise-types shown in Appendix 1.1 may give ideas for the production of some in-house materials. The design and production of such materials is the subject of the next chapter.

17.7 Introspect and discuss

1. Do you have any views on teaching ESAP? On what do you base them?
2. If you are familiar with ESAP in one subject-area, try to list the predominant language features of that subject. What are your main findings?
3. In the section 'Other concerns', three areas were noted. Are there any others that you would add from your experience?

4. Some suggestions for teaching ESAP have been made, grouped under several sub-headings (e.g. 'Asking questions'). From your experience, can you suggest further examples to add to the lists? Can you also propose additional groupings?

5. In the section on 'Individualisation/self-access' (re individual project), Peretz noted that there were advantages to the students in giving an ESAP oral presentation. Suggest what the advantages might be.

6. Three main ways were suggested for providing ESAP practice on an individualised/self-access basis: individual projects, audio-/video-cassettes, a small library. Can you suggest additional ways?

7. Several suggestions have been made for teaching ESAP. Which type of activity would you feel most comfortable teaching, and why?

8. Have you used any ESAP/ESP books in your teaching that both you and your students thought were good or useful? Which ones were they? Why were they successful?

9. Some examples of vocabulary exercises in economics are shown. Can you suggest any other types of vocabulary exercises that would be appropriate for ESAP?

10. Decide upon one academic discipline that you are familiar with, or have experience of teaching. Devise a suitable pyramid discussion (topic, and list of 15–20 choices of items).

11. Imagine that you have just finished teaching a course in ESAP for a particular discipline. Devise an appropriate questionnaire that you could give to the students in order to obtain feedback on the course and the books used.

18 Materials design and production

The purpose of this chapter is to consider the desirability and feasibility of teachers producing their own ESAP material for teaching. This may be done because there are no suitable books, or to supplement existing books; there may also be other reasons. First of all, we shall look at differing views on the subject, coupled with advice that has been proffered.

18.1 Against and for

One view is expressed by Hutchinson and Waters (1987) who consider that 'materials writing is best regarded as the last resort, when all other possibilities of providing materials have been exhausted'. Sheldon (1988) also remarks on 'the sheer labour-intensiveness of developing classroom materials'. Hutchinson and Waters offer a few hints for 'those who, in the end, feel they have to write new materials':

a) Don't re-invent the wheel. Use existing materials as a source for ideas.
b) It's better to work in a team, if only to retain your sanity.
c) Don't set out to write the perfect materials on the first draft. Materials can always be improved. Do what you can and try it out. Use what you learn from this experience to revise and expand the materials.
d) Don't underestimate the time needed for materials writing. It can be a very time-consuming business.
e) Pay careful attention to the appearance of your materials. If they look boring and scruffy, they will be treated as such.
f) Good luck!

Hutchinson and Waters consider that good materials contain:

– interesting texts;
– enjoyable activities which engage the learners' thinking capacities;
– opportunities for learners to use their existing knowledge and skills;
– content which both learner and teacher can cope with.

They then present a model which has helped them in writing their own

259

materials. In summary, it consists of four elements: input, content focus, language focus and task.

The opposite view is taken by Block (1991) who argues that teachers *should* produce materials and 'that, for at least part of the time, teachers should replace the commercial course book with a contribution of their own'. Block's reasons can be summarised as:

– contextualisation: to ensure relevancy and interest;
– timeliness: to ensure being up-to-date;
– 'the personal touch': to appeal directly to the students.

Block does not deny that materials writing is time-consuming but considers that 'the time spent is well worth it'.

Good practical advice on producing materials is given by Moore (1977) who sets out some criteria for the selection of texts to be used as the basis for exercises:

TOPIC   1. Is it interesting for students/teachers?
         2. Is the information accessible to students/teachers?
         3. Does it provide variety?
TYPE OF WRITING   1. Is it an authentic example of academic English?
         2. Is it of likely relevance for students?
EXEMPLIFICATION   1. Is it a clear illustration of conceptual structures and exponents selected?
         2. Does it exemplify an optimum range?
         3. Does it involve appropriate reading tasks?
DIFFICULTY   1. Is it at an appropriate level of linguistic difficulty?

Moore bases his advice on his involvement with the project that produced the *Reading and Thinking in English* series (OUP 1979–1980). He recommends a team approach to materials production rather than an individual one. After setting out a procedural guide to producing a unit, Moore proposes six types of criteria to be applied to each activity that is devised:

PURPOSE: Is the purpose clearly defined?
TYPE: Does the exercise type effectively and economically accomplish the purpose?
CONTENT: Is the ratio of language given/student task economic?
         Are instructions to students clear?
INTEREST: Is it interesting?
AUTHENTICITY: Is it a meaningful task?
         Is it challenging?
DIFFICULTY: Does it contain distracting difficulties?

Dubin and Olshtain (1986) examine in some detail the creation of materials and note that 'more attention needs to be paid to developing guidelines for writers', which they then proceed to do in the form of useful checklists. They distinguish between writing for a wider audience, which involves publication, and writing for a local audience, which is non-commercial. The latter is often known as 'in-house materials' and is the area we are concerned with. Dubin and Olshtain consider the implications of writing for a local audience. They note the problem of getting the right balance in the materials between following a step-by-step approach, with almost no scope for the teacher's initiative, and complete open-endedness for the teacher, who may not be able to manage it. They, therefore, comment that 'writers who deal with a local audience often find they must walk a tightrope'. We might feel, therefore, that Figure 10 (The course design balancing act) could apply equally well to materials writers, operating between the two poles of control and freedom.

18.2 Team writing

Materials writing, as Dubin and Olshtain (1986) point out, is often undertaken by a team of teachers or, at least, two or three co-authors. The reason for this is sometimes the magnitude of the task and the shortage of time. However, there can be distinct advantages in a joint effort, not the least of which is the level of quality achieved (Robinson 1991), as the materials are checked by the whole team. Other advantages are the mixture of talents, skills and different points of view that are brought to bear on the inevitable variety of tasks that need to be undertaken.

A number of the requirements for an ideal writing team are listed by Dubin and Olshtain (1986). An overriding need is for there to be trust among the individuals. Other needs include:

– members should complement each other, i.e. each should have a specialisation to offer (including: ideas, flair, imagination);
– an organiser should be responsible for allocating tasks and keeping to deadlines;
– an agreed procedure should exist for making final decisions.

A consequence of a team project is the raising of 'Who?' questions (Dubin and Olshtain 1986); for example – Who is responsible for organising the writing tasks? Who checks on the time taken in the writing, and the mounting costs? etc. Of course, difficulties can arise in team writing, for example, someone may be poor at keeping to deadlines, personality clashes can occur and strong differences of opinion may develop.

261

18.3 Recommended background reading

There are a number of articles and books by experienced textbook writers that discuss the relative merits of different approaches to materials design and writing. Anyone who proposes to produce materials (which can be, at the very least, very time-consuming) is strongly advised to see some of these first. The books and articles look at materials from the point of view of evaluation of the finished product as well as being useful for guidance for production. Aspects such as motivation, creativity, exercise typology, sequencing and grading, and various other criteria, are considered. The references are given in Appendix 1.3.

18.4 The need

A fairly wide range of books is now available to cater for most general study skills situations (see Chapters 9–15). The need is more likely to be for material that is directly related to the students' immediate or predicted needs. If the students can see a close connection between the content of the material and their study needs/wants, then there will be a strong motivating force for language learning. Such material is most likely to be subject-specific.

The following questions can act as prompts, and help to focus or clarify considerations or aspects of the materials to be devised and produced. There can be several questions and answers under each question-word; only a selection is given here. The questions can be considered in conjunction with the list of variables that follows.

1. *Why?*
   Why are the materials needed?
   – There is no suitable book.
   – Students attending particular courses at this university, need help with aspects of their studies. This is best catered for by producing some practice material locally, in conjunction with staff in their department. (Will the course be repeated, or is it a one-off? Is it economical of time, effort and cost to produce special materials? Can feedback be obtained to modify the materials for future use?)
2. *Who?*
   Who are the students?
   – Information is needed on: their age, maturity and sophistication, cultural background, language level, knowledge-level of their subject, their motivation, preferred learning styles, their numbers.
   Who are the teachers (who will be using the material)?

    – Information is needed on: their experience and proficiency, their familiarity with the discipline, their self-confidence in using new materials, how much help they will need, their teaching conditions.

3. *What?*

What materials are needed?
- Their place in a syllabus?
- Receptive/productive/integrated skills?
- Language and vocabulary content?
- Text/tape/video/computer . . .?
- For classroom/group or self-access use?
- Specific needs? e.g. practice material in listening and note-taking for lectures and seminars in their subject; structuring argumentative essays; practice in writing answers for examination questions (a lecturer in their department has agreed to co-operate).
- Type of practice/exercise-types (and grading/sequencing/length)?
- Answer key/notes?
- Variety (how is it to be achieved)?
- Resources available?

4. *Where?*

Where will the materials be used?
- In the students' own department or in the EAP centre?
- In a classroom (numbers of students?) with a teacher, or in a resource centre/language laboratory or self-access mode?
- On in-sessional/pre-sessional/specific courses? Number of hours available, and frequency?
- Facilities and equipment available?

5. *When?*

When will the course be held?

When is the material needed?

When will it be produced?
- Often the answer to the second question is 'yesterday'! This question serves as a reminder of the time-scale to be calculated and kept to for producing the materials. If there is time, small-scale piloting of materials usually pays dividends (unforeseen difficulties can be eliminated, instructions clarified, etc.).
- The third question needs examining carefully. Is a teacher or team to produce material in their own time? This may be feasible for a very limited amount of material but not for large-scale production. Material production takes a lot of time, and teachers need extra time for the writing and revising of it.

6. *How?*

How are the materials to be produced?
- By one teacher? By two, or a team?

- What quality controls will there be?
- Who will initiate and organise the production?
- How will responsibilities and writing share be allocated?
- How will the finished material be produced: on computer, printed, typed, photocopied, etc.? Who will do this?

18.5 Variables

In any materials writing, there are a number of variables to consider. These have been subsumed under the questions that were posed:

a) *Students* – their needs and learning objectives;
b) *Teachers* – their abilities, proficiency, and self-confidence;
c) *Syllabus* – the approach;
d) *Methodology* – its implementation;
e) *Resources* – their availability;
f) *Time* – availability;
g) *Finance* – amount.

Questions and comments have already been made about aspects of the above. We shall now look at two of these in more detail.

18.5.1 Students

The first step is to analyse what is needed. Exactly what is it that students need help with? Which language skills and study skills are the priority needs? If it is listening, for example, is it in lectures, seminars, tutorials or what? If it is writing, which kind: essays, reports, case-studies, dissertations, etc.? What exactly is the nature of the help or practice needed? Is it concerned with the structure of the writing, with the style, with the use of certain language functions, with appropriate vocabulary or what?

Before beginning to write the practice material, it will be invaluable to compile a list of students' language difficulties so that practice for these can be built into the exercises (Chapter 2 looked at methods of collecting data). Feedback from observation in the classroom, use of other practice material, checking of comprehension and, perhaps, testing of some items will provide a list of difficulties. For example, perhaps these could be divided into syntax and lexis, each sub-divided, as necessary, to provide further information. A list of language functions could also be made in the same way. An example is given below of such a list made for students of economics (Jordan 1977a).

Remedial syntax	Remedial lexis	
a) general	*a) general*	*b) subject specific*
articles	concerned with	supply of
prepositions	determined by	demand for
plurality: agreement –	depend (up)on	import from
subject/verb	consist of	export to
weak forms		development
contractions	on the whole	developed
	in general	developing
	in my opinion	underdeveloped
b) specific		undeveloped
	other/another	economic/economical
on the one hand …	this/these	agriculture/-ral
… on the other hand	who/which/that	industry/-rial
		standard of living
interrogatives:	raise/rise	cost of living
(i) word order	increase	balance of payments
(ii) do/does/did		terms of trade
	fall/reduce	disguised
stem+s (form)	lower/increase	unemployment
	decline	conspicuous
x-er than y		consumption
x more than y		entrepreneur
as … as		employer/employee
although (cf. but)		surplus/deficit
if …, then …		bottleneck
		labour intensive
		capital intensive
		buffer stock

18.5.2 *Resources*

What resources are available for use in devising practice material? If subject-specific practice is needed, is it possible to enlist the help of the appropriate department and staff? A discussion of this, with its difficulties and advantages exemplified, is contained in Brennan and van Naerssen (1989). Perhaps reading lists can be obtained, and books and journals borrowed. It may be possible to record short introductory talks (10–15 minutes) on subjects suitable for the students by tutors/lecturers: these can be extremely useful for intensive listening if exercises/worksheets are devised for class or self-access use. Full-length talks can also be used for note-taking practice, comprehension exercises and summary writing.

Departments might be willing to co-operate with EAP teachers by giving one or two (anonymous) specimens of good essays (or other writing) so that a model can be shown to students. It would be helpful if departments could say why the writing is good. Departments should be able to provide copies of previous years' exam questions for use in exam writing practice (see Chapter 15).

If you gain a certain understanding of, or familiarity with, a subject, you may be able to adapt a suitable text or some data, or to record a short talk. It is preferable, however, for a subject-specialist to be consulted to prevent various types of error. It should be noted that if articles are taken only from newspapers or magazines, instead of from academic journals, there is a danger that students will be exposed to journalistic style and journalese, not formal, academic style, which is what they most need to practise.

In the initial stages of producing material, there is a danger that you may lack self-confidence and hesitate before committing yourself to paper. This is understandable, with the desire to be as near-perfect as possible. However, it is far more efficient, in terms of time and usefulness, to produce something on paper, even if it is not perfect, so that students can try it out. It can always be improved and amended in the light of feedback. Teachers of English who are NNS may, understandably, be uncertain about some of the exercises they produce. In this situation, it is recommended that, if possible, they ask a NS to check their accuracy.

18.6 Materials: suggestions

18.6.1 Recorded talks

A) NOTE-TAKING

One of the most useful kinds of exercise for students is for them to take notes from subject-specific talks. Ideally, such talks will be 10–15 minutes long. If a talk has been recorded by a subject-specialist and it has been copied for class or self-access use, it will also need to be carefully transcribed. This is a very time-consuming, but necessary, procedure. If it is typed, with lines numbered every five lines, it is invaluable for constructing exercises and, later, for reference, checking answers and discussion. It is essential to have this so that students can compare spoken with written language. They can also learn a considerable amount about pronunciation, stress, rhythm and fluency by listening and reading at the same time.

There are different approaches to note-taking. The one(s) chosen may depend on the level of the students and/or the preferences of the students and teachers. One approach is to provide a framework for the notes, with each main point numbered and subsidiary points numbered differently or lettered. Another one is to provide 'word cues' so that students listen carefully for that part of the talk. Another is to list the discourse markers indicating the main points and changes of direction of the talk. Yet another may give a summary of the talk but leave a number of blanks to be filled by careful listening.

If there is not time to compose a note-taking exercise, but if the transcription has been completed, then a general rubric can be used to state that notes should be taken. The main points could possibly be indicated on the transcription for checking. This approach gives maximum flexibility in note-taking, and allows students to adopt any method or technique that they prefer. It is also advanced, as it is completely open and without guidance.

The example below shows the general rubric that can be used with self-access talks (without specific exercises). Examples of different approaches to note-taking can be seen in Chapter 12 and Appendix 1.1.

Instructions for use

Note-taking

Option 1 Listen to the lecture and, at appropriate places, stop the cassette and then write down the main points so far; then continue until the next appropriate stopping place, etc. Check the tape transcript.

Option 2 Listen to the whole lecture, understand as much as possible, and then make notes of the main points from memory. Check the tape transcript.

Option 3 Take the *tape transcript* from the folder read it at the same time as you listen to the cassette. This may help you to pronounce correctly some words that you did not already know. It may also help you to understand some new words. It may even help you to improve your reading speed.

IF NECESSARY, LISTEN TO THE CASSETTE MORE THAN ONCE.
PLEASE DO NOT WRITE ON, OR MARK, THE TRANSCRIPT

PLEASE REPLACE THE TAPE TRANSCRIPT IN THE FOLDER AFTER USE.

B) OTHER EXERCISES

Based on recorded talks, other exercises can be devised as needed, e.g. comprehension, language features, verbalising data and spoken numbers, assimilating various types of information and reproducing it in a different form (e.g. in a table: information transfer). Exercises in the form of worksheets can be placed in a folder, etc. in a self-access centre/

language laboratory, together with answer keys/lecture transcripts. An example is given below of the type of instruction that can accompany exercises based on self-access talks.

Please read this carefully before listening to the cassette

Procedure

1. The talk lasts for about six minutes: listen to it without stopping the cassette; concentrate on understanding as much as possible.
2. Rewind the cassette to the beginning of the talk.
3. Take a copy of *Exercise A* from the left-hand pocket in the folder. Listen to the talk and, as you are listening, write the answers to the questions. You may find it necessary to stop the tape while you are writing. If necessary, play parts of the tape again.
4. When you have finished, take the *Answer sheet* from the right-hand pocket in the folder. Correct your answers. *Replace the Answer sheet.*
5. Take a copy of *Exercise B* from the left-hand pocket. Rewind the tape and listen again. As you are listening to it, write in the missing words. You may find it necessary to stop the tape while you are writing.
6. Correct your answers from the *Answer sheet* in the right-hand pocket.
7. Finally – take from the right-hand pocket the *Text of Tape*. Make a note of any words that cause you difficulty.
    NOTE:
    Please return to the right-hand pocket the *Answer sheets* and *Text*.
    Keep your own copies of the exercises.

18.6.2 Communicative activities

A) DESCRIBE AND DRAW

In its simplest form, this activity involves students working in pairs, communicating information to each other. It also gives useful practice in using numbers and in describing non-verbal data. One student (looking at an illustration/diagram in a folder) describes a table, diagram, graph, chart, etc. to his/her partner, after first giving an overview of the data; the partner, without seeing the illustration, tries to draw the diagram, following the spoken instructions of the partner. S/he can ask questions of the partner in order to clarify the instructions/information. However, no helping gestures are allowed! It is not difficult to obtain suitable illustrations from most subjects for this activity. It helps students to focus on details of the language which are important for accuracy (see Jordan 1982).

Below is given the rubric from a folder containing an illustration, table, etc. This activity was referred to in Chapter 13, and an example is included in Appendix 1.1.

Describe and draw

Instructions (for Player A)

DO NOT OPEN THIS FOLDER UNTIL YOU HAVE READ THE INSTRUCTIONS BELOW.

1. In the folder you will find a picture. DO NOT SHOW THE PICTURE TO PLAYER B.
2. Tell Player B that s/he will need a pencil, a rubber and some paper.
3. Describe the picture to Player B. Give him/her a general description of the picture first. Tell Player B to draw what you describe. TRY NOT TO WATCH PLAYER B. Tell him/her that s/he may ask you questions.
4. When Player B has finished drawing, show him/her your picture. Compare the two pictures and discuss any language difficulties.

B) PYRAMID DISCUSSIONS

These have already been referred to, and exemplified, elsewhere, i.e. Chapters 7, 13 and 17, and in Appendix 1.1. They are a useful vehicle for developing students' confidence in speaking – in pairs, small groups and with the whole class. It is not necessary for the teacher to be a subject specialist in order to conduct the activity, as the students can volunteer the necessary items.

18.7 Possible problems in materials writing

Problems that may occur in materials writing may stem from a number of sources and will depend on local circumstances; they are also linked with the list of variables given earlier. Some of the main areas of difficulty that may need addressing are:

1. Shortage of time – for preparation and piloting of materials;
2. Insufficient money to finance additional teachers to help with teaching/writing;
3. Difficulty of obtaining access to subject-specific information, data, and the appropriate academic conventions of the target discourse community;
4. Lack of co-operation from staff in specialist departments;
5. Lack of self-confidence, experience, imagination, creativity;
6. Fear of lack of credibility with students.

18.8 Conclusion

In designing practice material, it is clearly important to select the best type of exercise or activity for the purpose. Some of the references given in Appendix 1.3 relating to the *recommended background reading* section earlier in the chapter will help. It is also worthwhile looking carefully at the types of exercise included in books: these will certainly give a large number of ideas and help to provide variety (e.g. multiple-choice, true/false, blank-fill, cloze, sentence completion, jumbled order, open-ended, information transfer, etc.). In the final analysis, the best type of exercise is the one that is the most effective in helping students to learn. This, in itself, suggests the value of classroom research; this dimension will be considered in the next chapter.

18.9 Introspect and discuss

1. What are your views on writing materials for ESAP? Have you ever produced any? What types? What particular difficulties, if any, did you have? What advice would you give to someone embarking on writing such materials for the first time?
2. Moore proposed six types of criteria to be applied to each activity that is devised. Select any activity or exercise from a book that you are familiar with, or an activity you have produced, and apply the criteria. How well does the activity perform? Would you add any other criteria?
3. What are the main advantages and disadvantages of team writing that should be added to those given? Would you prefer to write as an individual? Why/Why not?
4. A number of questions are posed relating to aspects of materials production (Why? Who? What? Where? When? How?). Under these headings, suggest other appropriate questions and considerations.
5. Some examples of students' difficulties with syntax and lexis in economics (Jordan 1977a) are given on page 265 in three columns. Which kind(s) of exercise would you suggest in order to practise some of them.
6. Apart from note-taking, can you suggest other suitable exercises to accompany recorded talks (a) on a self-access basis, and (b) on a group basis?
7. Devise a suitable describe and draw activity either for the social sciences or another discipline that you are familiar with.
8. Apart from describe and draw, which other ways could you suggest for giving practice in using non-verbal data (listening and speaking)?
9. At the end of the chapter, a short list was given of some of the

problems that might arise in materials writing. From your experience, or that of your colleagues, are there any other areas of difficulty that you would add? What solutions do you propose?

10. In writing exercise/practice material, it is imperative that the rubric/instructions are clearly written, especially for self-access material. It is essential that the language used is *not* more difficult/complex than the items being practised. Look carefully at the rubric/instructions for the *note-taking* practice and the activity *describe and draw* shown near the end of the chapter. Would you suggest modifying them in any way?

19 Concerns and research

In EAP teaching and institutions, in the designing and implementing of EAP courses, and in the EAP profession as a whole, a number of concerns or issues have emerged in recent years. Inevitably, these have varied from institution to institution, and from country to country. The fact that there are concerns often prompts investigations: these, in turn, can lead to research projects which, also in turn, may lead to solutions or suggestions for materials development, teaching techniques, etc.

The purpose of this chapter is to look at some of the areas of concern that exist at present, together with some that have been with EAP since its inception. This will lead in to a consideration of research methods that are appropriate for EAP. Finally, we shall note the variety of EAP areas that are currently under investigation.

19.1 Concerns

Some of the main concerns are listed below in the form of questions. No attempt is made to answer these: in some cases it will vary from place to place; in others, investigations are still under way. Many aspects are involved: finance, administration, organisation, specialist departments, materials, methodology, teaching and learning. The very fact of noting the questions will raise awareness of the difficulties and directions of EAP.

1. To what extent (i.e. time, numbers) should institutions provide EAP support classes/courses? Should there be cut-off levels of language adequacy above and below which students will not be accepted? Should the classes be voluntary/optional or compulsory/mandatory?
2. What level(s) of English should university departments insist on from students? (See Appendix 4 regarding EAP exams.)
3. What is the status of 'service EAP units/centres'? What is the professional status of EAP teachers/tutors? Is it on a par with other academic staff in mainstream departments? How do students and subject-specialists perceive the role of EAP? The question of status becomes important when problems arise over timetable clashes between EAP classes and specialist subject classes (sometimes EAP

tutors teach in 'unsociable' hours, e.g. lunch periods, late afternoons, etc.). Similar problems can arise over matters such as room bookings and the use of equipment when a service unit is housed in a larger department. Regrettably, the label 'Cinderella service' has sometimes been applied to EAP units.

4. To the concern above is attached one that is closely connected – finance or funding. On what basis is EAP support funded? Is the unit centrally funded, or by departments (pro rata), or by individual students? Or by a combination of these?
5. What is the most effective way of implementing EAP support classes/courses? Should classes be centralised and non-subject specific? Should EAP tutors be assigned to certain (larger) departments to give shared language support (ESAP)? Or is a mixture of the two approaches desirable? How far should classes be based on one disciplinary culture and its genres? How far is team-teaching desirable or possible? How far can academic activities (e.g. seminars, exam writing, etc.) be generalised across disciplines (and sub-disciplines)? Can EAP be taught without reference to specialist subjects or content?
6. How far is it possible to take learning styles and cultural attitudes into account on a mixed nationality course?
7. At what level should EAP materials be introduced to students? At elementary, or only at intermediate (plus), levels?
8. What is the best way to help students to study independently and to make use of self-access facilities, i.e. learner training and learner independence?
9. What causes some students to make more rapid progress than others on an EAP course, even though their starting levels may be similar? How can this be ascertained, and then made use of? What strategies are employed by successful students? How can they best be taught?
10. How far are EAP courses successful in preparing students for the reality of academic study in specialist departments?
11. Should one-to-one tutorials be provided on EAP courses if there are available staff, e.g. for correcting essays, dissertations, etc. and helping with individual speech difficulties? Are they cost effective?
12. What training, qualifications and experience are required for effective EAP teaching?

Other concerns have been voiced by Johns and Dudley-Evans (1991).

19.2 What is research?

A considerable amount of everyday teaching and dealing with learning difficulties is ad hoc and based on intuition, 'common sense', experience and trial and error. To some extent, this will always be so; one cannot anticipate every possible contingency. However, there are a number of situations where a systematic study can be conducted in order to obtain evidence, data, etc. which may support one's approach or suggest solutions to a difficulty. Put formally, research is:

> a systematic process of inquiry consisting of three elements or components (1) a question, problem or hypothesis, (2) data and (3) analysis and interpretation of data.
>
> (Nunan 1992)

The type of research conducted will usually be linked to the reason for doing it. The straightforward question 'Why do research?' can elicit a variety of answers. For some teachers in colleges and universities, the answer may well be that they are expected to as part of their contract of employment, and that it is essential for promotion. For some staff, it may not be easy to decide upon a research topic or method of investigation. The following sections may suggest ideas. A number of teachers have experienced difficulties in their teaching, or observed that students have particular problems, and try to find solutions. This is an example of *applied research*. Others have developed particular areas of interest in EAP and wish to pursue them in some depth. Yet others have a wish to add to knowledge in a certain area, perhaps finding evidence to support a theory: this may be termed *pure* or *basic research*.

There is another reason for undertaking research that is particularly valuable for EAP teachers. By doing their own research, teachers will be in a better position to help students who are also doing research and need help with English. Teachers will understand more easily the kinds of difficulties students are likely to experience, and may have very practical and relevant advice to offer, linked with English.

19.3 Action research

Before looking at research methods, it is useful to look at a popular form of small-scale research. Its main purpose is to find solutions to problems and to enable teachers to improve aspects of teaching/learning. It is usually classroom based (see Nunan 1990). For example, it may involve recording students while they are taking part in a discussion, and then analysing the speech. As a result of the analysis, it may be possible to see different ways of helping the students, perhaps by producing certain types of material. Alternatively, the results may confirm some action that has already been taken. Examples of this kind of action research are given in Jordan (1978a, 1990b). This kind of practical research is often a good starting-point for EAP teachers who want to undertake some limited research. It will involve one or more of the research methods listed below.

19.4 Research methods

Various research methods are listed below, together with some references to articles, etc. containing examples of research into EAP based on these methods. Some of the methods involve data collection similar to those referred to in Chapter 2 for needs analysis. The research methods can be divided into *quantitative* (e.g. test scores and other statistical analyses) and *qualitative* (e.g. interviews and subjective assessments). The results of one method can often act as a check on, or explanation of, those of other methods.

1. *Observation*: based in a classroom, or related to an observable learning situation, e.g. a language laboratory, written homework, etc. (e.g. Allwright 1988; Primrose 1993). As an instance, a systematic noting of errors in written work, either for the class as a whole, or for students individually, can help to indicate areas of greatest need for an improvement in accuracy. This may not, however, necessarily correlate with breakdowns in communication (e.g. Jordan 1988b). For those interested in looking at error analysis in depth, the following are recommended: Selinker (1972), Richards (1974), Corder (1981), Odlin (1989) and Ellis (1994).
2. *Case studies*: these can be of individuals over a period of time, i.e. longitudinal studies, or of groups at a particular point in time (or the same group over a period of time): some comparisons can be made (e.g. James 1984a, Dudley-Evans 1988b, McDonough and McDonough 1993). See also O'Brien, T. (1995) who compares a native-speaker undergraduate's performance in an examination and in a course-work essay.
3. *Diaries and diary studies*: these can be written by students and/or teachers over varying periods of time, from a day or two, to the length of a course – depending on the purpose of the study. An advantage of this approach is that it allows for both introspection and reflection, and can be informative as to difficulties and attitudes (e.g. O'Brien 1989, Parkinson and Howell-Richardson 1990).
4. *Questionnaires; interviews*: although these are separate methods, they are put together here as both are examples of elicitation

techniques, involving the recording of opinions and attitudes. Questionnaires, in particular, are frequently used in conducting surveys of classes, courses, etc. (e.g. Weir 1988c, Grundy 1993b, Jordan 1993). Some of the information gained from surveys can be put to very practical use: for example, sending an interpretation of the results to staff in specialist departments about their students' difficulties and expectations. Considerable care needs to be taken with regard to the wording of questionnaires in order to obtain the type of response hoped for. This aspect is examined by Low (1996) who considers the impact of intensifiers (e.g. very, extremely) and hedges (e.g. seem, tend) in questions.

5. *Tests*: these are used for a number of purposes, and there are various kinds of tests (see Chapter 5). In research, tests are an example of *numerical methods*, which can involve scores, frequencies, results and correlations (e.g. Coleman 1991). Data collection, of all kinds, needs analysis and interpretation.

In addition, there is *interaction analysis*, which looks at interpersonal encounters among students, and between students and teachers. Also, *experimental methods*, which may, for example, compare teaching techniques, or two groups of students. See Nunan (1992) for details of these two methods, and a useful glossary of key terms in research.

Many EAP teachers conduct small-scale research, either alone, or with a co-researcher, or in small groups. Apart from a desire to improve their teaching, materials and courses, they also use the research as a basis for conference papers and articles in journals. Both of these are excellent sources of information about ongoing research in EAP. Larger scale and full-time, joint research projects may be funded by a research grant, with a specific purpose that may benefit the institution. Invariably in research, questions will arise, as in test design, regarding reliability, validity and generalisability. These aspects, as well as details of research methods, are covered in the books listed in Appendix 1.4.

EAP research areas

19.5.1 General

Research areas in EAP are, in general, related to the following – either separately or combined:

a) *People*: the learner; the teacher; the subject tutor; roles and relationships;
b) *Places*: situations and contexts in which learning/teaching take place (lectures, seminars, tutorials, libraries, etc.);

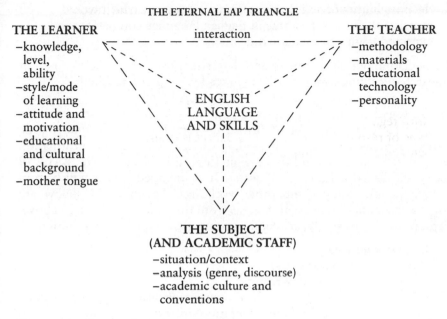

THE ETERNAL EAP TRIANGLE

THE LEARNER
–knowledge,
 level,
 ability
–style/mode
 of learning
–attitude and
 motivation
–educational
 and cultural
 background
–mother tongue

interaction

ENGLISH
LANGUAGE
AND SKILLS

THE TEACHER
–methodology
–materials
–educational
 technology
–personality

THE SUBJECT
(AND ACADEMIC STAFF)
–situation/context
–analysis (genre, discourse)
–academic culture and
 conventions

Figure 21   Research areas and links

c) *Language*: specialist subject; study skills; English language; mother
   tongue; testing;
d) *Materials/media*: books; audio-visual aids; technology.

The relationships between the above areas may be seen more easily in
Figure 21. Particular instances of EAP research follow.

19.5.2 Specific

McDonough (1986) discussed the potential for research which straddles
EAP courses and specialist subjects and/or subject departments. She
suggested a number of areas for investigation:

1. designing a reliable measure for assessing an individual's competence
   on a language course in relation to the study demands of the target
   department;
2. establishing a means by which a student's failure in end-of-year
   exams can be accurately assigned to difficulties caused by deficiency
   in language competence or deficiency in subject knowledge;
3. determining whether or not a student can grasp 'Westernised
   concepts of academic investigation' (i.e. separate from problems of
   language or subject);

4. the possibility of creating a predictive instrument which would measure the rate of progress in English language competence to be expected from a particular student.

As McDonough said, the issues that she raises share 'a number of research questions with general language learning and teaching'.

A survey of papers given at recent BALEAP Conferences (see Appendix 3), together with an analysis of ongoing research interests expressed by EAP staff at a number of British universities, indicate that a wide variety of areas are being addressed. In order to co-ordinate information on research into EAP, and to disseminate it in published form, BALEAP have established a Research Register. It is intended that it will help in linking people doing comparable work (see Appendix 3). Below are listed a selection of the research areas from the sources referred to above. Perhaps not surprisingly, academic writing attracts the most attention.

1. *Academic writing*
   - team writing on projects;
   - peer support in essay writing;
   - the importance of grammatical accuracy in subject-specific writing;
   - overall structures and argumentation; introductions and conclusions;
   - a comparison between argumentation in written and spoken academic discourse;
   - what makes an academic essay 'good' or 'successful' from a subject specialist's point of view?
   - the acquisition of technical vocabulary;
   - a comparison of NS and NNS teachers' attitudes to language errors;
   - types of spelling mistakes; effective methods of correction;
   - bibliographic presentation in different disciplines;
   - modality and 'hedging' in different disciplines;
   - the application of word-processing to a development of writing skills;
   - the compromising of standards in specialist departments regarding NNS students' written work.
2. *Reading*
   - developing critical reading approaches;
   - improving reading efficiency.
3. *Genre analysis*
   - academic essays in the social sciences;
   - tutorials;
   - extent to which academic activities, e.g. seminars, oral presentations, can be generalised across disciplines;

  - types of writing required from students in assessed course work, e.g. essays and reports;
  - law reports;
  - examination requirements in different disciplines.
4. *Spoken language*
  - assessing spoken language performance: ways to improve it on short courses;
  - academic discourse intonation;
  - interaction in one-to-one tutorials;
  - recording lectures and analysing structure and language.
5. *Evaluation and testing*
  - the most suitable entry and placement tests for different categories of students, e.g. undergraduates and postgraduates;
  - a comparison of different assessment procedures for students;
  - course evaluation and tracer studies;
  - devising language tests that are linked to learning experience and the target situation.
6. *Ethnographic*
  - the observation and description of academic activities in different disciplines, e.g. seminars, tutorials, lectures (academic conventions and appropriate behaviour);
  - academic cultural gaps between students and host university staff, especially in seminars and tutorials (conflicting expectations).
7. *Learner training*
  - learner training in the efficient use of information sources;
  - the most effective ways to prepare students for independent study.
8. *Others*
  - data-driven learning;
  - the potential of e-mail and computer conferencing to give support to learning and teaching;
  - bilingual concordancing;
  - mixed nationality courses and stereotypical attitudes;
  - raising awareness of, and dealing with, culture shock;
  - effective ways for EAP teacher development.

19.6 Conclusion

In the research areas, many of the current concerns will almost certainly continue for some time to come. They will undoubtedly include the following:

- aspects of academic writing;
- genre analysis at different levels;

– CALL;
– disciplinary cultures;
– learner independence;
– collaboration between EAP teachers and specialist subject
  departments.

The wide range of interests is an indication of the dynamic nature of EAP. It is also a healthy sign for the EAP profession; so, too, is the practical application of much of the research, frequently involving a marrying of the pragmatic and the eclectic.

As EAP develops, and teachers become more innovative, so the areas of interest of researchers change, and techniques become more refined. There is an understandable desire to research all aspects of EAP, and in greater depth and detail: this is laudable, and should be ultimately beneficial to students in many ways. However, a healthy balance needs to be maintained between research interests and the practical teaching of students. In this respect, EAP is no different from any other discipline.

19.7   Introspect and discuss

1. At the beginning of the chapter, a dozen areas of concern in EAP are listed. Which ones are most relevant to you? Add any other concerns that occur in your situation.
2. Can you suggest some suitable areas for action research in EAP, stemming from your classroom experience?
3. Do you have experience of any of the research methods listed? In which situation(s) did you use them, and with what result?
4. What kinds of difficulties would you envisage with some of the research methods? How could they be overcome or minimised?
5. *Figure 21* shows the main elements in research areas in EAP. Are there any modifications you would wish to make to the diagram? Why?
6. A wide-ranging list of specific research areas in EAP is given. Which ones interest you most? From your experience, are there any others you would want to add?
7. Finally ...
   Below is given a list of words commonly misspelt by NS in Britain (from McIlroy and Jones 1993). Within the context of EAP, which words are commonly misspelt by your students? Which strategies have you found effective in rectifying the errors?

Research undertaken in March 1992 by the RSA Examination Board revealed that up to half of Britain's office workers regularly misspell simple words. The 20 most misspelt were as follows:

Word	Percentage of workers who misspelt it
practice/practise	54
withhold	52
occurred	52
innovate	52
benefited	48
principal/principle	45
incur	44
grievance	40
concede	40
transferred	39
competent	37
calendar	35
warranty	35
acquire	34
liaise	34
truly	34
expedite	33
discrete/discreet	33
affect/effect	32
accommodation	32

Appendices

Index of appendices

Appendix 1 Recommended books and journals

1.1 Specimens of published/printed materials
(in chapter order)

Chapter 2

METHODS OF COLLECTING DATA

4 Examples of self-assessment procedures

a) Oskarsson (1980)

SPEAKING	
☐ I speak the language as well as a well-educated native.	5
☐	4.5
☐ I speak the language fluently and for the most part correctly. I have a large vocabulary so I seldom have to hesitate or search for words. On the other hand I am not completely fluent in situations in which I have had no practice with the language.	4
☐	3.5
☐ I can make myself understood in most everyday situations, but my language is not without mistakes and sometimes I cannot find the words for what I want to say. It is difficult for me to express myself in situations in which I have had no opportunity to practise the language. I can give a short summary of general information that I have received in my native language.	3
☐	2.5
☐ I can make myself understood in simple everyday situations, for example asking and giving simple directions, asking and telling the time, asking and talking about simpler aspects of work and interests. My vocabulary is rather limited, so it is only by a great deal of effort that I can use the language in new and unexpected situations.	2
☐	1.5
☐ I can just about express very simple things concerning my own situation and my nearest surroundings, for example asking and answering very simple questions about the time, food, housing and directions. I only have a command of very simple words and phrases.	1
☐	0.5
☐ I do not speak the language at all.	0

Appendix 1

b) Oskarsson (1980)

Sample questionnaire for self-assessment at T-level
[To be translated into the learner's native language]
Instruction: Imagine that you meet an English-speaking person from another country. He does not know anything about you and your country. Indicate your estimated command of the language by putting a cross in the appropriate box (*Yes* or *No*) for each statement.

1. I can tell him when and where I was born.	☐ Yes	☐ No
2. I can spell my name in English.	☐ Yes	☐ No
3. I can describe my home to him.	☐ Yes	☐ No
4. I can tell him what kinds of food and drink I like and don't like.	☐ Yes	☐ No
5. I can tell him about my interests (hobbies, interests in general, etc.).	☐ Yes	☐ No
6. I can tell him what I usually read (kinds of books, newspapers, magazines, textbooks, etc.).	☐ Yes	☐ No
7. I can ask him what newspapers there are in his own country.	☐ Yes	☐ No
8. I can tell him what I do in my free time.	☐ Yes	☐ No
9. I can ask him how to get to a certain place by public transport.	☐ Yes	☐ No
10. I can tell him what I think of art galleries.	☐ Yes	☐ No

c) Floyd (1984)

Self-Assessment Form
Below is a list of study skills required for university or college level work. Look at each item and decide which of the four possible responses best expresses your present situation regarding that skill. Circle the appropriate number:
1 'I can't do this (or I don't know how). Help needed urgently!'
2 'I'm not very good at this. Improvement necessary.'
3 'There is room for improvement, but this is not a big problem for me.'
4 'I feel I am quite good at this.'

The ability to:

a	read efficiently: at a normal speed of at least 300 wpm with about 70% comprehension	1	2	3	4
b	concentrate when reading or studying	1	2	3	4
c	understand what has been read	1	2	3	4
d	remember what has been read	1	2	3	4
e	assess reading difficulty	1	2	3	4
f	preview effectively	1	2	3	4
g	select key ideas quickly	1	2	3	4
h	recognize and use a wide vocabulary	1	2	3	4

i	get the most from a dictionary	1 2 3 4
j	make useful notes from books	1 2 3 4
k	enjoy reading	1 2 3 4
l	plan a week's study	1 2 3 4

d) Ward Goodbody (1993)

PRE-SESSIONAL COURSE QUESTIONNAIRE
In order to place you in the most suitable English class, we would like to know about what you think about learning English, your own opinion of your language skills, your previous experience, what you would like to learn and how you would like to learn. Please write as much as you can to help *us* to help *you*.

A Language Skills Assessment
1 Below is a nine-band scale used for assessing students' levels. Decide which level you think best describes your standard of English for each skill and write it in the appropriate space underneath.
Level 1 **Non-user:** Unable to use English.
Level 2 **Very Little English:** Uses single words and only understands single word messages.
Level 3 **Little English:** May understand general meaning in very simple situations, but often fails to communicate and understand.
Level 4 **Limited English:** Understands English in familiar situations, but has frequent problems in understanding and fluency. These can make communication a constant effort.
Level 5 **Modest English:** Has partial command of English coping with overall meaning in most situations, although some misunderstandings and lack of fluency could prevent communication.
Level 6 **Competent User:** Has a generally effective command of English, although occasional misunderstandings and lack of fluency could interfere with communication.
Level 7 **Good User:** Can operate in English, but with occasional inaccuracies or misunderstandings in some situations.
Level 8 **Very Good User:** Has full command of English in most situations but with some occasional minor inaccuracies, inappropriacies or misunderstandings possible in unfamiliar situations.
Level 9 **Expert User:** Has a full command of English. His/her English is appropriate, accurate and fluent with complete understanding.

Reading level	_____	Listening level	_____
Writing level	_____	Speaking level	_____

2 Have you any additional comments about your level?

3 What are you best at in English?

4 What do you find difficult?

B Previous Experience of Learning English
1 Describe your previous experience of learning English. You may mention, for example, size of class, type of English (reading. writing, grammar, discussion,

etc.) organisation of learning (pairs, groups, whole class) and the role of the teacher.

2　What has been your most helpful language learning experience so far inside or outside the class?

3　Who or what has motivated and encouraged you to learn English best in the past?

C　Aims for Pre-sessional English Course
1　What is your reason for attending this course?

2　Which skills do you wish to improve?
(please tick as appropriate)

Reading　general
　　　　　textbooks, journals
Writing　note-taking from texts
　　　　　note-taking from lectures
　　　　　essays
　　　　　reports and theses
　　　　　examinations
Listening　general conversation
　　　　　group discussion, e.g. seminars
　　　　　lectures
Speaking　general conversation
　　　　　group discussion, e.g. seminars
　　　　　giving a talk or presentation
　　　　　pronunciation
General vocabulary
Grammar
Everyday English
Using an academic library

3　Have you any additional comments or special needs you wish to mention?

D　Class Organisation and Management of Learning
1　You will be in a mixed nationality, mixed sex group, with a similar level to your own. You will work in pairs and small groups as well as a whole class. You will be expected to contribute to class discussion. What is your feeling about this?

Any other comments

7　*Surveys*

Questionnaire: Jordan and Mackay (1973)

SPOKEN ENGLISH: QUESTIONNAIRE
Estimate the number of hours per week spent listening to spoken English and speaking English. (Please answer the following questions in hours or fractions of an hour, e.g. $\frac{1}{4}$, $1\frac{1}{2}$ etc. If the answer is 'nothing' please write the word NIL.)

A English instruction — hours per week
1 English classes attended in the University _____
2 Use of Language Laboratory tapes _____
3 English classes attended outside the University _____
TOTAL _____

B Listening to spoken English
By native speakers only (do *not* include information already included in Section A) — hours per week
1 Lectures _____
2 Seminars/tutorials/classes _____
3 Serious discussion/conversation _____
4 Everyday small-talk (shopping etc.) _____
5 T.V. _____
6 Radio _____
7 Cinema/theatre _____
8 Records/tapes (personal, *not* Language Laboratory) _____
9 Other? Please specify _____
TOTAL _____

C Speaking English
To native English speakers only (do *not* include information already included in Sections A or B) — hours per week
1 University teachers _____
2 British colleagues/friends/acquaintances _____
3 Landlord/landlady (if British) _____
4 Shopkeepers, etc. _____
5 Others? please specify _____
TOTAL _____

D Speaking and listening to overseas students/people in English
hours per week
1 Fellow students _____
2 Other people _____
TOTAL _____

E General
1 How long have you been a) in Britain? _____ months
b) in Manchester? _____ months
2 When you first arrived in Manchester, what was your biggest problem with the English language?
_____
3 What is your biggest problem with the English language now?
_____
4 Has there been as much improvement in your English as you hoped or expected? (Yes or No) _____

5 Have you met as many British people as you would have liked?
(e.g. to practise spoken English with) (Yes or No)   _____
Why?/Why not? _____

6 Has it been difficult to meet British people? (Yes or No)   _____

7 What do you think is the reason why it has been difficult?
(If it has *not* been difficult, explain why not)

8 How many hours per week do you spend listening to and
speaking your own language?   _____
Why is this? _____

Name _____

Mother tongue _____

Home country _____

Manchester University Department _____

Today's date _____

8 *Structured interview*

Mackay (1978)
_____

STRUCTURED INTERVIEW   Ref. ID/Basic Info/75.
STUDENT VERSION   Faculty
Student's name: Subject
                                  Professor in charge

1 What proportion of the required reading in this course is available in
Spanish?
None ☐   0–24% ☐   25–49% ☐   50–74% ☐   75% or more ☐

2 Are texts in a language other than Spanish recommended reading material in
this course?
                                              Yes ☐   No ☐
(In what language(s) is/are the recommended material published?
                              most important _____
                              2nd most important _____)

3 In your opinion, is it NECESSARY to know a foreign language(s) in order to
PASS this course?
                                              Yes ☐   No ☐
(What language(s) is/are necessary?)

4 Do you consider it NECESSARY to know a foreign language in order to
GRADUATE in this field?
                                              Yes ☐   No ☐
a) What language(s) is/are necessary? _____
(in order of importance)

b) Why is it/are they needed? _____

5 Can you read in a foreign language?

Yes ☐   No ☐

(If affirmative, a) In what language(s)?

b) How frequently do you read in that/these languages?

Daily ☐   Weekly ☐   Monthly ☐   Occasionally ☐

c) How do you read?

fluently ☐
little difficulty ☐
some difficulty ☐
great difficulty ☐

d) What do you read?

basic texts ☐
professional journals ☐
theses/dissertations ☐
other (please specify) ☐

(if negative)

Would knowing a foreign language help you in your studies?

Yes ☐   No ☐

(If affirmative, what language(s)?
Why?)

6 What texts does your professor recommend you read in this course?

Author _____ Title _____

Which of these do you consider of greatest help in your studies?

7 How would you describe the usefulness of ENGLISH for graduating as a well-qualified professional in this field?

Necessary ☐   Convenient ☐   Unnecessary ☐

Chapter 3

EXPERIENCE AND EXPECTATIONS

Jordan (1993)
Summer 1988: 82 Students
(During Pre-Session Courses) (Manchester University)

Experience of studying in own country, and expectations of studying own subject in Britain

A. *Experience in own country:*

1 Had any instruction/help in:
   a. taking notes in lectures?   NO: 54%
   b. preparing a talk?   NO: 48%
   c. writing an essay?   NO: 32%

2 In a lecture is it customary to ask questions at the end?   YES: 84%
   Do you normally ask questions?   YES: 72%

3 In a seminar tutorial is it customary to:
   a. ask a question?   YES: 83%
   b. express one's own ideas?   YES: 76%
   c. express disagreement with a tutor's point of view?   YES: 61%

d. Do you normally do any of the above?	YES: 79%
4 Are college/university libraries in your country:	
a. open-access?	YES: 72%
b. closed-access?	YES: 40%
5 Were you given any formal instruction in using the library?	NO: 49%
6 When writing an essay etc.	
a. is 'long' considered better than 'short'?	YES: 34%
b. do tutors tell you exactly what to do?	YES: 49%
c. do you have difficulty in starting?	YES: 67%
7 Have you ever written an essay etc. in formal academic English?	NO: 50%

B. *Expectations re own subject in Britain:*

8 Do you expect your tutor to tell you precisely what to read?	YES: 54%
9 Do you expect your subject tutor to correct written English mistakes?	YES: 78%
10 Do you expect your tutor to show you an example of an essay etc.?	YES: 78%
11 Would you find it useful to see such an example?	YES: 96%
12 How often do you expect to meet your tutor?	
a. at least once a week:	83%
b. twice or more a week:	51%
c. 3, 4 or 5 times a week:	15%
13 What are the main differences you expect to find with your studies in Britain (compared with your own country)?	
a. System of teaching (methods; more practical; research techniques; supervision; seminars; contact with tutors; more help given; better organised)	37%
b. Better facilities (better libraries; more books, materials, technology)	28%
c. Only the language	12%
d. No differences	12%
14 a. Do you expect any difficulties with your studies?	YES: 62%
	NO: 37%
b. Difficulties expected:	
i. language and study skills	50%
ii. own subject	10%
iii. personal problems	10%

Chapter 4

EAP SYLLABUS

Example (1970s→1990s)

8-week Pre-sessional EAP Course (UK)
I. *Core components*
   1. *READING COMPREHENSION AND NOTE-TAKING*
      – prediction
      – recognising different writing functions
      – reading for general idea
      – reading for specific information
      – identifying relative importance of information
      – distinguishing between factual and non-factual information
      – distinguishing between explicit and implicit information
      – note-taking/information transfer
      – strategies for vocabulary development
   2. *ACADEMIC WRITING*
      – organising information into a coherent structure
      – expressing different writing functions
      – interpreting non-verbal information
      – employing appropriate register
      – using appropriate linking devices to produce cohesive text
      – achieving greater grammatical and lexical accuracy
      – employing usual conventions (see *Reference/Research Skills*)
   Short-term Target Activities for components 1, 2, and 5 (See below)
      i) *Library Project*
         Following an introduction to the University Library you will be assigned a set of tasks which will help familiarise you with the Library, particularly its organisation, the different catalogues (card: author and subject, computer and journal), and the location of the books and journals.
      ii) *Study Project*
         During the course you will be required to work on a literature-based project in the subject area of your main course of study/research, the product of which will be a text of 1,500–3,000 words, depending on the length of your course, and an oral presentation. You will receive tutorial guidance at each stage in the writing/presentation of this project.
         The aim of the project is two-fold, being designed:
         a) to give you practice in integrating the study skills worked on during the course;
         b) to enable you to further develop your study skills in English in the context of your specialist subject area.

3. *LISTENING COMPREHENSION AND NOTE-TAKING*
   – prediction
   – understanding native spoken English
   – recognising different language functions
   – listening for general idea
   – listening for specific information
   – identifying relative importance of information
   – recognising lecturer's signals
   – note-taking/information transfer
   – strategies for dealing with incomplete comprehension

4. *ACADEMIC SPEECH*
   – oral presentation : organising information into coherent structure
                        : speaking from notes
                        : using 'signals' to facilitate task of listener
                        : developing audience awareness
                        : operating with greater fluency
                        : achieving greater phonological, grammatical and
                          lexical accuracy
   – seminar strategies : taking the floor
                        : using notes
                        : requesting/providing clarification/information
                        : stating point of view
                        : supporting view expressed by another speaker
                        : challenging view expressed by another speaker

Short-term Target Activities for components 3 and 4:

  i) *Plenary Lectures/Group Seminars*
     There will be a series of lectures given by Guest Lecturers (from different University Departments) to all Pre-Session Course students. These will approximate to the normal lecture situation (i.e. use of lecture theatre, larger student body, use of different media, interference from background noise etc.). Each lecture will be followed by a seminar with the class tutor or the lecturer.

 ii) *Tutor Seminars*
     Each of your tutors will give a short talk on a topic of current/general interest, giving you the opportunity to practise listening to a 'live' talk and clarify/discuss points raised where necessary/relevant.

iii) *Student Seminars*
     Here, you will be required to give a talk on a subject of your choice to the rest of your group. This will give each student (a) practice in leading a seminar and (b) exposure to different varieties of English, as represented in the group. Student seminars will also be organised around a shared reading assignment, where each student will be responsible for reporting back on a specific aspect of the assignment.

 iv) *Interview/Questionnaire Project*
     Near the end of the course you will be involved in designing a questionnaire in order to conduct a small survey of a particular aspect of life in Britain, using people in the street as the database. You will work in pairs for this project and prepare an oral report for your group.

5. *REFERENCE/RESEARCH SKILLS*
   (both language and academic reference skills)
   – using a monolingual English dictionary
   – using a bibliography
   – using a library
   – surveying sources
   – referencing (i.e. citation/acknowledgement of sources)
   – writing footnotes
   – writing a bibliography
   The above skills will be covered at the appropriate stage in your work on
   the *Study Project* (see above).

6. *GRAMMAR/VOCABULARY WORKSHOP*
   This component is designed to allow for remedial/developmental language
   work, and thereby to complement the study skills focus of the course. You
   will be encouraged to develop your independence as a learner-user of
   English.

7. *LIFE IN BRITAIN*
   As the title suggests, the aim of this component will be to prepare you for
   non-academic life in Britain. This will involve language-oriented sessions
   focusing on 'survival' English, and information oriented sessions on
   aspects of British life and institutions. There will also be a minor project
   involving British newspapers.

8. *SELF-ACCESS*
   You will also have the opportunity to work independently (e.g. in the
   language laboratory) on a range of materials (audio-/video-taped, printed)
   to allow for greater individualisation of learning. Some of this work will
   be tutor-monitored (i.e. time-tabled with a specific tutor), but most of it
   will be self-monitored. Early on in the course, there will be learner-training
   sessions, including an introduction to self-assessment.

II. *EVALUATION/ASSESSMENT*
   i) *Tutorials*
      The major part of the course will be classroom-based. You will, however,
      have regular tutorials with your class tutor. The purpose of these will be
      (a) to enable your tutor to give you individualised feedback on your
      progress, (b) to give you the chance to discuss with your tutor any
      individual problems you may be having with an aspect of the language/
      course, and (c) to give you experience of this aspect of the target academic
      culture

   ii) *Evaluation*
      You will be encouraged to evaluate the course on a regular basis. At the
      end of the course, you will be invited to give your opinion of the course
      by answering a questionnaire. In planning the course each year, account
      is taken of students' comments on the previous year's course.

   iii) *Assessment*
      There will be self-, peer-, and tutor-assessment of your work/progress on
      the course. At the end of the course, there will be a written test of your
      ability to operate effectively in English for study purposes. You will

receive individual feedback on all tutor-assessments. After the course, a report will be sent to your department (and sponsor). This report will aim to assess your readiness for your proposed course of study/research.

EXAMPLES OF PROJECTS

Some examples of the type of projects referred to in the syllabus are included below. Projects 1 and 2 are individual; numbers 3 and 4 are for pairs of students.

1. *Library project:*

a. *Mixed subjects*

A. What is the call number and date of the 6th edition of *The Law of Nations* by James Brierly (reprinted 1972)?

B. How many copies of *The Norman Conquest* by R. A. Brown are available for borrowing? Where are they located?

C. Who is the co-author with Edgardo Browne of *Table of radioactive isotopes*? In which country was the book published?

D. What is the title of the 1929 book on the *American Revolution* by E. B. Greene? Can it be taken off a shelf and borrowed immediately?

E. If the 1967 copy of *Lenin and the Russian Revolution* is already out on loan, is there another copy that can be borrowed? If so, where is it located?

F. Steven McDonough's book on *language teaching* was published in 1981. What is its exact title? How many copies are there available for borrowing?

b. *Your own subject*

1. What is your academic subject? _____

2. What is the Dewey Decimal number range for books in your subject?

3. Where are the books located for your subject?
   Area: _____ Floor: _____ Range(s): _____

4. Give full details and the exact location of *one book* in your subject:
   Author (or *Editor* (surname & initials): _____

   Title: _____

   Publisher: _____

   Place of publication: _____

   Date of first publication: _____

   Date and number of latest edition or impression: _____

   Library call number: _____

   Exact location in the library: _____

   Area: _____ Floor: _____ Range: _____ Shelf: _____

5. Give the *title* and publishing details of one *journal* in your subject: _____

   _____

2. *Study project*
   Description: The purpose of the Project is to give you an opportunity to do some extended reading related to your own subject which you will then write up in English (max. 3000 words). The project may be one of the following:
   i) part of some current research, i.e. work that you are already doing;
   ii) a straightforward summary of an aspect of your subject;
   iii) an explanation of certain key concepts/procedures in your special subject;
   iv) an analysis of a problem area, in your own country, which relates to your special subject;
   v) one other aspect of your subject *but* only after consultation with your tutor.
   Schedule: The following should be submitted to your tutor for monitoring:
   Week 2: Specification sheet (listing subject, topic title, etc.)
   Week 3: Specimen notes and detailed outline
   Weeks 4/5/6: Samples of writing
   Week 7: Completed project
3. *Interview/questionnaire project*
   So far on the Pre-Session Course you have undertaken a Study Project which concentrates on academic writing. The *purpose* of this *Interview/questionnaire project* is to give you an opportunity to meet people, ask them questions, and to note their replies. It will also give you practice in devising a questionnaire, analysing results and giving a brief oral report.
   1. When you stop people to ask them questions, show them the *letter of explanation* from the Course Director. Also introduce yourself and politely ask them for their co-operation.
   2. *Good areas* to find people, apart from around the University, are: ...
   3. *Possible topics* for you to devise a questionnaire on are as follows:
      a) eating habits and preferences
      b) leisure activities
      c) reading habits
      d) pollution in the city
      e) TV programmes preferred
      f) accommodation problems in the city
      g) holiday habits
      h) library users' habits
      i) sports amenities
      j) transport problems in the city
      k) shopping habits
      l) choice of newspapers
      m) smoking habits
      n) *other suitable topics* (discuss with tutor)
   4. *AVOID THE FOLLOWING TOPICS*:
      Politics, religion, and very personal matters, e.g. salary, sex ... (if you are uncertain, discuss with your tutor)

5. Think carefully about the purpose of your questionnaire. Try to choose questions that will give you the information that you need. Check that you have the *correct question-word* and that the question is *grammatically correct* (otherwise people may misunderstand the question and give you the wrong information).

Note: For the project you will be paired with another student (who does not have the same mother tongue as yourself).

4. *Newspaper project*

ANALYSIS SHEET

Title of Newspaper:

1. Price	
2. Circulation	
3. Owners	
4. Political tendency	
5. Tabloid or full-size	
6. No. of pages	
7. Main headline	
8. No. of pages devoted to: a) International news	
b) Home News	
c) Sensational news	
d) Sports news	
e) Arts/entertainment	
f) Business and finance	
g) Special features	
h) Advertisements	
9. Proportion of picture to print	
10. Who do you think reads this newspaper?	
11. Would *you* read it (on a regular basis)? Why (not)?	

Note: You will work in pairs to complete the information in the table, obtaining the answers to questions 1–4 from the handout 'British Newspapers'. Check carefully through the newspaper that you have been allocated for the other answers. When you have finished the analysis, there will be a group discussion.

EXAMPLES OF TOPICS FOR STUDENT SEMINARS

The following topics can be talked about from the point of view of one country or, sometimes, two or more countries compared. Students often give introductory talks on their own specialist subject, or on aspects of life and culture in their own country. Some examples are as follows:
  – birth, marriage, death – customs
  – the family unit
  – equal opportunities for women
  – major festivals
  – systems of agriculture
  – the population explosion and its control
  – demographic changes
  – primary health programmes
  – sources of fuel and energy
  – the effectiveness of international law
  – political systems
  – food and diet
  – educational reform
  – the problems of higher education
  – water resources
  – the work of the UN agencies
  – AIDS
  – pollution
  – acid rain
  – natural disasters: earthquakes, floods, famine
  – the meaning of leisure
  – the principles of overseas aid
  – the influence of writers
  – the function of zoological gardens
  – crime and punishment
  – behavioural problems in children
  – the power of multinational corporations

Chapter 5

FEEDBACK: END-OF-COURSE QUESTIONNAIRE

c) Example

Questions should be answered by putting a tick (✓) in the appropriate box. (If you have any extra comments to make please write them on the back of the paper and number them.)

Section A

Course components (main ones only)

5=extremely valuable	4=valuable	3=of some value	2=of little value	1=of no value

Please give your opinion as to the value of the following:

1. Listening comprehension and note-taking   5☐ 4☐ 3☐ 2☐ 1☐
2. Academic writing   5☐ 4☐ 3☐ 2☐ 1☐
3. Reading comprehension   5☐ 4☐ 3☐ 2☐ 1☐
4. Academic speech   5☐ 4☐ 3☐ 2☐ 1☐
5. Language laboratory   5☐ 4☐ 3☐ 2☐ 1☐
6. Tutors' seminars   5☐ 4☐ 3☐ 2☐ 1☐
7. Students' seminars   5☐ 4☐ 3☐ 2☐ 1☐
8. Video sessions   5☐ 4☐ 3☐ 2☐ 1☐
9. Lectures and guest lectures   5☐ 4☐ 3☐ 2☐ 1☐
10. Oral activities   5☐ 4☐ 3☐ 2☐ 1☐

11. *Projects*:
    a) Personal project   5☐ 4☐ 3☐ 2☐ 1☐
    b) Library project   5☐ 4☐ 3☐ 2☐ 1☐
    c) Interview/questionnaire project   5☐ 4☐ 3☐ 2☐ 1☐
    d) Newspaper project   5☐ 4☐ 3☐ 2☐ 1☐
    e) TV project   5☐ 4☐ 3☐ 2☐ 1☐

Chapter 7

AWARENESS-RAISING AND LEARNER TRAINING

Exercise on taking notes: Gibbs (1981)

Taking notes

Instructions

Working alone
This first stage involves students taking notes from some source – a lecture, book, film, tape-slide or audio cassette. This can simply involve the students' last lecture before coming to the exercise, a special note-taking activity at the start of the exercise, or even, if this exercise is tacked on to the end of a normal lecture of your own, the students' notes from this lecture. The more recently the notes have been taken, the more vividly and completely will students be able to reconstruct how and why they were written.

Working in pairs (10 min.)
'In pairs, each of you in turn have a look at the other's notes and try to understand *why* they are written in the form they are. Which things are included and which left out, and why? What will they be used for? Ask the other person whatever questions you need in order to understand their notes. Spend about five minutes on each set of notes. At the next stage you will be asked to explain and justify your *neighbour's* notes to another pair.'

Working in fours (20 min.)
'In fours, I'd like each of you in turn to try to explain your neighbour's notes to the other pair. Why are the other's notes different from your own? Do the others *use* their notes in the same way as you do? Find out! You are not allowed to describe your *own* notes unless your neighbour is unable to.'

Working in fours (15 min.)
'Still in fours, can you see from your four sets of notes what makes them either "good" and useful notes or "poor" and useless notes? Can you form a list of those characteristics you have identified which you think are useful and those you think you should avoid? Elect a chairman to write down these characteristics so you have a list ready to report at the plenary. You have about fifteen minutes.

Working in plenary 15 min.)
'I'd like each group in turn to read out one item from its list. If what is read out is clear to the other groups and not contentious, then I'll write it up on the board under one of the two headings: "Good points about these notes" or "Bad points about these notes." If the points are unclear or contentious, I want others to clarify or object to them. I won't write anything up unless we can agree on it, and we are clear what it means.'

Continue until points are exhausted.

Chapter 9

STRATEGIES AND SKILLS

Providing a purpose: examples

a) *Glendinning and Holmström (1992)*

Unit I   Getting to know your textbook

During your studies, you will learn from your lecturers, your fellow students and from books. Your textbook is one of your most valuable sources of information. It is important that you know how to use it effectively.

This unit aims to develop the reading skills required for:
1. surveying a textbook
2. using an index
3. dealing with word problems

TO MAKE YOU THINK

Task I (Individual, then pairs)

Knowing the parts of a textbook is the first step to using it properly. Study this list of some of the parts of a textbook. Try to match the parts with the correct descriptions.

Parts of a textbook	*Descriptions*
1. front cover	a) the units of the book
2. title page	b) sources used by the author
3. publishing details	c) a list of the main topics by chapter
4. preface/introduction	d) a page containing title and author's name
5. acknowledgements	e) an alphabetical list of topics in detail
6. contents	f) publisher, place and date of publication
7. chapters	g) selling points, author information, positive reviews
8. references	h) thanks to people who have helped with the book
9. glossary	i) the author's aims and the coverage of the book
10. index	j) a mini-dictionary of specialist terms used
11. back cover (or dust jacket blurb)	k) title, author and often an illustration in colour

When you have finished, compare your answers with your neighbour. Use your dictionary to find definitions for these parts:
   appendix
   bibliography
   foreword

b) McGovern et al. (1994)

ACADEMIC SUCCESS

The topic of this unit involves educational theory. It is based on an analysis of students' attitudes and performance in further and higher education in Britain and the United States.

This unit will give you practice in:

1. Asking predicting questions and answering pre-reading questions about texts.
2. Skimming, scanning and detailed reading.
3. Guessing unknown vocabulary.
4. Understanding the use of generalisation and qualification.
5. Understanding text organisation.
6. Analysing a writer's references to time in text organisation.
7. Understanding the main ideas in a text.
8. Evaluating titles of texts.
9. Identifying a writer's attitude.
10. Evaluating a writer's attitude.
11. Understanding the characteristics of a writer's use of language.

PRE-READING TASKS

A. Consider the possible influence of the following on academic success:

(a) Reasons for studying
(b) Physical energy patterns or 'bio-rhythms'
(c) Study methods
(d) Intelligence
(e) Time spent studying
(f) Personality.

Which do you think are the *most* and the *least* important? Why?

Chapter 10

TEACHING/LEARNING VOCABULARY

b) Word networks (or thematic webs), Jordan (1990a)

D Useful vocabulary for describing universities.

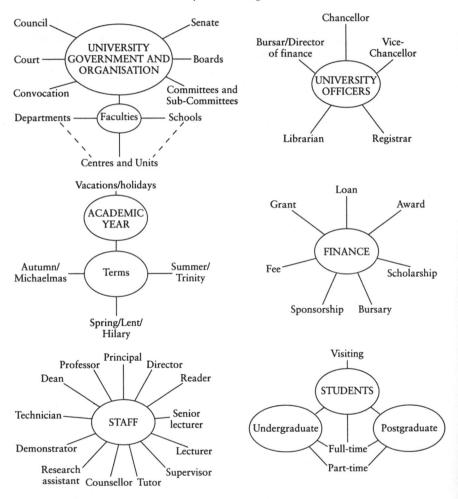

1. Can you think of any more words to add to the above lists?
2. Take the subject *Academic Reading*. Make a list of words for it (types of reading) in the same way as the above.

Chapter 11

THE PRODUCT APPROACH

a) Rhetorical-functional (Jordan (1990a) – Classification

Unit 7   Classification

When we divide something into groups, classes, categories, etc. we are *classifying* those items. The classification is normally made according to a criterion or several criteria (standards or principles on which judgements are based).

Stage 1   Criteria   1   Read the following carefully.

State Schools In England and Wales

The vast majority of children in Britain (87%) attend state (local authority) schools which provide compulsory education from the age of 5 to 16 years. These schools can be classified according to the age range of the pupils and the type of
5 education provided. Basically, there are two types of school: primary and secondary, although in some areas there are also middle schools. Primary schools cater for children aged 5–11, and secondary schools for ages 11–16 (and in some areas up to 18 years). Primary schools can be sub-divided into infant
10 schools (for ages 5–7) and junior schools (for ages 7–11).

Secondary schools are normally of one type for all abilities, viz. comprehensive schools. More than 90% of children in state schools attend this kind of school. In some areas middle schools exist as an extra level after primary school for children
15 aged 8 or 9 to 12 or 13. Pupils then transfer to senior comprehensive schools. In a small number of areas, pupils may be grouped according to their ability and selected by means of an examination at the age of 11. In these areas, grammar schools cater for those with academic ability and
20 secondary modern schools for those with less academic ability.

When pupils reach the age of 16 there may be three choices open to them. Firstly, they may leave school. Secondly they may stay on at school for two more years if it has a Sixth
25 Form. Thirdly, they may transfer to a Sixth Form College or a Tertiary College.

Now complete the following sentences which are based upon the text above.

a   Schools _____ the pupils' ages and the type of education.

b   There are _____ school: primary and secondary.

c   Primary schools _____ into infant and junior schools.

d   Secondary school pupils _____ their ability.

e   The *criterion* for classifying secondary schools is whether or not there is _____.

2   Below there are seven sentences, labelled a–g, which summarise the information in the passage. The sentences are in the wrong order. Put them into the correct order by writing the appropriate letter next to the numbers 1–7.

a   Most children go to comprehensive schools.

b   There may be three types of school: primary, middle and secondary.

c   At the age of sixteen, pupils may stay on at school, or leave and go to a college, or leave school altogether.

d   Exceptionally, children may take a selection exam at 11 years and go to either a grammar or a secondary modern school.

e   Most children go to state schools.

f   If children attend middle schools, they go on to senior comprehensive schools afterwards.

g   Primary schools comprise both infant and junior schools.

3a Look at *Diagram 1*. It shows a diagrammatic classification of state schools in England and Wales. If necessary read the text again and then complete *Diagram 1*, writing on the lines provided.

Diagram 1: State Schools in England and Wales

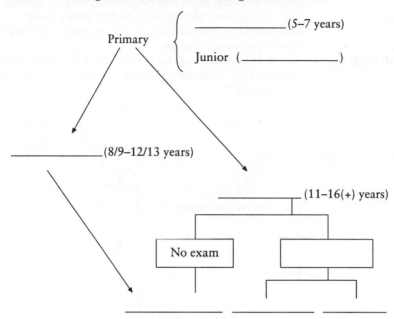

b Without looking at the text again, write a brief description of the information contained in *Diagram 1*. Begin your description:

    There are two types of school: primary and secondary. Primary schools can be sub-divided, according to age, into …

Note: If any help is needed with the language of classification in this exercise, or the following ones, turn to the *Structure and Vocabulary Aid* at the end of this unit (page 46).

4 Try to draw a classification diagram of the education system in your country. When you have completed it, write a brief description of it.

b) Academic genres

Swales and Feak (1994) – Constructing a research paper

Overview of the Research Paper

The overall rhetorical shape of a typical RP is shown in Figure 10.

    This diagram gives a useful indication of the out-in-out or general-specific-general movement of the typical RP. As the RP in English has developed over the last hundred years or so, the four different sections have thus become identified with four different purposes.

Appendix 1

Introduction (I)   The main purpose of the Introduction is to provide the rationale for the paper, moving from general discussion of the topic to the particular question or hypothesis being investigated. A secondary purpose is to attract interest in the topic—and hence readers.

Methods (M)   The Methods section describes, in various degrees of detail, methodology, materials, and procedures. This is the narrowest part of the RP.

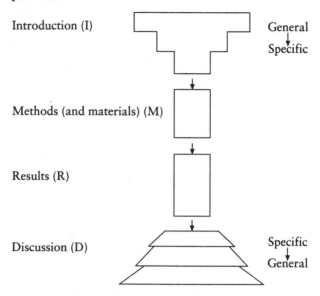

Figure 10   Overall shape of a research paper

Results (R)   In the Results section, the findings are described, by variable amounts of commentary.

Discussion (D)   The Discussion section offers an *increasingly generalized* account of what has been learned in the study. This is usually done through a series of "points," at least some of which refer back to statements made in the Introduction.

As a result of these different purposes, the four sections have taken on different linguistic characteristics. We summarize some of these in table 17. The first line of the table shows, for instance, that the present tense is common in Introduction and Discussions, but uncommon in Methods and Results.

Task One
In 1993 Dorothea Thompson published a useful RP on Results sections in biochemistry articles. She was particularly interested in what kinds of comments researchers made in their Results sections and whether researchers followed the guidelines in manuals. Here are eight sentences

TABLE 17. Frequencies of Selected Items in RP Sections

	Introduction	Methods	Results	Discussion
Present tense	high	low	low	high
Past tense	mid	high	high	mid
Passive voice	low	high	variable	variable
Citations/references	high	low	variable	high
Qualification	mid	low	mid	high
Commentary	high	low	variable	high

from her paper. Based on table 17 and on your own knowledge, can you guess from which of the sections they come? Mark each one *I*, *M*, *R*, or *D*. There are two sentences from each section. Work with a partner, if possible.

- 1. Only further research can determine the applicability of this study's findings to scientific disciplines outside bio-chemistry.
- 2. The data were analyzed both qualitatively and quantitatively.
- 3. Short communications and mini-reviews were excluded from the sample because these publications have different objectives and use a different format from that of the experimental research article.
- 4. The assumptions underlying this study are grounded largely in sociological accounts of the scientific enterprise (Knorr-Cetina, 1981; Latour, 1987; Latour and Woolgar, 1979).
- 5. These style guides are, at best, superficial descriptions of the content of these sections.
- 6. In 15 of the sample articles, these methodological narratives included explicit justifications for the selection of certain technical procedures, laboratory equipment, or alternatives to standard protocols.
- 7. Scientific style manuals reinforce the conception that Results sections simply present experimental data in a "cold," purely objective, expository manner (Council of Biology Editors, 1972; Day, 1988; Mitchell, 1968; Woodford, 1968).
- 8. In 38% of the JBC Results sections sampled, Kornberg and his co-authors directly relate their findings to those of earlier studies, as the following illustrate: . . .

THE PROCESS APPROACH

White and McGovern (1994) – Comparing and contrasting cities

COMPARING AND
CONTRASTING CITIES

TASK 2

Step 1

2.1 Think of two cities which interest you – they could be two cities in your own country, or a city in your own country and one of a comparable size in another country.

1. List at least three things which are the same or similar about these two cities.
2. List at least three things which are different.

2.2 In a group, compare the answers you have given to each question. Which things did you compare and contrast? Did they include things like location, population and industries?

Step 2

2.3 Work together to make a list of relevant headings for your points of similarity and difference, such as 'Location' or 'Population'. Group the points you listed in 2.1 under the appropriate headings or categories. For example, under which heading would you put the following points about Reading, a town in England?

- distribution and administration
- in the Thames valley
- about 200,000 people
- 40 miles west of London
- Digital, Hewlett Packard, Porsche UK

This is called *categorising* – in other words, organising information into groups, classes or categories according to similarities and differences.

The heading is sometimes called a *category*, *characteristic* or *criterion* (plural *criteria*). There are many forms of diagrams that can help you organise information in this way. Two examples are shown below. The diagram on the right is called a *classification diagram*.

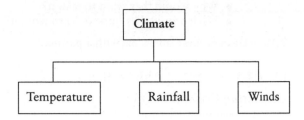

2.4 Now try to think of more points of similarity and difference between your two cities and place them under an appropriate heading.

2.5 Discuss what other headings – or categories – you have not included and add them to your list. For instance, do you have 'Cultural life' as one of your headings? Or 'Entertainment'?

2.6 Make a complete list of all of the main categories or headings that you have listed. Compare your headings with those of another person in your group.

Step 3

2.7 Now draw up a table like the one below. Several categories have been given as examples – you should fill in the table with your own categories as listed in 2.6.

Category	City A	City B
Location		
Population		
Industries		

2.8 Against each of the categories, make a note in your table of specific points relating to City A and to City B.

    If you don't have some of the information you need, ask other students in your group or refer to your teacher, who will suggest how you can find out what you need to know. Possible sources of information include:

- a travel book or reference book
- tourist information brochures
- information from travel agents or embassies.

2.9 When you have completed your table, you will have the basis for a comparison of the two cities chosen. Now ask yourself:

- Who (apart from your teacher) would want to read such a comparison?

- Why would they want to read it?
- What would they hope to learn from it?

2.10   Discuss these questions with a partner.

FEEDBACK AND EVALUATION

Correcting Code: J. P. O'Brien

ACADEMIC WRITING: ACCURACY

Correction of Written Work

Throughout the course, there will be shared responsibility for the correction of your written work.

When you submit a piece of writing, your tutor will return it to you having underlined any errors and indicated the type of error in each case (see Key attached). Your task will be to try and correct the errors, using your grammar and dictionary where necessary. Some class-time will be set aside during the Grammar Workshop for this purpose. Finally, your tutor will check your corrections.

It is hoped that this approach to correcting your work will help you in the following ways:

(1) to develop an awareness of your particular areas of weakness
(2) to become familiar with the more common grammatical rules of English through regular reference to the grammar
(3) to check your work more thoroughly
(4) to improve your accuracy in writing

KEY

Attached is a list of the symbols/abbreviations which will be used to indicate the type of error made. These will appear in the margin.

Note:

When doing a piece of writing, *please use alternate lines*. This will enable you to make any necessary corrections more easily. You should not rewrite your entire text.

ACADEMIC WRITING: ACCURACY

List of symbols/abbreviations for self-correction

Symbol/abbreviation   *Meaning*

vt	Verb tense, i.e. the wrong tense has been used
vf	Verb form, e.g. active/passive, progressive/non-progressive singular/plural, regular/irregular, perfective/non-perfective
a	Article usage, i.e. wrong usage
pr	Preposition, i.e. wrong usage
g	Miscellaneous grammatical errors, e.g. countable/uncountable nouns, pronouns
wc	Word class, i.e. the wrong class (noun, verb, adjective, adverb) of word has been used
wf	Word formation, i.e. wrongly formed word
v	Vocabulary, i.e. inappropriate use of word/phrase
wo	Word order, i.e. word/phrase in wrong position in sentence
expr.	Unidiomatic expression, i.e. not 'English'
ps	Phrase structure, e.g. *'s* v *of* genitive
ss	Sentence structure, e.g. no verb, two verbs without connective
sp	Spelling
p	Punctuation
⋏	Omission
?	Meaning unclear – rewrite
( )	Omit, i.e. word/phrase unnecessary
c	Connective, i.e. wrong usage
r	Register, e.g. use of spoken English in formal writing

Appendix 1

Chapter 12

LISTENING CUES

Markers: a) Lynch (1983)

Importance markers

In the last unit, you heard how the voice can be used to help listeners to recognise important information. Another way that a speaker can direct attention to specific points is by using phrases that 'mark' or indicate importance. Look at these examples:

A The central problem is that ...
B Clearly, ...   solutions are not going to be easy ...
C I ought to stress that ...

These three types of importance markers often occur in seminars and talks. We will now examine each type in turn.

Marker type A

Discussion point 1

Look at the table below. What other adjectives and nouns can you suggest, to add to those listed? Write in your suggestions.

Article	Adjective	Noun	Verb to be	
The	central	problem	is	that ...
A(n)	basic	point	was	etc.
One	....	....	will be	
Another	....	....	has been	
	....	....	must be	
	....	....	etc.	

Compare your additions with those of another student.

Listening exercise 1

Listen to the cassette. Write down the marker phrase (of type A) that each speaker uses.
1 'Preventive medicine': problems outside the doctor's control.
   Marker phrase: ....
2 'Development and aid': how to categorise the countries of the developing world.
   Marker phrase: ....
3 'Preventive medicine': one of the objectives.
   Marker phrase: ....

Listening exercise 2
Listen to those three extracts again. This time, note down the point or idea that the speaker wants to mark as important.

1 ....
2 ....
3 ....

(Marker Types B and C are treated in a similar way.)

b) Williams (1982)

Markers are devices that a speaker uses to divide up what he is saying. They help the listener to extract the main points from the talk, identify the introduction of a new topic, or follow successive stages in a line of reasoning. You heard the following markers in the *Age structure* talk. What was their significance?

1. '... I shall discuss two aspects of age structure ...' (What are *aspects of X*?)

2. '... what do I mean by this term "age structure"?' (Why did the speaker ask this question? What followed it?)

3. 'So much for age structures themselves.' (What does *so much for X* tell you, i.e. what is the relationship between the information before and after this marker?)

4. 'The point I am making, then, ...' (What type of information does this marker introduce? Why did the speaker use this marker?)

TAKING NOTES

Abbreviations and symbols: James *et al.* (1991)

HOW TO TAKE NOTES

The purpose of taking notes during a talk or a lecture is to help you concentrate on what the speaker is saying and to provide a summary for reference or revision later. The general principle in note-taking is to reduce the language by shortening sentences and words.

The following advice and exercises will help you to take notes more efficiently and should be read and completed before trying to do the *Guided Note-taking* exercises in each Unit.

1 *Generally, if you want to take quick notes you must*:
  a) omit completely certain sentences which are not essential to the main ideas;
  b) concentrate on the important sentences, i.e. those which give most information, and on the important words, i.e. usually nouns, sometimes verbs or adjectives;
  c) write in short phrases, rather than in complete sentences;
  d) use common symbols or signs and abbreviations (see below)
2 *You can show the connections between ideas by using*:
  a) *space*: the presentation of the notes is important – you should be able to see the main points clearly;

b) *numbers and letters* (as here), e.g. 1, 2, 3; (i), (ii), (iii); A, B, C; (a), (b), (c);
c) *underlining*, to draw attention to something or to emphasize something;
d) *common symbols and signs*, e.g.

∴	therefore	∵	because
✓	statement/answer is correct	×	statement/answer is wrong
?	question; is the statement correct	/	or (this/that = this *or* that)
& or +	and/plus	—	a dash (often used to join ideas and replace words or punctuation marks that have been omitted
" "	ditto (means the same as the words immediately above the ditto marks)	≠	does *not* equal, differs from, is the opposite of
=	is/are/have/has/equals		
→	leads to/results in/causes	↛	does *not* lead to/result in/cause

3 *Abbreviations*

a) Common general abbreviations. Many of these are to be found in an appendix in a dictionary; others are commonly used by English students. Some commonly used ones are shown below.

e.g.	for example	1st	first
i.e.	that is	2nd	second
etc.	et cetera: and so on	3rd	third etc.
cf.	compare	G.B.	Great Britain
viz.	namely	U.K.	United Kingdom
c. (or ca.)	about/approximately	Eng.	English
N.B.	note	Brit.	British
C19	nineteenth century similarly C20 etc.	Q.	question
		A.	answer
1920s	i.e. 1920–1929; similarly 1970s etc.		
approx.	approximately	no.	number
dept.	department	p./pp.	page/pages
diff.(s)	difficult(y)(-ies)	poss.	possible/possibly
excl.	excluding	prob.	probable/probably
govt.	government	probs.	problems
imp.	important/importance	re-	with reference to/concerning
incl.	including	ref.	reference
info.	information	sts.	students
lang.	language	tho'	though
ltd.	limited	thro'	through
max.	maximum	v.	very
min.	minimum		

Note: English students often shorten words ending in '-ion' by writing 'n' instead of these letters, e.g. 'attent^n' instead of 'attention'. Similarly words ending in '-ment' are often represented by 't' for the letters, e.g. 'develop^t' for 'development'.

b) Abbreviations of common words and phrases in an academic subject, e.g. an economist would abbreviate economics to econ., Gross National Product to G.N.P., balance of payments to b. of p. etc. These abbreviations will depend upon individual needs.

Guide note-taking:

a) space and clear organisation: Heaton and Dunmore (1992)

ACTIVITY
10.8

> The careful use of space in your notes, together with numbers and letters, will make them clear, well-organised and easy to remember. You should aim for this:
>
> Note-making 1. Use space →
>   (i) notes easy to read & remember
>   (ii) easy to add points later
>   2. Use numbers and letters →
>   (i) classify main and supporting points
>   (ii) show sequence
>
> instead of this:
>
> Note-making: Use space → notes easy to read & remember; easy to add points later. Use numbers and letters → classify main and supporting points; show sequence.

Task 1

A student has made the notes below from a talk about Antarctica. They do not make good use of space or numbers and letters. Rewrite these notes in the framework provided after the notes. Some words have been written already to help you.

Antarctica. Geography: Continent in S. hemisphere. Area = 5m sq miles; 66°S to S pole. Climate: av temp −50°C. Contains 95% world's ice; ice 2 miles thick in places. Life on land: humans (scientists), insects; life in sea: fish, whales. Early exploration: 2 expeditions 1911–12: first Norwegian, led by Amundsen; second British, led by Scott.

Antarctica
1. Geography
   (i) _____
   (ii) area
      (a) _____
      (b) 66°S→S pole
   (iii) Climate _____
   (iv) ice
      (a) _____
      (b) 2 miles thick in places
2. Life
   (i) _____
      (a) humans (scientists)
      (b) _____
   (ii) in sea
      (a) _____
      (b) _____
3. _____
   (i) Norwegian, led by Amundsen
   (ii) _____

ACTIVITY
10.9

You are going to hear a talk about Peru, a country in South America. Make your own notes as you listen. Try to use space and numbers and letters to make your notes clear.

b) word cues and discourse markers: *James et al.* (1991)
   i) word cues:
   Unit 3   Stage 3   Guided Note-taking
   Complete the following as you listen to the Stage 3 talk.
   Title: ....
   4 most   :

   1   Understand what lecturer says ....
       cannot ....
       Often poss. to understand much by ....
       ....

   2   What's imp.?
       Most imp. info. = ... make sure ....
       ....
       implies
       Good lecturer   ....
       ....or... signals
       Explicit =   write it down!
       Indirect = ... or .... etc.
                         = sth. imp.
                         ....
                         ....
                         = sth. incidental
   ii) discourse markers:
   Unit 3   Stage 3   Alternative Guided Note-taking
   Listen to Stage 3 talk and take notes using the lecturer's signals (listed below) to help you. These can be written in the book or on a separate piece of paper.

Lecturer's signals	Notes
Today I'm going to analyse	
Firstly	(1) ....
	....
	....
	....
	....
But how does the student decide what's important? ... It is, in fact, the second of the four skills I want to talk about today	(2) ....
	....
	....
... for example	....
	....
It's worth remembering that ... also	....
	....
	....

c) branching notes: Wallace (1980)

Branching notes

This is a type of note-taking which is especially useful when you have not been given an outline of the lecture. It enables you to develop your notes as the lecture proceeds, in a flexible way. It is also argued that this type of layout makes it easier to recapture the speaker's original message and to see the relationships between ideas more clearly.

MR BROWN
31.5.78

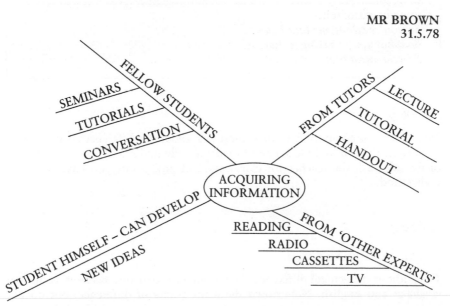

Appendix 1

Chapter 13

SEMINARS

Questions: Lynch and Anderson (1992)

SEMINAR SKILLS: GETTING CLARIFICATION
When using a foreign language, we have to get used to dealing with situations where we do not understand, or only partly understand, what the speaker has said. In a seminar, where time may be short, it is important to make it clear to the speaker precisely what your problem is. If you ask a very general question you may find that the speaker simply produces a repetition of what they said before.

Useful phrases

Non-comprehension
   I'm sorry, I didn't understand what you said about (X).
                catch
           could you repeat
   What does (X) mean?

Partial comprehension
   What did you mean when you said (X)?
   Could you be more specific about (X)?
         expand a little on   *what you said about (X)?*
         give an example of
         explain in more detail

Getting confirmation
   So you're telling me that I can't ...?
   So what you're saying is that ...?
   So you mean that ...?

Listening

Your teacher is going to play you a short talk about the differences between two languages: English and Outlandic. Listen carefully and make notes. At the end of the talk, ask the teacher for clarification of any points you have not fully understood.

Speaking

STAGE I: PREPARATION

Think about the general differences in grammatical structure between your own language and English. Note down the main points of difference, but do not write complete sentences. Among the other things you could consider are: tenses, articles, word order, pronouns and question forms.

STAGE 2: PRACTICE

Using your notes, describe the differences to a partner. Limit your talk to around five minutes. Allow them to ask you for any additional clarification that they feel they need. Be prepared to expand or exemplify what you have said.

Then exchange roles of speaker and listener.

STAGE 3: PRESENTATION

Form a new trio with two other students. Take turns at giving your talk as the others take notes. Answer the questions that your listeners may need to ask you. Think in particular about ways of making clearer the points that your Stage 2 partner asked you to clarify.

STAGE 4: EVALUATION

Were you able to make the differences clearer the second time? Are there still points that you would like the teacher to help you to put into English?

Summary

As a listener in a seminar you should not feel embarrassed about asking the speaker to repeat or clarify ideas that you were unable to follow first time round. But time (and patience) can quickly be used up if you do not make clear what it is that needs clarification.

Discussions:

a) Wallace (1980)

The language of discussion

Usually the purpose of a seminar is to discuss ideas, not mainly to learn facts, although facts are important as evidence to support the ideas. When one of the other participants expresses an idea or opinion, you have to decide what your own thoughts are:

1 *You agree.* If so, do you agree completely, or do you think he is only partly right? Have you any arguments, facts etc. which support the speaker's point of view?
2 *You disagree.* There is nothing wrong in disagreeing with a speaker. But always respect other people's views, and remember: you may be mistaken!
3 *You don't know.* You may be looking for more evidence, or you may not quite have understood what the speaker is trying to say.

Exercise 9
Here are some useful expressions for indicating whether you agree, disagree or don't know:

Appendix 1

Agree
I couldn't agree more.
On the whole, I think the speaker's arguments are fair.

Disagree
I'm afraid I can't agree with Mr X on this matter.

Don't know
Is the speaker saying ...?
Am I correct in assuming ...?

Under which heading would you put each of these expressions?

1 I'm sorry, I can't accept Mr X's point of view.
2 I think the speaker is right in what he says.
3 I'm afraid I'm not convinced.
4 I'm afraid I didn't quite get the speaker's last point. Could he go over it again, please?
5 All right. I take your point.
6 May I suggest another explanation?
7 Could I ask the speaker for his views on ...
8 By and large, I would accept the speaker's views (but ...)
9 I'm not sure that I entirely agree with Mr X.
10 Could I ask Mr X what he means by ...

b) James (1984b)
   1 Below are nine ways of expressing agreement with a statement. Fill in as many spaces as you can. Then listen to the tape. Check your answers.
      • Big universities tend to be impersonal.
      1 Yes, I think s_____ too.   6 That's ab_____ right.
      2 I c_____ agree more.   7 Yes. I ag_____.
      3 That's wh_____ I think too. 8 That's ex_____ what I think.
      4 I'm af_____ it's true.   9 I m_____ say I think you're right.
      5 I have to ad_____ you're right.

   2 Classify the above forms of agreement by writing each one in its appropriate box.

agree reluctantly	agree	agree enthusiastically
I'm af_____ it's true.	Yes, I think s____ too.	I c_____ agree more.

3 Read the following opinions to your
partner who will (a) agree with them and
(b) add his/her own reasons or comments

- Generalisations about national
character can be very misleading.
- Loneliness can be a big problem
for those who study abroad.

- Different cultures favour
different ways of studying.
- If you want to live abroad
successfully, you have to learn
how to behave differently.

(The exercise continues with a similar treatment of disagreement.)

c) Heaton and Dunmore (1992):

ACTIVITY
7.5

In discussions it is important to be able to express your
opinion clearly and to support your argument with reasons
and examples.

Below is a list of five means of transport:

bus plane bicycle train ship

Individually, number them from 1 to 5, using the cost of travel
in your country as a criterion (1 = the most expensive; 5 = the
cheapest).

Now work in groups of four or five. Explain your order to
the other members of the group. Do you all have the same
order? If not, why?

Next, as a group, think of two other ways which can be used
to compare the five means of transport. Decide on the best
order from 1 to 5.

Finally, present your two new orders in the form of a table to
your class and explain why you chose those orders.

ORAL PRESENTATIONS

a) Pyramid discussions: Jordan and Nixson (1986)

Pyramid discussion A pyramid discussion is a device whereby students are
encouraged to take part in discussion by gradually increasing the size of the
discussion group, starting with the individual, then building up to two students,
then four, then eight, until the whole group is involved. The procedure is as
follows:

1 First, students should individually select three items, as instructed, from the
list given in the exercise. The order of their three choices is not important.
2 Then each student, in turn, should call out the numbers of his/her choices.
Write these on the blackboard for all to see.

		A	B	C	D	etc.
e.g.	*student*	12	3	4	1	
	choices	14	7	7	7	
		20	10	12	10	

3 After this, put the students in pairs so that they have, as far as possible, at least one choice in common (e.g. A and C, B and D above).

4 In pairs the students should then try to persuade each other to make changes in their choices so that at the end of a certain time limit (perhaps five minutes) they both agree on three choices. If necessary, they can compromise on new choices or 'trade-off' choices. The pairs' three choices are then noted on the blackboard.

5 Pairs should then be placed together who have at least one choice the same ... and so the procedure continues until all of the class are involved.

6 If a pair or group finish their discussion before other groups, they can prepare arguments to defend their choices so that they are ready to meet another group.

7 While they are discussing, students will be practising the language of persuasion: agreement, disagreement, suggestion, qualification and compromise.

2 Group activity: Pyramid discussion

a Individually select the *three* most important requirements from the list below that you think will help a developing country to improve its economic development. The order of the three choices is not important. The time-scale of the items below in the process of economic development can be interpreted as you wish – either short- or long-term.

b The procedure for continuing this activity is described on page 8.

1 a good standard of education in schools for all (or most) children
2 adult literacy
3 a low birth rate
4 good health for the working population
5 a small percentage of the population employed in agriculture
6 modernisation of agricultural techniques
7 higher productivity per worker (in agriculture and industry)
8 a large amount of foreign aid
9 a high rate of import substitution
10 a high propensity to save
11 an effective tax system
12 greater equality of distribution of income
13 the growth of financial institutions
14 a high rate of investment in industry
15 government direction or control of investment and production
16 an increase in exports and export earnings
17 diversification of exports, especially exports of manufactured goods
18 an abundance of natural resources
19 more efficient allocation of scarce resources
20 political stability

What are likely to be the three biggest problems for students studying abroad?
1 adjusting to different food
2 adjusting to a different climate
3 homesickness
4 being a foreigner in a different culture
5 culture shock
6 adapting to different customs and habits
7 using a foreign language for study purposes
8 loneliness
9 adapting to new styles of teaching and learning
10 adapting to greater independence
11 thinking critically in a foreign language
12 organising and using time efficiently
13 paraphrasing and summarising in a foreign language
14 uncertainty about standards of work expected
15 the adjusting of expectations to reality
16 participating in discussions
17 relations with academic staff
18 continuous writing in a foreign language

b) Preparation for a short talk: Forman *et al.* (1990)

Now you are ready to draw up your final plan. You should keep the following points in mind.

a **Introduction**	You will need to	*(i)* introduce the general topic
		(ii) explain the structure of your talk
	Can you think of suitable phrases for these stages?	
b **Talk content**	For ease of reference, the points that you want to make should be reduced to key words only. You should not read from your notes.	
c **Visuals**	Flow charts, diagrams, mind maps, graphs and so on can be very effective ways of presenting information.	
	But you will have to consider how you will display them – on a blackboard – in poster form – on an overhead projector The visuals should be simple and have an immediate impact.	
d **Conclusion**	In order to make sure that your main points are clear, you might summarise them at this stage and draw a general conclusion.	

Now, prepare the notes you are going to talk from and any visuals you have decided to use.

Appendix 1

Notes on delivery

Timing	Your time is limited in this case to 3 minutes.
Pace	Your speed of delivery should allow listeners enough time to take in what you are saying. On the other hand, too slow a pace can be boring.
Voice	You should be heard by everybody in the room. This involves projecting your voice to the far corners.
Stance	When speaking, face your audience. If you are referring to a visual, don't turn your back on your listeners. Don't speak to the blackboard.
Audience contact	Try to speak to all your listeners and not just a section.

c) Peer evaluation: Lynch (1988a)

Seminar Evaluation Sheet
(Please complete this sheet by *filling in* the spaces or by *circling* the items.)

1. What do you think were the strengths of the presentation?
2. Were you able to follow the main points?
   YES   WITH DIFFICULTY   NO
3. Would you be able to summarise the talk for someone else?
   YES   WITH DIFFICULTY   NO
4. Was the presentation well organized?
   YES   GENERALLY   NO
5. Did the speaker show clearly when they were moving to a new point?
   YES   GENERALLY   NO
6. Did they make good use of visual support (e.g. hand-outs, blackboard, overhead projector) to make their points clearer?
   YES   NOT ALWAYS   NO
7. Was their speed of speaking appropriate?
   YES   TOO FAST   TOO SLOW
8. Was the loudness appropriate?
   YES   NOT LOUD ENOUGH TOO LOUD
9. Did they give sufficient explanation of technical vocabulary?
   YES   NOT ALWAYS   NO
10. Was the amount of information appropriate?
    YES   TOO LITTLE   TOO MUCH
11. How would you judge the speaker's eye-contact with the listeners?
    GOOD   UNEQUAL   INSUFFICIENT
12. If you had serious difficulties in following the talk, were they any of the following?
    speed of speaking   poor organization
    accent   grammar
    loudness   poor signalling of new points
    Mention any other problems here:
13. What advice would you give the speaker for future seminar presentations?

d) Teacher's evaluation: Mason (1995)

PRESENTATION EVALUATION FORM

NAME OF PRESENTER _____

ASSESSED BY: _____

OVERALL IMPRESSION: _____

PREPARATION:

CLEAR OBJECTIVE	YES/NO
SPEAKER HAD CONSIDERED THE AUDIENCE	YES/NO
CONTENT – relevant to topic	YES/NO
too much suitable amount	too little

ORGANISATION:

CLEAR, LOGICAL STRUCTURE	YES/NO
GOOD INTRO/LINK TO NEXT SPEAKER/ CONC.	YES/NO
(depending on position in group)	
REFERRED TO QUESTIONS?	YES/NO

DELIVERY:

BODY LANGUAGE (mannerisms, posture, positioning, etc.) _____

EYE CONTACT	enough	YES/NO
	shared round audience	YES/NO
VISUAL MATERIALS	were there any?	YES/NO
	too much on transparencies	YES/NO
	positioning OK?	YES/NO

spelling/other errors on transparencies:

VOICE PROJECTION:	loud enough?	YES/NO
PACE: too fast	fine	too slow
INDEPENDENCE OF NOTES:		YES/NO

GRAMMAR & VOCABULARY:	**PRONUNCIATION:**

Appendix 1

VERBALISING DATA

Elsworth (1982)

How do you say '346,521,978'? It's easy if you think of the figure in groups, with three numbers in each group. After the first number in the group, you say *hundred and*; and at the comma say *thousand* or *million*.

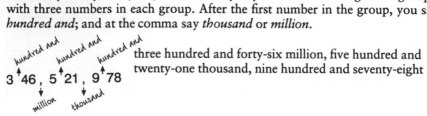

three hundred and forty-six million, five hundred and twenty-one thousand, nine hundred and seventy-eight

If there are '0's in the figure, you don't say them.

100,002 *a hundred thousand and two*
100,020 *a hundred thousand and twenty*
100,120 *a hundred thousand, one hundred and twenty*

Exercise 5 Say these numbers: a) 58,942   b) 645,932,461   c) 2,000,020
                       d) 461,902,431   e) 729,414,986   f) 333,021,603

Now listen to the tape, and write the numbers here:

g) _____   h) _____   i) _____   j) _____   k) _____
l) _____   m) _____   n) _____   o) _____   p) _____

Chapter 14

DICTIONARIES

Dictionary practice: alphabetical ordering and using the dictionary quickly: O'Brien and Jordan (1985)

Exercise 2 Put the following groups of letters or words in the order in which you would find them in the dictionary by numbering them,
e.g. mi ... (2); me ... (1); mu ... (3)
a bl ... ( ); be ... ( ); br ... ( )
b di ... ( ); dr ... ( ); dor ... ( ); dre ... ( ); din ... ( ); dar ... ( );
   drea ... ( )
c real( ); rarity( ); really( ); rear( ); rare( ); reality( ); rarefied( ).
d growl( ); grocer( ); ground( ); groan( ); grouse( ); grope( ); group( ).

326

Saving time
You can save time if you know that:
1 the first quarter ($\frac{1}{4}$ – or 25 per cent of the pages) of a dictionary usually contains words that begin with a, b, c and d (a–d);
2 the second quarter of a dictionary usually contains words that begin with e, f, g, h, i, j, k, l (e–l);
3 the third quarter contains m, n, o, p, q, r, s (m–s);
4 the last quarter contains t, u, v, w, x, y z (t–z).

Exercise 3 *Speed exercise*
(You should do all the speed exercises as quickly as you can.)
In which *quarter* of the dictionary will you find the following? Write 1st, 2nd, 3rd or 4th after each word.

1 ornate	_____	5 literature	_____
2 means	_____	6 accurate	_____
3 view	_____	7 jargon	_____
4 phenomenon	_____	8 renaissance	_____

Exercise 4 *Speed exercise*
Here are some words and some *guide-words*.
Find the correct guide-words for each word and write the letter in the space next to the word. The first one has been done for you.

Words		*Guide-words*		
1 ornate	e	a item/jade	f orotund/otherwise	
2 means	____	b jaffa/jaw	g persuasive/petrify	
3 jargon	____	c May/mean	h petro-/phenomenon	
4 phenomenon	____	d meander/meat	i reline/reminisce	
5 renaissance	____	e ordure/ornithology	j reminiscence/render	

USING THE LIBRARY

a) The Dewey Decimal System and Library of Congress Classification: O'Brien and Jordan (1985)

The Dewey Decimal System
Main outline

```
000 General Works
100 Philosophy
200 Religion
300 Social Sciences
400 Language
500 Natural Science
600 Technology
700 Fine Arts (e.g. painting)
800 Literature
900 History
```

Each of these divisions can be subdivided many times. Let us look at how this works in the Social Sciences.

300–399 The Social Sciences

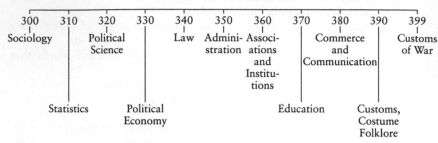

Library of Congress Classification System

In this classification system there are 26 main divisions based upon the letters of the English alphabet. After the first letter a further letter is added to provide a subdivision. Further subdivisions are then created by using numerals to follow the letters, e.g. D–History; DT–History of Africa; DT 515 History of Nigeria.

Library of Congress Classification System
A: General works, Polygraphy
B1: B–BJ: Philosophy
B2: BL–BX: Religion
C: Auxiliary – Sciences of History
D: General and Old World History
E–F American History
G: Geography, Anthropology, Folklore, Manners and Customs, Recreation
H: Social Sciences
J: Political Science
K: Law
L: Education
M: Music
N: Fine Arts
P–PA: Philology, Linguistics, Classical Philology, Classical Literature
PB–PH: Modern European Languages
PG: in part – Russian Literature
PJ–PM: Languages and Literatures of Asia, Africa, Oceania, America, Mixed
            Languages, Artificial Languages
PN, PR, PS, PZ: Literature (General), English and American Literature, Fiction
            in English, Juvenile Literature
PQ, 1: French Literature
PQ, 2: Italian, Spanish, and Portuguese Literature
PT, 1: German Literature
PT, 2: Dutch and Scandinavian Literatures
Q: Science
R: Medicine
S: Agriculture, Plant and Animal Industry, Fish Culture, and Fisheries, Hunting
   Sports

T: Technology
U: Military Science
V: Naval Science
Z: Bibliography and Library Science

b) *Library use*: Williams (1982)

5 Practical work in the library
Complete at least six of the following

YOU NEED TO KNOW IF THE LIBRARY HAS ...	FIND OUT (from the catalogue) ...	FIND OUT (from the book itself) ...
a book written by Bruce *Cooper*, about *writing reports*	a) the title of the book b) the class number c) the publisher	whether the book contains a chapter on *illustrations* (YES/NO)
a book entitled *A Dictionary of Biological Terms* (or similar)	a) the place of publication b) its location in the library c) the number of pages it contains d) the class number	the meaning of the term *lagopodous*
any book on the subject of *energy conservation*	a) the author b) the title c) the date of publication d) the class number	whether the book contains information on a) electric cars (YES/NO) b) domestic solar heating (YES/NO)
any book about FORTRAN programming	a) the title b) the publisher c) its location in the library d) the class number	whether the book explains *Simpson's Rule* (YES/NO)

(The exercise continues with another six items.)

Appendix 1

REFERENCES

Footnotes: Smith and Smith (1990)

EXERCISE 7.15

Read through these footnotes, and then answer the following questions.
1 Shaver, H., 1977, *Malaria and the Political Economy of Public Health*, pp. 557–9.
2 Ibid., p. 623.
3 Ibid.
4 Calder, R., 1964, *Two Way Passage: A Study of the Give and Take of International Aid, passim*.
5 Shaver, op. cit., p. 563.
6 Cf. in this connection of the work of P. Goubert.
7 Djukanovic, V., *et al.*, 1957, 'Alternative Approaches to Meeting Basic Health Needs in Developing Countries', *WHO Technical Report*, no. 392, p. 6.
8 Jackson, R. (ed.), 1960, *Preventative Medicine in World War II*, vol. 1, p. 47.
9 Ibid., vol. II, p. 69.
10 Edmonds, R. T., 1983, 'The ineffectiveness of DDT Residual Spraying in the Jordan Valley', MS, University of Amman.

(a) What is the title of the work referred to in footnote 3?
(b) Why are these references not in alphabetical order?
(c) Did Djukanovic write all of *WHO Technical Report*, no. 392?
(d) What is the title of the book referred to in footnote 5?
(e) When was the book referred to in footnote 9 published?
(f) Why is the title of the work referred to in footnote 10 not in italics?
(g) Is it likely that the article referred to in footnote 10 will be in your library? Why?
(h) Which of the books by P. Goubert has the writer referred to?
(i) Why is there no reference to a page number in footnote 3?

Bibliographies: Lynch and McGrath (1993)

Putting Principles into Practice:
Examples of References

The following should not be taken as the only way of setting out references, but they are complete, consistent, clear and correct.

BOOKS
1. one author
   Wallace, M. 1980. *Study Skills in English*. Cambridge: Cambridge University Press.
2. two authors
   Brookes, A. and P. Grundy. 1990. *Writing for Study Purposes*. Cambridge: Cambridge University Press.
3. three or more authors
   See (2). It is necessary to list all the authors.
4. second or subsequent edition
   Turabian, K. 1973 (4th ed.) *A Manual for Writers of Term Papers, Theses and Dissertations*. Chicago: University of Chicago Press.
5. edited volume (one editor)
   James, G. (Ed.) 1984. *The ESP Classroom – Methodology, Materials, Expectations*. Exeter Linguistic Studies 7. University of Exeter.
6. edited volume (two or more editors)
   Geddes, M. and G. Sturtridge. (Eds.) 1982. *Individualisation*. Oxford: Modern English Publications.
7. no obvious author or editor
   British Council. 1980. *The Teaching of Listening Comprehension*. ELT Documents Special. London: The British Council.

PAPERS IN BOOKS
8. paper in volume referred to elsewhere in bibliography
   James, K. 1984. Mr Suleiman, the buttoning of cauliflowers and how I learnt to love the abstract. In James (Ed.) 1984: 58–68.
9. paper in volume not referred to elsewhere in bibliography
   St John, M. 1988. Attitudinal changes to self-access in EAP. In Brookes, A. and P. Grundy (Eds.) 1988. *Individualisation and Autonomy in Language Learning*. ELT Documents 131. London: Modern English Publications/The British Council: 126–35.

ARTICLES IN JOURNALS
10. one author
    Hyland, K. 1990. A genre description of the argumentative essay. *RELC Journal* 21.1: 66–78.
11. two or more authors
    See (2) and (3) above.

Appendix 1

OTHER

12. unpublished conference paper
    McGrath, I. 1991. Text use in the language classroom. Paper presented at 1st International Conference of LATEUM/MAAL, Moscow. September 1991.
13. unpublished work
    Lynch, T. n.d. Writing academic essays. Mimeo. IALS, University of Edinburgh.
14. McKinlay, J. 1983. An analysis of the discussion section of medical journal articles. Unpublished M.A. dissertation. University of Birmingham.
15. lecture (one of series)
    Ferguson, G. 1992. The scope of curriculum and syllabus studies. Lecture in M.Sc. option course on Language Programme Design. Department of Applied Linguistics, University of Edinburgh.

Chapter 15

WRITING PRACTICE

Reading instructions carefully: Heaton and Dunmore (1992)

> ACTIVITY
> 14.2
>
> You should always read the instructions very carefully before you begin to write any answers in an examination.

You will need a clean sheet of paper for this short test. Read all the instructions carefully before you start. Work as quickly as you can. You have only five minutes to complete the test.

1 Write your name in the top left-hand corner of the page.
2 Write today's date in the top right-hand corner.
3 Under the date, make a note of the present time.
4 Leave a line and then write the title of this book under your name.
5 Write the names of the authors on the next line, putting a circle round their surnames.
6 Draw a small rectangle below each name.
7 Write the number 32 in the first box and the number 12 in the second box.
8 Multiply these numbers and write the answer in a small circle to the right of the small rectangle.
9 Write the name of your favourite subject on the next line.
10 Why is this your favourite subject? Give a reason.
11 Now write the name of the subject in which you always score the highest mark. Underline the name if it is the same as that of your favourite subject. Put a cross after the name if the subject is different from your favourite subject.

12 On the next line state briefly what you find most difficult to master in English.

13 How many years have you been learning English? Put the answer to this question in a triangle.

14 When you have reached this stage of the test, call out your name twice and then continue with the remainder of the test.

15 Now turn over your page. At the top of the page write the title of the unit in this book which you have found most useful.

16 In the middle of the page draw the symbol which means *therefore* or *consequently*.

17 To the right of this symbol and on the line below write one word for which you can use the symbol ↑.

18 In the top half of this page draw an example of a simple pie chart.

19 Turn over your page to the front side and sign your name in the bottom right-hand corner.

20 Now that you have finished reading all the instructions carefully, do only the first three tasks which are listed.

Chapter 16

APPROPRIACY

Report conversion: Hamp-Lyons and Heasley (1987)

Using the information in this text, write a description of the findings of the study. Try to use a general-specific structure.

Cholesterol: the killer is convicted

A 10-year study of 3806 typical American men has shown that a cut in the cholesterol in their diet has saved lives.

Doctors have argued for years that America's predilection for food that is high in saturated fats is striking down men and women in their prime with heart disease, the country's biggest killer. High levels of cholesterol in the blood coat blood vessels with plaque, which causes angina and prompts surgery that costs billions of dollars each year.

But the hypothesis that low-fat diets and drugs could save lives had never been carefully tested until the National Heart, Lung and Blood Institute began its study 10 years ago.

One group of subjects embarked on a low-fat diet supplemented by cholestyramine, a drug that attacks cholesterol, taken several times a day. The other group also dieted but, unknowingly, took a placebo instead of the drug. After one year, cholesterol levels dropped among both groups, but eventually the drug easily outperformed the diet, reducing the risk of heart disease by 19 per cent, and heart attacks by 24 per cent.

(New Scientist)

Appendix 1

The result of the conversion might look something like the following:

> There is general acceptance among the medical profession that the high incidence of fatal heart disease can be attributed to a diet high in cholesterol. A high cholesterol level causes plaque to form on blood vessels, which results in angina. A study was conducted at the National Heart, Lung and Blood Institute in the United States over a period of ten years and involving 3806 'typical' men. The subjects were divided into two groups, both of which followed a low-fat diet. However, in the case of the first group, this was supplemented by cholestyramine, an anti-cholesterol drug, while the second received a placebo. The results showed a fall in the level of cholesterol among both groups but the reduction was significantly greater in the case of the first, the risk of heart disease being decreased by 19 per cent and heart attacks by 24 per cent.
>
> (J. P. O'Brien)

It is recognised that the exercise above is artificial and that the content of the original is retained, some of which would be inappropriate for a genuine academic text. However, the exercise does achieve one objective, and that is to help students to become aware of register through the resulting discussion.

Chapter 17

EXAMPLE OF ECONOMICS

From Jordan and Nixson (1986):

a) *Vocabulary*: i) from recognition to open:
Word study

Exercise 1A
Alternative vocabulary

Below is a list of words (and line numbers) from the text (1–19). Next to them is a list of synonyms or explanations, in mixed order (a–s). Match the words from the text with their synonyms.

1 presupposes (14)	a	creates
2 homogeneous (22)	b	stock or reservoir
3 incentives (23)	c	notions
4 term (27)	d	faced
5 live off (29)	e	assumes, takes for granted
6 lack (34)	f	small-scale, minor
7 coupled (36)	g	obtain money from, depend or rely on
8 shifted (41)	h	light open shoes with straps
9 pool (45)	i	expression
10 livelihood (53)	j	payment, reward
11 target (54)	k	similar, uniform
12 remuneration (56)	l	employment, earning a wage (living)
13 conceptualisations (60)	m	moved, transferred
14 reliance (63)	n	combined, joined
15 petty (66)	o	carried out, put into effect
16 sandals (68)	p	dependence
17 poses (78)	q	encouragement, motivation
18 confronted (81)	r	want, need, deficiency
19 implemented (82)	s	objective, mostly affected

Exercise 1B
Explanation

The following words are taken from the text (line numbers are given). Can you explain their meanings as used in the text? Use a dictionary if necessary.
1 disguised unemployment (12)
2 recycling (67)

Open exercise

Show that you understand the meanings of the words given below, and that you can use them correctly, by composing sentences that in some way explain their meaning (perhaps by giving a definition).
e.g. An *employee* is a person who works for someone else in return for payment.

1 full employment	3 unemployed	5 employer
2 seasonal unemployment	4 work-force	6 labourer

ii) information transfer:

TABLE 1.1 Economic growth

GNP per person (1980 dollars)	1950	1960	1980
Industrial countries	4130	5580	10660
Middle-income countries	640	820	1580
Low-income countries	170	180	250

Average annual growth (per cent)	1950–1960	1960–1980
Industrial countries	3.1	3.3
Middle-income countries	2.5	3.3
Low-income countries	0.6	1.7

Source: World Bank (1981), Figure 1.1, p. 6

Now look at Table 1.1 in the text. The following sentences are based on the information in it. Complete the sentences using the *correct forms* of the following words: *rise, raise, increase*. Remember to decide if a verb or a noun is required, which verb tense is appropriate, and whether to use singular or plural.

1 Comparing 1960 with 1950, GNP per person in industrial countries _____ by $1450.
2 In 1960, compared with 1950, there was _____ of $180 in the GNP per person in middle-income countries.
3 From 1950 to 1960 the GNP per person was _____ by only $10 for the low-income countries.
4 In 1980 the GNP per person had continued _____ in all groups of countries.
5 From 1960 to 1980 there were sharp _____ in the GNP per person in industrial and middle-income countries compared with the _____ from 1950 to 1960.

b) *Language function: cause and effect* – from recognition to open:

1 Some sentences have been taken from the text and slightly shortened. They are separated into the parts of 'cause' and 'effect'. Find the sentences in the text and write down the appropriate verb or phrase (connective) that links them.
   a The absence of foreign competition _____ the development of high-cost, inefficient, monopolistic and over-diversified industrial sectors. (26)
   b Widespread government intervention in these economies _____ distortions in both product and factor markets. (28)
   c Overvalued exchange rates _____ the continued balance of payments problems of the LDCs. (31)
   d Export-led industrialisation _____ a dependence on foreign capital and technology. (84)
   Now look carefully at the following sentence: it is organised differently from

the sentences above. Find the connective, and say which part is the 'cause'
and which part is the 'effect'.
  e As a result of this trend, there has been a significant change in the
     composition of LDC exports.
2 **Open exercise** Complete the following sentences by first adding an appropriate connective and then the remainder of the sentence.
  a A rapid increase in urban population ...
  b Increased employment opportunities in LDCs ...
  c Low incomes ...

c) *Writing and discussion activities*:
(From a unit on 'Poverty and Inequality')

1 Writing: A case study of poverty
Define poverty as it exists in your country. Describe a group of people that are
known to be poor in your country: give some indication of their poverty and
what you consider to be the causes of that poverty.

2 Group activity: Pyramid discussion
The procedure for conducting this activity is described on pages 7–8. Select from
the list below what you consider to be the three most important causes of
poverty in LDCs. The order of the three choices is not important.

  1 unemployment/disguised unemployment
  2 early death of the main wage-earner
  3 large families/insufficient family planning
  4 illness/malnutrition/poor medical facilities
  5 bureaucratic corruption
  6 illiteracy/poor education
  7 high rents in rural areas
  8 inefficient government administration
  9 inequalities in the distribution of income and wealth
 10 limited access to land and other factors of production
 11 inadequately developed infrastructure
 12 lack of local credit facilities
 13 inefficient land utilisation
 14 poor climate and lack of natural resources
 15 insufficient investment for industrialisation

 16 low wages/income
 17 low productivity
 18 drink/gambling
 19 discrimination
 20 inflexible religions

(From a unit on 'Urbanisation and Employment')

1 Writing: Essay
Describe the employment situation in your country. Where appropriate refer to
different types of unemployment (see Exercise 2 Employment) and any other
aspects of employment mentioned in the text.

Appendix 1

2 Group activity: Discussion – role-play
Minimum wages

Imagine that you are the minister, in the government of an LDC, responsible for fixing minimum wage levels in all sectors of the economy. Look at the list of 12 occupations in the table below. Decide on the order of the 12 occupations: write the highest wage first (1) and the lowest last (12). (Actual wages in monetary terms are not required, just the order.) Note that several jobs can be at the same level if you wish.

Individually decide on the order of the occupations and then discuss your order with others in a group. Be prepared to justify the order you have chosen (and think of the effects on the economy). Bear in mind some of the following, possible criteria for determining wage levels: production *v*. service, scarce *v*. plentiful supply, skilled *v*. unskilled, working conditions, demand, differentials, limited resources, social desirability ...

nurse	secondary school teacher
farm labourer	policeman/woman
bank clerk (cashier)	shop assistant
road builder (labourer)	civil servant
university lecturer	factory worker (semi-skilled)
civil engineer	medical doctor

Chapter 18

MATERIALS: SUGGESTIONS

Communicative activities: describe and draw: Jordan (1982)
The Trend to Monopoly in British Manufacturing

(Share of top hundred companies in manufacturing output)

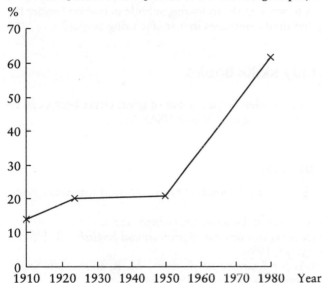

The Trend to Monopoly in British Manufacturing

Introduction. This is a graph containing one curve which shows the percentage share of the top companies in manufacturing output in particular years. The percentage share is indicated on the vertical axis and the years on the horizontal axis.

Description. About five centimetres from the left-hand edge of your paper draw a vertical line roughly eight centimetres long. Above it put the symbol for percentage (%). On this vertical axis mark off divisions at intervals of about one centimetre. At the very bottom, to the left of the mark at the base, put a zero. To the left of each mark going up the axis put the numbers, in tens, from ten to seventy.

Now draw the horizontal axis of the graph, also about eight centimetres long. Just to the right of the horizontal line write the word 'year'. Mark this line off in seven divisions at intervals of about one centimetre. On the extreme left, under the vertical axis, put in figures the year nineteen ten. Under the next mark put nineteen twenty. Then under the rest of the marks put the dates every ten years until the last one, which is nineteen eighty.

On the graph plot the following positions and put a very small cross for each one. Start with nineteen ten: on the vertical axis put a small cross by fourteen per cent. The next position is nineteen twenty-four with twenty per cent. After this comes nineteen fifty with twenty-one per cent. Finally comes nineteen eighty with sixty-one per cent.

When you have finished plotting the positions, draw a single line joining up the crosses from the first one for nineteen ten to the last one at nineteen eighty.

The final thing to do is to write in the following subtitle in brackets under the main title: 'Share of top hundred companies in manufacturing output.'

1.2 Selected study skills books

The following are selected examples. Some are out of print. Other books can be found in the ELT publishers' catalogues (UK and USA).

a) Integrated study skills books

A Study Skills Handbook – M. and G. Smith. Oxford: Oxford University Press, 1990.
Campus English – D. Forman *et al*. London: Macmillan, 1990.
ESP Ideas: Recipes for teaching academic and professional English – R. Holme. Harlow, Essex: Longman, 1996.
Language and Study Skills for Learners of English – M. R. Romanoff. Englewood Cliffs, N.J.: Prentice Hall Regents, 1991.
Learning to Study in English – J. B. Heaton and D. Dunmore. London: Macmillan, 1992.
Panorama – R. Williams. London: Longman, 1982.
Studying in English – J. B. Heaton. London: Longman, 1975.
Study Skills for Colleges and Universities in Africa – M. Montgomery. London: Longman, 1982.
Study Skills for Higher Education – J. Floyd. London: Collins, 1984.
Study Skills for Students of English – R. C. Yorkey. New York: McGraw-Hill, 1982.
Study Skills in English – M. J. Wallace. Cambridge: Cambridge University Press, 1980.

b) Academic reading

Academic Challenges in Reading – H. T. Abdulaziz and A. D. Stover. Englewood Cliffs, New Jersey: Prentice Hall Regents, 1989.
Academic Reading: A Content-Based Approach – L. W. Holschuh and J. P. Kelley. New York: St. Martin's Press, 1988.
Academic Reading and Study Skills for International Students – L. Rosenthal

and S. B. Rowland. Englewood Cliffs, N.J.: Prentice Hall Regents, 1986.

Approaches to Academic Reading and Writing – M. L. Arnaudet and M. E. Barrett. Englewood Cliffs, N.J.: Prentice Hall Regents, 1984.

English Vocabulary in Use – M. McCarthy and F. O'Dell. Cambridge: Cambridge University Press, 1994.

Exploring Academic Discourse – R. B. Kaplan and P. A. Shaw. Rowley, Mass.: Newbury House, 1983.

Lexis: Academic Vocabulary Study – A. Burgmeier, G. Eldred and C. B. Zimmerman. Hemel Hempstead: Phoenix ELT, 1991.

Practical Faster Reading – G. and V. Mosback. Cambridge: Cambridge University Press, 1976.

Reading – D. McGovern *et al.* Hemel Hempstead: Phoenix ELT, 1994.

Reading and Thinking in English – J. Moore (Ed.) Oxford: Oxford University Press, 1979–80.

Reading Choices – D. Jolly. Cambridge: Cambridge University Press, 1982.

Reading Comprehension Course – D. D. Sim and B. Laufer-Dvorkin. London: Collins, 1982.

Reading Faster: A Drill Book – E. Fry. Cambridge: Cambridge University Press, 1963.

Skills for Learning – University of Malaya/Nelson, 1980–81.

Skills for Reading – K. Morrow. Oxford: Oxford University Press, 1980.

Study Reading – E. H. Glendinning and B. Holström. Cambridge: Cambridge University Press, 1992.

Study Skills for Reading – E. Davies and N. Whitney. London: Heinemann, 1984.

Teaching Faster Reading: A Manual – E. Fry. Cambridge: Cambridge University Press, 1963.

c) Academic writing

I) FUNCTIONAL-PRODUCT APPROACH:

Academic Writing Course – R. R. Jordan. London: Collins, 1990; Nelson, 1992; Longman, 1995.

Becoming a Writer – R. Wong, E. H. Glendinning and H. Mantell. New York: Longman Inc., 1987.

Communicate in Writing – K. Johnson. London: Longman, 1981.

Paragraph Development – M. L. Arnaudet and M. E. Barrett. Englewood Cliffs, N.J.: Prentice Hall Regents, 1990.

Skills in Action – D. Sellen. London: Hulton Educational, 1982.

Think and Link – J. Cooper. London: Edward Arnold, 1979.

Write Ideas – E. H. Glendinning and H. Mantell. London: Longman, 1983.

II) GENRE APPROACH:

Academic Writing for Graduate Students – J. M. Swales and C. B. Feak. Ann Arbor: University of Michigan Press, 1994.

Appendix 1

How To Write Essays – J. Clanchy and B. Ballard. Melbourne: Longman Cheshire, 1992.
The Process of Composition – J. M. Reid. Englewood Cliffs, N.J.: Prentice Hall Regents, 1988.
Writing Laboratory Reports – T. Dudley-Evans. Melbourne, Victoria: Nelson Wadsworth, 1985.
Writing Up Research – R. Weissberg and S. Buker. Englewood Cliffs, N.J.: Prentice Hall Regents, 1990.

III) PROCESS APPROACH:

Academic Writing: Techniques and Tasks – I. Leki. New York: St. Martin's Press, 1989.
Feedback: essential writing skills for intermediate students – J. Sherman. Oxford: Oxford University Press, 1994.
Interactive Writing – A. Kwan-Terry. London: Prentice Hall International, 1988.
Process Writing – R. White and V. Arndt. London: Longman, 1991.
Read, Write, Revise: A Guide to Academic Writing – M. J. Schenck. New York: St. Martin's Press, 1988.
Study Skills for Academic Writing – J. Trzeciak and S. E. Mackay. Hemel Hempstead: Phoenix ELT, 1994.
Study Writing – L. Hamp-Lyons and B. Heasley. Cambridge: Cambridge University Press, 1987.
Writing – R. White and D. McGovern. Hemel Hempstead: Phoenix ELT, 1994.
Writing as Thinking: A Guided Process Approach – M. Frank. Englewood Cliffs, N.J.: Prentice Hall Regents, 1990.
Writing for Study Purposes – A. Brookes and P. Grundy. Cambridge: Cambridge University Press, 1990.

d) Lectures and note-taking

Listening Comprehension and Note-taking Course – K. James *et al*. London: Nelson, 1991.
Listening to Lectures – J. McDonough. Oxford: Oxford University Press, 1978.
Study Listening – T. Lynch. Cambridge: Cambridge University Press, 1983.
Text to Note – A. Adkins and I. McKean. London: Nelson, 1983.
Understanding Academic Lectures – A. Mason. Englewood Cliffs, N.J.: Prentice Hall Regents, 1983.

e) Speaking for academic purposes

Count Me In – S. Elsworth. London: Longman, 1982.
Defining and Verbalising – M. Fletcher and R. Hargreaves. London: Evans, 1980.

342

Figures in Language: Describe and Draw – R. R. Jordan. London: Collins, 1982.

Speak to Learn – K. James. London: Collins, 1984.

Speech Communication for International Students – P. Dale and J. C. Wolf. Englewood Cliffs, N.J.: Prentice Hall Regents, 1988.

Springboard to Success – P. Skillman and C. McMahill. New Jersey: Prentice Hall Regents, 1995.

Study Speaking – T. Lynch and K. Anderson. Cambridge: Cambridge University Press, 1992.

f) Reference/research skills

Developing Reference Skills – T. O'Brien and R. R. Jordan. London: Collins, 1985.

Research Matters – L. Hamp-Lyons and K. B. Courter. Cambridge, Mass.: Newbury House, 1984.

DICTIONARIES

Examples only are given; further information is available from publishers' catalogues.

a) Native speaker's dictionaries:

The Concise Oxford Dictionary of Current English
Collins English Dictionary

b) Pronouncing dictionaries:

The English Pronouncing Dictionary – Daniel Jones. Cambridge University Press
Longman Pronunciation Dictionary – J. C. Wells

c) Specialist subject dictionaries:

The Penguin Dictionary of Chemistry, etc.
Collins Dictionary of Sociology, etc.

d) Thesaurus:

The Oxford Thesaurus (An A–Z Dictionary of Synonyms)
Roget's Thesaurus of English Words and Phrases – Longman
Penguin Roget's Thesaurus

e) Learner's dictionaries:

Oxford Advanced Learner's Dictionary of Current English.
Worksheets (photocopiable): free – Oxford University Press
Longman Dictionary of Contemporary English.
Longman Dictionary Skills Handbook – J. McAlpin
Collins COBUILD English Language Dictionary
Cambridge International Dictionary of English

BBC English Dictionary
Harrap's Essential English Dictionary
Intermediate level dictionaries:
Oxford Wordpower Dictionary
   Worksheets (photocopiable) free
Longman Active Study Dictionary of English
   (with built-in workbook)
Longman Language Activator Workbook – S. Maingay and C. Tribble
Collins COBUILD Essential English Dictionary Workbook – C. Owen
(See *EFL Gazette*, April 1995, for a survey review of five up-to-date learner's dictionaries: Collins COBUILD, Longman, Oxford, Harrap's, Cambridge.)

LANGUAGE REFERENCE BOOKS:

The Cambridge Encyclopedia of Language – D. Crystal. 1987.
The Cambridge Encyclopedia of the English Language – D. Crystal. 1995.

g) Examination Skills

Answering Examination Questions – P. M. Howe. London: Collins, 1983.

1.3 Subject-specific (ESAP); and materials design and writing

i) ESAP surveys/overviews

a) The following are good background surveys which look at theoretical bases, methodology and materials, as well as containing extensive bibliographies.
   State of the art articles:
Coffey, B. 1984. ESP – English for Specific Purposes. *Language Teaching*, 17 (1).
Strevens, P. 1977. Special-purpose Language Learning: A Perspective *Language Teaching and Linguistics: Abstracts*, 10 (3).
Tickoo, M. L. (Ed.) 1988. ESP: State of the Art. SEAMEO RELC, Singapore, *Anthology Series 21*.
   Excellent books that survey the whole field of ESP with very extensive bibliographies:
Robinson, P. C. 1980. *ESP (English for Specific Purposes)*: the present position
Robinson, P. C. 1991. *ESP Today: A Practitioner's Guide*
   Concise and well-annotated articles that give a broad overview of key areas of interest in ESP within the period 1960s to late 1980s, with bibliographies:
Flowerdew, J. 1990. English for Specific Purposes – a selective review of the literature. *ELT Journal*, 44 (4).
Johns, A. M. 1991. English for Specific Purposes (ESP): Its History and Contributions. In M. Celce-Murcia (Ed.) *Teaching English as a Second or Foreign Language*.

A *useful article* that surveys the scope and distinguishing features of ESP, from the 1970s to 1991, with a discussion of questions and controversies:

Johns, A. M. and T. Dudley-Evans. 1991. English for Specific Purposes: International in Scope, Specific in Purpose. *TESOL Quarterly*, 25 (2).

An *excellent book* that explains and illustrates the main developments in ESP (mainly EST) by means of an appraisal of the major ESP books, from the early 1960s to the early 1980s, with some later additions. It shows the relationships between 15 key publications – 11 articles and 4 extracts from textbooks – and adopts the following format: setting, text and commentary, activities, evaluation and related readings.

Swales, J. 1985 and 1988. *Episodes in ESP*. A source and reference book on the development of English for Science and Technology.

b) The following are more specialised articles, or collections of papers, that focus on various disciplines in ESAP.

Selinker, L., E. Tarone and V. Hanzeli. 1981. *English for Academic and Technical Purposes* (Studies in Honor of Louis Trimble).

Maher, J. 1986. English for Medical Purposes. *Language Teaching*, 19 (2). (state-of-the-art article)

Bhatia, V. K. 1987. Language of the law. *Language Teaching*, 20 (4). (state-of-the-art article)

Dudley-Evans, T. and W. Henderson (Eds.) 1990. *The Language of Economics: The Analysis of Economics Discourse. ELT Documents 134.*

Henderson, W., T. Dudley-Evans and R. Backhouse (Eds.) 1993. *Economics and Language*. London: Routledge

West, R. 1994. Needs Analysis in Language Teaching. *Language Teaching*, 27 (1). (state-of-the-art article: covers EGAP and ESAP as well as EOP)

ii) *ESAP books for students*

AGRICULTURE

Agriculture. Yates, C. St. J. 1989. Phoenix ELT.

BUSINESS STUDIES

Business Studies. James, C. V. 1989. Phoenix ELT.
English for Business Studies. Moore, B. and C. Parsons. 1981. Phoenix ELT.

COMPUTER SCIENCE

Oxford English for Computing. Boeckner, K. and P. C. Brown. 1993. Oxford University Press.
Computer Science. Walker, T. 1989. Phoenix ELT.

ECONOMICS

Language for Economics. Jordan, R. R. and F. I. Nixson. 1986. Nelson.

Appendix 1

A Rapid Course in English for Students of Economics. McArthur, T. 1973.
  Oxford University Press.
English for Economics. Mead, R. 1985. Longman.
Economics. Yates, C. St. J. 1989. Phoenix ELT.

ELECTRONICS

Oxford English for Electronics. Glendinning, E. H. and J. McEwan. 1993.
  Oxford University Press.

ENGINEERING

General Engineering. Johnson, C. M. and D. Johnson. 1988. Phoenix ELT.
Oxford English for Electrical and Mechanical Engineering. Glendinning, E. and
  N. Glendinning. 1995. Oxford University Press.

LAW

English for Law. Riley, A. 1991. Phoenix ELT.
English Law and Language. Russell, F. and C. Locke. 1992. Phoenix ELT.

MEDICINE

English in Medicine. Glendinning, E. and B. Holmström. 1987. Cambridge
  University Press.
Medicine. James, D. V. 1989. Phoenix ELT.

SCIENCES

Basic English for Science. Donovan, P. R. 1978. Oxford University Press.
Earth Sciences. Yates, C. St. J. 1988. Phoenix ELT.
English for Science. Zimmerman, F. 1989. Phoenix ELT.

SCIENCES AND SOCIAL SCIENCES

Academic Reading and Study Skills for International Students. Rosenthal, L.
  and S. B. Rowland. 1986. Phoenix ELT.

SOCIAL SCIENCES

Reading Skills for the Social Sciences. Haarman, L., P. Leech and J. Murray.
  1988. Oxford University Press.

a) *ESAP major British series*

  1) *English Studies Series* (Oxford University Press): 1964–1971.
  2) *Listening to Lectures* (Oxford University Press): 1978.
  3) *English in Focus* (Oxford University Press): 1974–1980.
  4) *Nucleus* (Longman): 1976–1980.
  5) *English for Academic Purposes Series* (Phoenix ELT): 1988–1989.

346

b) Specialised dictionaries

Useful series of subject-specific dictionaries, for teachers and students, are:
i)   *The Penguin Dictionary of ...* e.g. Botany, Chemistry, Civil Engineering, Economics, Electronics, Geography, Geology, Mathematics, Physics, Politics, Psychology, Science, Sociology.
ii) *Collins Dictionary of ...* e.g. Astronomy, Biology, Economics, Environmental Science, Law, Medicine, Personal Computing, Philosophy.
iii) *Peter Collin Specialized Dictionaries* e.g. Agriculture, Banking and Finance, Business, Law, Medicine, Information Technology, Computing, Ecology and Environment.
     (Peter Collin Publishing, 1 Cambridge Road, Teddington, Middlesex, TW11 8DT, England.)

iii) Materials design and writing

Alderson, J. C. 1980. A Process Approach to Reading at the University of Mexico. In The British Council: *Projects in Materials Design. ELT Documents Special.* (contains a number of exercise-types with examples)
Cunningsworth, A. 1984. *Evaluating and Selecting EFL Teaching Materials.* Heinemann.
Cunningsworth, A. 1995. *Choosing Your Coursebook.* Heinemann.
Dubin, F. and E. Olshtain. 1986. *Course Design.* Cambridge University Press.
Grellet, F. 1981. *Developing Reading Skills.* Cambridge University Press. (contains a useful list of reading comprehension exercise-types together with numerous examples)
Hutchinson, T. and A. Waters. 1982. Creativity in ESP Materials or 'Hello! I'm a Blood Cell'. *Lancaster Practical Papers in English Language Education,* Vol. 5: *Issues in ESP.*
Hutchinson, T. and A. Waters. 1984. How communicative is ESP? *ELT Journal,* 38 (2).
Hutchinson, T. and A. Waters. 1987. *English for Specific Purposes: A learning-centred approach.* Cambridge University Press.
James, K. 1977. Note-taking in lectures: problems and strategies. In Cowie and Heaton (Eds.) *English for Academic Purposes.* BAAL/SELMOUS.
Johnson, K. 1982. *Communicative Syllabus Design and Methodology.* Pergamon.
Jordan, R. R. 1978. Language Practice Material for Economists. In Mackay and Mountford (Eds.). *English for Specific Purposes.* Longman.
Jordan, R. R. 1984. Motivation in ESP: a case study of methods and materials for Economics. In James (Ed.) *The ESP Classroom.* Exeter Linguistic Studies, 7.
McDonough, J. 1978. Designing exercises for listening. *Modern English Teacher,* 6 (4).
McDonough, J. 1983. Steps in the design of academic listening materials. In Jordan (Ed.) *Case Studies in ELT.* Collins.
McDonough, J. 1984. *ESP in Perspective: A Practical Guide.* Collins.

McDonough, J. and C. Shaw. 1993. *Materials and Methods in ELT*. Blackwell. (contains a useful chapter on *adapting* materials)

Mackay, R. and A. J. Mountford. 1978. *English for Specific Purposes*. Longman. (contains several useful case studies of materials and textbook design)

Mountford, A. J. 1988. Factors influencing ESP materials production and use. In Chamberlain and Baumgardner (Eds.) *ESP in the Classroom: Practice and Evaluation. ELT Documents*, 128.

Nunan, D. 1988. *Syllabus Design*. Oxford University Press.

Robinson, P. C. 1991. *ESP Today: A Practitioner's Guide*. Phoenix ELT (includes a useful survey of references to materials writing, with comments on a team approach to writing)

Sheldon, L. E. (Ed.) 1987. *ELT Textbooks and Materials: Problems in Evaluation and Development. ELT Documents*, 126.

Sheldon, L. E. 1988. Evaluating ELT textbooks and materials. *ELT Journal*, 42 (4).

Williams, D. 1983. Developing criteria for textbook evaluation. *ELT Journal*, 37 (3).

1.4   Research

Bell, J. 1993. *Doing Your Research Project*. Open University Press.

Blaxter, L., C. Hughes and M. Tight. 1996. *How to Research*. Open University Press.

Brown, J. D. 1988. *Understanding Research in Second Language Learning*. Cambridge University Press.

Butler, C. S. 1985. *Statistics in Linguistics*. Blackwell.

Cohen, L. and L. Manion. 1994. *Research Methods in Education*. Routledge.

Cryer, P. 1996. *The Research Student's Guide to Success*. Open University Press.

Hopkins, D. 1993. *A Teacher's Guide to Classroom Research*. Open University Press.

McDonough, J. and S. McDonough. 1997. *Research Methods for English Language Teachers*. Arnold.

Nunan, D. 1990. 'Action Research in the Language Classroom': Chapter 5 in Richards, J. C. and D. Nunan (Eds.) 1990. *Second Language Teacher Education*. Cambridge University Press.

Nunan, D. 1992. *Research Methods in Language Learning*. Cambridge University Press.

Oppenheim, A. N. 1992. *Questionnaire Design, Interviewing and Attitude Measurement*. Pinter (London).

Orna, E. and G. Stevens. 1995. *Managing Information for Research*. Open University Press.

Phillips, E. M. and D. S. Pugh. 1994. *How to get a Ph.D.* Open University Press.

Rowntree, D. 1981. *Statistics without Tears*. Penguin.

Seliger, H. W. and E. Shohamy. 1989. *Second Language Research Methods.* Oxford University Press.
Weir, C. and J. Roberts. 1994. *Evaluation in ELT.* Blackwell. (note: although about evaluation, the methods are appropriate for research into EAP viz. interviews, questionnaires, classroom observation)

Appendix 2   Educational technology

2.1   The language laboratory

A number of institutions have language laboratories which are under-used. This is wasteful of an excellent resource that can be used either for group sessions or for self-access/library-mode purposes. Apart from the array of listening/speaking material available commercially, other material can be developed to provide a bank of EGAP/ESAP cassettes, worksheets and folders (see Chapter 18). The material would need to be divided into *categories*: e.g.

1. pronunciation, stress and intonation
2. listening and reading
3. listening and speaking
4. listening and comprehension (with some writing)
5. listening and note-taking
6. grammar
7. EGAP
8. ESAP (various subjects)

and *levels* (perhaps colour-coded for easy recognition): e.g.

a   elementary
b   lower intermediate
c   upper intermediate
d   advanced

Students need guidance in using the language laboratory in order to obtain the maximum benefit. This is, perhaps, best achieved by an introductory, practical session, combined with printed advice to act as a reminder, an example of which is given below.

WORKING IN THE LANGUAGE LABORATORY

Use the language laboratory for about 30 minutes at a time. It is difficult to work in a concentrated way for longer, so take a short break after half-an-hour.

Procedure for using a tape-course:

REMEMBER

- Most courses are designed to give practice in *listening* and *speaking* (with very little reading).
- If you look at the book **all the time** while listening to the tape, you are really practising reading – and this will defeat the purpose of the course.
- If you try to finish several exercises or pages before comparing your voice

with the master voice, you will probably forget what the first exercise was about.

– Do not try to **race** through the book. It is more important to work carefully and methodically.

THEREFORE

1. Listen carefully to the tape.
2. Speak when told to do so (when the 'pause' occurs).
3. Try to imitate the master voice as closely as possible.
4. Do not look at the book at first, especially if you are imitating a dialogue or completing a short exercise which contains an example of what to do. By listening and speaking only (not reading) you will be practising in a more realistic and useful way.
5. Look at the book if it is necessary as part of the exercise e.g. to answer a question or give a reply based upon some information in the book (perhaps in a picture or diagram).
6. Also look at the book:

   if you have a particular difficulty (perhaps some unknown words that make it difficult to understand the sentence);

   if you want to check afterwards the spelling etc. of the words used.
7. When you have completed one dialogue or one or two short exercises, rewind the tape to the beginning of the exercise and listen to your voice: compare it carefully with the master voice.
8. If you notice any differences between the master voice and your voice or if you had difficulty in doing any of the exercises, rewind the tape to the beginning of the exercise and do it again, trying to improve on the previous attempt. Then listen once again to check your accuracy. Then proceed to the next exercise.

Monitoring

Basic to the use of a language laboratory is the matter of monitoring. Clearly, there is little purpose in students practising listening/speaking if they simply reinforce errors or make no progress. Consequently, monitoring by a tutor is necessary, who can then pinpoint difficulties and help a student to correct them, or/and students need to be taught how to monitor themselves. An example of the help/advice that can be given to a student is given below.

Being self-critical and monitoring yourself:

When you are comparing your voice with the master voice, notice particularly the following aspects of spoken English. There may be difficulties in each area.

1. **Pronunciation.** Are you pronouncing **each sound** and **each word** in the same way as the master voice? If not, perhaps you are **producing** the sound wrongly (e.g. your tongue may be in the wrong position).

   For example, **the sounds underlined** in the following words are all different; can you produce them correctly?

   thin, tin; then, den,

   this, these; can, can't

fine, vine, wine; pine, bind
He walks to work. (Remember: pronounce the final 's' in 'walks')

2. **Stress.** Are you putting the correct stress on the **correct syllable** of the **correct word** in the sentence?
   For example, **the syllable underlined** in the following words has the main stress; can you say the words correctly?
   economics, economist
   He's not going. He isn't going.
   Some nouns and verbs are spelled the same but have a different stress e.g.

the objects	(noun)
he objects	(verb)

   Remember: putting the main stress on a different word in the same sentence can change the meaning or emphasis of a sentence e.g.
   You're going to wash the car. (i.e. not the bicycle)
   You're going to wash the car. (i.e. not drive it)

3. **Intonation.** Is your **voice rising** and/or **falling** in the same way and in the same place as the master voice?
   The rise or fall may occur in different places in a sentence but it is especially important **at the end of a sentence.**
   For example the two questions below have different intonation patterns:
   What's the time?   (the voice **falls**: this is normal with questions beginning with a question-word e.g. what, where, when, why, how, who, ...)
   Have you the time?   (the voice **rises**: this is normal with questions beginning with an auxiliary verb e.g. have, has, had, is, are, etc.)

4. **Fluency.** Are you **joining your words together in groups** in the same way as the master voice?
   Being fluent does not mean that you try to speak quickly; it means that you say the words in groups, allowing a 'natural' pause to occur where the master voice puts one (e.g. to take a breath). Try to avoid making a pause after **every** word, as it sounds unnatural.

Student/tutor record sheet

In order to encourage progress, it is useful for a student to maintain a record sheet of use made of material in the laboratory. Similarly, if a tutor monitors students, he/she should keep a record for checking progress. It can be very simply designed, similar to the example on page 353 (adapted as necessary for students or tutors).

Language Laboratory Books

The books below give information about organising a language laboratory and developing material for use in it.
Dakin, J. 1973. *The Language Laboratory and Language Learning*. Longman.
Ely, P. 1984. *Bring the Lab Back to Life*. Pergamon.

Name ——————————— Tutor ———————————

Date	Booth No.	Book title: Unit/Ex. Page	Cassette No.	Difficulties (Diagnosis)	Recommendations/ Progress

Hayes, A. 1980. *Language Laboratory Management: A Handbook for Teachers*. Modern English Publications: Macmillan.

2.2   Resource/self-access centres

Self-access learning centres (or resource centres) are an ideal facility for EAP centres or courses as they provide flexibility, optional use of resources and materials, and an individualised approach. Sheerin, S. 1991. ('Self-access', state-of-the-art article, *Language Teaching*, 24(3)) gives a useful overview of self-access centres: in particular, she looks at the practical aspects of implementation, the management and administration of the centres, and the organisation and classification of the materials. She also examines the problem of learner resistance to the change in their role, 'taking responsibility for their learning and participating in the decision-making which affects their learning'. Sheerin provides a very extensive bibliography on many aspects of self-access (see also Sheerin, S. 1989. *Self-access*. Oxford University Press).

Before investing the time, energy and money needed to establish and run a self-access centre, a number of questions have to be asked and answered to allow an informed decision to be made about the type of system most suitable for implementation. Miller, L. and P. Rogerson-Revell. 1993. ('Self-access systems', *ELT Journal*, 47(3)) compare four types of self-access systems, giving examples of each. They stress the importance of considering certain basic questions:

1. Why set up a self-access centre?
2. Who will use the facility?
3. What human resources are available to help establish and manage a self-access centre?

They suggest that 'the rationale for establishing a self-access centre may be based on one or a combination of the following reasons': financial, pedagogical, ideological, and prestigious.

O'Dell, F. 1992. ('Helping teachers to use a self-access centre to its full potential', *ELT Journal*, 46(2)) considers the problems facing teachers, and the subsequent solutions, when self-access centres are established by organisations.

1. Teachers need to know what the centre contains.
2. Teachers need to know what to do in the centre (a) with their classes, and (b) as counsellors in self-study time.
3. Teachers need to feel confident about working in the centre.

The solutions that are proposed by O'Dell can be summarised as:

a) providing induction materials for new members of staff;
b) building up a substantial bank of lesson materials and activities covering the different language skills, built around topics or language areas;
c) providing reference material and handouts for counselling sessions;
d) providing on-going training seminars for staff in the development and use of materials, and ideas for the use of the centre.

Teaching staff should be involved in the establishment and development of self-access centres. In this way, the centres are likely to be more effective in meeting students' needs. Waite, S. 1994. ('Low-resourced self-access with EAP in the developing world: the great enabler?', *ELT Journal*, 48(3)) describes the experience of starting a small self-access centre in a university in a 'low income country'. By centrally involving the teaching team, and proceeding step by step, Waite shows that 'the establishment of quite basic, low-tech, self-access facilities can have a disproportionate and positive effect on the provision of language support within an institution'.

The needs of learners in self-access centres are examined by Barnett, L. and G. Jordan 1991. ('Self-access facilities: what are they for?', *ELT Journal*, 45(4)). The first need is for a clear and comprehensive classification and indexing system so that students can see what materials are available. The next step is to link materials so that paths of study can be created and followed. A main need, in order to obtain maximum benefit from the materials, is for learner training and the development of learner strategies.

In the context of learner training, Aston, G. 1993. ('The learner's contribution to the self-access centre', *ELT Journal*, 47(3)) describes a successful experiment in a university self-access centre. The centre was the focus for a project in which students were involved in improving the facilities and access. This was done by investigation and use and, after discussion, producing leaflets for other users. They also made recommendations for improvements.

The actual contents of a self-access centre are considered by McDonough, J. and C. Shaw, 1993. (*Materials and Methods in ELT*. Blackwell):

'the self-access or resource centre should ideally contain the following software and hardware:
  – resource room(s) incorporating all materials
  – consultation room(s) for individual counselling
  – listening (self-monitoring) section or laboratory

- computer assisted facilities with programmes on vocabulary, testing, reading and communication games
- video facilities
- wall charts analysing at a quick glance all materials available
- classified folders, drawers or boxes containing all the materials available in the centre
- answer sheets, or self-correcting keys where appropriate'.

McDonough and Shaw also give careful consideration to the types of material and their accessibility to students by means of orientation worksheets.

A very useful series of small books has been published by the British Council in Manchester as *self-access guides*:

- *Self-access: setting up a centre*. McCall, J. 1992.
- *Self-access: appropriate technology*. Moore, C. 1992.
- *Self-access: preparation and training*. Sturtridge, G. 1992.
- *Self-access: appropriate material*. Carvalho, D. 1993.
- *Self-access: classification and retrieval*. 1995.

A useful introduction to self-instruction is provided in Dickinson, L. 1987. *Self-instruction in Language Learning*. Cambridge: Cambridge University Press.

2.3 Computer Assisted Language Learning (CALL)

'It is one of the ironies of EAP support teaching that those students with the greatest need are those who can least afford the time away from their studies' (Nesi, H. 1993. Self-Access System for English Language Support. *ReCALL*, 8, May). Nesi lists other reasons why students fail to attend language classes. They include: timetable difficulties, different needs from others in a group, etc.

Nesi's rationalisation of the students' needs indicated that a supplementary EAP support system was needed, with ease of access a high priority and materials readily available. Nesi and colleagues at the University of Warwick tackled the problem by 'setting up a package of self-access material on the university computer network'. This became known as 'the CELTE package' (Centre for English Language Teacher Education). With about a hundred networked computer workstations at Warwick, most of them accessible to students for most of the day and night, a neat solution seems to have been found. Nesi describes the five phases of setting up the CELTE package of self-access EAP materials.

The materials that the Warwick students use are divided into four main sections: language functions, grammar and usage, vocabulary and topics. Having decided on the language area they wish to practise, the students then choose an appropriate exercise from one of six programs in the package: 'Matchmaster', 'Choicemaster', 'Pinpoint', 'Gapmaster', 'Vocab' or 'Eclipse'. These programs are all from WIDA *Software* (see below); they have been found to be very user-friendly and have attractive screen displays. The feedback obtained from students is positive, indicating that the provision of self-access language materials on the university computer network has fulfilled a real need.

The use of computers and computer programs on EAP courses need not depend on a university network. Computers may be available in self-access centres or in classrooms for individual use. The use of them, for many students, provides its own motivation.

The use of computer conferencing (CC) in a university EAP context in Finland is described and discussed by Leppänen, S. and P. Kalaja. 1995. (Experimenting with computer conferencing in English for Academic Purposes. *ELT Journal*, 49(1)). CC was used for discussions and for writing as a process. They found that students had 'greater freedom in conducting the discussions' and that 'they came to do most of the "talking" on their own'; ... 'the number of comments the students received on their writings increased, and more importantly, the comments differed in quality from those made by the tutor who preferred the traditional red pen to CC'.

CALL: suggested books for teachers

Note: Computers and CALL are changing quickly as technology develops. Consequently, in general, books before 1985 are now out of date with regard to the technology that is described.

Abdulaziz, M., W. Smalzer and H. Abdulaziz. 1985. *The Computer Book.* Hemel Hempstead: Prentice Hall International.

Brumfit, C., M. Phillips and P. Skehan (Eds.) 1985. *Computers in English Language Teaching* (A view from the classroom). *ELT Documents*, 122.

Davies, G. and J. Higgins. 1985. *Using Computers in Language Learning: A Teacher's Guide*. London: CILT.

Hardisty, D. and S. Windeatt. 1989. *CALL*. Oxford: Oxford University Press.

Higgins, J. and T. Johns. 1984. *Computers in Language Learning*. London: Collins ELT. (an early book, out of print, but still of interest and use)

Jones, C. and S. Fortescue. 1987. *Using Computers in the Language Classroom*. London: Longman. (out of print, but still a good introduction to CALL)

Leech, G. and C. N. Candlin. (Eds.) 1986. *Computers in English Language Teaching and Research*. London: Longman.

Levy, M. and A. Green. 1995. CALL Bibliography for Postgraduate Study. *System*, 23(1). (this provides a comprehensive listing of key writings, published up to May 1994, that constitute recommended reading for study and research in CALL at postgraduate level)

Lonergan, J. 1991. A decade of development: educational technology and language learning. *Language Teaching*, 24(1) (state-of-the-art article, with extensive bibliography)

Pennington, M. C. and V. Stevens. 1992. *Computers in Applied Linguistics*. Clevedon, Avon, UK: Multilingual Matters.

Tribble, C. and G. Jones. 1990. *Concordances in the Classroom: A Teaching Handbook*. London: Longman.

Relevant journals

CALL Review. (Journal of the IATEFL Computer Special Interest Group – formerly 'MUESLI News': see Appendix 3.4)
Journal of Computer Assisted Learning. Oxford: Blackwell Scientific Publications.
ReCALL. (Journal of the CTI Centre for Modern Languages, University of Hull: see below)
System. Oxford: Pergamon.

Other sources of information

a) The CTI Centre for Modern Languages ('Computers in Teaching Initiative')
    Centre for Modern Languages
    School of European Languages and Cultures
    The University of Hull
    Cottingham Road
    Hull HU6 7RX, England   (Tel: 01482–466373/465872)
    The Centre provides advice and information on all aspects of CALL. Its services are aimed primarily at teachers in the UK higher education sector; it maintains an extensive library of software. Its journal *ReCALL* is issued twice a year, and its newsletter, *ReCALL NewsSheet*, comes out 2–3 times a year. *ReCALL* is free of charge to academics working in universities, colleges and schools in the UK. Other organisations and individuals may subscribe to the journal. Several publications are for sale, including a *Software Guide* and a *CALL Bibliography*.
b) The British Council:
    English Studies Information Service (ELIS) publish:
        Computer-Assisted Language Learning: An Annotated Bibliography
        Computer-Assisted Language Learning: Select Bibliography
c) Centre for Information on Language Teaching and Research (CILT):
        Atkinson, T. 1992. *Hands off! It's my go. IT in the Languages Classroom.* CILT/NCET.
        Hewer, S. 1990. *Making the most of IT skills*
        Rendall, H. 1990. *Making the most of micro-computers*
        CILT Information Sheets on various aspects of technology
d) Learning Methods Branch,
    Employment Department
    Moorfoot
    Sheffield S1 4PQ, England
    Two wide-ranging survey-reports have been produced for the Employment Department, by the University of East Anglia and the Bell Educational Trust (1990): *Educational Technology in Modern Language Learning* (in the secondary, tertiary and vocational sectors), and the University of East Anglia (1992): *New Perspectives in Modern Language Learning*. These two reports give an overview, with details, of the use of computers in teaching, and contain bibliographies and useful addresses.

e) WIDA Software,
2 Nicholas Gardens,
London W5 5HY   (Tel: 0181 567 6941)
WIDA produces an extensive catalogue of software and books for teachers and learners of languages, including authoring programs and programs on CD-ROM. Of interest to EAP students is *CALLEAP*, a program produced in conjunction with Eurocentres and NEAB. It consists of 21 exercises which include: finding missing words, word building, finding and correcting mistakes in a text, answering questions about a written text and analysing data in a table (the authors are Tony Sibbons and Gary Motteram).

Appendix 3 BALEAP (The British Association of Lecturers in English for Academic Purposes), and the Survey

BALEAP was founded in 1972. Initially, it was known as SELMOUS (The Group for 'Special English Language Materials for Overseas University Students'). The name reflected the main priority at the time, which was to produce appropriate teaching materials. In 1989 the name was changed to BALEAP, in order to indicate the reduction in emphasis on materials and the increase in professionalism of member institutions on a broader front. This entails not only high standards of teaching on EAP courses, but also research, and adequate administrative and pastoral procedures. Membership is open to British university departments which provide courses in EAP for overseas students. The current membership is more than 60 British universities.

Members of BALEAP subscribe to a *Code of Practice* which sets standards for courses in EAP/study skills. Since 1991 BALEAP has operated an *Accreditation Scheme* whereby members' courses are visited by assessors. The Scheme is recognised by the British Council, which is represented on the Accreditation Scheme Committee (BASC). A full account of the Scheme is contained in an article by June O'Brien (EAP Course Evaluation and Quality Assurance) in *Evaluation and Course Design in EAP*, edited by M. Hewings and T. Dudley-Evans, *Review of ELT*, 6(1). Phoenix ELT, 1996. The Code of Practice is described by C. Weir and J. Roberts in *Evaluation in ELT*, Blackwell, 1994 (in Appendix 4.1, which lists the criteria for assessment, together with a checklist of the necessary documentation).

Every two years (in March/April of the 'odd' years, viz. 1991, 1993, etc.), BALEAP organises a national conference, open to all, to report on research and developments in EAP. Following the conference, a selection of papers is normally published (see below). Since 1991, one-day conferences have also been organised, each one focusing on a particular aspect of EAP (e.g. Law, Academic Writing, CALL, ...): these are known as *Professional Interest Meetings* (PIMs).

In 1995 a *BALEAP Research Register* was started. The purpose is to list the EAP research activities being conducted by staff in member institutions, with a view to linking people doing comparable kinds of work. Initially, the information is being stored on a database; afterwards, it will be made more generally available in booklet form. The Register will be updated annually; it is maintained by:

Jo McDonough, Director EFL Unit
Department of Language and Linguistics
University of Essex
Wivenhoe Park
Colchester Essex CO4 3SQ

In 1995 a *Register of Tutors* for short-term contracts was also initiated. The names of qualified and experienced teachers of EAP are entered on a database which is accessed by BALEAP member institutions for use on short courses.

BALEAP Survey

Between November 1991 and February 1992 I circulated an EAP course questionnaire to all BALEAP members (41 at that time). An 80% response rate provided sufficient information for authoritative comments to be made on the design and content of EAP courses. The questionnaire covered a number of areas relevant to EAP, including needs analysis, research findings, EAP and other components included on EAP courses, percentage of time allocated to components, books and other materials used, subject-content of course material, and specimens of timetables and feedback questionnaires.

A full account of the Survey is contained in my paper 'A Survey of BALEAP EAP Courses' (from the 1993 BALEAP Conference) published in the proceedings, edited by M. Hewings and T. Dudley-Evans (1996) – as above.

BALEAP publications

1977:   *English for Academic Purposes*, A. P. Cowie and J. B. Heaton (Eds.) BAAL/SELMOUS, University of Reading.

1977:   *SELMOUS Occasional Paper No. 1*, K. Johnson (Ed.) University of Reading.

1978:   *Pre-sessional Courses for Overseas Students*, R. R. Jordan (Ed.) *ETIC Occasional Paper*, The British Council.

1978:   *Pre-sessional English Language Courses in Britain Today*, J. Price (Ed.) SELMOUS/ETIC, The British Council.

1980:   *Study Modes and Academic Development of Overseas Students*, G. M. Greenall and J. E. Price (Eds.) *ELT Documents 109*, The British Council.

1981:   *The ESP Teacher: Role, Development and Prospects*, J. McDonough and T. French (Eds.) *ELT Documents 112*, The British Council.

1984:   *Common Ground: Shared Interests in ESP and Communication Studies*, R. Williams, J. Swales and J. Kirkman (Eds.) *ELT Documents 117*, Phoenix ELT.

1984:   *The ESP Classroom*, G. James (Ed.) *Exeter Linguistic Studies*, Vol. 7, University of Exeter.

1988:   *Academic Writing: Process and Product*, P. Robinson (Ed.), *ELT Documents 129*, Phoenix ELT.

1988:   *Individualization and Autonomy in Language Learning*, A. Brookes and P. Grundy (Eds.) *ELT Documents 131*, Phoenix ELT.

1991:   *Socio-Cultural Issues in English for Academic Purposes*, P. Adams, B. Heaton and P. Howarth (Eds.) *Developments in ELT* series, Phoenix ELT.

1993:   *Language, Learning and Success: Studying through English*, G. M. Blue (Ed.) *Developments in ELT* series, Phoenix ELT.

1996:   *Evaluation and Course Design in EAP*, M. J. Hewings and T. Dudley-Evans (Eds.) *Developments in ELT* series, Phoenix ELT; and *Review of ELT*, 6 (1).

Contact address for information

At present, the chair of BALEAP and its secretariat rotates among members every two years. Consequently, enquiries can be made to the English Language Unit or Language Centre of any member university, or to:

BALEAP Secretary
c/o ELT Unit
University of Manchester
Manchester M13 9PL
England
Tel: 0161 275 2000

Appendix 4 EAP exams and examining bodies

The main public exams listed here are examples of *proficiency tests* (commented on in Chapter 5). The biggest, in terms of student numbers, are the *IELTS* test and *TOEFL*. They are used for admission purposes by universities and other academic institutions world-wide; increasingly, third-country training is provided for these two exams. NEAB's exam, *UETESOL*, is also used for admission to UK universities. (Two of the Cambridge Exams are also recognised for admission purposes in the UK, i.e. *Certificate of Proficiency* and *Certificate in Advanced English*.)

Full accounts of the above exams, and many others, and how they compare, are contained in Davies and West (1989), the best overall guide. There is also a useful survey of the same exams in Carroll and West (1989) and Simmonds (1985), and an appraisal of the *TOEFL* by Traynor (1985). Castillo (1990) describes the *RELC Test of Proficiency in EAP*, with which it is of interest to compare the above public exams.

A very clear and useful table of comparison between many of the exams is provided in the second edition of the English-Speaking Union's Framework chart – *English Language Examinations from Britain* (R. West and G. Walsh 1993). The Framework consists of a nine-level scale, with exams grouped according to the type of English tested: General, Business, Study, and Young Learners; the scale is reproduced below. The nine bands used by *IELTS* in its overall band scores are similar to these.

Full details of the entry requirements of all British higher education institutions are contained in *The British Council English Language Entrance Requirements in British Higher Education* (HMSO).

a) The IELTS (International English Language Testing System)

The *IELTS Handbook* contains basic information about the test and the types of questions and tasks in it. It also gives examples of questions.

The *IELTS Specimen Materials* pack contains sample reading, writing, listening and speaking papers (including a sample listening cassette), and provides information on the format and content of the *IELTS* test.

	**THE ENGLISH-SPEAKING UNION'S NINE-LEVEL SCALE**
Uses an extensive range of language equivalent to that used in own language.	**9**
Uses a full range of language with proficiency approaching that in own language, with occasional minor problems.	**8**
Uses the language effectively in most situations with few problems. Communication is effective and consistent, with few hesitations and uncertainties.	**7**
Uses the language competently in a variety of situations but with noticeable problems. Communication is usually effective. When difficulties arise communication is recovered with ease.	**6**
Uses the language adequately in familiar situations. Rather frequent problems but usually succeeds in communicating general message.	**5**
Uses a basic range of language sufficient for familiar and non-pressuring situations. Frequent problems restrict prolonged communication, but message communicated with repetition and/or assistance.	**4**
Uses a limited range of language adequate for short communication and practical needs. Problems cause frequent breakdown of communication, but message usually recovered with repetition and/or assistance.	**3**
Uses a narrow range of language, adequate for basic communication. Basic communication is possible with assistance.	**2**
Uses a few words or phrases such as greetings, and recognises some public notices or signs.	**1**

(From West and Walsh 1993)

Contact address for information

IELTS Subject Officer
University of Cambridge Local Examinations Syndicate
1 Hills Road
Cambridge CB1 2EU UK   *Tel*: 01223 553311

Note: Publications that are useful for students preparing for *IELTS* are:
How to prepare for IELTS, R. de Witt (The British Council, Manchester)

IELTS: Strategies for Study, M. Garbutt and K. O'Sullivan (NCELTR, Macquarie University, Sydney, Australia)
Passport to IELTS, D. Hopkins and M. Nettle (Phoenix ELT; revised edition, 1995)
Cambridge Practice Tests for IELTS 1, V. Jakeman and C. McDowell (Cambridge University Press, 1996).

b)   *The UETESOL (NEAB) (University Entrance Test in English for Speakers of Other Languages: Northern Examinations and Assessment Board – the successor to the former JMB)*

Contact address for information

Northern Examinations and Assessment Board (NEAB)
Devas Street
Manchester M15 6EX   *Tel*: 0161 953 1180

c)   *TOEFL (Test of English as a Foreign Language: Educational Testing Service, USA)*

Contact address for information

Test of English as a Foreign Language
Educational Testing Service
PO Box 6155
Princeton
NJ 08541–6155
USA   *Tel*: 609 921 9000

References

Abbott, G. 1981. Encouraging communication in English: a paradox. *ELT Journal*, 35 (3).

Abdulaziz, H. T. and A. D. Stover. 1989. *Academic Challenges in Reading*. Englewood Cliffs, N.J.: Prentice Hall Regents.

Adkins, A. and I. McKean. 1983. *Text to Note*. London: Edward Arnold/Nelson.

Alderson, J. C. 1980. A process approach to reading at the University of Mexico. In the British Council. *Projects in Materials Design*. ELT Documents Special.

Alderson, J. C. (Ed.) 1985. *Evaluation: Lancaster Practical Papers in English Language Education*. Vol. 6.

Alderson, J. C. 1988. Testing and its administration in ESP. In D. Chamberlain and R. J. Baumgardner (Eds.) *ESP in the classroom: practice and evaluation. ELT Documents 128*.

Alderson, J. C. and A. Beretta. 1992. *Evaluating Second Language Education*. Cambridge: Cambridge University Press.

Alderson, J. C. and A. Hughes (Eds.) 1981. *Issues in language testing. ELT Documents 111*.

Alderson, J. C. and B. North (Eds.) 1991. *Language Testing in the 1990s. Developments in ELT*. Hemel Hempstead: Phoenix ELT.

Alderson, J. C. and A. Waters. 1982. A course in testing and evaluation for ESP teachers or 'How bad were my tests?'. In A. Waters (Ed.) *Issues in ESP: Lancaster Practical Papers in English Language Education*. Vol. 5.

Allen, J. P. B. and H. G. Widdowson (Eds.) 1973–78. *English in Focus* series. Oxford: Oxford University Press.

Allison, D. and R. Webber. 1984. What place for performative tests? *ELT Journal*, 38 (3).

Allison, D. and S. Tauroza. 1995. The effect of discourse organisation on lecture comprehension. *English for Specific Purposes*, 14 (2).

Allwright, J. 1988. Don't correct – reformulate! In P. C. Robinson (Ed.) *Academic writing: process and product. ELT Documents 129*.

Allwright, R. 1982. Perceiving and pursuing learner's needs. In M. Geddes and G. Sturtridge (Eds.) *Individualisation*. Oxford: Modern English Publications.

Allwright, R. L., M. P. Woodley and J. M. Allwright. 1988. Investigating reformulation as a practical strategy for the teaching of academic writing. *Applied Linguistics*, 9 (3).

Archer, C. M. 1986. Culture bump and beyond. In J. M. Valdes (Ed.) *Culture Bound*. Cambridge: Cambridge University Press.

References

Arnaudet, M. L. and M. E. Barrett. 1984. *Approaches to Academic Reading and Writing*. Englewood Cliffs, N.J.: Prentice Hall Regents.

Arnaudet, M. L. and M. E. Barrett. 1990, 2nd ed. *Paragraph Development*. Englewood Cliffs, N.J.: Prentice Hall Regents.

Bachman, L. F. 1990. *Fundamental Considerations in Language Testing*. Oxford: Oxford University Press.

Bachman, L. and A. Palmer. 1992. *Language Testing in Practice*. Oxford: Oxford University Press.

Baker, D. 1989. *Language Testing*. London: Edward Arnold.

Baker, M. 1988. Sub-technical vocabulary and the ESP teacher: an analysis of some rhetorical items in medical journal articles. *Reading in a Foreign Language*, 4 (2).

Ballard, B. 1984. Improving student writing: an integrated approach to cultural adjustment. In R. Williams, J. Swales and J. Kirkman (Eds.) *Common Ground: Shared Interests in ESP and Communication Skills. ELT Documents: 117*.

Ballard, B. and J. Clanchy. 1984. *Study Abroad: A Manual for Asian Students*. Kuala Lumpur: Longman Malaysia Sdn. Berhad.

Ballard, B. and J. Clanchy. 1991. *Teaching Students from Overseas*. Melbourne: Longman Cheshire.

Bannock, G., R. E. Baxter and E. Davis. 1992, 5th ed. *The Penguin Dictionary of Economics*. London: Penguin Books.

Barron, C. 1991. Material thoughts: ESP and culture. *English for Specific Purposes*, 10 (3).

Bartram, M. and R. Walton. 1991. *Correction*. Hove: Language Teaching Publications.

Bates, M. and T. Dudley-Evans (Eds.) 1976–85. *Nucleus*. London: Longman.

Beard, R. and J. Hartley. 1984. *Teaching and Learning in Higher Education*. 4th Edition. London: Harper and Row.

Beattie, G. W. 1982. The dynamics of university tutorial groups. *Bulletin of the British Psychological Society*, vol. 35.

Bell, J. 1993, 2nd edn. *Doing Your Research Project*. Milton Keynes: The Open University.

Benson, M. J. 1994. Lecture listening in an ethnographic perspective. In J. Flowerdew (Ed.) *Academic Listening: Research Perspectives*. Cambridge: Cambridge University Press.

Bhatia, V. K. 1987. Language of the Law. *Language Teaching*, 20 (4).

Bhatia, V. K. 1993. *Analysing Genre: Language Use in Professional Settings*. London: Longman.

Blatchford, C. H. 1986. Newspapers: vehicles for teaching ESOL with a cultural focus. In J. M. Valdes (Ed.) *Culture Bound*. Cambridge: Cambridge University Press.

Bligh, D. A. 1971/72. *What's the Use of Lectures?* London: Penguin Education.

Bligh, D. A., G. J. Ebrahim, D. Jaques and D. Warren-Piper. 1975. *Teaching Students*. Exeter University Teaching Services.

Block, D. 1991. Some thoughts on DIY materials design. *ELT Journal*, 45 (3).

Bloor, M. 1985. Some approaches to the design of reading courses in English as a Foreign Language. *Reading in a Foreign Language*, 3 (1).

Bloor, M. and T. Bloor. 1988. Syllabus negotiation: the basis of learner autonomy. In A. Brookes and P. Grundy (Eds.) *Individualization and Autonomy in Language Learning. ELT Documents 131.*

Bloor, M. and T. Bloor. 1991. Cultural expectations and socio-pragmatic failure in academic writing. In P. Adams, B. Heaton and P. Howarth (Eds.) *Developments in ELT: Socio-Cultural Issues in EAP.* Hemel Hempstead: Phoenix ELT.

Bloor, M. and M. J. St John. 1988. Project writing: the marriage of process and product. In P. C. Robinson (Ed.) *Academic Writing: Process and Product. ELT Documents 129.*

Blue, G. M. 1988a. Individualising academic writing tuition. In P. C. Robinson (Ed.) *Academic Writing: Process and Product. ELT Documents 129.*

Blue, G. 1988b. Self-assessment: The limits of learner independence. In A. Brookes and P. Grundy (Eds.) *Individualization and Autonomy in Language Learning. ELT Documents 131.*

Blue, G. M. 1991. Language learning within academic constraints. In P. Adams, B. Heaton and P. Howarth (Eds.) *Socio-Cultural Issues in English for Academic Purposes. Developments in ELT.* Hemel Hempstead: Phoenix ELT.

Blue, G. M. 1993. Nothing succeeds like linguistic competence: the role of language in academic success. In G. M. Blue (Ed.) *Language, Learning and Success: Studying through English. Developments in ELT.* Hemel Hempstead: Phoenix ELT.

Blue, G. and P. Grundy. 1996. Team evaluation of language teaching and language courses. *ELT Journal, 50* (3).

Bowers, R. 1980. The individual learner in the general class. In H. B. Altman and C. V. James (Eds.) *Foreign Language Teaching: Meeting Individual Needs.* Oxford: Pergamon Press.

Bowers, R. 1992. Memories, metaphors, maxims and myths: language learning and cultural awareness. *ELT Journal, 46* (1).

Boyle, R. 1993. Distance learning and the pre-sessional ESP course. In K. Richards and P. Roe (Eds.) *Distance Learning in ELT. Review of ELT, 3* (2).

Boyle, R. 1996. Modelling oral presentations. *ELT Journal, 50* (2).

Bramki, D. and R. Williams. 1984. Lexical familiarization in economics text and its pedagogic implications in reading comprehension. *Reading in a Foreign Language, 2* (1).

Breen, M. P. 1984. Process syllabuses for the language classroom. In C. J. Brumfit (Ed.) *General English Syllabus Design. ELT Documents 118.*

Breen, M. P. 1985. Authenticity in the language classroom. *Applied Linguistics, 6* (1).

Breen, M. P. 1987. Contemporary paradigms in syllabus design. Part I in *Language Teaching, 20* (2). Part II in *Language Teaching, 20* (3).

Breen, M. P. and C. N. Candlin. 1987. Which materials?: a consumer's and designer's guide. In L. E. Sheldon (Ed.) *ELT Textbooks and Materials: Problems in Evaluation and Development. ELT Documents 126.*

Brennan, M. and M. van Naerssen. 1989. Language and context. *ELT Journal, 43* (3).

References

Brett, P. 1994. A genre analysis of the results section of sociology articles. *English for Specific Purposes*, 13 (1).

Brieger, N. and A. Jackson. 1989. *Advanced International English*. Hemel Hempstead: Prentice Hall International.

The British Council. 1981. J. McDonough and T. French (Eds.) *The ESP teacher: role, development and prospects*. ELT Documents 112.

Brookes, A. and P. Grundy. (Eds.) 1988. *Individualization and autonomy in language learning*. ELT Documents 131.

Brookes, A. and P. Grundy. 1990. *Writing for Study Purposes*. Cambridge: Cambridge University Press.

Brooks, N. 1986. Culture in the classroom. In J. M. Valdes (Ed.) *Culture Bound*. Cambridge: Cambridge University Press.

Brown, G. 1978. *Lecturing and Explaining*. London: Methuen.

Brumfit, C. 1993. Culture and success: a general model, and its applicability for EAP learners. In G. M. Blue (Ed.) *Language, Learning and Success: Studying through English. Developments in ELT*. Hemel Hempstead: Phoenix ELT.

Budd, R. 1989. Simulating academic research: one approach to a study-skills course. *ELT Journal*, 43 (1).

Butler, J. 1990. Concordancing, teaching and error analysis: some applications and a case study. *System*, 18 (3).

Buzan, T. 1977a. *Speed Reading*. Revised edition. Newton Abbot: David and Charles.

Buzan, T. 1977b. *Speed Memory*. Newton Abbot: David and Charles.

Buzan, T. 1981. *Make the Most of Your Mind*. New edition. London: Pan Books.

Buzan, T. 1982. *Use Your Head*. Revised edition. London: Ariel Books / BBC.

Buzan, T. 1986. *Use Your Memory*. London: BBC Publications.

Cambridge University Press. 1995. *How to Choose An English Dictionary: A short guide*. Cambridge.

Campbell, C. 1990. Writing with others' words: using background reading text in academic compositions. In B. Kroll (Ed.) *Second Language Writing*. Cambridge: Cambridge University Press.

Campbell, V. 1973. Report: *The Communications Problems of Overseas Students in British Technical Education*. London: North East London Polytechnic.

Campion, M. E. and W. B. Elley. 1971. *An Academic Vocabulary List*. Wellington: Council for Educational Research.

Candlin, C., C. Bruton, J. Leather and E. Woods. 1977. *Doctor-Patient Communication Skills (DOPACS)*. Chelmsford: Graves Medical Audio-Visual Library.

Candlin, C. N., J. M. Kirkwood and H. M. Moore. 1975. Developing study skills in English. In E.T.I.C., *English for Academic Study: Problems and Perspectives*. London: The British Council.

Candlin, C. N., J. M. Kirkwood and H. M. Moore. 1978. *Study skills in English: theoretical issues and practical problems*. In R. Mackay and A. Mountford (Eds.) *English for Specific Purposes*. London: Longman.

Carroll, B. J. 1980. *Testing Communicative Performance.* Oxford: Pergamon Press.

Carroll, B. J. and P. J. Hall. 1985. *Make Your Own Language Tests.* Oxford: Pergamon Press.

Carroll, B. J. and R. West. 1989. *E.S.U. Framework.* London: Longman.

Carter, R. 1987. Vocabulary and second/foreign language teaching. *Language Teaching*, 20 (1).

Carter, R. 1988. Vocabulary, cloze and discourse: an applied linguistic view. In R. Carter and M. McCarthy (Eds.) *Vocabulary and Language Teaching.* London: Longman.

Carter, R. and M. McCarthy. 1988. *Vocabulary and Language Teaching.* London: Longman.

Casanave, C. P. and P. Hubbard. 1992. The writing assignments and writing problems of doctoral students: faculty perceptions, pedagogical issues, and needed research. *English for Specific Purposes*, 11 (1).

Castillo, E. S. 1990. Validation of the RELC Test of Proficiency in English for Academic Purposes. *RELC Journal*, 21 (2).

Cawood, G. 1978. Seminar strategies: asking for repetition or clarification. In R. R. Jordan (Ed.) Pre-sessional courses for overseas students. ETIC occasional paper. London: The British Council.

Chamberlain, D. and R. J. Baumgardner. (Eds.) 1988. *ESP in the classroom: practice and evaluation. ELT Documents 128.*

Chambers, F. 1980. A re-evaluation of needs analysis in ESP. *The ESP Journal*, 1 (1).

Chandrasegaran, A. 1986. An exploratory study of EL2 students' revision and self-correction skills. *RELC Journal*, 17 (2).

Channell, J. 1981. Applying semantic theory to vocabulary teaching. *ELT Journal*, 35 (2).

Channell, J. 1988. Psycholinguistic considerations in the study of L2 vocabulary acquisition. In R. Carter and M. McCarthy (Eds.) *Vocabulary and Language Teaching.* London: Longman.

Channell, J. 1990. The student-tutor relationship. In M. Kinnell (Ed.) *The Learning Experiences of Overseas Students.* The Society for Research into Higher Education and Open University Press.

Channell, J. 1994. *Vague Language.* Oxford: Oxford University Press.

Charles, M. 1990. Responding to problems in written English using a student self-monitoring technique. *ELT Journal*, 44 (4).

Chaudron, C. 1988. *Second Language Classrooms: Research on Teaching and Learning.* Cambridge: Cambridge University Press.

Chaudron, C., L. Loschky and J. Cook. 1994. Second language listening comprehension and lecture note-taking. In J. Flowerdew (Ed.) *Academic Listening: Research Perspectives.* Cambridge: Cambridge University Press.

Chaudron, C. and J. C. Richards. 1986. The effect of discourse markers on the comprehension of lectures. *Applied Linguistics*, 7 (2).

Chirnside, A. 1986. Talking for specific purposes. In D. Harper (Ed.) *ESP for the University. ELT Documents 123.*

References

Christison, M. A. and K. J. Krahnke. 1986. Student perceptions of academic language study. *TESOL Quarterly*, 20 (1).

Clanchy, J. and B. Ballard. 1992. *How to Write Essays*. Melbourne: Longman Cheshire.

Clarke, D. F. 1989. Communicative theory and its influence on materials production. *Language Teaching*, 22 (2).

Clarke, D. F. 1991. The negotiated syllabus: what is it and how is it likely to work? *Applied Linguistics*, 12 (1).

Clarke, D. F. and I. S. P. Nation. 1980. Guessing the meanings of words from context: strategy and techniques. *System*, 8 (3).

Clerehan, R. 1995. Taking it down: note taking practices of L1 and L2 students. *English for Specific Purposes*, 14 (2).

Coffey, B. 1984. ESP–English for Specific Purposes. *Language Teaching*, 17 (1).

Cohen, A. D. and M. C. Cavalcanti. 1990. Feedback on compositions: teacher and student verbal reports. In B. Kroll (Ed.) *Second Language Writing*. Cambridge: Cambridge University Press.

Coleman, H. 1987. Teaching spectacles and learning festivals. *ELT Journal*, 41 (2).

Coleman, H. 1991. The testing of 'appropriate behaviour' in an academic context. In P. Adams, B. Heaton and P. Howarth (Eds.) *Socio-cultural issues in English for Academic Purposes. Review of ELT*, 1 (2).

Cooper, J. 1979. *Think and Link*. London: Nelson.

Corder, S. P. 1981. *Error Analysis and Interlanguage*. Oxford: Oxford University Press.

Cortazzi, M. 1990. Cultural and educational expectations in the language classroom. In B. Harrison (Ed.) *Culture and the language classroom. ELT Documents 132*.

Cortazzi, M. 1994. Narrative analysis. *Language Teaching*, 27 (3).

Cotterall, S. 1995. Developing a course strategy for learner autonomy. *ELT Journal*, 49 (3).

Cowan, J. R. 1974. Lexical and syntactic research for the design of EFL reading materials. *TESOL Quarterly*, 8 (4).

Cowie, A. P. and J. B. Heaton (Eds.) 1977. *English for Academic Purposes*. Reading: British Association for Applied Linguistics.

Cunningsworth, A. 1983. Needs analysis – a review of the state of the art. *System*, 11 (2).

Cunningsworth, A. 1984. *Evaluating and Selecting EFL Teaching Materials*. Oxford: Heinemann ELT.

Cunningsworth, A. 1987. Coursebooks and conversational skills. In L. E. Sheldon (Ed.) *ELT Textbooks and Materials: Problems in Evaluation and Development. ELT Documents 126*.

Cunningsworth, A. and P. Kusel. 1991. Evaluating teachers' guides. *ELT Journal*, 45 (2).

Davies, E. and N. Whitney. 1984. *Study Skills for Reading*. London: Heinemann Educational.

Davies, F. 1988. Designing a writing syllabus in English for Academic Purposes:

process and product. In P. C. Robinson (Ed.) *Academic Writing: Process and Product, ELT Documents 129.*

Davies, S. and R. West. 1989. *The Longman Guide to English Language Examinations.* London: Longman.

DeCarrico, J. and J. R. Nattinger. 1988. Lexical phrases for the comprehension of academic lectures. *English for Specific Purposes,* 7 (2).

De Leeuw, M. and E. De Leeuw. 1965. *Read Better, Read Faster.* London: Penguin Books.

Dickinson, L. 1987. *Self-instruction in Language Learning.* Cambridge: Cambridge University Press.

Dickinson, L. 1992. *Learner Autonomy 2: Learner training for language learning.* Dublin: Authentik.

Dickinson, L. and A. Wenden (Eds.) 1995. Special issue on autonomy, self-direction and self-access in language teaching and learning. *System,* 23 (2).

Dougill, J. 1987. Not so obvious. In L. E. Sheldon (Ed.) *ELT textbooks and materials: problems in evaluation and development. ELT Documents 126.*

Dubin, F. and F. Olshtain. 1986. *Course Design.* Cambridge: Cambridge University Press.

Dudley-Evans, A. 1984a. The team teaching of writing skills. In R. Williams, J. Swales and J. Kirkman (Eds.) *Common Ground: Shared Interests in ESP and Communication Studies. ELT Documents 117.*

Dudley-Evans, T. 1984b. A preliminary investigation of the writing of dissertation titles. In G. James (Ed.) *The ESP Classroom. Exeter Linguistic Studies,* Vol. 7.

Dudley-Evans, T. 1985. *Writing Laboratory Reports.* Melbourne: Nelson Wadsworth.

Dudley-Evans, T. (Ed.) 1987. *Genre analysis and ESP. English Language Research Journal,* Vol. 1.

Dudley-Evans, T. 1988a. A consideration of the meaning of 'discuss' in examination questions. In P. C. Robinson (Ed.) *Academic writing: process and product. ELT Documents 129.*

Dudley-Evans, T. 1988b. One-to-one supervision of students writing M.Sc. or Ph.D. theses. In A. Brookes and P. Grundy (Eds.) *Individualization and autonomy in language learning, ELT Documents 131.*

Dudley-Evans, T. 1991. Socialisation into the academic community: linguistic and stylistic expectations of a Ph.D. thesis as revealed by supervisor comments. In P. Adams, B. Heaton and P. Howarth (Eds.) *Socio-Cultural Issues in English for Academic Purposes. Developments in ELT.* Hemel Hempstead: Phoenix ELT.

Dudley-Evans, T. 1993. Variation in communication patterns between discourse communities: the case of highway engineering and plant biology. In G. M. Blue (Ed.) *Language, Learning and Success: Studying through English. Developments in ELT.* Hemel Hempstead: Phoenix ELT.

Dudley-Evans, T. 1994. Variations in the discourse patterns favoured by different disciplines and their pedagogical implications. In J. Flowerdew (Ed.) *Academic Listening: Research Perspectives.* Cambridge: Cambridge University Press.

References

Dudley-Evans, T. and M. Bates. 1987. The evaluation of an ESP textbook. In L. E. Sheldon (Ed.) *ELT Textbooks and Materials: Problems in Evaluation and Development. ELT Documents 126.*

Dudley-Evans, T. and W. Henderson. 1990a. *The language of economics: the analysis of economics discourse. ELT Documents 134.*

Dudley-Evans, T. and W. Henderson. 1990b. The organisation of article introductions: evidence of change in economics writing. In T. Dudley-Evans and W. Henderson (Eds.) *The language of economics: the analysis of economics discourse. ELT Documents 134.*

Dudley-Evans, A. and T. F. Johns. 1981. A team teaching approach to lecture comprehension for overseas students. *The Teaching of Listening Comprehension, ELT Documents Special.*

Dudley-Evans, T. and J. Swales. 1980. Study modes and students from the Middle East. In G. M. Greenall and J. E. Price (Eds.) *Study modes and academic development of overseas students, ELT Documents 109.*

Dunkel, P. 1988. The context of L1 and L2 students' lecture notes and its relation to test performance. *TESOL Quarterly,* 22 (2).

Dunkel, P. and S. Davy. 1989. The heuristic of lecture notetaking: perceptions of American and international students regarding the value and practice of notetaking. *English for Specific Purposes,* 8 (1).

Dunmore, D. 1989. Using contextual clues to infer word meaning: an evaluation of current exercise types. *Reading in a Foreign Language,* 6 (1).

ETIC. 1975. *English for Academic Study: problems and perspectives.* ETIC Occasional Paper. London: The British Council.

Edge, J. 1983. Reading to take notes and to summarise: a classroom procedure. *Reading in a Foreign Language,* 1 (2).

Ellis, G. and B. Sinclair. 1989. *Learning to Learn English.* Cambridge: Cambridge University Press.

Ellis, R. 1994. *The Study of Second Language Acquisition.* Oxford: Oxford University Press.

Elsworth, S. 1982. *Count Me In.* London: Longman.

Ewer, J. R. 1983. Teacher training for EST: problems and methods. *The ESP Journal,* 2 (1).

Ewer, J. R. and G. Hughes-Davies. 1971. Further notes on developing an English programme for students of science and technology (1). *English Language Teaching,* 26 (1).

Ewer, J. R. and G. Latorre. 1969. *A Course in Basic Scientific English.* London: Longman.

Fanning, P. 1981. Academic essay-writing. *Modern English Teacher,* 9 (1).

Fanning, P. 1993. Broadening the ESP umbrella. *English for Specific Purposes,* 12 (2).

Fathman, A. K. and E. Whalley. 1990. Teacher response to student writing: focus on form versus content. In B. Kroll (Ed.) *Second Language Writing.* Cambridge: Cambridge University Press.

Ferris, D. R. 1995. Student reactions to teacher response in multiple-draft composition classrooms. *TESOL Quarterly,* 29 (1).

Fisher, J. 1990. Factors influencing the design of syllabi and support materials for non-native speakers studying economics. In T. Dudley-Evans and W. Henderson (Eds.) *The language of economics: the analysis of economics discourse. ELT Documents 134.*

Fletcher, M. and R. Hargreaves. 1980. *Defining and Verbalising.* London: Evans Brothers.

Flowerdew, J. 1986. Cognitive style and specific-purpose course design. In *English for Specific Purposes,* 5 (2).

Flowerdew, J. 1990. English for Specific Purposes – a selective review of the literature. *ELT Journal,* 44 (4).

Flowerdew, J. 1993. An educational, or process, approach to the teaching of professional genres. *ELT Journal,* 47 (4).

Flowerdew, J. (Ed.) 1994. *Academic Listening: Research Perspectives.* Cambridge: Cambridge University Press.

Flowerdew, J. and L. Miller. 1995. On the notion of culture in L2 lectures. *TESOL Quarterly,* 29 (2).

Floyd, J. 1984. *Study Skills for Higher Education.* London: Collins.

Ford, C., A. Silverman and D. Haines. 1983. *Cultural Encounters.* Oxford: Pergamon.

Forman, D., F. Donoghue, S. Abbey, B. Cruden and I. Kidd. 1990. *Campus English.* Hemel Hempstead: Phoenix ELT.

Frank, M. 1990. Writing as Thinking: A Guided Process Approach. Englewood Cliffs, N.J.: Prentice Hall Regents.

Fried-Booth, D. L. 1986. *Project Work.* Oxford: Oxford University Press.

Friederichs, J. and H. D. Pierson. 1981. What are science students expected to write? *ELT Journal,* 35 (4).

Fry, E. 1963a. *Teaching Faster Reading: A Manual.* Cambridge: Cambridge University Press.

Fry, E. 1963b. *Reading Faster: A Drill Book.* Cambridge: Cambridge University Press.

Furneaux, C., C. Locke, P. Robinson and A. Tonkyn. 1991. Talking heads and shifting bottoms: the ethnography of academic seminars. In P. Adams, B. Heaton and P. Howarth (Eds.) *Socio-Cultural Issues in English for Academic Purposes. Developments in ELT.* Hemel Hempstead: Phoenix ELT.

Furneaux, C., P. Robinson and A. Tonkyn. 1988. Making friends and influencing tutors: strategies for promoting acculturation in the EAP classroom. In A. Brookes and P. Grundy (Eds.) *Individualization and autonomy in language learning. ELT Documents 131.*

Gaffield-Vile, N. 1996. Content-based second language instruction at the tertiary level. *ELT Journal,* 50 (2).

Gairns, R. and S. Redman. 1986. *Working with Words.* Cambridge: Cambridge University Press.

Geddes, M. and G. Sturtridge. 1979. *Listening Links.* London: Heinemann.

Gee, S., M. Huxley and D. Johnson. 1984. Teaching Communication Skills and English for Academic Purposes: A Case Study of a Problem Shared. In R. Williams, J. Swales and J. Kirkman (Eds.) *Common Ground: Shared Interests in ESP and Communication Skills. ELT Documents 117.*

References

Geoghegan, G. 1983. *Non-Native Speakers of English at Cambridge University.* Cambridge: Bell Educational Trust.

Gibbs, G. 1977. Can students be taught how to study? *Higher Education Bulletin,* 5 (2).

Gibbs, G. 1981. *Teaching Students to Learn.* Milton Keynes: Open University Press.

Glendinning, E. and B. Holmström. 1992. *Study Reading.* Cambridge: Cambridge University Press.

Glendinning, E. and H. Mantell. 1983. *Write Ideas.* London: Longman.

Greenall, G. M. and J. E. Price (Eds.) 1980. *Study modes and academic development of overseas students. ELT Documents 109.*

Grellet, F. 1981. *Developing Reading Skills.* Cambridge: Cambridge University Press.

Grundy, P. 1993a. *Newspapers.* Oxford: Oxford University Press.

Grundy, P. 1993b. Student and supervisor perceptions of the role of English in academic success. In G. M. Blue (Ed.) *Language, Learning and Success: Studying through English. Review of ELT,* 3 (1).

Hadfield, J. 1992. *Classroom Dynamics.* Oxford: Oxford University Press.

Halliday, M. A. K. 1978. *Language as Social Semiotic.* London: Edward Arnold.

Halliday, M. A. K., A. McIntosh and P. Strevens. 1964. *The Linguistic Sciences and Language Teaching.* London: Longman.

Hamp-Lyons, L. 1983. Survey of materials for teaching advanced listening and note-taking. *TESOL Quarterly,* 17 (1).

Hamp-Lyons, L. 1988. The product before: task-related influences on the writer. In P. C. Robinson (Ed.) *Academic writing: process and product. ELT Documents 129.*

Hamp-Lyons, L. and K. B. Courter. 1984. *Research Matters.* Cambridge, Mass.: Newbury House.

Hamp-Lyons, L. and B. Heasley. 1984. Survey review: textbooks for teaching writing at the upper levels. *ELT Journal,* 38 (3).

Hamp-Lyons, L. and B. Heasley. 1987. *Study Writing.* Cambridge: Cambridge University Press.

Hartley, J. and C. Knapper. 1984. Academics and their writing. *Studies in Higher Education,* 9 (2).

Harvey, P. D. 1983. Vocabulary learning: the use of grids. *ELT Journal,* 37 (3).

Hawkey, R. 1980. Needs analysis and syllabus design for specific purposes. In H. B. Altman and C. V. James (Eds.) *Foreign Language Teaching: Meeting Individual Needs.* Oxford: Pergamon Press.

Hawkins, S., I. K. Davies, K. Majer and J. Hartley. 1981. *Getting Started: Guides for Beginning Teachers,* 2nd Ed. Oxford: Blackwell.

Heaton, J. B. 1975. *Studying in English.* London: Longman.

Heaton, J. B. (Ed.) 1982. *Language Testing.* Modern English Publications.

Heaton, J. B. 1988, new edition. *Writing English Language Tests.* London: Longman.

Heaton, J. B. 1990. *Classroom Testing.* London: Longman.

Heaton, B. and D. Dunmore. 1992. *Learning to Study in English.* London: Macmillan.

Heaton, J. B. and N. D. Turton. 1987. *Longman Dictionary of Common Errors and Workbook*. London: Longman.

Henderson, W. and T. Dudley-Evans. 1990. Introduction: the analysis of economics discourse. In T. Dudley-Evans and W. Henderson (Eds.) *The language of economics: the analysis of economics discourse. ELT Documents 134*.

Henderson, W. and P. Skehan. 1980. The team teaching of introductory economics to overseas students. *Team Teaching in ESP, ELT Documents 106*.

Herbert, A. J. 1965. *The Structure of Technical English*. London: Longman.

Hewings, A. 1990. Aspects of the language of economics textbooks. In T. Dudley-Evans and W. Henderson (Eds.) *The language of economics: the analysis of economics discourse. ELT Documents 134*.

Hewings, A. and W. Henderson. 1987. A link between genre and schemata: a case study of economics text. In T. Dudley-Evans (Ed.) *Genre Analysis and ESP. English Language Research Journal*, Vol. 1.

Hewings, M. 1988. The individualization of pronunciation improvement. In A. Brookes and P. Grundy (Eds.) *Individualization and autonomy in language learning. ELT Documents 131*.

Hewings, M. 1991. The interpretation of illustrations in ELT materials. *ELT Journal*, 45 (3).

Hewings, M. 1993a. *Pronunciation Tasks*. Cambridge: Cambridge University Press.

Hewings, M. 1993b. The end! How to conclude a dissertation. In G. M. Blue (Ed.) *Language, Learning and Success: Studying through English. Developments in ELT*. Hemel Hempstead: Phoenix ELT.

Higgins, J. J. 1966. Hard Facts. *ELT Journal* (formerly *English Language Teaching*), 21 (1).

Hill, B. 1994. Self-managed learning. *Language Teaching*, 27 (4).

Hohl, M. 1982. Necessary English at the University of Petroleum and Minerals, Dharhran, Saudi Arabia: A Faculty Survey. *TEAM*, no. 42.

Holes, C. D. 1972. An investigation into some aspects of the English language problems of two groups of overseas postgraduate students at Birmingham University. MA thesis, University of Birmingham.

Holliday, A. 1994a. The house of TESEP and the communicative approach: the special needs of state English language education. *ELT Journal*, 48 (1).

Holliday, A. 1994b. *Appropriate Methodology and Social Context*. Cambridge: Cambridge University Press.

Holliday, A. and T. Cooke. 1982. An ecological approach to ESP. *Lancaster Practical Papers in English Language Education*, 5 (*Issues in ESP*). University of Lancaster.

Holschuh, L. W. and J. P. Kelley. 1988. *Academic Reading*. New York: St. Martin's Press.

Hopkins, A. and T. Dudley-Evans. 1988. A genre-based investigation of the discussion sections in articles and dissertations. *The ESP Journal*, 7 (2).

Hornby, A. S. 1954. *A Guide to Patterns and Usage in English*. Oxford: Oxford University Press.

Hornby, A. S. 1959. *The Teaching of Structural Words and Sentence Patterns.* Oxford: Oxford University Press.

Horowitz, D. 1986a. Essay examination prompts and the teaching of academic writing. *English for Specific Purposes,* 5 (2).

Horowitz, D. 1986b. Process, not product: Less than meets the eye. *TESOL Quarterly,* 20 (1).

Houghton, D. and P. King. 1990. What it makes sense to ask: students' and lecturers' questions in English for development economics. In T. Dudley-Evans and W. Henderson (Eds.) *The language of economics: the analysis of economics discourse. ELT Documents 134.*

Howe, P. M. 1983. *Answering Examination Questions.* London: Collins ELT.

Howe, P. 1988. Teaching examination techniques at Buckingham. In P. C. Robinson (Ed.) *Academic writing: process and product. ELT Documents 129.*

Howe, P. M. 1990. The problem of the problem question in English for Academic Legal Purposes. *English for Specific Purposes,* 9 (3).

Howe, P. M. 1993. Planning a pre-sessional course in English for Academic Legal Purposes. In G. M. Blue (Ed.) *Language, Learning and Success: Studying through English. Developments in ELT.* Hemel Hempstead: Phoenix ELT.

Huang, G. F. 1985. The productive use of EFL dictionaries. *RELC Journal,* 16 (2).

Huckin, T. N. 1988. Achieving professional communicative relevance in a 'generalized' ESP classroom. In D. Chamberlain and R. J. Baumgardner (Eds.) *ESP in the Classroom: Practice and Evaluation. ELT Documents 128.*

Hughes, A. (Ed.) 1988. *Testing English for university study. ELT Documents 127.*

Hughes, A. 1989. *Testing for Language Teachers.* Cambridge: Cambridge University Press.

Hughes, G. H. 1986. An argument for culture analysis in the second language classroom. In J. M. Valdes (Ed.) *Culture Bound.* Cambridge: Cambridge University Press.

Hunter, I. M. L. 1957/64. *Memory.* Revised edition. London: Penguin Books.

Hutchinson, T. 1988. Making materials work in the ESP classroom. In D. Chamberlain and R. J. Baumgardner (Eds.) *ESP in the classroom: practice and evaluation. ELT Documents 128.*

Hutchinson, T. and A. Waters. 1982. Creativity in ESP materials or 'Hello! I'm a blood cell'. *Lancaster Practical Papers in English Language Education* Vol. 5: *Issues in ESP.*

Hutchinson, T. and A. Waters. 1984. How communicative is ESP? *ELT Journal,* 38 (2).

Hutchinson, T. and A. Waters. 1987. *English for Specific Purposes: A learning-centred approach.* Cambridge: Cambridge University Press.

Hyland, K. 1994. Hedging in academic writing and EAP textbooks. *English for Specific Purposes,* 13 (3).

Imhoof, M. and H. Hudson. 1975. *From Paragraph to Essay.* London: Longman.

Jackson, J. and L. Bilton. 1994. Stylistic variations in science lectures: teaching vocabulary, *English for Specific Purposes*, 13 (1).

James, D. V. 1989. *EAP Series: Medicine*. Hemel Hempstead: Phoenix ELT.

James, K. 1977. Note-taking in lectures: problems and strategies. In A. P. Cowie and J. B. Heaton (Eds.) *English for Academic Purposes*. University of Reading: BAAL/SELMOUS.

James, K. 1980. Survey of University of Manchester overseas post-graduate students' initial level of competence in English and their subsequent academic performance: Calendar year 1977. In G. M. Greenall and J. E. Price (Eds.) *Study modes and academic development of overseas students*. *ELT Documents 109*.

James, K. 1983. The teaching of spoken English to overseas students in a British university. In R. R. Jordan (Ed.) *Case Studies in ELT*. London: Collins ELT.

James, K. 1984a. The writing of theses by speakers of English as a Foreign Language: the results of a case study. In R. Williams, J. Swales and J. Kirkman (Eds.) *Common ground: shared interests in ESP and communication studies*. *ELT Documents 117*.

James, K. 1984b. *Speak to Learn*. London: Collins ELT.

James, K. 1993. Helping students to achieve success in the information structuring of their academic essays. In G. M. Blue (Ed.) *Language, Learning and Success: Studying through English. Developments in ELT*. Hemel Hempstead: Phoenix ELT.

James, K., R. R. Jordan, A. Matthews and J. P. O'Brien. 1979/91. *Listening Comprehension and Note-taking Course*. London: Collins/Nelson.

Jarvis, J. 1983. Two core skills for ESP teachers. *The ESP Journal*, 2 (1).

Jenkins, S., M. K. Jordan and P. O. Weiland. 1993. The role of writing in graduate engineering education: a survey of faculty beliefs and practices. *English for Specific Purposes*, 12 (1).

Johns, A. M. 1981. Necessary English: a faculty survey. *TESOL Quarterly*, 15 (1).

Johns, A. M. 1988a. The discourse communities' dilemma: identifying transferable skills for the academic milieu. *English for Specific Purposes*, 7 (1).

Johns, A. M. 1988b. Reading for summarising: an approach to text orientation and processing. *Reading in a Foreign Language*, 4 (2).

Johns, A. M. 1993. Written argumentation for real audiences: suggestions for teacher research and classroom practice. *TESOL Quarterly*, 27 (1).

Johns, A. M. and T. Dudley-Evans. 1991. English for Specific Purposes: International in scope, specific in purpose. *TESOL Quarterly*, 25 (2).

Johns, C. 1978. Seminar discussion strategies. In R. R. Jordan (Ed.) Pre-sessional courses for overseas students. *ETIC occasional paper*. London: The British Council.

Johns, C. M. and T. F. Johns. 1977. Seminar discussion strategies. In A. P. Cowie and J. B. Heaton (Eds.) *English for Academic Purposes*. University of Reading: BAAL/SELMOUS.

Johns, T. F. 1981. Some problems of a world-wide profession. In J. McDonough and T. French (Eds.) *The ESP teacher: role, development and prospects*. *ELT Documents 112*.

References

Johns, T. 1986. Micro-concord: a language learner's research tool. *System*. 14 (2).

Johns, T. 1991. Should you be persuaded – two samples of data-driven learning materials. In T. Johns and P. King (Eds.) Classroom concordancing. *ELR Journal*, Vol. 4.

Johns, T. 1994. From printout to handout: grammar and vocabulary teaching in the context of data-driven learning. In T. Odlin (Ed.) *Perspectives on Pedagogical Grammar*. Cambridge: Cambridge University Press.

Johns, T. and F. Davies. 1983. Text as a vehicle for information: the classroom use of written texts in teaching reading in a foreign language. *Reading in a Foreign Language*, 1 (1).

Johns, T. F. and A. Dudley-Evans. 1980. An experiment in team teaching of overseas postgraduate students of transportation and plant biology. *Team Teaching in ESP. ELT Documents 106*.

Johnson, K. 1981. *Communicate in Writing*. London: Longman.

Johnson, K. 1982. *Communicative Syllabus Design and Methodology*. Oxford: Pergamon.

Johnson, K. 1988. Mistake correction. *ELT Journal*, 42 (2).

Jolly, D. 1982. *Reading Choices*. Cambridge: Cambridge University Press.

Jones, J. F. 1995. Self-access and culture: retreating from autonomy. *ELT Journal*, 49 (3).

Jordan, R. R. 1977a. English for Academic Purposes – Economics. In K. Johnson (Ed.) *SELMOUS Occasional Paper*, 1. Reading: University of Reading.

Jordan, R. R. 1977b. Identification of problems and needs: a student profile. In A. P. Cowie and J. B. Heaton (Eds.) *English for Academic Purposes*. University of Reading: BAAL/SELMOUS.

Jordan, R. R. 1978a. Motivation in ESP. *Modern English Teacher*, 6 (4).

Jordan, R. R. 1978b. Language practice material for economists. In R. Mackay and A. Mountford (Eds.) *English for Specific Purposes*. London: Longman.

Jordan, R. R. 1980. *Looking for Information*. London: Longman.

Jordan, R. R. 1981. Comment Améliorer l'Anglais Écrit de l'Étudiant Étranger en Université Britannique. Paris: *Études de Linguistique Appliquée*, Vol. 43.

Jordan, R. R. 1982. *Figures in Language: Describe and Draw*. London: Collins ELT.

Jordan, R. R. (Ed.) 1983. *Case Studies in ELT*. London: Collins ELT.

Jordan, R. R. 1984. Motivation in ESP: a case study of methods and materials for economics. In G. James (Ed.) *The ESP Classroom*. University of Exeter: *Exeter Linguistic Studies*, Vol. 7.

Jordan, R. R. 1988a. The introductory paragraph in economics essays and examinations. In P. C. Robinson (Ed.) *Academic writing: process and product. ELT Documents 129*.

Jordan, R. R. 1988b. Developing student writing – a subject tutor and writing tutors compare points of view. In P. C. Robinson (Ed.) *Academic writing: process and product. ELT Documents 129*.

Jordan, R. R. 1989. English for Academic Purposes (EAP). *Language Teaching*, 22 (3).

Jordan, R. R. 1990a; 2nd ed. *Academic Writing Course*. London: Nelson/ Longman.

Jordan, R. R. 1990b. Pyramid discussions. *ELT Journal*, 44 (1).

Jordan, R. R. 1990c. He said: quote ... unquote. In T. Dudley-Evans and W. Henderson (Eds.) *The language of economics: the analysis of economics discourse*. *ELT Documents 134*.

Jordan, R. R. 1993. Study skills: experience and expectations. In G. M. Blue (Ed.) *Language, Learning and Success: Studying through English. Developments in ELT*. Hemel Hempstead: Phoenix ELT.

Jordan, R. R. 1996a. A survey of BALEAP EAP courses. In M. J. Hewings and T. Dudley-Evans (Eds.) *Evaluation and course design in EAP*. *Review of ELT*, 6 (1).

Jordan, R. R. 1996b. Reviews: quick guide. Books for study skills/EAP. *Modern English Teacher*, 5 (4).

Jordan, R. R. 1997. What's in a name? *English for Specific Purposes*, 16 (1).

Jordan, R. R. and R. Mackay. 1973. A survey of the spoken English problems of overseas postgraduate students at the Universities of Manchester and Newcastle upon Tyne. *Journal of the Institutes of Education of the Universities of Newcastle upon Tyne and Durham*, 25 (125).

Jordan, R. R. and F. I. Nixson. 1986. *Language for Economics*. London: Nelson.

Kaplan, R. B. and P. A. Shaw. 1983. *Exploring Academic Discourse*. Rowley, Mass.: Newbury House.

Keh, C. L. 1990. Feedback in the writing process: a model and methods for implementation. *ELT Journal*, 44 (4).

Kennedy, C. and R. Bolitho. 1984. *English for Specific Purposes*. Hemel Hempstead: Phoenix ELT.

Kennedy, J. and S. Hunston. 1982. *Patterns of Fact*. London: Edward Arnold.

Khidhayir, M. and D. Du Boulay. 1994. Assessing student presentations on pre-sessional courses. At the BALEAP Professional Interest Meeting, Spoken English in EAP Contexts, at CALS, University of Reading, December 1994.

King, P. 1989. The uncommon core. Some discourse features of student writing. *System*, 17 (1).

Kirkland, M. R. and M. A. P. Saunders. 1991. Maximizing student performance in summary writing: managing cognitive load. *TESOL Quarterly*, 25 (1).

Kramsch, C. 1993. *Context and Culture in Language Teaching*. Oxford: Oxford University Press.

Kroll, B. (Ed.) 1990. *Second Language Writing*. Cambridge: Cambridge University Press.

Kruse, A. F. 1979. Vocabulary in context. *ELT Journal*, 33 (3).

Kusel, P. A. 1992. Rhetorical approaches to the study and composition of academic essays. *System*, 20 (4).

Kwan-Terry, A. 1988. *Interactive Writing*. Hemel Hempstead: Prentice Hall International.

Lavery, C. 1993. *Focus on Britain Today*. (Teacher's Book) Hemel Hempstead: Phoenix ELT.

Lebauer, R. S. 1984. Using lecture transcripts in EAP lecture comprehension courses. *TESOL Quarterly*, 18 (1).

References

Lee, W. Y-C. 1995. Authenticity revisited: text authenticity and learner authenticity. *ELT Journal,* 49 (4).

Leki, I. 1989. *Academic Writing.* New York: St. Martin's Press.

Leki, I. and J. Carson. 1994. Students' perceptions of EAP writing instruction and writing needs across the disciplines. *TESOL Quarterly,* 28 (1).

Levy, M. 1990. Concordances and their integration into a word-processing environment for language learners. *System,* 18 (2).

Little, D. 1989; 1993. *Self-access systems for language learning: a practical guide.* Dublin: Authentik; and London: CILT.

Littlewood, W. 1981. *Communicative Language Teaching.* Cambridge: Cambridge University Press.

Long, M. H. and G. Crookes. 1992. Three approaches to task-based syllabus design. *TESOL Quarterly,* 26 (1).

Low, G. 1996. Intensifiers and hedges in questionnaire items and the lexical invisibility hypothesis. *Applied Linguistics,* 17 (1).

Lynch, T. 1983. *Study Listening.* Cambridge: Cambridge University Press.

Lynch, T. 1988a. Peer evaluation in practice. In A. Brookes and P. Grundy (Eds.) *Individualization and autonomy in language learning. ELT Documents 131.*

Lynch, T. 1988b. Teaching examination answer writing: process, product or placebo? In P. C. Robinson (Ed.) *Academic writing: process and product. ELT Documents 129.*

Lynch, T. 1994. Training lecturers for international audiences. In J. Flowerdew (Ed.) *Academic Listening: Research Perspectives.* Cambridge: Cambridge University Press.

Lynch, T. and K. Anderson. 1991. Do you mind if I come in here? – a comparison of EAP seminar/discussion materials and the characteristics of real academic interaction. In P. Adams, B. Heaton and P. Howarth (Eds.) *Socio-Cultural Issues in English for Academic Purposes. Developments in ELT.* Hemel Hempstead: Phoenix ELT.

Lynch, T. and K. Anderson. 1992. *Study Speaking.* Cambridge: Cambridge University Press.

Lynch, T. and I. McGrath. 1993. Teaching bibliographic documentation skills. *English for Specific Purposes,* 12 (3).

McCarthy, M. 1991. *Discourse Analysis for Language Teachers.* Cambridge: Cambridge University Press.

McCarthy, M. and R. Carter. 1994. *Language as Discourse: Perspectives for Language Teaching.* London: Longman.

McDonough, J. 1978a. *Listening to Lectures (Biology, Computing, Government, Mechanics, Sociology).* Oxford: Oxford University Press.

McDonough, J. 1978b. Designing exercises for listening. *Modern English Teacher,* 6 (4).

McDonough, J. 1983. Steps in the design of academic listening materials. In R. R. Jordan (Ed.) *Case Studies in ELT.* London: Collins ELT.

McDonough, J. 1984. *ESP in Perspective: A Practical Guide.* London: Collins ELT.

McDonough, J. 1986. English for Academic Purposes: a research base. *English for Specific Purposes,* 5 (1).

McDonough, J. and S. McDonough. 1993. From EAP to chemistry: risking the anecdotal. In G. M. Blue (Ed.) *Language, Learning and Success: Studying through English. Review of ELT*, 3 (1).

McDonough, J. and C. Shaw. 1993. *Materials and Methods in ELT*. Oxford: Blackwell.

McDonough, S. 1985. Academic writing practice. *ELT Journal*, 39 (4).

McEldowney, P. L. 1982a. *Practice for the JMB Test in English (Overseas)*. London: Nelson.

McEldowney, P. L. 1982b. *English in Context*. London: Nelson.

McGovern, D., M. Matthews and S. E. Mackay. 1994. *Reading*. Hemel Hempstead: Phoenix ELT.

McIlroy, J. and B. Jones. 1993. *Going to University*. Manchester: Manchester University Press.

Mackay, R. 1978. Identifying the nature of the learner's needs. In R. Mackay and A. Mountford (Eds.) *English for Specific Purposes*. London: Longman.

Mackay, R. and M. Bosquet. 1981. LSP curriculum development – from policy to practice. In R. Mackay and J. D. Palmer (Eds.) *Languages for Specific Purposes*. Rowley, Mass.: Newbury House.

Mackay, R. and J. D. Palmer (Eds.) 1981. *Languages for Specific Purposes: Program Design and Evaluation*. Rowley, Mass.: Newbury House.

Mackay, R., S. Wellesley and E. Bazergan. 1995. Participatory evaluation. *ELT Journal*, 49 (4).

McKenna, E. 1987. Preparing foreign students to enter discourse communities in the U.S. *English for Specific Purposes*, 6 (3).

Maddox, H. 1963. *How to Study*. London: Pan Books.

Madsen, H. S. 1983. *Techniques in Testing*. Oxford: Oxford University Press.

Maher, J. 1986. English for Medical Purposes. *Language Teaching*, 19 (2).

Makaya, P. and T. Bloor. 1987. Playing safe with predictions: hedging, attribution and conditions in economic forecasting. *Written Language: British Studies in Applied Linguistics*, no. 2. London: CILT/BAAL.

Makino, T-Y. 1993. Learner self-correction in EFL written compositions. *ELT Journal*, 47 (4).

Maley, A. 1981. Games and problem solving. In K. Johnson and K. Morrow (Eds.) *Communication in the Classroom*. London: Longman.

Manchester University. 1979. *Teaching and Learning in the University of Manchester Faculty of Science: A Survey of Student Attitudes*. Manchester: Manchester University Students' Union Education Office.

Marshall, S. 1991. A genre-based approach to the teaching of report-writing. *English for Specific Purposes*, 10 (1).

Martin, A. V. 1976. Teaching academic vocabulary to foreign graduate students. *TESOL Quarterly*, 10 (1).

Mason, A. 1983. *Understanding Academic Lectures*. Englewood Cliffs, N.J.: Prentice Hall Regents.

Mason, A. 1994. By dint of: student and lecturer perceptions of lecture comprehension strategies in first-term graduate study. In J. Flowerdew (Ed.) *Academic Listening: Research Perspectives*. Cambridge: Cambridge University Press.

References

Mason, D. 1995. Project work with students of household sciences. *ESP SIG Newsletter*. January. Whitstable, Kent: IATEFL.

Matthews, A., M. Spratt and L. Dangerfield. 1985. *At the Chalkface*. London: Edward Arnold.

Meara, P. 1980. Vocabulary acquisition: a neglected aspect of language learning. *Language Teaching and Linguistics: Abstracts*, 13 (4).

Melton, C. D. 1990. Bridging the cultural gap: a study of Chinese students' learning style preferences. *RELC Journal*, 21 (1).

Mendonca, C. O. and K. E. Johnson 1994. Peer review negotiations: revision activities in ESL writing instruction. *TESOL Quarterly*. 28 (4).

Montgomery, M. 1982. *Study Skills for Colleges and Universities in Africa*. London: Longman.

Montgomery, M. 1991. *Study Skills for GCSE and A Level*. London: Charles Letts.

Moody, K. W. 1974. *Frames for Written English*. Oxford: Oxford University Press.

Moore, J. D. 1977. The preparation of rhetorically-focused materials for Columbian university students. In the British Council, *English for Specific Purposes: An International Seminar*, at Paipa, Bogota, Columbia.

Moore, J. (Ed.) 1979/80. *Reading and Thinking in English*. Oxford: Oxford University Press.

Morrison, J. W. 1974. An investigation of problems in listening comprehension encountered by overseas students in the first year of postgraduate studies in sciences in the University of Newcastle upon Tyne, and the implications for teaching. MEd thesis, University of Newcastle upon Tyne.

Morrow, K. 1977. Authentic texts and ESP. In S. Holden (Ed.) *English for Specific Purposes*. London: Modern English Publications.

Morrow, K. 1980. *Skills for Reading*. Oxford: Oxford University Press.

Morrow, K. 1981. Principles of communicative methodology. In K. Johnson and K. Morrow (Eds.) *Communication in the Classroom*. London: Longman.

Mosback, G. and V. Mosback. 1976. *Practical Faster Reading*. Cambridge: Cambridge University Press.

Mountford, A. 1988. Factors influencing ESP materials production and use. In D. Chamberlain and R. J. Baumgardner (Eds.) *ESP in the classroom: practice and evaluation. ELT Documents 128*.

Munby, J. 1978. *Communicative Syllabus Design*. Cambridge: Cambridge University Press.

Murphy, D. F. 1980. Taking notes in engineering lectures. *Lancaster Practical Papers in English Language Education*, 3 (3).

Nation, I. S. P. (Ed.) 1986. *Vocabulary Lists: Words, Affixes and Stems*. Victoria University of Wellington (New Zealand), English Language Institute, Occasional Publications No. 12.

Nation, P. 1989. Improving speaking fluency. *System*, 17 (3).

Nation, I. S. P. 1990. *Teaching and Learning Vocabulary*. New York: Newbury House/Harper Collins.

Nation, P. and D. Crabbe, 1991. A survival language learning syllabus for foreign travel. *System*, 19 (3).

Nattinger, J. 1988. Some current trends in vocabulary teaching. In R. Carter and M. McCarthy (Eds.) *Vocabulary and Language Teaching*. London: Longman.

Nesi, H. and J. Skelton. 1987. The structure of oral presentations. *ESPMENA Bulletin*, no. 24.

Norrish. J. 1983. *Language learners and their errors*. Hemel Hempstead: Phoenix ELT.

North, S. 1990. Resource materials for library project work. *ELT Journal*, 44 (3).

Northedge, A. 1990. *The Good Study Guide*. Milton Keynes: The Open University.

Nunan, D. 1988a. *Syllabus Design*. Oxford: Oxford University Press.

Nunan, D. 1988b. *The Learner-Centred Curriculum*. Cambridge: Cambridge University Press.

Nunan, D. 1990. Action research in the language classroom: Chapter 5. In J. C. Richards and D. Nunan (Eds.) *Second Language Teacher Education*. Cambridge: Cambridge University Press.

Nunan, D. 1991. *Language Teaching Methodology*. Hemel Hempstead: Phoenix ELT.

Nunan, D. 1992. *Research Methods in Language Learning*. Cambridge: Cambridge University Press.

Nunan, D. 1993. *Introducing Discourse Analysis*. London: Penguin English.

Nuttall, C. 1996. *Teaching Reading Skills in a Foreign Language*. Oxford: Heinemann ELT.

O'Brien, J. P. 1989. Diary-keeping as evaluation. Paper given at the ninth SELMOUS (BALEAP) conference at Leeds University: *Socio-Cultural Issues in EAP*. Unpublished paper. ELTU, University of Manchester.

O'Brien, J. 1996. EAP course evaluation and quality assurance. In M. J. Hewings and T. Dudley-Evans (Eds.) Evaluation and course design in EAP. *Review of ELT* 6 (1).

O'Brien, T. 1988. Writing for continuous assessment or examinations – a comparison of style. In P. C. Robinson (Ed.) *Academic writing: process and product*. *ELT Documents 129*.

O'Brien, T. 1995. Rhetorical structure analysis and the case of the inaccurate, incoherent source-hopper. *Applied Linguistics*, 16 (4).

O'Brien, T. and R. R. Jordan. 1985. *Developing Reference Skills*. London: Collins ELT.

O'Malley, J. M. and A. U. Chamot. 1990. *Learning Strategies in Second Language Acquisition*. Cambridge: Cambridge University Press.

Odlin, T. 1989. *Language Transfer: Cross-Linguistic Influence in Language Learning*. Cambridge: Cambridge University Press.

Okoye, I. 1994. Teaching technical communication in large classes. *English for Specific Purposes*, 13 (3).

Olsen, L. A. and T. N. Huckin. 1990. Point-driven understanding in engineering lecture comprehension. *English for Specific Purposes*, 9 (1).

Oskarsson, M. 1980. *Approaches to Self-assessment in Foreign Language Learning*. Oxford: Pergamon.

References

Ostler, S. E. 1980. A survey of academic needs for advanced ESL. *TESOL Quarterly*, 14 (4).

Oxford, R. L., M. E. Hollaway and D. Horton-Murillo, 1992. Language learning styles: research and practical considerations for teaching in the multicultural tertiary ESL/EFL classroom. *System*, 20 (4).

Paltridge, B. 1995. Analyzing genre: a relational perspective, *System*, 23 (4).

Parkinson, B. and C. Howell-Richardson, 1990. Learner diaries. In C. Brumfit and R. Mitchell (Eds.) *Research in the language classroom, ELT Documents 133.*

Pass, C. and B. Lowes. 1993; 2nd ed. *Collins Dictionary of Economics.* Glasgow: HarperCollins.

Peretz, A. S. 1988. Student-centered learning through content-based instruction: use of oral report projects in the advanced EFL reading class. *Reading in a Foreign Language*, 5 (1).

Phillips, M. K. 1981. Toward a theory of LSP methodology. In R. Mackay and J. D. Palmer (Eds.) *Languages for Specific Purposes.* Rowley, Mass.: Newbury House.

Phillips, M. K. and C. C. Shettlesworth. 1978. How to ARM your students: a consideration of two approaches to providing materials for ESP. In R. A. Hawkey (Ed.) *English for Specific Purposes. ELT Documents 101.*

Pilbeam, A. 1987. Can published materials be widely used for ESP courses? In L. E. Sheldon (Ed.) *ELT textbooks and materials: problems in evaluation and development. ELT Documents 126.*

Plaister, T. 1968. Reading instruction for college level foreign students. *TESOL Quarterly*, 2 (3).

Potter, M. 1991. *International Issues.* Hemel Hempstead: Phoenix ELT.

Prabhu, N. S. 1987. *Second Language Pedagogy.* Oxford: Oxford University Press.

Price, J. E. 1977. Study skills – with special reference to seminar strategies and one aspect of academic writing. In S. Holden (Ed.) *English for Specific Purposes.* London: MEP.

Price, J. E. 1978. Seminar strategies: agreement and disagreement. In R. R. Jordan (Ed.) Pre-sessional courses for overseas students. *ETIC Occasional Paper.* London: The British Council.

Primrose, C. 1993. English as a Foreign Library. In G. M. Blue (Ed.) *Language, Learning and Success: Studying through English. Developments in ELT.* Hemel Hempstead: Phoenix ELT.

Rea-Dickins, P. 1994. Evaluation and English language teaching. In *Language Teaching*, 27 (2).

Rea-Dickins, P. and K. Germaine. 1992. *Evaluation.* Oxford: Oxford University Press.

Reid. J. M. 1987. The learning style preferences of ESL students. *TESOL Quarterly*, 21 (1).

Reid, J. M. 1988; 2nd ed. *The Process of Composition.* Englewood Cliffs, N.J.: Prentice Hall Regents.

Richards, J. C. 1974. *Error Analysis: Perspectives on Second Language Acquisition.* London: Longman.

Richards, J. C. 1983. Listening comprehension: approach, design, procedure. *TESOL Quarterly*, 17 (2).

Richards, J. C., J. Platt and H. Platt. 1992. *Longman Dictionary of Language Teaching and Applied Linguistics*. London: Longman.

Richards, J. C. and T. S. Rodgers, 1986. *Approaches and Methods in Language Teaching*. Cambridge: Cambridge University Press.

Richards, K. and J. Skelton. 1991. How critical can you get? In P. Adams, B. Heaton and P. Howarth (Eds.) *Socio-Cultural Issues in English for Academic Purposes. Developments in ELT*. Hemel Hempstead: Phoenix ELT.

Richards, R. T. 1988. Thesis/dissertation writing for EFL students: an ESP course design. *English for Specific Purposes, 7* (3).

Richterich, R. (Ed.) 1983. Introduction to *Case studies in identifying language needs*. Oxford: Pergamon (Council of Europe).

Richterich, R. and J. L. Chancerel. 1977/80. *Identifying the Needs of Adults Learning a Foreign Language*. Oxford: Pergamon Press.

Robinson, P. C. 1980. *ESP (English for Specific Purposes): the present position*. Oxford: Pergamon Press.

Robinson, P. C. (Ed.) 1988. *Academic writing: process and product. ELT Documents 129*.

Robinson, P. C. 1991. *ESP today: A Practitioner's Guide*. Hemel Hempstead: Phoenix ELT.

Romanoff, M. R. 1991. *Language and Study Skills for Learners of English*. Englewood Cliffs. N.J.: Prentice Hall Regents.

Rost, M. 1990. *Listening in Language Learning*. London: Longman.

Rowntree, D. 1970/76. *Learn How to Study*. London: Macdonald.

Rubin, J. and I. Thompson. 1983. *How to be a More Successful Language Learner*. New York: Heinle & Heinle.

Rudzka, B., J. Channell, Y. Putseys and P. Ostyn. 1981. *The Words You Need*. Hemel Hempstead: Phoenix ELT. (also: *More Words You Need*, 1985).

St. John, M. J. 1987. Writing processes of Spanish scientists publishing in English. *English for Specific Purposes, 6* (2).

St. John, M. J. 1992. Keeping tests abreast of language learning developments. *English Studies Information. Issue 9, EFL Examinations*. Manchester: The British Council.

Salager-Meyer, F. 1994. Hedges and textual communicative function in medical English written discourse. *English for Specific Purposes, 13* (2).

Salimbene, S. 1985. *Strengthening Your Study Skills: A Guide for Overseas Students*. Rowley, Mass.: Newbury House.

Saville-Troike, M. 1984. What *really* matters in second language teaching for academic achievement? *TESOL Quarterly, 18* (2).

Schenck, M. J. 1988. *Read, Write, Revise*. New York: St. Martin's Press.

Schmuck, R. A. and P. A. Schmuck. 1971. *Group Processes in the Classroom*. Dubque, Iowa: W. C. Brown.

Scholfield, P. 1982. Using the English dictionary for comprehension. *TESOL Quarterly, 16* (2).

Selinker, L. 1972. Interlanguage. *IRAL, 10* (3).

Selinker, L. 1979. On the use of informants in discourse analysis and language for specialized purposes. *IRAL, 17* (3).

References

Selinker, L., E. Tarone and V. Hanzeli. (Eds.) 1981. *English for Academic and Technical Purposes*. Rowley, Mass.: Newbury House.

Sellen, D. 1982. *Skills in Action*. Amersham, Bucks: Hulton Educational.

Shalom, C. 1993. Established and evolving spoken research process genres: plenary lecture and poster session discussions at academic conferences. *English for Specific Purposes*, 12 (1).

Shaw, P. 1991. Science research students' composing processes. *English for Specific Purposes*, 10 (3).

Sheerin, S. 1991. Self-access. *Language Teaching*, 24 (3).

Sheldon, L. E. (Ed.) 1987. *ELT textbooks and materials: problems in evaluation and development*. *ELT Documents 126*.

Sheldon, L. E. 1988. Evaluating ELT textbooks and materials. *ELT Journal*, 42 (4).

Sherman, J. 1992. Your own thoughts in your own words. *ELT Journal*, 46 (2).

Silva, T. 1990. Second language composition instruction: developments, issues and directions in ESL. In B. Kroll (Ed.) *Second Language Writing*. Cambridge: Cambridge University Press.

Sim, D. D. and B. Laufer-Dvorkin. 1982. *Reading Comprehension Course: selected strategies*. London: Collins ELT.

Sim, D. D. and B. Laufer-Dvorkin. 1984. *Vocabulary Development*. London: Collins ELT.

Simmonds, P. 1985. A survey of English language examinations. *ELT Journal*, 39 (1).

Sinclair, J. 1991. *Corpus, Concordance, Collocation*. Oxford: Oxford University Press.

Sinclair, J. M. and R. M. Coulthard. 1975. *Towards an Analysis of Discourse*. Oxford: Oxford University Press.

Sinclair, J. M. and A. Renouf. 1988. A lexical syllabus for language learning. In R. Carter and M. McCarthy (Eds.) *Vocabulary and Language Teaching*. London: Longman.

Skehan, P. 1980. Team teaching and the role of the ESP teacher. In G. M. Greenall and J. E. Price (Eds.) *Study modes and academic development of overseas students*. *ELT Documents 109*.

Skehan, P. 1988. Language Testing. Part I. *Language Teaching*, 21 (4). no. 4. 1989. Language Testing. Part II. *Language Teaching*. 22 (1).

Skehan, P. 1989. *Individual Differences in Second Language Learning*. London: Edward Arnold.

Skehan, P. 1996. A framework for the implementation of task-based instruction, *Applied Linguistics*, 17(1).

Skelton, J. 1988a. The care and maintenance of hedges. *ELT Journal*, 42 (1).

Skelton, J. 1988b. Comments in academic articles. In P. Grunwell (Ed.) *Applied Linguistics in Society: British Studies in Applied Linguistics No. 3*. London: CILT/BAAL.

Smith, M. and G. Smith 1990. *A Study Skills Handbook*. Oxford: Oxford University Press.

Spack, R. 1988. Initiating ESL students into the academic discourse community: How far should we go? *TESOL Quarterly*, 22 (1).

Spencer, D. H. 1967. *Guided Composition Exercises*. London: Longman.

SRA Reading Laboratory, Researchlab, Reading for Understanding. Henley-on-Thames: Science Research Associates Ltd., 1974.

Stevens, V. 1991. Classroom concordancing: vocabulary materials derived from relevant, authentic text. *ESP Journal*, 10 (1).

Stieglitz, E. L. 1983. A practical approach to vocabulary reinforcement. *ELT Journal*, 37 (1).

Strevens, P. 1977. Special purpose language learning: a perspective. *Language Teaching and Linguistics: Abstracts*, 10 (3).

Strodt-Lopez, B. 1991. Tying it all in: asides in university lectures. *Applied Linguistics*, 12 (2).

Sturtridge, G. 1977. Using simulation in teaching English for Specific Purposes. In S. Holden (Ed.) *English for Specific Purposes*. London: Modern English Publications.

Sullivan, T. 1979. *Writing*. Cambridge: National Extension College.

Summers, D. 1988. The role of dictionaries in language learning. In R. Carter and M. McCarthy (Eds.) *Vocabulary and Language Teaching*. London: Longman.

Swales, J. 1971. *Writing Scientific English*. Walton-on-Thames: Nelson.

Swales, J. 1981. Aspects of article introductions. *University of Aston ESP Research Reports*, No. 1.

Swales, J. 1982. Examining examination papers. *English Language Research Journal*, Vol. 3.

Swales, J. 1983. Developing materials for writing scholarly introductions. In R. R. Jordan (Ed.) *Case Studies in ELT*. London: Collins ELT.

Swales, J. 1984. Research into the structure of introductions to journal articles and its application to the teaching of academic writing. In R. Williams, J. Swales and J. Kirkman (Eds.) *Common ground: shared interests in ESP and communication studies*. *ELT Documents 117*.

Swales, J. 1985. *Episodes in ESP*. Oxford: Pergamon. 1988. Hemel Hempstead: Prentice Hall International.

Swales, J. 1986. Citation analysis and discourse analysis. *Applied Linguistics*, 7 (1).

Swales, J. 1987. Utilising the literatures in teaching the research paper. *TESOL Quarterly*, 21 (1).

Swales, J. 1988. Discourse communities, genres and English as an international language. *World Englishes*, 7 (2).

Swales, J. 1990. *Genre Analysis*. Cambridge: Cambridge University Press.

Swales, J. M. 1994. From the editors. *English for Specific Purposes*, 13 (3).

Swales, J. M. 1995. The role of the textbook in EAP writing research. *English for Specific Purposes*, 14 (1).

Swales, J. M. and C. B. Feak. 1994. *Academic Writing for Graduate Students*. Ann Arbor: University of Michigan Press.

Tabachnick, B. R. 1969. Improving reading skills. In B. Tiffen (Ed.) *A Language in Common*. London: Longman.

Tadros, A. A. 1984. Materials for law students: learning to use the library. *ESPMENA Bulletin*, no. 17.

References

Tauroza, S. and D. Allison. 1994. Expectation-driven understanding in information systems lecture comprehension. In J. Flowerdew (Ed.) *Academic Listening: Research Perspectives*. Cambridge: Cambridge University Press.

Thompson, G. and Y. Ye. 1991. Evaluation in the reporting verbs used in academic papers. *Applied Linguistics*, 12 (4).

Thompson, S. 1994. Frameworks and contexts: a genre-based approach to analysing lecture introductions. *English for Specific Purposes*, 13 (2).

Thorp, D. 1991. Confused encounters: differing expectations in the EAP classroom. *ELT Journal*, 45 (2).

Tinkham, T. 1993. The effect of semantic clustering on the learning of second language vocabulary. *System*, 21 (3).

Tomalin, B. and S. Stempleski. 1993. *Cultural Awareness*. Oxford: Oxford University Press.

Tomlins, J. 1993. Principles and design of materials for academic discussion. Unpublished dissertation for MEd TESOL, Faculty of Education, University of Manchester.

Tonkyn, A., C. Locke, P. Robinson and C. Furneaux. 1993. The EAP teacher: prophet of doom or eternal optimist? – EAP teachers' predictions of students' success. In G. M. Blue (Ed.) *Language, Learning and Success: Studying through English. Developments in ELT*. Hemel Hempstead: Phoenix ELT.

Traynor, R. 1985. The TOEFL: an appraisal. *ELT Journal*, 39 (1).

Trim, J., R. Richterich, J. van Ek and D. Wilkins. 1973/80. *Systems development in adult language learning*. Strasbourg: Council of Europe/Oxford: Pergamon.

Trzeciak, J. and S. E. Mackay. 1994. *Study Skills for Academic Writing*. Hemel Hempstead: Phoenix ELT.

Tudor, I. 1993. Teacher roles in the learner-centred classroom. *ELT Journal*, 47 (1).

Tyler, A. E., A. A. Jefferies and C. E. Davies. 1988. The effect of discourse structuring devices on listener perceptions of coherence in non-native university teacher's spoken discourse. *World Englishes*, 7 (2).

Underhill, A. 1985. Working with the monolingual learners' dictionary. In R. Ilson (Ed.) *Dictionaries, lexicography and language learning*, ELT Documents 120.

Underhill, N. 1987. *Testing Spoken Language*. Cambridge: Cambridge University Press.

Underhill, N. 1991. *Focus on Studying in Britain*. Hemel Hempstead: Phoenix ELT.

University of Malaya. 1980–1981. *Skills for Learning: Foundation, Development, Progression, Application*. London: Nelson/UMP.

Valdes, J. M. (Ed.) 1986. *Culture Bound*. Cambridge: Cambridge University Press.

Valette, R. M. 1986. The culture test. In J. M. Valdes (Ed.) *Culture Bound*. Cambridge: Cambridge University Press.

Wallace, M. J. 1980. *Study Skills in English*. Cambridge: Cambridge University Press.

Wallace, M. J. 1982. *Teaching Vocabulary*. London: Heinemann Educational Books.

Ward Goodbody, M. 1993. Letting the students choose: a placement procedure for a pre-sessional course. In G. M. Blue (Ed.) *Language, learning and success: Studying Through English. Developments in ELT*. Hemel Hempstead: Phoenix ELT.

Waters, M. and A. Waters. 1992. Study skills and study competence: getting the priorities right. *ELT Journal*, 46 (3).

Waters, M. and A. Waters. 1995. *Study Tasks in English*. Cambridge: Cambridge University Press.

Weir, C. J. 1984. The Associated Examining Board's Test in English for Academic Purposes (TEAP). In R. Williams, J. Swales and J. Kirkman (Eds.) *Common Ground: Shared Interests in ESP and Communication Studies. ELT Documents 117*.

Weir, C. J. 1988a. The specification, realization and validation of an English language proficiency test. In A. Hughes (Ed.) *Testing English for university study. ELT Documents 127*.

Weir, C. J. 1988b. *Communicative Language Testing*. University of Exeter: *Exeter Linguistic Studies*, Vol. 11.

Weir, C. 1988c. Academic writing – Can we please all the people all the time? In P. C. Robinson (Ed.) *Academic writing: process and product. ELT Documents 129*.

Weir, C. 1992. *Understanding and Developing Language Tests*. Hemel Hempstead: Phoenix ELT

Weir, C. and J. Roberts. 1994. *Evaluation in ELT*. Oxford: Blackwell.

Weissberg, B. 1993. The graduate seminar: another research-process genre. *English for Specific Purposes*, 12 (1).

Weissberg, R. and S. Buker. 1990. *Writing Up Research*. Englewood Cliffs, N.J.: Prentice Hall Regents.

Wenden, A. and J. Rubin. 1987. *Learner Strategies in Language Learning*. Hemel Hempstead: Phoenix ELT.

West, M. 1953. *A General Service List of English Words*. London: Longman.

West, R. 1987. A consumer's guide to ELT dictionaries. In L. E. Sheldon (Ed.) *ELT textbooks and materials: problems in evaluation and development. ELT Documents 126*.

West, R. 1994. Needs analysis in language teaching. *Language Teaching*, 27 (1).

White, R. V. 1988a. Academic writing: process and product. In P. C. Robinson (Ed.) *Academic writing: process and product. ELT Documents 129*.

White, R. V. 1988b. *The ELT Curriculum: Design, Innovation and Management*. Oxford: Basil Blackwell.

White, R. and V. Arndt. 1991. *Process Writing*. London: Longman.

White R. and D. McGovern. 1994. *Writing*. Hemel Hempstead: Phoenix ELT.

White, R., M. Martin, M. Stimson and R. Hodge. 1991. *Management in English Language Teaching*. Cambridge: Cambridge University Press.

Widdowson, H. G. 1979. *Explorations in Applied Linguistics*. Oxford: Oxford University Press.

Widdowson, H. G. 1981. English for Specific Purposes: criteria for course design. In L. Selinker, E. Tarone and V. Hanzeli (Eds.) *English for Academic and Technical Purposes*. Rowley, Mass.: Newbury House.

Wijasuriya, B. S. 1971. The occurrence of discourse-markers and intersentence connectives in university lectures and their place in the testing and teaching of listening comprehension in English as a foreign language. M. Ed. thesis University of Manchester.

Wilkins, D. A. 1976. *Notional Syllabuses*. Oxford: Oxford University Press.

Williams, D. 1983. Developing criteria for textbook evaluation. *ELT Journal*, 37 (3).

Williams, R. 1982. *Panorama*. London: Longman.

Willing, K. 1988. *Learning Styles In Adult Migrant Education*. Sydney: NCELTR, Macquarie University.

Willing, K. 1989. *Teaching How To Learn: Learning Strategies in ESL*. Sydney: NCELTR, Macquarie University.

Willis, D. 1990. *The Lexical Syllabus*. London: Collins ELT/COBUILD.

Wilson, J. 1986. Task-based language learning. In D. Harper (Ed.) *ESP for the university*. *ELT Documents 123*.

Wong, R., E. Glendinning and H. Mantell. 1987. *Becoming a Writer*. New York: Longman.

Wong, V., P. Kwok and N. Choi, 1995. The use of authentic materials at tertiary level. *ELT Journal*, 49 (4).

Wright, A. 1993. *Suggestions for Presenters of Talks and Workshops*. Whitstable, Kent: IATEFL.

Xue, G-Y. and I. S. P. Nation. 1984. A university word list. *Language, Learning and Communication*, 3 (2).

Yalden, J. 1987. *Principles of course design for language teaching*. Cambridge: Cambridge University Press.

Yates, C. St. J. 1989. *EAP Series: Economics*. Hemel Hempstead: Phoenix ELT.

Yorkey, R. C. 1970; 1982. *Study Skills for Students of English*. New York: McGraw-Hill.

Yu, Y. 1995. Using a radio station on campus for English learning: recent developments in China. *System*, 23 (1).

Zamel, V. 1983. The composing processes of advanced ESL students: Six case studies. *TESOL Quarterly*, 17 (2).

Zamel, V. 1985. Responding to student writing. *TESOL Quarterly*, 19 (1).

Zughoul, M. R. and R. F. Hussein. 1985. English for higher education in the Arab World: a case study of needs analysis at Yarmouk University. *ESP Journal*, 4 (2).

Subject Index

References in italic indicate figures or tables.

Author Index

Author index